Using Critical Theory

"I know of no other book on critical theory for beginning and intermediate students that offers the same depth and breath. It offers thorough and clear applications of each theory while its rhetorical tone puts students at ease as they attempt to think about the world in new and different ways ... [this] is the perfect text for students new to critical theory and stands in a league of its own."

Gretchen Cline, *Muskegon Community College, USA*

Explaining both why theory is important and how to use it, Lois Tyson introduces beginning students of literature to this often daunting area in a friendly and approachable style. The new edition of this textbook is clearly structured with chapters based on major theories that students are expected to cover in their studies.

Key features include:

- coverage of all major theories including psychoanalysis, Marxism, feminism, lesbian/gay/queer theories, postcolonial theory, African American theory, and a new chapter on New Criticism (formalism)
- practical demonstrations of how to use these theories on short literary works selected from canonical authors including William Faulkner and Alice Walker
- a new chapter on reader-response theory that shows students how to use their personal responses to literature while avoiding typical pitfalls
- new sections on cultural criticism for each chapter
- new "further practice" and "further reading" sections for each chapter
- a useful "next-step" appendix that suggests additional literary examples for extra practice.

Comprehensive, easy to use, and fully updated throughout, *Using Critical Theory* is the ideal first step for students beginning degrees in literature, composition, and cultural studies.

Lois Tyson is Professor of English at Grand Valley State University, USA. She is the author of *Critical Theory Today: A User-Friendly Guide* (2nd edition, Routledge, 2006).

Using Critical Theory

How to read and write about literature

Second edition

Lois Tyson

Routledge
Taylor & Francis Group

LONDON AND NEW YORK

First edition published as *Learning for a Diverse World* 2001
by Routledge

This edition published as *Using Critical Theory* 2011
by Routledge
2 Park Square, Milton Park, Abingdon, Oxon OX14 4RN

Simultaneously published in the USA and Canada
by Routledge
711 Third Avenue, New York, NY 10017

Routledge is an imprint of the Taylor & Francis Group, an informa business

British Library Cataloguing in Publication Data
A catalogue record for this book is available from the British Library

Library of Congress Cataloging in Publication Data
Tyson, Lois, 1950-
    Using critical theory: how to read and write about literature / Lois Tyson.
        p. cm.
    Includes bibliographical references and index.
    1. Criticism. 2. Critical theory. I. Title.
    PN98.S6T973 2011
    801'.95 – dc22
                    2011008274

ISBN: 978-0-415-61616-4 (hbk)
ISBN: 978-0-415-61617-1 (pbk)
ISBN: 978-0-203-80509-1 (ebk)

Typeset in Bembo
by Taylor & Francis Books

Printed and bound in Great Britain by
CPI Group (UK) Ltd, Croydon, CR0 4YY

For Mac Davis and the late Stephen Lacey,
who both know that a good teacher is one
who remains a good student.

Contents

Preface for instructors

If you're planning to use this book in your undergraduate classroom, then you know that critical theory is no longer considered an abstract discipline for a select group of graduate students, as it was fifteen or twenty years ago. Personally, I don't think critical theory should ever have been limited to that mode of thinking or to that audience. In its most concrete and, I think, most meaningful form, critical theory supplies us with a remarkable collection of pedagogical tools to help students, regardless of their educational background, develop their ability to reason logically; to formulate an argument; to grasp divergent points of view; to make connections among literature, history, the society in which they live, and their personal experience; and of special importance on our shrinking planet, to explore human diversity in its most profound and personal sense: as diverse ways of defining oneself and one's world. From this perspective, critical theory is an appropriate pedagogical resource not only for advanced literature courses, but for the kinds of meat-and-potatoes courses that many of us teach: foundation-level literature courses; introduction-to-literary-studies courses; diversity courses; and composition courses that stress critical thinking, social issues, or cultural diversity.

Creating pedagogical options

For most of us who see the pedagogical potential of critical theory, the question then becomes: "How can I adapt critical frameworks to make them useful to students new to the study of literature and to the social issues literature raises?" That is precisely the question *Using Critical Theory* attempts to answer by offering you: (1) a reader-response chapter to help students recognize and make interpretive use of their personal responses to literature; (2) seven carefully selected theoretical approaches to literary interpretation—introducing the fundamentals of New Critical, psychoanalytic, feminist, lesbian/gay/queer, African American, and postcolonial theories—from which to choose; and (3) five different ways to use each of these approaches through the vehicle of our "Interpretation exercises," the step-by-step development of sample interpretations of the five literary works reprinted at the end of this book. Now, the key word here is *choice*. I think we do our best teaching when we adapt our materials to our own pedagogical goals and teaching styles. For example, you can employ *Using Critical Theory* to structure an entire course, to create a unit or units on specific theoretical approaches, or to supplement the teaching of specific literary works with an increased repertoire of possible interpretations. To provide maximum flexibility, each chapter is written to stand on its own, so you can choose which of the selected theoretical frameworks you want to use. Each interpretation exercise is also written to stand on its own, so you can choose which of the selected literary works you want to use.

I hope the structure of these chapters will facilitate your own creation of classroom activities and homework assignments. For example, students can work in small groups to find the textual data required by a given interpretation exercise, and that activity can be organized in a number of ways. Each group can work on a different section of the same interpretation exercise, thereby each contributing a piece of the puzzle to a single interpretation. Or each group can work on a different interpretation exercise from a single chapter, thereby using concepts from the same theory to complete interpretation exercises for different literary works. Or if students feel they fully understand a given interpretation exercise, you might invite them to develop one of the alternative interpretations suggested in the "Focusing your essay" section at the end of each interpretation exercise or to develop an interpretation of their own. Finally, once the class has become acquainted with a few different theories, different groups of students can use different theoretical approaches to collect textual data from the same literary work, thereby getting an immediate sense of the ways in which concepts from different critical theories can foreground different aspects of the same literary work or foreground the same aspect of a literary work for different purposes.

Similarly, the "Basic concepts" sections of Chapters 3 through 9 can be used to generate activities by having students apply these concepts to short literary works other than those used in this book. For example, students can be given—singly, in pairs, or in small groups—one of the basic concepts of a single theory and asked to find all the ways in which that concept is illustrated in or relevant to any literary work you assign. Or you might allow students to select one of the basic concepts of a theory the class is studying and explain to their classmates how an understanding of that concept helps illuminate the lyrics of a song of their own choosing, a magazine advertisement, a video game, or some other production of popular culture.

To whatever uses you put this book, I think you'll find that the seven theoretical approaches it introduces, taken in any combination, provide a *comparative* experience, a sense of how our perceptions can change when we change the lens through which we're looking. In this way, these theories, all of which are in current academic use, can help students develop a concrete, productive understanding of the diverse world in which we live. Our five literary works—Emily Dickinson's "I started Early—Took my Dog" (c. 1862),

William Faulkner's "A Rose for Emily" (1931), Ralph Ellison's "The Battle Royal" (1952), Alice Walker's "Everyday Use" (1973), and Jewelle Gomez's "Don't Explain" (1987)—were chosen because each lends itself to our selected theories in ways that are accessible to novices and that are typical of the kinds of perspectives on literature each theory offers us. Thus, each interpretation exercise serves as a template for future literary analysis. In addition, our five literary works are heavily weighted in favor of fiction because I have found that most novices respond most readily to stories and, indeed, most of the drama and much of the poetry we offer our introductory-level literature and composition students have a perceptible narrative dimension. Thus, the interpretive skills and strategies students learn here will carry over to the interpretation of works from other literary genres, genres which are represented in each chapter's "Questions for further practice" and in the "Literary works for further practice" provided in Appendix F.

Responding to pedagogical challenges

Of course, *Using Critical Theory* is not intended as a complete introduction-to-literature textbook: for example, it does not define such basic literary vocabulary as *plot, character, setting, stage directions, rhyme*, or *meter*. Nevertheless, the book addresses several common problems encountered by students new to the study of literature, problems which I suspect you've encountered in the classroom many times. For example, Chapter 1, "Critical theory and you," explains, among other things, the difference between an opinion and a thesis, the purpose of a literary interpretation, and how we can analyze the meaning of a literary work without knowing what the author intended. Chapter 2, "Using concepts from reader-response theory to understand our own literary interpretations," includes an explanation of the difference between a symbolic interpretation justified by the literary work and a symbolic interpretation arbitrarily imposed by a reader's personal response to the work. This same chapter also explains the difference between a text's representation of human behavior and its endorsement of that behavior, which students' personal responses to a literary work often lead them to confuse. Chapter 3, "Using concepts from New Critical theory to understand literature," aims to solidify students' understanding of thesis-and-support argumentation, which remains an area of pedagogical frustration for many of us. Moreover, the interpretation exercises provided in Chapters 4 through 9, in addition to their primary function as sample literary applications of our remaining selected theories, are all lessons in close reading, for each exercise guides students through the process of collecting textual evidence to support the interpretation at hand. Students are thus encouraged to see the equal importance of two aspects of current critical practice that they often mistakenly believe are mutually exclusive: (1) that there is more than one valid interpretation of a literary text; and (2) that every interpretation requires adequate textual support. The goal here is to correct a misconception you've probably encountered in the classroom all too often: once students have accepted that there is no single correct interpretation of a literary work, they frequently conclude that their own interpretations do not need to be supported with textual evidence. Finally, Chapter 10, "Holding on to what you've learned," in addition to its other functions, brings students back to the kind of personal connection that opens Chapter 1: how their study of critical theory can help them understand, develop, and articulate their personal values within the context of the changing world in which they live.

Perhaps you will find, as I have, that this last connection—between students' sense of themselves as individuals and the cultures that shape them—is the most valuable connection the study of critical theory can help students make. For it is a connection that has the capacity to spark imaginative inquiry in every domain of their education. And it seems to me that few things motivate students more thoroughly—if we can just find the keys that open those doors—than their own imaginations.

Acknowledgments

My sincere gratitude goes to the following friends and colleagues for their many and varied acts of kindness during the writing of this book: the late Forrest Armstrong, Kathleen Blumreich, Brent Chesley, Patricia Clark, Dianne Griffin Crowder, Michelle DeRose, Milt Ford, Roger Gilles, Chance Guyette, Michael Hartnett, Avis Hewitt, Rick Iadonisi, Regina Salmi, Christopher Shinn, Gary Stark, Veta Tucker, and Brian White.

Special thanks also go to Dean Frederick Antczak; to Grand Valley State University for its generous financial support of this project; and to my editors at Routledge, Emma Nugent and Polly Dodson.

Finally, the deepest appreciation is expressed to Hannah Berkowitz, Jeremy Franceschi, Gretchen Cline, and, especially, Mac Davis for service above and beyond the call of friendship—and to Lenny Briscoe for his untiring and invaluable support.

Permissions

Chapter 1

Critical theory and you

If you're reading this textbook, then you've probably got a lot on your plate right now. You might be preparing to enter college. Or you might be in your first or second year of undergraduate studies. Perhaps you're taking your first literature course. If you're specializing in literary studies, at this point you might be a bit concerned about what you've gotten yourself into. If you're not specializing in literary studies, you might be wondering if you can get away with skipping this part of the course or putting forth a minimal effort. After all, you might be thinking, "What does critical theory have to do with me?" As I hope this book will show you, critical theory has everything to do with you, no matter what your educational or career plans might be.

What does critical theory have to do with me?

First, most of my students find that the study of critical theory increases their ability to think creatively and to reason logically, and that's a powerful combination of vocational skills. You will see, for example, how the skills fostered by studying critical theory would be useful to lawyers in arguing their cases and to teachers in managing the interpersonal dynamics that play out in their classrooms. In fact, as you read the following chapters I think you will find that critical theory develops your ability to see any given problem from a variety of points of view, which is a skill worth having no matter what career you pursue.

As important, if not more important, than your future role on the job market is your future role as a member of the global community. Many people are coming to realize that the numerous and diverse cultures inhabiting planet Earth each has its own history of struggle and achievement as well as its own part to play on the modern stage of national and world events. However, while each culture has its own unique heritage, we share the need to learn to live together, to learn to work with and for one another, if we want our planet to survive. And the issue becomes more complex when we realize that cultures don't occupy tidy bins determined by race or ethnicity alone. In reality, cultures consist of patchworks of overlapping groups that define themselves in terms of many factors, including race, ethnicity, religion, gender, sexual orientation, and socioeconomic class.

It's easy for each of us to think ourselves tolerant of cultural groups other than our own, to believe that we are unbiased, without prejudice. But it's not meaningful to say that we are tolerant of groups about which we know little or nothing. For as soon as our tolerance is tested we might find that the tolerance we thought we had doesn't really exist. For example, take a minute to think about the schools you attended before you entered college. Didn't the student population of at least one of those schools, if not all of them, divide itself into social groups based largely on the kinds of cultural factors listed above? If your school had a diverse student body, didn't students tend to form *close* bonds only with members of their own race? Didn't students from wealthy, socially prominent families tend to stick together? Didn't students from poorer neighborhoods tend to stick together as well? Didn't students with strong religious ties tend to be *close* friends with students of the same religion? If your school environment was safe enough for gay students to identify themselves, wasn't there a social group based on gay sexual orientation, which may have been subdivided into two more groups: gay male and gay female students? You can see the strength of these cultural ties if your school had athletic teams made up of students from diverse backgrounds. The athletes may have bonded with their teammates at school, but how many of them formed *close* out-of-school friendships with athletes of a different race, class, or sexual orientation?

Of course, it seems natural for us to form close ties with people who share our cultural background because we have so much in common. The unfortunate thing is that we tend to form only superficial relationships, or none at all, with people from other cultural groups. And worse, we tend to classify other groups according to misleading stereotypes that prevent us from getting to know one another as individuals. We might even find ourselves looking at members of another group as if they were creatures from another planet, "not like us" and therefore not as good, not as trustworthy, and in worst-case scenarios, not as human. One solution to this problem is to begin to understand one another by learning to see the world from diverse points of view, by learning what it might be like to "walk a mile in another person's moccasins." And though it might sound like a big claim, that is precisely what critical theory can help us learn because it teaches us to see the world from multiple perspectives.

Naturally, critical theory has specific benefits for students of literature. For example, critical theory can increase your understanding of literary texts by helping you see more in them than you've seen before. And by giving you more to see in literature, critical theory can make literature more interesting to read. As you'll see in the following chapters, critical theory can also provide you with multiple interpretations of the same literary work, which will increase the possibility of finding interesting essay topics for your literature classes. Finally, a practice that is increasing in popularity in literary studies is the application of critical theory to cultural productions other than literature—for example, to movies, song lyrics, and television shows—and even to your own personal experience, which will help you see more and understand more of the world in which you live.

What will I learn about critical theory from this book?

So now that I've been trying to convince you of the value of critical theory for the last several paragraphs, perhaps it's time to explain in some detail what critical theory is. If you've looked at the table of contents of this textbook, you've probably discovered that what is commonly called *critical theory* actually consists of several critical theories. And what is most interesting, each theory focuses our attention on a different area of human experience—and therefore on a different aspect of literature—and gives us its own set of concepts with which to understand the world in which we live and the literature that is part and parcel of our world. Think of each theory as a different lens or a different pair of eyeglasses through which we see a different picture of the world and a different view of any literary text we read. To help you get a feel for how each critical theory changes what we see in a literary work, here's a brief overview of the theories from which we'll draw in this book.

Reader-response theory focuses on how readers make meaning—on what happens to us as we read a particular literary work. It asks us to analyze how, exactly, we interact with a given text as we read and interpret it. In Chapter 2 we'll use concepts from this theory to help you understand some of the personal sources of your own individual interpretations of literature—that is, to help you understand why each of us tends to interpret particular literary texts the way we do. For this reason, Chapter 2 won't show you how to analyze literary texts; instead, it will help you understand the ways in which we bring our own beliefs and experiences to our literary interpretations. In addition, Chapter 2 will offer you ways of dealing with the personal, subjective nature of interpretation. Once you're in touch with the personal factors influencing your interpretations, you'll be ready to bring that awareness to subsequent chapters in which we use concepts from different critical theories to analyze literary works.

Whereas reader-response theory focuses on the experiences of the reader during the act of reading, *New Critical* theory focuses exclusively on the ways in which language operates in a literary text to make meaning. Chapter 3 will provide concepts from New Critical theory to help you interpret literature thematically—that is, in terms of a literary text's meaning as a whole concerning general topics about human experience, such as love and hate, tradition and change, the initiation into adulthood, conformity and rebellion, and the like. And in order to help you analyze how a text's meaning is linked to its language, this chapter will help increase your understanding of such literary devices as, for example, setting, characterization, point of view, ambiguity, imagery, symbol, and metaphor. Many of you will be familiar with this approach because it resembles the way we are usually taught to interpret literary works in high-school or preparatory-school literature classes. In addition, Chapter 3 will help you improve and expand your ability to generate a thesis (a debatable opinion that forms the main point of your interpretation) and to support your thesis with evidence from the literary work you are interpreting. Taken together, then, Chapters 2 and 3 should help you develop both the self-awareness and interpretive skills that will serve you well as you move on to the critical theories offered in the following chapters.

Chapters 4 through 9 introduce you to a range of critical theories that I believe you will find very interesting as well as very helpful to your study of literature. In Chapter 4, we'll use concepts from *psychoanalytic theory* to interpret literature. Psychoanalytic theory asks us to examine the emotional causes of the characters' behavior and to view a given story, poem, or play as the unfolding of the characters' personal psychological dramas. In contrast, *Marxist theory*, as we'll see in Chapter 5, asks us to look at the ways in which characters' behavior and plot events are influenced by the socioeconomic conditions of the time and place in which the characters live. From a Marxist perspective, all human experiences, including personal psychology, are products of the socio-economic system—which is usually some sort of class system—in which human beings live. In Chapter 6, we'll see how *feminist theory* asks us to look at the ways in which traditional gender roles, which cast men as naturally dominant and women as naturally submissive, affect characters' behavior and plot events. *Lesbian*, *gay*, and *queer theories*, as Chapter 7 demonstrates, ask us to examine the ways in which literary works reveal human sexuality as a complex phenomenon that cannot be fully understood in terms of what is currently defined as heterosexual experience. In Chapter 8, we'll see how *African American theory* focuses our attention on the many different ways in which race and racial issues operate in literary texts. *Postcolonial theory*, as we'll see in Chapter 9, asks us to look at the ways in which literature offers us a view of human experience as the product of a combination of cultural factors, including race, class, gender, sexual orientation, and cultural beliefs and customs.

Finally, Chapter 10, "Holding on to what you've learned," offers shorthand overviews both of the critical theories you encountered in Chapters 2 through 9 and of the interpretation exercises provided to help you learn to use these theories. In addition, Chapter 10 revisits the relationship between critical theory and cultural criticism discussed later in this chapter. Chapter 10 closes by examining a question implied by our use of reader-response concepts in Chapter 2, which is also a question raised whenever any critical theory attempts to promote cultural understanding and the appreciation of cultural difference: How can critical theory help us understand, develop, and give voice to our personal values, particularly as those values affect and are affected by the values of others?

Of course, there are many more critical theories than those introduced here. For example, in addition to the theories we draw upon in this book, courses in critical theory may include units on structuralism, deconstruction, new historicism, rhetorical criticism, or Jungian theory, among others. The theories I've chosen for you were selected because I believe you will find them most helpful as you develop your understanding of literature and most relevant to your life. And these theories will lay a strong foundation for further study in critical theory, should you choose to pursue your education in that direction.

Analogously, the five literary texts that appear at the end of this book (Appendices A–E) and are used for our interpretation exercises were chosen for specific reasons. Each text shows you something useful about our selected theories. And collectively, these literary works offer a range of authorial voices in terms of race, gender, and sexual orientation. These works include Emily Dickinson's poem #520, "I started Early—Took my Dog" (c. 1862); William Faulkner's story "A Rose for Emily" (1931); Ralph Ellison's "The Battle Royal," which is the first chapter of his well-known novel *Invisible Man* (1952); a story by Alice Walker entitled "Everyday Use" (1973); and Jewelle Gomez's story "Don't Explain" (1987). Although, as you can see, we focus primarily on fiction, our theories can be used to interpret any genre of literature. For like short stories and novels, most plays and poems contain a narrative element—they tell a story—and stories usually offer us the best starting places for learning to use concepts from critical theory.

One secret for developing a good initial relationship to critical theory is to not expect of yourself more than you should at this stage of the game. For example, although you should be able to understand the interpretation exercises I offer you in each chapter—or be able to ask questions about those exercises that will allow your instructor to help you—you should not expect yourself, at first, to come up with similar interpretations completely on your own. At this point in your acquaintance with theory, it is quite natural that you should need some guidelines to help you develop your own theoretical interpretations. The "Interpretation exercises" found in Chapters 3 through 9 offer those guidelines: each interpretation exercise demonstrates a different aspect of the theory at hand and thus serves as a model for analyzing literature on your own.

In addition, to help insure that you take one step at a time, each chapter presents only the basic concepts of the theory it addresses. This will help you get a firm grasp of the theory at hand without overwhelming you with the kind of full-blown explanations of each theory you would need in a course devoted exclusively to critical theory. If you want to learn more about a particular theory, I suggest you try "Taking the next step" at the end of any chapter that especially interests you. There you will find "Questions for further practice," to help you gain experience using the theoretical concepts you've learned in that chapter by applying them to additional literary works, and a selected bibliography, "Suggestions for further reading," to guide you to additional discussions of the critical theory at hand. Finally, Appendix F, "Additional literary works for further practice," recommends a range of specific titles that lend themselves readily to our selected critical theories.

To customize *Using Critical Theory* for your own purposes, you can study just those theories that interest you or that your instructor selects for you. Each chapter is written to stand on its own and will make sense without requiring you to read other chapters. Once you have read the chapters you've selected, it might also be useful to "read across" those chapters, so to speak, by rereading the different interpretations of the same literary work offered in different chapters. See what happens, for example, as Alice Walker's "Everyday Use" is interpreted through the successive lenses of the theories you've studied. You will notice, especially if you look at all of the interpretation exercises offered for any one of our literary pieces, that some theories work better than others for analyzing a particular text. Indeed, literary works tend to lend themselves more readily to interpretation through some theoretical frameworks than through others. For this reason, our interpretation exercises analyze our sample literary works in the order in which those works are most accessible to the theory being used in that chapter.

Clearly, the ability to pick the appropriate theory for a literary work you want to interpret, or to pick an appropriate literary work for a theory you want to use, is a skill worth developing. For most of us, it's a question of trial and error. We experimentally apply different theories to a piece of literature we want to analyze until we find one that yields the most interesting and perhaps the most thorough interpretation. Of course, the ability to use any given theory to analyze any given text differs from person to person, so the key is to find the combination of theory and literary text that works *for you*. In fact, you might see some of the ways in which different readers can use the same theory to come up with different readings of the same literary work if you or your instructor interprets any of our five literary texts in ways that differ from the interpretation exercises I offer you.

Critical theory and cultural criticism

One of the most eye-opening and enjoyable features of critical theory is the way it can be used to practice cultural criticism. Contrary to what you might be thinking, *cultural criticism* does not refer to the evaluation of works of "high" culture, such as opera, ballet, symphonic music, or Renaissance painting. Rather, cultural criticism sees works of "high" and "popular" culture as equally important expressions of the societies that produce them. Indeed, cultural criticism often crosses the line between the two, for instance, by analyzing a work of "high" culture alongside a popular version of that work in order to see what similarities and differences the two can reveal about the societies from which they emerged. Think, for example, of Shakespeare's *Romeo and Juliet* (c. 1595) and *West Side Story* (directed by Robert Wise and Jerome Robbins, 1961), a musical film adaptation of Shakespeare's play set amidst New York City gang rivalry in the late 1950s.

Cultural criticism focuses primarily, however, on works of popular culture, on productions intended for popular consumption, such as movies, television and radio shows, song lyrics, "pulp" fiction, cartoons, games, toys, television and magazine ads, fairy tales, urban legends, children's books and curriculum materials, self-help books, beauty contests, professional sports, state fairs, and the like. And as this list indicates, cultural criticism also crosses the line between forms of entertainment and information. So let's think of cultural criticism as any analysis of any production of popular culture that seeks to understand what that production is "saying" to members of the culture that produced it. Let me explain.

As you develop your ability to interpret literature using concepts from different critical theories, you'll probably catch yourself noticing new things—related to one or more of these concepts—about your favorite television program, about a movie you've recently seen, or even about a comic strip in the newspaper or a magazine ad. That is, you'll probably start practicing cultural criticism without realizing that you're doing so. For as we've just seen, television shows, movies, comic strips, advertisements, and just about any other cultural production intended for the general public are all examples of popular culture. They all grow out of a particular set of customs and values generally shared by a particular population. Therefore, they all reveal something about the culture that creates them, whether they intend to do so or not.

One way to discover what popular-culture productions reveal about the culture that creates them—that is, one way to practice cultural criticism—is to analyze the cultural "messages" these productions send to the members of that culture or, as cultural critics put it, the *cultural work* these productions perform in reflecting, reinforcing, or transforming the values, beliefs, and perceptions of the culture that produces them. And concepts from the critical theories we'll study in this book can help us do just that. For as we'll see shortly, in addition to sharpening our interpretive skills, concepts from each critical theory provide a foundation for asking specific questions about cultural productions, questions that will help us "decode," so to speak, the cultural messages being sent by those productions. Let me offer you two brief examples of cultural criticism suggested by my students. Although you may be familiar with these examples, you may not have thought of them as instances of cultural criticism.

Suppose I want to analyze the availability of a certain doll intended for pre-teen American girls; offered with a variety of hair colors, eye colors, and apparel; and extremely popular nationwide: the "doll of the year," so to speak, which every girl owns or wants to own. If I pay particular attention to the dolls' physical features in terms of their apparent race or ethnicity, I can use concepts from African American, postcolonial, and psychoanalytic theories to help me answer questions like the following. Do most or all of these dolls have white skin and Anglo-European facial features? Do most of them have blond or light-brown hair and blue or light-colored eyes? If the toy company that makes these dolls has produced a version intended as an African American doll, does that version have tan rather than medium-brown or dark-brown skin? Does that version have the same Anglo-European features as the white dolls? Can the African American version of the doll be found as readily in stores—especially in stores located in racially integrated regions—as the white versions? Can Latina, Asian American, or Native American versions of the doll be found readily in stores located where these Americans live and shop? How does a parent of color decide, when there are no ethnic versions of the coveted doll available locally, whether or not to give his or her child a white version of the doll? What does it mean if a young girl of color prefers a white version or would reject a medium- or dark-brown version of the doll?

In short, what cultural message does the racially based limited availability of these dolls send to the doll-purchasing and doll-receiving members of the community concerning the value of certain kinds of dolls? And what message is being sent concerning the value of certain kinds of little girls? What dangers to children's self-image and self-esteem are inherent in racially or ethnically biased marketing? Ideally, of course, children of all races and ethnicities would want to play with dolls of all races and ethnicities. How does the limited availability of anything but white dolls discourage this ideal? Can you find a brand of doll, or of any kind of children's plaything, that offers more equitable multicultural representation and availability? It might be interesting to analyze the cultural messages sent by two such different toys. For, as noted earlier, although productions of popular culture often reflect and reinforce the values, beliefs, and perceptions of the culture that creates them, those productions also can transform the values, beliefs, and perceptions of the culture that creates them.

Similarly, I can use concepts from postcolonial and Marxist theories to help me examine video games intended for teenaged boys and marketed in many countries. I might analyze, for instance, video games in which players try to accumulate some form of wealth or social rank by shooting as many as possible of the enemy figures that appear on the screen. The following questions might help me discover the cultural messages being sent by such games. What do the enemy figures look like? Do their physical features or apparel make them look less than or other than human? In other words, is the enemy dehumanized in some way? Why are the accumulation of great wealth and the acquisition of high social rank such motivating rewards? Why is competition against other players often an important part of the game? People who are not interested in cultural criticism would probably respond to these questions by saying, "It's human nature to dehumanize our enemies, to be strongly motivated by the prospect of accumulating great wealth and acquiring high social rank, and to enjoy competition." If you are interested in cultural criticism, however, you will want to know how concepts from postcolonial and Marxist theories can offer you ways of responding to these questions quite differently by showing you the connections between the rules governing a given video game and the values supporting the culture that creates and plays that game.

To approach this kind of video game from a different perspective, we might use concepts from feminist theory and from gay, lesbian, and queer theories to analyze the definition of masculinity—and perhaps the definition of femininity—promoted by these games. What masculine qualities does a player need in order to play the game successfully? What masculine qualities seem to be valued in the world created by the game? What personal qualities are devalued or seem to be irrelevant? Are female figures present in the game? What do they look like, and how are they dressed? What kinds of behavior do they exhibit? How do male and female figures relate to figures of the opposite sex? How do they relate to figures of the same sex? What seems to be the role of the female figures in the game?

The issue here isn't whether or not we play any particular kind of video game or whether we approve or disapprove of any particular kind of video game. Rather, the issue here is our ability to notice and interpret the messages we receive every day from video games and from all the other modes of popular entertainment and information that are so much a part of our culture that we may not give them a second thought.

These examples might seem, at this point, rather simple. As you become acquainted with concepts from our critical theories, however, you'll see how the everyday products and practices we take for granted are, in fact, much more complex and interesting than most of us realize. To that end, each chapter's "Food for further thought" section includes an extended example of the ways in which cultural criticism relates to the critical theory addressed in that chapter. You will also find, included in the list of "Questions for further practice" that closes each chapter, an opportunity to apply the theory at hand to a production of popular culture in addition to the literary works to which these questions primarily apply. Chapter 10, the final chapter, offers further discussion of the relationship between critical theory and cultural criticism and includes guidelines for a cultural analysis of an episode from an old television series still popular today. When you reach the final chapter, I think you'll be in a position to appreciate that the cultural analysis suggested there is somewhat more complicated than it might appear to the uninitiated eye.

Three questions about interpretation most students ask

By this point, I hope I've answered most of the questions you have about our reasons for studying critical theory and the ways in which this book can help you get started. However, there are three questions that seem to come up whenever students interpret literature and especially when they begin to use critical theories to help them develop their interpretations. So let's take a brief look at those questions now.

My interpretation is my opinion, so how can it be wrong?

Yes, your interpretation *is* your opinion. That's what it's supposed to be. In fact, the definition of the word *thesis* is *debatable opinion*, and your thesis is the main point of your argument when you write a paper that offers an interpretation of a literary work. But notice the word *debatable* in the definition of the word *thesis*. When you're giving your interpretation of a literary work, you're not saying "I like this work" or "I don't like this work." True, "I like this work" and "I don't like this work" are opinions that can't be wrong. (Your instructor can't tell you that you're wrong unless your instructor wants to suggest that you're lying about your opinion!) But that kind of opinion is not an interpretation. It's not a thesis because it's not debatable.

A reader's interpretation doesn't tell us whether or not he or she likes a given literary work. An interpretation tells us what the reader thinks the literary work *means*. An interpretation is thus an opinion that is debatable. Your interpretation, therefore, can be judged right or wrong by other readers, just as you can judge their interpretations right or wrong. So the point in offering an interpretation is not just to state what you think the literary work means—not just to give your opinion—but to use evidence from the literary work to explain why you think your interpretation is valid. Interpreting a literary work, then, is like being both a detective and a lawyer: first you have to figure out what you think the work means; then you have to "make a case" for your opinion that will be as convincing to others as you can make it.

Do authors deliberately use concepts from critical theories when they write literary works?

Once students begin to use critical theories to interpret literature, they often see so many theoretical concepts in literary works that they think the authors must have put those concepts there on purpose. How else, many students wonder, could these critical theories show us so much about literature? The truth is, however, that authors may or may not deliberately use concepts from critical theories when they write literary works. Let's use psychoanalytic theory as an example.

We are told that D.H. Lawrence knew some of Freud's theories and deliberately used psychoanalytic concepts when he wrote *Sons and Lovers*, a novel that focuses on a young man's rather consuming and self-destructive oedipal attachment to his mother. But many authors were unfamiliar with psychoanalysis—or with any of the critical theories we use today—when they wrote literary works. Shakespeare, for example, lived and died long before Sigmund Freud developed his psychoanalytic approach to understanding human behavior. Yet we can use psychoanalytic concepts to interpret Shakespeare's plays and sonnets, for instance, to understand his characters' motivations or to gain insight into some of the psychological forces operating in the society represented in his work. For Freud didn't invent the psychological forces that motivate human beings. As he himself stated, Freud simply observed those psychological forces and gave them names. That is, Freud discovered something that had always existed and that would continue to exist whether or not anyone ever discovered it: the human psyche.

Shakespeare, therefore, didn't need psychoanalytic theory to create his emotionally complex and psychologically conflicted characters. All he had to do was represent human behavior accurately: his characterizations automatically included the operations of the human psyche. However, while Shakespeare didn't need psychoanalytic theory to create his masterpieces, psychoanalytic theorists believe that psychoanalytic concepts can help us understand the work of Shakespeare and other writers more profoundly than we might be able to do without those concepts. And indeed, all schools of critical theory, including those upon which we draw in this book, make the same kinds of arguments for the usefulness of their approaches to literary interpretation.

How can we interpret a literary work without knowing what the author intended the work to mean?

When we interpret a literary work we assume that it may contain more meanings or fewer meanings or different meanings from those the author intended it to have. After all, writers are human beings. Sometimes what they produce goes beyond their expectations, beyond what is called *authorial intention*. On the other hand, sometimes a literary work doesn't live up to what its author intended it to mean: sometimes authors fail to achieve their intentions. And even if literature were nothing more than the embodiment of authors' intended meanings, we usually don't know, or can't be certain, what an author intended a particular work to mean. Many authors whose works we read are long dead, and there is no record of their intended meaning.

Some authors, however, wrote essays in which they explained what they wanted their work to mean, and, of course, many authors are alive and can tell us what they intended their work to mean. Yet even then, we still have to face the problem of whether a given literary work achieves the author's intention, fails to achieve the author's intention, or is even richer and more complex than the author expected it to be. All we really have to go on is the literary work itself, even when we know the author's intention. So that's what we go on: the literary work itself. Our interpretation can draw on historical elements relevant to the author's life and times, but our interpretation must be supported by adequate evidence—elements of plot, characterization, dialogue, setting, imagery, and so forth—from the literary text. Therefore, even when we feel that our interpretation must be what the author intended the work to mean, we generally say "the text seems to intend" or "the text implies" rather than "the author seems to intend" or "the author implies."

Why feeling confused *can* be a good sign

Perhaps one of the most unfortunate things about formal education is that it trains us to fear failure to such a degree that we become afraid to take risks. At the first feeling of confusion we often become terrified. When confronted with a new subject or even a new idea, the first time we silently say the words "I don't get it"—the first time we feel confused—we usually experience any number of negative reactions that generally involve giving up without a fight: "Why should I waste my time when I'm not going to understand this anyway?" That is, we assume that our confusion is a sign of probable, if not inevitable, failure.

Confusion, however, *can* mean just the opposite when we're learning something new. It can mean that we've let go of an old, comfortable way of seeing things in order to see something new. Because we're trying to see something new, however, we can't quite get a firm grasp of it immediately. It's like crossing a river: we're temporarily stuck in the middle. We've let go of the riverbank on which we were comfortably seated, but we've not yet reached the bank on the other side. This experience is especially common when we're learning critical theory because critical theory requires that we temporarily let go of old ways of seeing things—old ways of seeing literature, society, ourselves—in order to see them in new ways.

So whatever your experience as you work your way through this textbook, remember that it's natural to feel confused at times. In fact, I think you should honor your confusion because it means that you've been courageous enough to let go of your usual way of understanding things in order to try a new way that you haven't quite grasped yet. You've let go of the riverbank in order to cross to the other side of the river. Although it may take a little while to get to that other side, you can't even begin the journey if you don't let go of solid ground. And no matter how you look at it, that's a brave and a very worthwhile act.

Chapter 2

Using concepts from reader-response theory to understand our own literary interpretations

Why should we learn about reader-response theory?

Most of us are intrigued, I think, by the prospect of learning something interesting or useful about ourselves. That's precisely what reader-response theory offers us, and perhaps that's why it has become a popular framework for the study of literature.

There are, however, several different kinds of reader-response theory, and they aren't all interested in the same kinds of self-knowledge. Some reader-response approaches examine the ways in which our literary interpretations are influenced by social factors: for example, by the social or cultural group with which we identify, by the system of education that tells us what literary works are important and how they should be interpreted, or even by the classmates whose opinions influence our responses as we read literary works together. Other reader-response approaches analyze literary works themselves in order to determine how our responses are guided by the way a work is written: for instance, the amount of information provided about characters and plot, the order in which that information is provided, and the attitude of the narrator that provides it. Finally, some reader-response approaches try to determine how our responses to literary works are influenced by our personal experiences, by the emotional or psychological dimension of our daily lives: for example, our likes and dislikes, our loves, our fears, our desires, and our memories.

It is this last kind of reader-response theory that we are interested in here. For despite their differences, all reader-response theories have one important thing in common. They all believe that readers play an active role in *making meaning when they read*. So let's begin at this common point by focusing, in this chapter, on the following question: how does each of us make meaning when we read a literary work? And to find answers to this question, let's use a reader-response approach that helps us examine the emotional events that occur within us as we read. For although we might believe that our literary interpretations are completely objective and based solely upon "what happens" in a story, poem, or play, in fact a good deal of what we think happens in a literary text, and what we think the text means, comes from the history of our personal experiences, which acts as a kind of emotional filter through which we perceive the literary work. It seems reasonable, then, to see if we can improve our ability to understand and enjoy literature by improving our ability to understand the role that our personal responses play in our literary interpretations.

One well-known framework for exploring the personal dimension of our individual reading processes is offered by Norman Holland,[1] who suggests that we respond to literary texts in much the same way that we respond to experiences in our daily lives. Holland believes that each of us has what he calls an *identity theme*, which is the pattern of our emotional challenges and coping strategies by which we respond to people and events on an everyday basis. To offer a simple example, if I don't trust people who remind me of my emotionally manipulative Aunt Betty, then I won't trust literary characters who remind me of her. And if I deal with my negative feelings about my Aunt Betty by refusing to see anything good in her at all—by reducing her to her character flaw so that I don't have to deal with her emotionally—then I will deal in the same way with literary characters that remind me of her: by refusing to see anything good in them at all.

In short, the same kinds of people, places, and events that create anxiety and activate my defenses in my everyday life will create anxiety and activate my defenses when I see representations of those kinds of people, places, and events in—or project them onto—a literary work. For obvious reasons, Holland calls this reading experience, which can occur for different reasons at multiple points throughout our reading of a literary work, the *defense mode*. To go back to the example of Aunt Betty, I will go into defense mode as soon as I spot a literary character that reminds me of her because, although I'm probably not aware of it, this reminder makes me anxious. My defenses are activated because I feel in need of some emotional protection.

When we are in defense mode, we will interpret what we are reading, not in a manner that reflects the actual words on the page, but in a manner that reduces our anxiety. In other words, we will imagine that the troubling passage means whatever our defenses require it to mean at that point in time. Holland calls this part of the reading process the *fantasy mode*. For example, my defenses having been raised by encountering a literary character that reminds me of my Aunt Betty, I will see only the negative side of the portrayal even if the character is portrayed positively in some respects. Most probably without realizing it, I will view this character in a very limited way so that—just as I do in my relationship with my Aunt Betty—I can avoid dealing with the emotions it will otherwise create in me.

For many of us, however, it is rather difficult to know when we are in defense mode or fantasy mode. For these two modes occur in order to keep us from knowing something we don't want to know about ourselves and, therefore, about the literary work we are reading. How, then, can we use Holland's ideas to help us discover how our personal reading responses operate to influence our interpretation of literature?

Perhaps the following common reading experiences can serve as vehicles for the kinds of responses described by Holland. That is, they can provide us with a hands-on, "up-close-and-personal" method to get in touch with and put into words the specific ways in which we are responding to a given literary work. In order to do so, these "response vehicles" focus on some of the very specific kinds of relationships that can occur between ourselves and various elements of a literary work.

Response vehicles

Personal identification

Personal identification is the experience of seeing ourselves in a literary character, often without knowing that we are doing so. We feel that we understand how this character feels and what motivates his or her behavior because we believe that the character feels as we would feel in his or her circumstances and is influenced by the same motivations that would influence us in a similar situation.

reader = character

The familiar character

Sometimes a literary character seems familiar to us because that character reminds us of someone we know, often someone important in our lives in the past or in the present, although we may not realize that this "recognition" is taking place. A character may remind us of a friend, family member, spouse, former sweetheart, teacher, roommate, classmate, or anyone else we've known at any point in our lives. Perhaps a character physically resembles, shares some personality traits with, or behaves like someone we know or used to know.

Character = friend/family

The familiar plot event

A plot event can be as brief and/or simple as a character's picking up a pen or as long and/or complex as a son discovering his father in a hotel room with a strange woman. Sometimes a plot event seems familiar to us because, whether we realize it or not, the event reminds us of something we've seen or experienced ourselves. Unless asked to do so, we may not notice that we are relating personally to a particular plot event because plot events are generally numerous, and our attention is often focused on the plot events that are, according to our teacher or textbook, central to the meaning of the literary work.

reader experience = plot experience (story)

The familiar setting

Sometimes a literary setting seems familiar to us because its geographic location or physical appearance evokes memories of a place with which we associate important experiences that occurred there or with which we associate an

subconscious (margin note)

important time in our life, although we may not realize that we are making this kind of connection. Personal responses to a literary setting are often more subtle than other kinds of personal responses to literature because many readers regard setting as a backdrop that doesn't require attention in its own right.

reader location = story location

Response exercises

Given our focus, in this chapter, on learning to understand the personal sources of our own literary interpretations rather than to analyze literary works, we won't do the kinds of interpretation exercises you will find in subsequent chapters, chapters that focus on different ways to understand literature. Instead of exercises that analyze each of the five sample literary works included at the end of this book, we'll use our response vehicles and one of our sample literary works—Alice Walker's "Everyday Use" (1973; see Appendix D)—to generate response exercises you can use whenever you want to explore the role played by your personal responses in your interpretation of a literary work. The sample responses that follow each exercise are intended to illustrate the wide variety of responses that can be elicited by these exercises as well as the fact that different exercises can elicit similar responses. Later in the chapter, we'll examine the ways in which your personal responses can either help or hinder your ability to interpret literature. Finally, we'll explore the ways in which your personal responses can be used to help you generate topics for interpreting literature that are meaningful to others as well as to yourself.

In order to perform the exercises below, you first need to read Alice Walker's story "Everyday Use," which appears at the end of this book. If you've not already read this story, please do so now. Then take a sheet of paper and try the following exercises. For each exercise, give whatever answers accurately reflect your feelings, even if you sometimes give the same answer to more than one question.

Personal-identification exercise

1   Which character do you like most?
2   Which character do you dislike most?
3   For which character do you feel most sorry?
4   Which character do you admire most?
5   To which of the above four questions did you have the strongest emotional response? (It doesn't matter what kind of emotion you experienced. Just pick the question that caused the strongest feeling in you.) Write down again here the character you named in answering that question.
6   How do you see yourself in the character you named in question 5? List all the things you have in common with this character. (You may have things in common with this character that don't come immediately to mind. Think about it.) Your job in question 6 is to describe as

completely as possible all the ways in which you personally identify with this character.

7   This is the crucial, final step. Now that you know some of the ways in which you personally identify with this character, how might that identification have influenced your interpretation of the story? For example, might your personal bond with this character have influenced your interpretation of this character, of another character, or of a particular event in the story? Write down your answer in as much detail as possible. (Try your best to answer this question thoroughly, but don't worry if, at this point in time, you're unable to do so as fully as you'd like.)

Our answer to question 7 is the key to understanding an important aspect of our emotional relationship to the story and, therefore, an important source of our interpretation of it. Let's see how my interpretation of "Everyday Use" might change according to which character I identify with most strongly.

Suppose, for instance, I identify most strongly with Maggie because, like her, I'm a quiet, shy person or had a sibling whom I felt was given more advantages or attention than I was. In that case, I might interpret Dee (Wangero)— because of her insensitivity to Maggie—in a wholly negative manner as a shallow, selfish, insensitive person, and I'd probably make light of the few positive qualities the text clearly gives her. I might even suspect that Dee started the fire that burned down the family's former home, although the story provides no clear evidence to support such a suspicion. In addition, I might argue that Mrs. Johnson (Mama) has been a less-than-perfect mother in favoring Dee over Maggie or in underestimating Maggie's talents. And I might dislike Hakim because of his apparent insensitivity to, and even dismissal of, Maggie.

In contrast, what if, instead, I identify with Dee? For example, suppose that, like Dee, I chose a path different from that of my family or have felt misunderstood by my family. In that case, I would probably interpret Dee more positively, as a character with understandably conflicted feelings toward her mother and sister and an understandable desire to live her own life. Although I would have to admit that Dee has some unfortunate traits, I would probably be more aware of her good points—including her less obvious good points—than would other readers. I might focus, for instance, on her remarkable achievements despite the biases of race, class, and gender that have stood in her way. And I might notice the textual evidence that suggests her desire to be appreciated by her mother and sister rather than treated as an outsider. In addition, I might argue that Mrs. Johnson has been a less-than-perfect mother in favoring Maggie over Dee or in failing to bridge the emotional distance between herself and Dee that has existed since Dee's childhood. Indeed, even my interpretation of Hakim's behavior toward Mrs. Johnson and Maggie will be influenced by whether or not I think him "good enough" for Dee.

Now what if, instead of identifying with either sister, I identify with Mrs. Johnson? Suppose, for example, I have children of my own and can understand what a difficult job it must have been for Mrs. Johnson to raise two daughters by herself on a low income. In that case, I might interpret Dee negatively based largely on her failure to appreciate all her mother has done for her. And I might argue further that it would be unfair of readers to blame Mrs. Johnson in any way for Dee's problems because I would be aware of all the ways in which Mrs. Johnson is a hardworking, devoted mother who loves Dee and who wishes she could please her successful daughter (just look at Mrs. Johnson's dream about appearing on television) despite Dee's insensitive air of superiority. In addition, I might find Maggie sympathetic, not just because she is shy and has suffered many serious hardships, but because Maggie clearly loves her mother, and the two are very close. And I might dislike Hakim because I think he is condescending and insensitive to Mrs. Johnson.

Finally, let's consider what might happen if, instead, I identify with Hakim, Dee's boyfriend. For instance, suppose that, like Hakim, I am attracted to a religious culture different from that of the older generation in my community or that, like him, I am not considered classically handsome. In either case, I might find vicarious satisfaction in Hakim's having won himself a beautiful girlfriend who shares his values. From this perspective, I might interpret Dee positively, in a manner that is especially sympathetic to her desire for a more affluent life and to her ambivalent feelings toward Mrs. Johnson and Maggie, who would probably seem to me unnecessarily rude to Hakim. But if I am put off by what I feel is Dee's lack of attention to Hakim—after all, she doesn't seem to interact with him any more than do her mother and sister—I might end up with a negative interpretation of all three female characters.

Remember, these are just examples of the ways in which our literary interpretations can be influenced by our personal identification with a character. Your experience with this exercise might lead you in a very different direction. Perhaps, for instance, you will find that your identification with a literary character is based on a trait that you don't like or about which you feel conflicted. In that case, the exercise might offer you the opportunity for helpful self-reflection. Whatever you discover, the goal here is to use your discovery to help you understand the personal sources of your literary interpretation.

Familiar-character exercise

When a character reminds us of someone we know or knew in the past, we may have responses similar to those elicited when we identify with a character. Which of these two exercises puts us more closely in touch with the sources of our literary interpretation will depend, of course, on the relationship between our personal history and the literary text in question.

1   Write down the names of all the characters in the literary work that you are able to remember. If you can't remember some characters' names, use some other way of identifying them.

2 Of the characters you've just listed, write down the names of those that seem somehow familiar to you. Perhaps they remind you, a great deal or just a little bit, of someone you know or someone you knew in the past. "Try each character on," so to speak, in your imagination. (Maybe you're not immediately sure why some characters seem familiar. Think about it.) Then list as many characters as you can that seem in any way familiar to you.

3 List again, vertically, the names of all the characters you identified in question 2. Beside each character's name, write the name of the person of whom that character reminds you.

4 To which of the pairs of names you listed in question 3 did you have the strongest emotional response? (It doesn't matter what kind of emotion you experienced. Just pick the pair of names that caused the strongest feeling in you.) Write down here that pair of names.

5 Think about the connection between the two names in the pair you wrote down in question 4. List all the things they have in common. Do they have some sort of physical resemblance? Do they share one or more personality traits? Do they, in some way, behave similarly? (They may have things in common that don't come immediately to mind. Think about it.) Your job in question 5 is to describe as completely as possible all the similarities you can find between the two.

6 This is the crucial, final step. Now that you know some of the ways this character reminds you of someone you know or used to know, how might that personal connection have influenced your interpretation of the story? For example, might a similarity between this character and someone you know or used to know have influenced your interpretation of this character, of another character, or of a particular event in the story? Write down your answer in as much detail as possible. (Try your best to answer this question thoroughly, but don't worry if, at this point in time, you're unable to do so as fully as you'd like.)

Our answer to question 6 is the key to understanding an important aspect of our emotional relationship to the story and, therefore, an important source of our interpretation of it. Let's see how my interpretation of "Everyday Use" might change depending on my responses to the character I find most familiar.

For instance, suppose I find Maggie most familiar because she reminds me of a quiet, shy classmate I had in grammar school. Suppose, too, this classmate's great hesitancy to speak irritated the teacher repeatedly and made our classmates impatient, thereby making me nervous and impatient. In that case, I might feel impatient, even irritated, with Maggie, and I might see her as her own worst enemy: she wouldn't be so overlooked by Dee, and by everyone else, if she weren't such a scared little mouse. Although many readers find Maggie extremely sympathetic, I might blame her for her own problems in order to get some emotional distance from her because, whether or not I realize it, she makes me feel guilty. She reminds me of my shy grammar-school classmate and, looking back, I feel I should have been kinder to her. Such a reaction to Maggie might lead me to interpret Mrs. Johnson as unfairly biased in Maggie's favor and/or inept as a mother. (After all, Mrs. Johnson should have taught Maggie to stand up for herself.) In addition, I might interpret Dee and Hakim sympathetically because Dee's impatience with Maggie, and Hakim's indifference to her, reminds me of my own insensitivity toward my shy young classmate. Or just as possibly, my guilty feelings about my classmate might make me want to prove to myself that I am not insensitive. In that event, I might interpret Dee and Hakim very negatively in order to show myself that I am not like them, that I strongly disapprove of insensitive people.

Suppose, instead, that Mrs. Johnson feels most familiar to me because she reminds me of one of my parents. If I was especially close to that parent, this similarity could increase my tendency to sympathize with Mrs. Johnson and trust her perceptions of the events she narrates, seeing in her only a hardworking mother devoted to both her daughters and severely underappreciated, even mistreated, by Dee and Hakim. Indeed, Mrs. Johnson is frequently interpreted in just such a positive manner. What if, however, Mrs. Johnson somehow reminds me of a parent who has a tendency to be passive-aggressive. (A passive-aggressive person will not admit to having negative feelings but nevertheless reveals those feelings in subtle ways so that people who are subjected to them cannot easily defend themselves.) In that case, whereas other readers might find Mrs. Johnson amusing or insightful in some of her humorous responses to Dee and Hakim, I might see her as passive-aggressive in a way that somewhat undercuts, for me, what many consider her very positive portrayal. I might see Mrs. Johnson's passive-aggressive behavior, for example, in her alleged inability to understand Dee's reason for calling herself Wangero and in her attempt to trivialize her daughter's new name by saying to Dee, "Ream it [your new name] out again." And I might see her passive-aggressive attitude in her repeated internal references to Hakim as "Asalamalakim" and "the barber" and in her silent conjecture that Hakim might not know how to shake hands. Such a response to Mrs. Johnson might lead me to a more sympathetic reading of Dee and Hakim. Indeed, I might even conclude that Maggie's shyness and uncertainty are, in part, the result of her mother's passive-aggression.

Similarly, my interpretation of Dee and Hakim will change depending on whether of not I find them familiar, individually or as a couple, and depending on how I feel about the person or persons in my own life of whom they remind me. For example, suppose Dee and Hakim remind me of a couple I admire because of their determination to have a better life and their success in achieving it or because their shared values make them seem to me enviably compatible. In this case, I might see Dee and Hakim as a successful young couple frustrated by the apparent refusal of Mrs. Johnson and Maggie to try to achieve a better life. Or I might deem the couple's attitude toward Mrs. Johnson and Maggie as the understandable product of youthful impatience with anything old-fashioned. In contrast, if Dee and Hakim put me in mind of a couple I dislike, then of course I will interpret the characters' relationship negatively. Perhaps I will find it superficial, a relationship of convenience based on nothing more meaningful than a mutual desire for display.

Remember, these are just examples of the ways in which our literary interpretations can be influenced by our personal connection to a familiar character. Your experience with this exercise might lead you in a very different direction. In fact, you may find that this exercise produces responses similar to those described in the personal identification exercise, for these two exercises can operate as two different routes to the same destination. Whatever you discover, the goal here is to use your discovery to help you understand the personal source of your literary interpretation.

Familiar-plot-event exercise

1   Which plot event did you find most satisfying or enjoyable?
2   Which plot event did you find most disturbing?
3   Which plot event did you find most surprising?
4   Which plot event did you find least important? That is, which plot event do you feel the story probably could do without?
5   To which of the above four questions did you have the strongest emotional response? (It doesn't matter what kind of emotion you experienced. Just pick the question that caused the strongest feeling in you.) Write down again here the plot event you named in answering that question.
6   What is your personal relationship to the plot event you named in question 5? List everything about this plot event that seems familiar to you. (There may be familiar elements in this plot event that don't come immediately to mind. Think about it.) Your job in question 6 is to describe as completely as possible all the ways in which you feel personally connected to this plot event.
7   This is the crucial, final step. Now that you know some of the ways in which you feel personally connected to this plot event, how might this connection have influenced your interpretation of the story? For example, might your personal connection to this plot event have influenced your interpretation of this event, of another plot event, or of a particular character in the story? Write down your answer in as much detail as possible. (Try your best to answer this question thoroughly, but don't worry if, at this point in time, you're unable to do so as fully as you'd like.)

Our answer to question 7 is the key to understanding an important aspect of our emotional relationship to the story and, therefore, an important source of our interpretation of it. Let's see how my interpretation of "Everyday Use" might change according to the plot event with which I most connect.

Suppose, for example, Mrs. Johnson's opening comment that she and Maggie cleaned the yard yesterday afternoon and made it so pleasant—or one of the other little events that show the closeness between Mama and Maggie—reminds me of the closeness between my mother and my sister, a closeness that I don't feel I really share. In that case, my feeling of uncertainty about my bond with my mother and sister, or my rivalry with my sister for my mother's love, might lead me to focus so strongly on the evidence of Mama's bond with Maggie that I don't pay close attention to much else in the story. As a result, I might feel that "Everyday Use" is primarily about Dee's emotional exclusion from her family. In fact, I might see all of Dee's achievements as efforts to impress her mother and thereby win her love. Hakim might therefore appear to me to be Dee's attempt to prove, both to her family and herself, that someone loves her, that she is worthy of love. From this perspective, I would probably find Mrs. Johnson and Maggie insensitive, even selfish: they're too focused on each other, on their common interests and shared experiences, to be aware of Dee's loneliness in the past or in the present.

In contrast, what if the arrival of Dee and Hakim reminds me of the "I'm-more-successful-than-you parade" that occurs every time my brother-in-law arrives to visit me with his high-end car, his designer clothes, and his latest high-tech "toy"? I might feel so put off by the "performance" Dee and Hakim put on before Mrs. Johnson and Maggie—their less privileged, coun-trified "audience"—that I don't remember in great detail what happened beyond that point in the story. Perhaps the only feeling of certainty I will have about the story is that Dee and Hakim are a superficial, selfish, insensitive young couple who visit Dee's very nice family for no other reason than to show off what they believe is their superiority.

Finally, suppose I recently inherited my mother's family heirlooms, which I plan to treat very carefully so that I will be able to pass them on to my own children? Perhaps, as a result, I won't like the fact that Mrs. Johnson gives the family's heirloom quilts to Maggie to "spoil." I might think Mrs. Johnson's impulsive decision to do so is a terrible mistake. Therefore, I might not find Mrs. Johnson as wise nor Dee as selfish nor Maggie as sympathetic as I might otherwise have found them. Indeed, I might understand quite well Dee's desire to have a few of the small domestic items—such as the butter-churn lid and dasher—that were made by family members who have passed away. Thus what many readers view as Dee's superficial attitude toward her mother's possessions—she wants them just for display because such homemade items have become fashionable—might seem to me to be Dee's sincere appreciation for their sentimental and historical significance.

Remember, these are just examples of the ways in which our literary interpretations can be influenced by our personal connection to a plot event. Your experience with this exercise might lead you in a very different direction. Perhaps, for instance, you will find that your personal connection to a particular plot event is based on something that you yourself did in the past and about which you feel especially proud or especially embarrassed. In that case, the exercise might offer you an opportunity for self-reflection that might help you better appreciate your achievement or understand your embarrassment. Whatever you discover, the goal here is to use your discovery to help you understand the personal sources of your literary interpretation.

Familiar-setting exercise

For many of us, setting may seem less influential than character and plot in eliciting our personal responses to a literary work. Although our reactions to setting are often subtle, they can nevertheless affect our reading experience in important ways.

1   Try to identify the region, country, or part of the world in which it seems to you the literary work is set. (Is the setting urban, suburban, rural, wilderness, or something else? Is the climate or the weather described? If so, what's it like, to the best of your recollection?)

2   What is the time period in which the literary work seems to you to be set? Be as general or specific as you think appropriate.

3   Is the setting characterized by architecture, landscaping, furnishings, or consumer products that you associate with wealth, poverty, middle-class life, or something else?

4   Is there some element in the work that gives you a sense of place (a feeling of "being there," in a specific locale, as you read) although you don't actually see that element or it's not always considered an aspect of setting? For example, are you struck by the way characters speak (their accent, use of regional vernacular, or use of formal speech); by the way they dress; or by references to an important element of community life, such as a company that employs most members of the community or a popular place of religious worship?

5   To which of the above four questions did you have the strongest emotional response? (It doesn't matter what kind of emotion you experienced. Just pick the question that caused the strongest feeling in you.) Write down again here your answer to that question.

6   What is your relationship to the aspect of setting you named in answer to question 5? List everything about this aspect of setting that seems familiar to you. (There may be familiar elements in this aspect of setting that don't come immediately to mind. Think about it.) Your job in question 6 is to describe as completely as possible all the ways in which you feel personally connected to this aspect of setting.

7   This is the crucial, final step. Now that you know some of the ways in which you feel personally connected to this aspect of setting, how might that connection have influenced your interpretation of the story? For example, might your connection to this aspect of setting have influenced your interpretation of the setting as a whole, of a character, or of a particular event in the story? Write down your answer in as much detail as

possible. (Try your best to answer this question thoroughly, but don't worry if, at this point in time, you're unable to do so as fully as you'd like.)

Our answer to question 7 is the key to understanding an important element in our emotional relationship to the story and, therefore, an important source of our interpretation of it. Let's see how my interpretation of "Everyday Use" might change according to the way I feel connected to some aspect of its setting.

Suppose, for example, I miss my childhood days growing up on a farm or have happy memories associated with any kind of rural location. In that case, I might consider the Johnson home a very happy place and Mrs. Johnson and Maggie—because they have remained there—very happy people. Mama and Maggie have their home, and they have each other. Maggie is marrying a local, country-bred youth like herself, so she and John Thomas will surely set up housekeeping near Mrs. Johnson. My belief that the simple life is the best life might lead me to overlook or underestimate the hardships Maggie and her mother have endured and the insecure future they face due to their lack of education and economic opportunities. In fact, if my nostalgia for the country-side is strong enough, I might not readily see Maggie's scarred body and poor vision, nor the low self-esteem to which these physical challenges have contributed, as important drawbacks. Analogously, I might feel sorry for Dee and Hakim because, having lived city lives for so long, they are beyond the reach of such genuine happiness. Or I might think that Dee is not nearly as smart as she thinks she is—or that she's smart in the wrong way—because she never valued the country life into which she was born.

In contrast, suppose I felt trapped in the rural community of my youth. Or suppose I have always lived in a city with plenty to do and can't imagine enjoying, or even enduring, what seems to me the dead-end boredom of rural life. In either case, I would not envy Mrs. Johnson and Maggie their country life. Perhaps I might share Dee's impatience with them for accepting without a murmur a life that seems to me so much less than it could be. If my relief at escaping my own limited upbringing is strong enough, I might even feel that Mama's giving the quilts to Maggie is a mistake typical of her lack of adequate concern about the future. For, as Dee rightly observes, Maggie will not save these heirlooms but ruin them by using them as bedcovers. On the other hand, I might sympathize with Mrs. Johnson and Maggie because they "got stuck" in an environment that I can think of only in negative terms. If I feel sorry for them, I might think that Dee should use her success to help her family. She hated rural life enough to go to great lengths to escape it, so she should know the severe limitations with which her mother and sister live. How can she be so selfish and uncaring? Of course, if I feel guilty for having been the only member of my family to "get away," I might either defend Dee (in order to defend myself) or attack her (in order to prove to myself that I'm not like her).

Finally, what if, instead of responding primarily to the physical aspects of setting, I respond most strongly to the emotional atmosphere—the spiritual setting—I feel is created in "Everyday Use" by the story's references to the church? Perhaps the importance of Christianity in my own life leads me to notice with particular interest the economic and psychological support the church provides, as seen in the money it raised to send Dee to college and in Mama's mention of singing hymns. In this case, I will most probably interpret Mrs. Johnson and Maggie, and the life they lead together, in very positive terms because I will see these two characters as people, like myself, in whose lives the church plays an important role. I might see their hardships as important factors in their lives, not because their hard times reveal the social and economic oppression Mrs. Johnson and Maggie have suffered, but because these hardships are the trials that have purified and enlightened the two women. And from this perspective, I might view Dee and Hakim either with disdain, as two unrepentant sinners who have rejected their Christian roots, or with sympathy, as two lost sheep adrift in a materialistic world and in great need of spiritual guidance.

Remember, these are just examples of the ways in which our literary interpretations can be influenced by our personal connection to an aspect of setting. Your experience with this exercise might lead you in a very different direction. Perhaps, for instance, you will find that your personal response to an aspect of setting is neither wholly positive nor wholly negative, but a mixture of both. In that case, your response to certain characters or plot events also might be mixed. Or you might have more trouble than some of your classmates in making up your mind about the story. Whatever you discover, the goal here is to use your discovery to help you understand the personal sources of your literary interpretation.

Of course, your responses to the characters, plot events, and setting of "Everyday Use" might resemble some of the responses described above or be entirely different. And keep in mind that our personal responses don't always involve emotional relationships to characters, plot events, or settings. Sometimes an image represented in a literary work will trigger a pleasant or unpleasant memory that will influence our reading experience and, therefore, our interpretation of the work. For instance, the image of Maggie standing shyly in the doorway of her house might trigger an important memory that will influence the way we interpret Maggie, another character, or the story as a whole. At other times our belief systems, or *ideologies*, will agree or clash with those represented in the text. For example, some readers might share Hakim's religious sympathies; others might share Mrs. Johnson's. Some readers might be especially appalled by the racism that robbed Mrs. Johnson of her rightful education; others might not consider racism a particularly important problem. Naturally, when our beliefs agree or clash with those represented in the text, this experience, too, often produces an emotional response. We may feel personally affirmed or even elated when our beliefs are in harmony with those represented in the text. Analogously, we may feel personally undermined or angry when our beliefs conflict with those represented in the text. And our interpretation of the text will probably change accordingly. In any case, the big question is this: what should we do about the significant role our personal responses play in our interpretation of literature?

How our personal responses can help or hinder interpretation

I think most instructors would agree that there is a role our personal responses should play in our interpretation of literature and a role they shouldn't. We should let our personal responses work for us by allowing them to engage us as much as possible in what we read. After all, if we have no personal response whatsoever to a literary work, we will probably find it boring, though in some instances a lack of personal response might be a way of avoiding a text that, if we let ourselves respond to it, would be too troubling or emotionally threatening. For example, if "Everyday Use" reminds me too much of a painful conflict I have with a member or members of my own family, I might be unable to concentrate on the story, rush through it, or leave it unfinished, without realizing that there is a personal reason why I couldn't "get into" the story. However, it is well worth the effort sometimes required to connect with a literary work because a personal connection to the text can increase our motivation to reread it, to pay attention to descriptive details that might help us understand it, and to work hard on developing an argument in support of our interpretation of it, which is what most literature-class-writing assignments ask us to do. As we've seen, all of the interpretive possibilities described in the previous section result from personal responses to "Everyday Use." Indeed, a personal relationship to the text can often lead us to develop more profound interpretations than we thought we could produce.

While our personal responses can thus play a very positive role in our understanding of literature, it's not unusual for a personal response to cause us to misunderstand a literary work in part or as a whole. As you probably know, there can be many different interpretations of a piece of literature. There is no one correct interpretation that we are all supposed to find. For most literary texts have enough ambiguities—things that can be interpreted in more than one way—to allow numerous readings that would be considered legitimate by most instructors. However, what makes an interpretation strong is usually the evidence we supply from the literary text to support it: characters' physical appearance, dialogue, and behavior; plot events; details of setting; imagery; and so forth. But a personal response to a text can also interfere with our perception of the evidence the text supplies. For example, if the physical description of Hakim, in "Everyday Use," reminds me of someone I dislike intensely, I might conclude that he has caused the rift between Dee and her family that he is a manipulative young man up to no good, although it's probably safe to say that the text offers no evidence to support such an interpretation. We must therefore try to remain open to the possibility that we have missed or misinterpreted something in any work we read. We can do this by keeping an open mind when our instructor or our classmates offer opinions that differ from our own. And when someone else's viewpoint challenges our own, we can go back to the text to check our initial perception and try to find evidence that will either correct or justify that perception.

The "symbolic leap"

One fairly reliable sign that our personal response to a literary work is interfering with our understanding of that work is what I would call the "symbolic leap." A symbolic leap occurs when you decide, without any support from the text, that some image you find in the text is a symbol, and then you develop an interpretation based on that symbol. In fact, once you make one symbolic leap in your reading of a text, you are very liable to make others in order to try to justify your first. For example, let's look again at the misreading of Hakim just mentioned. If that character's similarity to a person I dislike leads me to see Hakim as "trouble without a cause" and blame him for Dee's estrangement from her family, I will have difficulty finding textual evidence to back me up. But my negative personal response to Hakim will probably lead me to feel that everything associated with that character has some negative meaning, and that feeling will lead me straight into a symbolic leap.

I might, for example, decide that the long, thin hair hanging from the end of Hakim's chin, which Mrs. Johnson compares to a mule's tail, is a symbol of evil because it is, at least to me, serpent-like and because when Maggie sees it she makes the kind of sound you make, says Mrs. Johnson, when you suddenly see a wriggling snake in your path. This symbolic leap would make me very happy because I could use it to develop a reading of the story in which Hakim represents the biblical serpent in the Garden of Eden. Then, to back up my serpent-in-the-Garden-of-Eden interpretation, I would make other symbolic leaps. For example, I would see the Johnson farm as a symbol of the human condition before its fall from grace—that is, as the Garden of Eden before Eve took the apple offered by the serpent. Dee, then, would become for me the symbol of the fallen Eve, who can never return to live in the paradise represented by the Johnson farm. And so forth. At this point, I could probably find textual evidence that would seem to support my argument: in many ways, Mrs. Johnson and Maggie are both content with their life on the farm, where they apparently lead traditional Christian lives, whereas Dee seems restless, is worldly, and, as far as her mother knows, is "living in sin" with Hakim.

Such textual evidence, however, can't really help me because I haven't justified my initial symbolic leap: my initial claim that Hakim's beard is a symbol of evil. And I can't justify that claim because it's based not on the story but on my desire to see Hakim as a bad person because of the bad person of whom he reminds me. In fact, my blaming Hakim for Dee's family problems ignores, among other things, the fact that Dee was at odds with her family even when she was a young girl, long before she met Hakim. In other words, in this example I haven't been interpreting Hakim. I've been interpreting someone in real life whom I dislike and then ascribing those characteristics to Hakim. This kind of misinterpretation can be valuable, if you can figure out why it happened, because it can help you understand something about yourself. But in general, it probably won't help you understand the story.

The difference between representing and endorsing human behavior

Another way in which our personal response to a literary work can cause us to misunderstand that work occurs when we confuse a text's representation of a particular human behavior with the text's endorsement of that behavior. For example, a literary work might depict child abuse, but that doesn't mean the work endorses child abuse. In fact, many literary texts depict cruelty, injustice, and other destructive behaviors in order to expose them, in order to show readers that such behaviors deserve our disapproval or even our active resistance. Let's take an example from a text with an especially clear attitude toward one of the negative behaviors it represents: Ralph Ellison's "The Battle Royal" (1952), which appears at the end of this book (see Appendix C). As you'll see, "The Battle Royal" portrays a social gathering of white civic leaders who have invited a group of young black men to entertain them by fighting one another in a grotesquely punishing, group "boxing" match. Clearly, the text depicts very racist behavior. However, "The Battle Royal" does not endorse the racism it depicts. On the contrary, we know that the text's attitude is critical of racism because the racist civic leaders are very negatively portrayed and because the outcomes of their racist behavior are so harmful.

Sometimes, however, the fear, anger, or outrage we may feel in response to the behavior portrayed in a literary text can make us forget to examine the text's own attitude toward that behavior. If we're not careful, we might assume that a work is racist because it depicts racist behavior, that it is sexist because it depicts sexist behavior, and so forth. As the example of "The Battle Royal" illustrates, one way to learn a text's attitude toward the behavior it represents is to examine whether the characters performing that behavior are sympathetically or unsympathetically portrayed and whether the outcomes of their behavior are depicted as constructive or destructive. In other words, in order to fully understand the purpose of a literary work, we must determine if the work is asking us to approve or disapprove of the characters and events it represents.

Perhaps more important, however, we need to be aware that our judgment of a text's attitude toward such issues as race, class, gender, and sexual orientation will probably be influenced strongly by our own evolving attitudes toward these issues, just as we saw earlier that our interpretation of a literary work will probably be influenced by our personal feelings toward one of its characters, plot events, or some aspect of its setting. The problem of how to know when we're analyzing the text and when we're responding, instead, only to a personal belief or experience that we've projected onto the text is not a problem we can solve once and for all. It's a problem that continually recurs for all readers. So think of it as an ongoing challenge, and your skill at spotting the strengths and weaknesses in your own literary interpretations will develop over time.

Using our personal responses to generate paper topics

Although our personal responses to literature can lead us astray, they are also, as we saw earlier, frequently the source of our deepest insights. In addition, exploring your personal response to a literary work can help you come up with paper topics that are especially interesting to you, and when your topic interests you, you're more likely to write a strong paper that will interest your readers, as well. Let's see what kinds of topics might be generated by some of the examples of personal responses to "Everyday Use" provided earlier. Let's consider, for instance, what paper topics might result from a positive personal response to one of the characters. A popular category of topic that comes immediately to mind is called *character analysis*. For a character analysis, you would interpret a single character: the meaning of that character's behavior, its motives, its relationship to other characters, the purpose it serves in the story, and so forth. For example, a positive response to Maggie might lead to a paper entitled "Don't Judge a Book by Its Cover: An Analysis of Maggie in Alice Walker's 'Everyday Use,'" in which you would present all the textual evidence you could find to show that Maggie has more going for her than her sister or even her mother realizes. You would cite, for example, her excellent memory, her knowledge of family history, her ability to quilt, her willingness to help her mother with household tasks, and the ample evidence of her good nature. You might also argue that Maggie's engagement to John Thomas, despite Mrs. Johnson's apparent belief that the young man has little to offer, is no small achievement given Maggie's shyness, her feelings about her appearance, her family's rather low opinion of her abilities, and the way in which both her mother and the church community seem to have overlooked her needs (such as her medical needs as a result of the fire) in their efforts to fulfill Dee's.

Analogously, a positive response to Dee might result in a paper entitled "She's Not as Bad as She Seems: An Analysis of Dee in Alice Walker's 'Everyday Use,'" in which you would defend Dee by presenting all the textual evidence you could find to show that she does care about her family and that she must have a good deal of intelligence and internal fortitude to have accomplished what she has accomplished, given that her race, class, and gender must have presented many obstacles to her success. Of course, you would have to acknowledge Dee's negative qualities, for they are her most obvious qualities, but you would argue that there is also an admirable side to Dee that we shouldn't overlook. You might also research the Black Pride Movement of the late 1960s and early 1970s, the time in which the story is set, in order to argue that

Dee's attempt to reclaim her African roots is a legitimate one that should be respected, though you might agree with the point the story seems to make that Dee should better appreciate her family and be sensitive to the obstacles that have kept Mrs. Johnson and Maggie from achieving the kind of financial success she has achieved.

Certainly, you could find similar ways to write about Mrs. Johnson and Hakim, though Hakim would be a more difficult subject because we know so little about him. But let's take a moment, instead, to discuss briefly another popular topic-category—called *thematic analysis*—that you might find useful for interpreting "Everyday Use" in terms of your personal response to the story. For a thematic analysis, you would interpret the story in terms of a specific theme, or the point the story seems to make about a particular topic. In "Everyday Use," we see such topics as parenting, family relations, success, independence, heritage, and non-conformity. A positive or negative response to a character, plot event, or an aspect of setting could lead you to write a thematic analysis of heritage. For the definition of heritage seems to be the crux of the Johnson family's disagreement, a disagreement embodied in the differences among family members' clothing, lifestyle, and attitude toward the Johnsons' homemade furniture and quilts. On the one hand, Mrs. Johnson and Maggie believe that one's real heritage resides in one's family history; on the other hand, Dee believes that African Americans' real heritage lies in their African roots. Such a paper might be entitled "A Battle of Self-Perceptions: Defining One's Heritage in Alice Walker's 'Everyday Use'" and might address such questions as why these characters define heritage so differently, which definition the story supports, and whether or not you agree with the story's position on this topic.

Another thematic analysis, which could result from a positive or negative response to Dee, might address the point you think the story makes about the topic of non-conformity. Dee is an American, and the United States prides itself on its history of non-conformity, for example, its break with old-world European traditions. Indeed, non-conformity is generally considered a virtue in America. Yet Dee, who has struck out on her own path and accomplished a good deal against heavy odds, is rather negatively portrayed. Such a paper, which might be entitled "The Price Was High: Non-Conformity in Alice Walker's 'Everyday Use,'" would analyze the story's message about non-conformity. Is "Everyday Use" suggesting that non-conformity sometimes requires a certain amount of self-centered behavior, that an individual's leap forward necessarily leaves someone behind? Or is the story telling us that non-conformity should not always be a source of pride, that one's personal progress should not be achieved at the expense of one's family ties? Or finally, is the story suggesting that what we take to be non-conformity might be, in reality, simply conformity to the standards of a different group of people? Just as you would do in a character analysis, you would have to support your claims in a thematic analysis with textual evidence.

Food for further thought

Thinking it over

If you've worked through all of the interpretation exercises offered in this chapter, you should feel quite familiar with the basic approaches to discovering your personal responses to literary works and understanding how those responses operate as the sources of your literary interpretations. We've seen how your own reader responses can be explored by examining

1   Your personal identification with a literary character.
2   Your relationship to a literary character that reminds you of someone important in your life.
3   Your relationship to a plot event that reminds you of something important that occurred in your life or in the life of someone close to you.
4   Your relationship to a literary setting that reminds you of someplace important in your life.

We also discussed how such discoveries as these can occur concerning other aspects of literary representation, such as images that we find striking and ideologies about which we have an opinion or to which we have an emotional response. Indeed, an important benefit of our response exercises in this chapter is that they focus our attention on and show us the significance of literary elements that we otherwise might not have noticed: for example, descriptive details concerning characters' physical appearance, body language, and behavior; brief, subtle plot events; and aspects of setting that otherwise might have faded into the background. So let your personal response be your guide in expanding the repertoire of literary elements you are able to recognize, to which you are able to articulate your response, and as a result, with which you are able to produce more thorough and personally satisfying literary interpretations.

Moreover, you might try contrasting one of your completed response exercises with that of another reader. For the ways in which our personal responses differ from someone else's can offer us additional insights into our own reading processes and into the literary work to which we're both responding. How did my reactions to specific items from the response exercise differ from those of another reader? Did I overlook some aspect of the literary work, or see something that another missed, because of my personal response? If I contrast my responses from more than one response exercise with those of other readers, will I find a pattern in the way I react to certain kinds of characters, plot events, or settings? Perhaps, for example, I tend to trust uncritically characters who in some way fit the "wise-old-man" type and, for this reason, have difficulty seeing when that type of character is, in fact, manipulative, selfish, dangerous, or characterized negatively in any other way. Or perhaps

I tend to overlook descriptive details because I'm so focused on "what happens next," and thus miss out on the emotional response—and the information that would help guide my interpretation of the work—those details can provide. Because we all have different reader responses, we all have different strengths and challenges when it comes to literary interpretation. Knowing, as best we can, where our strengths and challenges lie can go a long way in helping us respond to literature with more emotional depth and use our responses more productively to interpret literary works.

Reader-response theory and cultural criticism

Consider, also, the productions of popular culture you can examine in an attempt to discover something new about your own response mechanisms. For all our response exercises can be used to explore our responses to and interpretations of such productions of popular culture as movies, television shows, television and magazine ads, video and board games, comic books, and even the packaging of some consumer products. Is a person or persons depicted in the magazine ad or video game? Is a plot, however brief, given or implied? Is a setting of some sort depicted? In short, if a cultural production has a character or characters, a plot, and/or a setting, then our response exercises should prove helpful in understanding how we relate to that production. Indeed, our response exercises can help us explore the ways in which such cultural productions operate to influence or even manipulate our responses to them. In this way, our response exercises can help us begin to try our hand at *cultural criticism*, which, as we saw in Chapter 1, attempts to analyze the productions of popular culture in order to discover the cultural "messages" they send, or the cultural work they perform, whether deliberately or not. These cultural messages can have a strong influence on how we see ourselves, other people, and the world in which we live, all without our realizing their effect.

Television commercials for Hallmark greeting cards, for example, generally market their product by telling a "mini-story" to which, presumably, most viewers can relate. One of my favorites is called "Brother of the Bride" (directed by Joe Pytka, 2008).[2] In this ad, we see a young man, probably in his early twenties, at his sister's wedding reception. It is immediately evident that Brother—rather pudgy, sweet-looking but not classically handsome—has a gift for saying the wrong thing. First, he offends a young woman he's trying to compliment when he tells her, "You look like you've lost a ton of weight!" Next, his attempt at a little male bonding fails miserably when he remarks that a good-looking young woman across the room is "high maintenance," and the young man to whom he is speaking answers resentfully, "That's my fiancée." Finally, Brother's effort to exchange a friendly greeting with Barbara, his father's third wife, backfires when he addresses her as Kate, which is the name of Dad's second wife. So when our blundering protagonist stands up at the bride's table to toast his sister, many of the wedding guests, as well as the bride and groom, clearly expect the worst. However, the toast is perfectly worded and quite moving. Everyone can now see Brother's good heart, and their smiling faces bespeak their warm approval. The camera zooms in to show us that Brother has read his toast from a Hallmark card as he finishes up by saying, "I didn't actually write those words, but I do mean them." The bride hugs Brother as the wedding guests applaud. Now that the guests have seen this side of Brother, their goodwill towards him does not diminish as the commercial closes on his final gaffe: "Eat up, everyone. My mom paid, like, two grand for that cake."

Now, I know this commercial is telling us, more or less, "When you're looking for the perfect words, you'll find them in a Hallmark card." However, let's consider the commercial in terms of the emotional responses viewers might experience, for I suspect that most viewers would experience some kind of emotional response to this commercial. Most of us probably experience some degree of social anxiety when "mingling," know someone like Brother, or at least have attended weddings or other large social gatherings. I know that when I mingle with others socially, I always worry that, like Brother, I'll say the wrong thing and inadvertently annoy or even hurt someone. So I used our "personal identification exercise," described earlier in this chapter, and found that I do, in fact, identify with Brother. That's why I felt so anxious as I watched Brother's social ineptitude alienate the people with whom he sought positive interactions. And that's why I was very relieved when his toast turned out so well. Yes, when I saw that he'd read his toast from a Hallmark card, I laughed and said, "Give me a break." And no, I didn't run right out and buy a Hallmark card. But when I think about it, I'm sure that, on some level, I now associate Hallmark cards with a feeling of relief, of emotional pressure removed, and that fact could influence my greeting-card purchases in the future both in terms of the brand of cards I buy and the frequency with which I buy them.

For our purposes here, I used my personal response to this commercial to help me find the cultural messages that had pushed my emotional buttons, so to speak. In other words, I used my personal response to see if I could discover some of the cultural work "Brother of the Bride" performs, whether it does so deliberately—in order to sell Hallmark cards—or not. To begin, why did Brother's social failures trigger my own anxiety? Well, like him, I want very much to have positive interactions with people I encounter in social situations, and I fear that, as it is in his case, my good intentions might not be enough. Wait a minute. Now that I think back, it occurs to me that Brother's behavior isn't really that bad. I think I based my judgment of him on the cold, rather hostile responses he receives for relatively minor social blunders because those are the responses I fear I'll receive during social interactions. Can't the wedding guests with whom he speaks recognize a friendly face when they see one? Are people so easily offended that they can't see Brother's sincere desire to please? Why do they appreciate him only after he gives his wonderful toast? Maybe I'm right to be anxious in social situations: it's so easy to alienate people. Okay, I can see that the most important effect this commercial has had on me is to increase my fear that I won't find the right words during social interactions, that I'll inadvertently alienate people. Does this mean I'll buy more Hallmark cards? I don't know. But now I have an idea about the cultural message this commercial might be sending.

If my personal response is, in fact, based on the content of the commercial, then the commercial is probably sending the following cultural message: *People will overlook our shortcomings but only if we can find the right words to show them that our good qualities make up for our failings. So the right words are essential to social success, even if we have to get those words from a greeting card. Indeed, unless we're really sure of ourselves, it's probably prudent to have some mistrust of our own words.* With this hypothesis as my starting point, I should be able to use concepts from psycho-analytic and Marxist theories to analyze the ways in which this commercial encourages social anxiety in the viewer in order to sell greeting cards, which the commercial suggests is a safer, more effective, and easier way to express my feel-ings than trying to express them in my own words. Yes, I'm suggesting that once you become familiar with Chapter 4's concepts from psychoanalytic theory and with concepts from the social theories addressed in subsequent chapters, you'll be in a position to analyze the productions of popular culture with greater insight and understanding. However, as I hope my own response to "Brother of the Bride"—and this chapter as a whole—has demonstrated, a clear grasp of your own response mechanisms will provide you with an excellent place to start.

★★★

Of course, before you can do anything with your personal response to a lit-erary work, to a production of popular culture, or to anything else, you need to know what that response is. So it might be a good idea to practice analyzing your own responses by using our response exercises to discover your personal responses to some of the literary texts that appear at the end of this book. These exercises should work especially well with a literary work to which you have a particularly strong emotional reaction. But you might be pleasantly surprised to find that they can also help you become more interested in a literary work that you don't like at first or that you think had no effect on you at all.

So don't be too quick to dismiss a literary work because your first response to it is not a positive one. For in attempting to write conscientious answers to the questions posed in our interpretation exercises, you might learn that you had a more meaningful response to the work than you realized. The effort to think carefully and write a detailed account of what was going on for you as you read a literary work can bring to the front of your mind feelings and ideas about the work that you didn't even realize you were having. In addition, it can spark creativity in you that you didn't know was there. And that's one of the best responses any of us can have to literature—to let an author's creativity spark our own.

Taking the next step

Exercises for further practice

1 Write a journal entry or an essay describing, in as much detail as possible, a productive experience you had using one of our response exercises to explore your personal response to a literary work. Include the personal connection to the work that you discovered in doing the exercise, and explain how this connection influenced your interpretation of some element in the work. Did your exploration lead you to see something new in the work or in yourself as a reader? Was your response to or opinion of some element in the work changed or confirmed by your exploration? Explain.

2 Select a literary work that you read recently and didn't like very much. (Perhaps the characters didn't interest you, or perhaps you disliked one or more of them. Or perhaps the plot seemed boring or meaningless to you.) Using all four of our response exercises, try to discover a personal connection you have to this work to help you explore the source of your dislike or lack of interest. Did one or more of our response exercises lead you to a better understanding than you originally had of some element of the work? Explain.

3 When given the choice of two or more literary works for an essay assignment, it can be difficult to know which one to choose. In order to help you decide, list together the names of the characters you remember most vividly from both, or all three, works. Drawing on this list, use the personal-identification and familiar-character exercises to help you discover which of the works elicits your strongest personal response. This is probably the work you should consider choosing for your essay assignment. To gather more ideas for your interpretation of this work, use the familiar-plot-event and familiar-setting exercises to help you find additional elements in the work you might otherwise overlook.

4 Partner with another reader. Contrast one of your completed personal-identification exercises with one of your partner's. Choose an exercise in which you both responded to the same literary work but identified with different characters. In what specific ways does your interpretation of the work differ from that of your partner? How might you attribute some or all of these differences in interpretation to your personal identifications with different characters? More importantly, did you overlook some aspect of the literary work, or see something that your partner missed, because of your personal response? Repeat this process three more times, each time with a different reading partner, a different literary work, and a different response exercise. Your goal is to learn as much as you can about your reading strengths on which you can build, and the reading challenges on which you need to work.

5   As we saw earlier in this chapter, cultural criticism cannot depend on
    reader–response concepts alone. However, your personal response to a
    production of popular culture can often serve as a useful first step in that
    direction. For example, what is your favorite movie—one you've seen
    many times and remember vividly? Try all four of our response exercises
    to help you discover what it is about this movie that keeps you coming
    back, though by now you know "what's going to happen next" and can
    probably talk along with much of the dialogue. Specifically, how does
    this movie in some way tell *your* story, perhaps not your whole story, but
    an important part of it, an important part of yourself of which you may
    or may not be fully aware? What elements in the movie seemed to "push
    your emotional buttons," so to speak? In short, see if our response exercises
    can help you discover something you don't know about the meaningful
    connection between you and your favorite movie. Depending on what
    you discover about the movie during this process, you might consider it a
    candidate, as you read subsequent chapters, for cultural criticism from a
    psychoanalytic; Marxist; feminist; gay, lesbian, or queer; African American;
    or postcolonial perspective.

Suggestions for further reading

Booth, Wayne C. "General Rules, IV: Emotions, Beliefs, and the Reader's Objectivity."
    The Rhetoric of Fiction. University of Chicago Press, 1961. 119–47.
Fish, Stanley. *Is There a Text in this Class?: The Authority of Interpretive Communities*.
    Cambridge, MA: Harvard University Press, 1980. (See, especially, "Literature in the
    Reader: Affective Stylistics," 22–67; and "How to Recognize a Poem When You See
    One," 322–37.)
Holland, Norman. "Unity Identity Text Self." *PLMA* 90 (1975): 813–22. Rpt. in *Reader-
    Response Criticism: From Formalism to Post-Structuralism*, ed. Jane P. Tompkins. Baltimore:
    The Johns Hopkins University Press, 1980. 118–33.
——. *5 Readers Reading*. New Haven: Yale University Press, 1975. (See, especially, "The
    Answer: Four Principles of Literary Experience," 113–29.)
Rosenblatt, Louise. *The Reader, the Text, the Poem: The Transactional Theory of the Literary
    Work*. Carbondale: Southern Illinois University Press, 1978. (See, especially, "The Poem
    as Event," 6–21; and "Efferent and Aesthetic Reading," 22–47.)
Tompkins, Jane P. "The Reader in History: The Changing Shape of Literary Response."
    Reader-Response Criticism: From Formalism to Post-Structuralism. Baltimore: The Johns Hopkins
    University Press, 1980. 201–32.
Tyson, Lois. "Reader-Response Criticism." *Critical Theory Today: A User-Friendly Guide*.
    2nd ed. New York: Routledge, 2006. 169–207.

Notes

1   Holland's theory of reading—variously referred to as *transactive, subjective*, and *psycholo-
    gical* reader-response theory—is explained in his "Unity Identity Text Self." *PLMA* 90
    (1975): 813–22. Rpt. in *Reader-Response Criticism: From Formalism to Post-Structuralism*,

ed. Jane P. Tompkins. Baltimore: The Johns Hopkins University Press, 1980. 118–33. Holland also discusses his theory in "The Answer: Four Principles of Literary Experience." *5 Readers Reading*. New Haven: Yale University Press, 1975. 113–29.

2 "Brother of the Bride" is available online at http://www.youtube.com/watch?v=7 ZdIjnkDpMo.

Chapter 3

Using concepts from New Critical theory to understand literature

Why should we learn about New Critical theory?

Have you ever taken a literature course in which you were asked to write an essay explaining what a literary work means? And were you required to provide examples from the literary work to back up your interpretation? If so, you were probably using concepts from New Critical theory to write your paper, although you might not have known it at the time.

New Criticism isn't new anymore: its heyday lasted from the late 1940s until the late 1960s. It was rightly considered "new" then because it offered a way of understanding literature that was radically different from the interpretive approaches it replaced. But you'll still see New Criticism discussed in literature and theory anthologies (sometimes under the name *formalism*) because its method of literary analysis is still used today. The basic concepts you'll see later in this chapter are still used to teach high-school and college students how to interpret and support, or defend, their interpretations of literature. In fact, New Critical interpretative tools have become such a fundamental part of our introduction to literary studies that we're often told simply that this method is the correct or accepted way to analyze literature without reference to the New Critical theory on which it is based.

Before "The New Criticism" (as it was called) arrived on the post-World-War-II scene, the study of literature usually meant one of two things: (1) the attempt by a literary critic or historian to determine *authorial intention*—what did the author *intend* the work to mean?—by studying the author's life and times; or (2) the attempt by a gifted, educated reader to express in an interesting and engaging manner his or her personal impressions of the work. Thus, a literary work meant only what the author intended it to mean or what a "professional" reader felt it meant.

How can we be sure, however, what the author intended the work to mean? And even if we could be sure, what if the author inadvertently created something other than what he or she intended? Because we can't know the answers to these questions, New Critics called the use of authorial intention to determine the meaning of a literary work the *intentional fallacy*, or the false belief in an author's intended meaning.

Similarly, how can we know that a given reader's impressions—even the impressions of a gifted, educated reader—can be counted on to reveal the meaning of a literary work? Aren't impressions guided by emotions? What if the reader's impressions are based on an emotional response rather than a response to the actual content of the literary work? Because we can't know the answers to these questions, New Critics called the use of a reader's impressions to determine the meaning of a literary work the *affective fallacy*, or the false belief in a reader's emotional response.

In short, neither the study of authorial intention nor the provision of a talented reader's impressions focuses on the literary work, or the *text itself*, as New Critics called it. And for New Criticism, the text itself is the only place we can look to find its meaning. Exactly where in the literary text should we look for its meaning? According to New Criticism, we should look at the ways in which a text's *literary language* operates to create a complex meaning that can stand on its own as an object of art. Does this idea seem rather abstract? Don't worry. It's not as difficult as it might sound. Let me explain.

Just as a great painting is a complex art object made of a unique combination of paints on canvas and a great symphony is a complex art object made of a unique combination of musical sounds, a literary text is a complex art object made of language. In order to understand a literary text, then, we need to understand the complex workings of the unique combination of words—and other literary devices, or techniques—of which it is made. So any claim about what a text means must have *textual support*, or evidence that backs up the claim that is based on the words found in the text itself. Sound familiar? Most of us are taught to analyze literature by backing up our opinion of the text's meaning with textual support: evidence of characters' speech, actions, and physical appearance; descriptions of plot events and setting; and so forth.

Indeed, we can begin to use New Critical theory to understand literature by asking the following two questions about the literary text we want to interpret: (1) What does the text mean? (What is the message communicated by the text as a whole?); and (2) How can I support my claim about the text's meaning with textual evidence? So gaining a more thorough knowledge of how to analyze textual evidence—of how to analyze the language of which a literary text is made—is an effective way to deepen our appreciation of literature and improve our ability to interpret it.

As New Criticism observed, *literary language* is different from other kinds of language. For example, scientific language and most everyday language are used to communicate practical matters as clearly as possible: What changes have scientists reported in the fish population of the Ohio River over the last decade? When was the last time I went fishing on the Ohio River? As these two questions illustrate, scientific and everyday language depend on the literal, or actual, meaning of words. If I refer to a river literally, as I did in the two questions above, I am referring to a physical body of water of substantial length that flows in one direction and contains aquatic life forms. In contrast, literary language frequently employs such literary devices as *figurative language*, or language that implies something more than or other than itself. For instance, if I refer to a river figuratively, I might be using the word *river* to invoke the idea of a journey, nature, life, or anything that a river can reasonably "figure," or "stand for." Being "sent up the river" is thus a figurative phrase for being sent on a journey to prison. And "crossing the river" is a figurative phrase for crossing from one phase of life to another or for crossing over from life to death. Even when a literary work uses language for its literal meaning, that language is usually chosen for its ability to produce associations with other words. For example, the word *mother* literally means *female parent*; however, the word *mother* produces associations such as *nurture*, *affection*, and *comfort*. And as we'll see later in the chapter, there are many more literary devices that contribute to the unique quality of literary language.

New Criticism has been replaced by the kinds of interpretive approaches discussed in the other chapters of this book, not because of its methodology—its attention to the operations of literary language—but because of its narrow definition of great literature and great literary interpretation and its dismissal of reader response as an important factor in literary analysis. We no longer believe, as New Critics did, that all great literature derives from the European male literary tradition (which they saw as universally meaningful) and that there is only one "best" interpretation of every literary work. Nor do we believe it is possible for readers to put aside their personal responses and interpret literature with complete objectivity. However, New Criticism's focus on the text itself has remained a foundational element of literary studies. In fact, New Criticism's insistence on textual evidence to support our literary interpretations is shared by all the interpretive approaches we'll use in the following chapters.

Although it's important that you read through the "Basic concepts" section that follows, don't be too concerned if you don't feel you thoroughly understand every one. You'll begin to understand these concepts much better when we use them later in this chapter to help us interpret the literary texts that appear at the end of this book. And you'll see that these fundamental New Critical concepts can help us understand other works of literature, as well.

Remember, too, that I'm offering you my own literary analyses in the interpretation exercises provided later in this chapter. You might use the same New Critical concepts I use but come up with different interpretations of your own. If you disagree with any of the analyses I offer in these exercises, don't be afraid to look in the literary text in question for evidence that will support your viewpoint. A literary text can support a number of different interpretations, even when readers are using concepts from the same theory.

Basic concepts

Theme

Every literary text can address any number of topics, such as love, the family, the effects of social pressure on the individual, the conflict between good and evil, the initiation into adulthood, and the like. Although the terms *topic* and *theme* are often used interchangeably, strictly speaking a theme is what a literary text says about a given topic. For example, while "family conflict" is a topic, "the family can be a source of painful emotional conflict as well as a source of emotional support" and "family conflict can sometimes result in a deeper, more meaningful family harmony" are themes. A literary text's theme is the overall meaning, or message, the text communicates, and New Critics believed that a great literary work has a theme that contributes to our understanding of what it means to be human. Of course, today we realize that a literary text can support more than one theme, but we still use New Critical strategies to support our interpretation.

Formal elements

While *theme* refers to the content of a literary work—what the work means— *form* refers to the literary devices and language, or *form*al elements, used to get that meaning across. Literary devices include the kinds of literary "tools" with which you are probably familiar: among many others, plot, narrator, characterization, and setting. How should the plot, or the events of the story, be laid out? Who should narrate, or tell, the story? How many and what kinds of characters should be employed? Where should the story take place? What should be the narrator's attitude toward the story's characters, events, and setting? The answers to these questions help give each literary work its unique form. The following literary devices are additional examples of the many kinds of formal elements important to our understanding of how a literary work communicates its theme.

Tension—In a literary text, tension is created by the interplay between two opposing concepts, such as conformity and rebellion, belonging and alienation, harmony and conflict, or tradition and change. The central, or most important tension in a literary text is generated by the two opposing concepts that most reflect the meaning of the text as a whole. A text's central tension is thus the clearest signpost to its theme. For instance, the tension between the opposing concepts *tradition* and *change* might generate a theme like one of the following: "The uncritical desire for change can result in a wholesale abandonment of traditions that are still meaningful"; "Change can be a difficult but necessary remedy for outmoded traditions that do more harm than good"; or "Tradition and change are both necessary elements for the health of any human community." As these three examples illustrate, the theme of a literary text might "take sides" by favoring one concept in the opposition over the other. Or the theme might consist of some combination of the two.

Ambiguity—A literary text exhibits ambiguity whenever a word, image, or plot event can have two or more different meanings. For example, a young woman rescuing her sister from a burning car might be seen as a representation of the young woman's love for her sister, of the bond between the two young women, of the rescued sister's helplessness (her need to be "rescued" in general) or of the rescued sister's strength (she's a "survivor" in general). Or this plot event might mean all of the above because plot events, like events in human life, can have all of these meanings at the same time. In a literary text, ambiguity is not considered a flaw, as it would be in scientific or everyday language, because ambiguity enriches the text by contributing to its depth and complexity.

Of course, not all possible interpretations of the meaning of a plot event, or of any literary device, are appropriate. For instance, although the burning car in the above example might have many possible meanings—fire, for example, can be associated with destruction, hell, strong emotions, sexual desire, and purification—this doesn't mean that any or all of these associations would be useful for a conscientious interpretation of this plot event. For in order to be meaningful, our interpretation of any part of a literary text must make sense in terms of our interpretation of the text as a whole: it must fit with all the other formal elements in the text and with the text's theme.

Imagery—Close your eyes and imagine a tall fir tree covered with snow and sparkling in the winter sunshine. You've just experienced an image. An image is a mental picture created by a word or words used to describe the physical appearance of a person, place, object, or event. Imagery can also consist of descriptive language related to the other four senses, but it's usually visual. A literary representation of our imaginary young woman rescuing her sister from a burning car, discussed above, might include a number of images, such as the image of flames reflected in flowing gasoline; of a young woman's arms reaching through a broken car window; or of two young women, clothes torn and dirty, leaning against the solid trunk of a nearby tree.

Images often occur in symbols, metaphors, and similes, all three of which are forms of comparison, and I will offer you a simple definition of each below. Remember, however, that the ability to correctly identify an image by one of these three labels isn't nearly as important as the ability to analyze how an image or a series of images operates in a text: how it is associated with certain ideas or experiences; how it creates a particular mood; in short, how it helps us interpret the meaning of a passage in a literary text or even the text as a whole.

Consider, for example, the different effects of the following three images: (1) a white picket fence bordering a tidy green lawn; (2) a white picket fence gathered in a bundle, tied together with wire, sitting among numerous other bundles of fencing in a home-improvement store; and (3) a white picket fence fallen on its side, smudged heavily with dirt, a number of pickets broken or missing, lying along one edge of a vacant lot strewn with old bricks, rotting boards, weeds, and litter. These images are associated with very different ideas and experiences, create very different moods, and would help us interpret the, presumably, very different meanings of the literary passages in which they appeared.

Symbol—"Most of us have to earn our bread." This sentence means that most of us have to work for a living because the word *bread* symbolizes life. As this example illustrates, a symbol has both literal and figurative meaning. Bread is, literally, a form of food made largely of flour and water that is eaten by human beings. Figuratively, the word *bread* can be used to figure, or stand for, ideas that have similar qualities. Bread sustains life, so it can symbolize life. Or it can symbolize other things that sustain life, as when the phrase *I need more bread* (or *dough!*) *to pay my rent* is used to mean that I need more money. Money can sustain life because it can buy what we need to sustain life. So the word *bread* can also be used to symbolize money.

Metaphor—"My grandmother is a treasure." If I meant this statement literally, I'd be claiming that my grandmother is a large amount of gold or precious gems. But unlike a symbol, a metaphor has only figurative meaning. And it links together two persons, things, or ideas that are, in a literal sense, *not* similar. The figurative meaning of "My grandmother is a treasure" is that my grandmother is a wonderful person, a person of great human value. So while I can legitimately say that the word *treasure* is a metaphor for my grandmother—that is, while I can use the word for its figurative meaning alone—I can't say that *treasure* is a symbol of my grandmother.

Simile—While "My grandmother is a treasure" is a metaphor, "My grandmother is like a treasure" or "My grandmother is as valuable as a treasure" is a simile. Think of a simile as a metaphor that uses *like* or *as*. A metaphor can be considered a more direct, and therefore stronger comparison. (Can you see, for instance, that "The final exam was a nightmare" has more punch than "The final exam was like a nightmare"?) I'm not suggesting that one device is better than the other. Rather, the use of one device or the other depends on the purpose for which it is used.

Unity

New Critics considered unity, or what they called *organic unity*, the most important quality of a literary text. A text has unity when its theme and formal elements work together as an inseparable whole. Put simply, when a text has unity, *what* it means can't be separated from *how* it means. In a unified text, every character, every plot event, every image, every tension, every ambiguity— in short, all the text's formal elements—contribute to the representation of the text's theme. At various points in the text, there will certainly be contradictory or conflicting meanings created by a particular plot event, ambiguity, image, or other formal element. But these conflicting meanings add to the richness and depth of the text as long as they work together in a shared contribution to the meaning of the text as a whole—that is, to the text's theme.

Let's consider an example. Conflicting meanings can be produced by the combination of both very positive and very negative qualities in the representation of a literary character. (For me, the Reverend Dimmesdale in Nathaniel Hawthorne's *The Scarlet Letter* and Willy Loman in Arthur Miller's *Death of a Salesman* come to mind.) At any given point in the text, and even after we've finished reading it, we may very well feel conflicted in our response to such characters because the text offers opposing elements in its portrayal of them. However, this kind of characterization is considered complex rather than self-contradictory if it contributes to the meaning of the work as a whole: for instance, if the character's duality helps explain certain plot events or justifies the mixed response to him of other characters. In addition, a character composed of conflicting elements can contribute to the quality of the text by being more believable and more interesting than a character who is all good or all evil, or what is called a *cardboard*, or *one-dimensional* character.

Close reading and textual evidence

When we're new to the study of literature we often focus most of our attention on major plot events and characters' behavior. "What happens?" and "How do I feel about the characters?" are questions that form the basis of many a new student's understanding of a literary text. In contrast, close reading consists of careful attention to every aspect of a literary work, including and especially to the text's formal elements, in order to accurately and meaningfully interpret the text: to determine the text's theme, as we see it, and to show how all the characters, plot events, settings, images, and other formal elements contribute to that theme. Close reading is how we provide thorough, detailed textual evidence to support our interpretation of a literary text. How do characters' behavior, physical appearance, and dialogue show that my interpretation of the text is correct? How do the images used to describe the setting reinforce the meaning I see in the text? How does the narrator's attitude toward the text's characters and events (does the narrator seem approving, disapproving, or neutral?) support my ideas? My opinion of what a text means is important to me and perhaps to those who agree with me. However, my opinion of what a text means, when conscientiously backed up by the textual evidence needed to support my opinion, becomes more convincing to those with interpretations different from mine as well as more meaningful to myself and to those who agree with me.

★★★

There are, of course, additional concepts used to interpret literature from a New Critical perspective, but these are enough to get us started. The interpretation exercises that follow will probably remind you of the thematic essays—interpretations of the text's meaning—you may have written for a literature class. In fact, the title of each exercise reflects the categories you'll see used in literature anthologies that are organized by theme. Like the rest of this chapter, these exercises are intended to help you improve your ability to identify a text's theme and analyze how that theme is "carried" by the text's formal elements. Let's begin our interpretation exercises by analyzing a story that offers us several useful examples of our New Critical concepts: Alice Walker's "Everyday Use."

Interpretation exercises

Appreciating the importance of tradition: Interpreting "Everyday Use"

Alice Walker's "Everyday Use" (1973; see Appendix D) consists almost entirely of the interactions among family members—Mrs. Johnson and her daughters Dee and Maggie—during a single afternoon. And those interactions consist almost entirely of differences that split the family in two: differences between Dee, who has been away at a big-city college and learned new ways of relating to herself and her world, and her mother and sister, who have remained together in their humble country home and in their adherence to family traditions. Thus, although set in a specific place and time—rural Georgia during the Black Pride movement of the late 1960s and early 1970s—"Everyday Use" focuses on a topic relevant to almost any place and time. That topic is the eternal tug-of-war between tradition and change.

Specifically, Dee has come home for a brief visit, presumably to introduce her boyfriend Hakim to her mother and sister Maggie. Dee and Hakim are as fashionably modern in their outlook as Mama and Maggie are traditionally old-fashioned. Readers may differ in their opinions concerning the opposed viewpoints expressed in "Everyday Use." However, our task here is to discover the viewpoint endorsed by the text and to explain how we know what that viewpoint is. In other words, with our topic in mind, our task is to discover the text's theme, or meaning as a whole, and to support that discovery with formal elements from the text itself. In order to fulfill this task, we must identify: (1) the central, or most important tension operating in the story, which will guide us to the story's theme and help us lay the groundwork for our interpretation; (2) the story's theme; and (3) the formal elements in the story that support the theme we have identified, thereby showing that our interpretation of the story is valid.

The text's central tension

As our topic suggests, the central tension operating in "Everyday Use" seems to be the tension between tradition and change represented by the differing viewpoints of, on the one hand, Dee and Hakim, and on the other hand, Mrs. Johnson and Maggie. To confirm that we've correctly identified the text's central tension and lay our interpretive groundwork, it can help to brainstorm a list of the oppositions related to our topic and embodied in plot events; in characters' behavior, attitudes, or physical appearance; and in the text's imagery. So let's start by finding evidence in the story of the following oppositions.

1   The clothing and hairstyles of Dee and Hakim vs. those of Mama and Maggie.
2   The ways in which Hakim greets Mama and Maggie vs. the ways in which Mama and Maggie respond to his greetings.
3   Dee's beliefs vs. Mama's beliefs about family names.
4   Dee's knowledge vs. Mama and Maggie's knowledge of family history.
5   Dee's attitude vs. Mama and Maggie's attitude toward the family home.
6   Dee's attitude vs. Mama and Maggie's attitude toward the family's handcrafted furniture.
7   Dee's attitude vs. Mama and Maggie's attitude toward the family's handcrafted quilts.
8   Dee's knowledge vs. Mama and Maggie's knowledge of the craft of quilting.

As expected, all of these examples cluster around the tension between Dee and Hakim's abandonment of family traditions and Mama and Maggie's loyalty to those traditions. And as the textual data just gathered indicate, the lines of disagreement among the characters are clearly drawn. Dee and Hakim believe that their cultural heritage, their real roots, are African, and family traditions are either outmoded—like quilting and furniture-making, the hand-me-down results of which are lovely relics to be kept as mementoes—or offensive, such as naming one's children names that originally belonged to the families of slave-owners. Mrs. Johnson and Maggie, in contrast, believe that their family traditions *are* their cultural heritage and that those traditions are to be kept alive by passing them down from one generation to the next.

The text's theme

As we've just seen, the central tension in "Everyday Use" is the tension, or opposition, between two contrasting attitudes toward family traditions. We will discover the text's theme by asking, Which side of this tension does the text promote, or portray more favorably? Or does the text favor some combination of both? I think most readers will readily feel that the story favors Mama and Maggie's loyalty to family traditions because most readers find Mama and Maggie much more likeable than Dee and Hakim. And as we'll see in the next section, Mama and Maggie are portrayed much more sympathetically (that is, their portrayals make it easier for readers to feel with them and for them) than Dee and Hakim. Indeed, literary texts often show approval of a character by portraying that character sympathetically, and conversely, disapproval is often shown by means of an unsympathetic portrayal.

   In the next section, moreover, we will do a close reading of the story in search of additional formal elements supporting our *thesis* (our debatable opinion, which is the main point of our interpretation) that the text promotes loyalty to family traditions. If we don't find such textual evidence or don't find enough of it or find conflicting textual evidence that doesn't fit our interpretation, we will have to amend our thesis to fit the textual evidence we find. However, at this point, we might reasonably argue that the text's theme can be stated as follows: *The adoption of new ideas about cultural heritage should not result in the abandonment of family traditions, for these traditions keep us connected to our family history and contribute to the emotional bond among family members.*

Textual evidence: Formal elements that support the text's theme

Let's take another look at our statement of the story's theme in order to determine the kind of textual evidence we need to support our claim that we have correctly identified the theme. To make sure that we don't miss anything, we'll divide our statement of the theme into its component parts.

Components of the theme

1   The adoption of new ideas about cultural heritage
2   should not result in the abandonment of family traditions,
3   for these traditions keep us connected to our family history
4   and contribute to the emotional bond among family members.

Now we can formulate the questions that will serve as guidelines in our search for textual evidence to support our claim.

Questions to guide our search for textual support

1   In "Everyday Use," what are the Johnsons' family traditions?
2   What new ideas about cultural heritage are adopted by Dee and Hakim?
3   How does the text indicate that Mama and Maggie's loyalty to family traditions keeps the two women connected to their family history and contributes to their close emotional bond?
4   How does the text indicate that Dee and, by association, Hakim are mistaken to have abandoned family traditions?
5   How does the text's portrayal of its main characters promote its theme concerning the importance of family traditions? (Remember: literary texts often show approval of a character by means of a sympathetic portrayal, and, conversely, disapproval is often shown by means of an unsympathetic portrayal.)

If we can find the textual evidence—including such formal elements as characterization, plot events, setting, imagery, ambiguity, and so forth—that answers each of these questions, then we will be able to support our thesis. That is, we will be able to show that our statement of the story's theme is valid. So let's translate these questions into the specific textual evidence we need to find in the story.

Finding our textual evidence

1   Find textual evidence that the Johnson family traditions include, for
    example, the following:

    a   the knowledge of family names and relationships going back to before
        the Civil War,
    b   keeping a particular name alive in the family by giving that name to
        one child in each generation,
    c   the knowledge of family history concerning the crafting of household
        furniture and other family items still used by Mama and Maggie,
    d   the ability to quilt,
    e   love of home, and
    f   the belief that family traditions should be part of everyday life, put to
        "everyday use."

2   Find textual evidence, including the following, that Dee and Hakim have
    adopted new ideas about cultural heritage.

    a   How do Dee and Hakim express their new ideas about cultural
        heritage through their new names, clothing, and hairstyles?
    b   How does Dee feel about the place Mama and Maggie call home?
    c   What does Dee plan to do with the family's handcrafted household
        items that she takes with her when she and Hakim leave—and with
        the family's handcrafted quilts that she wants to take?

3   Find textual evidence, including the following, that Mama and Maggie's
    loyalty to family traditions keeps them connected to their family history
    and contributes to their close emotional bond.

    a   Identify the past family members whom Mama and Maggie remember
        in association with family traditions.
    b   Although Maggie will put the handcrafted quilts Mama gives her to
        "everyday use"—and they will eventually wear out—how will she be
        able to ensure that the quilting tradition will live on in the family?
    c   Find the passages—especially the story's opening and closing
        paragraphs—that describe Mama and Maggie's shared love of home.
        What is the effect of the language used in these passages, for example,
        such phrases as "swept clean as a floor," "come and sit and look,"
        "sat ... enjoying," and "the two of us"?
    d   Mama and Maggie's love of home—and of each other—is also
        implied in the passage describing Mama's rescue of Maggie, long ago,
        from the fire that consumed their former home. What is the effect of
        the language used in this passage, including the following examples?

        i   What is the effect of the image conveyed when Mama says, "I can
            still ... feel Maggie's arms sticking to me"?

ii   Find the ambiguities (the possible meanings) present in this image. Consider, for example, that it can be seen as a metaphor for an emotional bond, a mother's emotional strength, a daughter's emotional weakness (she needs to be emotionally rescued), and a daughter's emotional strength (she's an emotional survivor). Can you think of additional meanings?

iii Which of the possible meanings associated with this image contribute to our interpretation of Mama and Maggie's relationship?

e Find the passage that describes Mama's taking the handcrafted quilts— which embody Johnson family history—from Dee and giving them to Maggie.

i   What is the effect of Mama's reference to being touched by the spirit of God?

ii   What is the effect of Mama's words, "hugged Maggie to me" (rather than simply "hugged Maggie")?

iii What is the effect of Mama's words "snatched the quilts" (rather than, say, "took the quilts") and "Miss Wangero" (rather than just "Wangero")?

4 Find textual evidence, including the following, that Dee and, by association, Hakim are mistaken to have abandoned family traditions.

a What is Dee missing out on in her relationship with her family?

b Find textual evidence that Dee, whether or not she realizes it, wants her mother's approval.

c Do we see any evidence that Mama and Dee lack the kind of bond Mama and Maggie share?

d Does Dee have knowledge of the Johnson family history or traditional skills that she can pass on to her children?

e Does Dee's relationship with Hakim seem to offer her the kind of bond that is missing between herself and her family?

5 Find evidence that the text's portrayal of its main characters promotes its theme concerning the importance of family traditions. Note that these portrayals are presented through Mrs. Johnson's eyes, from her point of view, because she is the story's first-person narrator. In this way, the text "takes Mama's side," so to speak, and encourages the reader to trust Mama's perceptions.

a Find evidence that the text offers sympathetic portrayals of Mama and Maggie, the representatives of family tradition, including, for example, the following:

i   the hard work Mama has done on the farm to support her daughters and help send Dee to college;

     ii the obstacles Mama has faced throughout her life;

    iii Mama's appreciation of Dee's new dress and willingness to learn Dee's new name;

    iv Maggie's willingness to help her mother, including Maggie's willingness to give up the quilts to Dee, and

    v the obstacles Maggie has faced throughout her life.

  b Find evidence that the text offers unsympathetic portrayals of Dee and Hakim, who reject family tradition, including, for example, the following:

    i Dee's insensitive use of her camera, which reveals her attitude toward Mama and Maggie's home as an object of curiosity;

    ii Hakim's insensitivity to Maggie's shyness;

    iii Dee's careless dismissal of Maggie's ability to remember family history;

    iv Dee's selfish appropriation of household items still being used by Mama and Maggie, including Dee's insensitive interaction with Mama concerning the quilts already promised to Maggie, and

    v Mama's awareness—seen in her dream—that Dee doesn't appreciate or even accept her mother for who she is.

Focusing your essay

Given the textual evidence you've collected, I think you can feel confident focusing your essay on the ways in which "Everyday Use" illustrates the importance of family traditions. Specifically, you should be able to support your thesis that the text's theme is as follows: The adoption of new ideas about cultural heritage should not result in the abandonment of family traditions, for these traditions keep us connected to our family history and contribute to the emotional bond among family members.

Although some of the textual evidence you've gathered paints rather unflattering portraits of Dee and Hakim, it doesn't suggest that their insensitive behavior can be blamed on the Black Pride movement. For one thing, the text provides abundant evidence of Dee's insensitivity prior to the advent of the movement. The point here is that newfound connections to our cultural past—no matter how self-affirming and inspiring—should not lead us to abandon thoughtlessly the traditions embraced by our family, for our family may have an important cultural heritage of its own.

Of course, you don't have to limit yourself to the analysis of the story I've offered you. You might want, instead, to see what themes are revealed when the text is explored through different topics. For example, given that various kinds of aspirations are represented in the story, you might want to examine "Everyday Use" in terms of the topic of personal success. Is there a single kind of personal success illustrated in the story, or does the text illustrate more than one kind? What seem to be the requirements for and/or consequences of personal success in the story? From the answers to these questions, can we infer the text's definition

of what it means to be successful? Or perhaps, given the various kinds of hardship portrayed in the story, you would like to examine the text's representation
of human responses to the obstacles life can place in our path. Which characters
overcome significant obstacles in their lives? How and to what extent do they
do so? What can thereby be inferred concerning the text's opinion of the
human capacity to endure hardship and to thrive? This topic might reveal the
ways in which Mama, Maggie, and Dee have a good deal in common.

Perhaps, rather than focusing on a thematic analysis, you would like to use
our New Critical concepts to analyze a particular character in the story. For a
conscientious character analysis can contribute a great deal to our understanding
of the text's meaning as a whole. Of course, in this case, characterization,
rather than theme, would be the focus of your thesis. Nevertheless, you
would still use the same kinds of textual evidence for a character analysis that
you would use for a thematic analysis: characterization, plot events, setting,
imagery, tension, ambiguity, and so forth. Consider, for instance, the following
sample of the kinds of specific textual evidence you would need for a character
analysis of Mrs. Johnson. Among other things, you would need to examine
the tensions embodied in her relationship with Dee (such as the tensions
between tradition and change, self-doubt and self-confidence, rural life and urban
life, experience and youth, and the like) as well as the tensions embodied within
Mama's own character (such as the tensions between her positive and negative
self-images, her positive and negative feelings about each of her daughters, and
the like). And you would need to pay special attention to images and ambiguities
associated with Mama, such as those you might find in her dream, her memories of the time when both her daughters lived with her, her memories of the
house fire that destroyed the family's former home, and her experience in
giving Maggie the quilts coveted by Dee. What ideas or values does the
character of Mrs. Johnson represent? Does your character analysis bring to light
a topic that you otherwise might not have considered, such as the conflicts
inherent in parental love? In short, what does a thorough understanding of Mrs.
Johnson contribute to our understanding and appreciation of "Everyday Use"?

Whatever your interpretation, be sure you understand the New Critical
concepts you choose to employ, compose a clear statement of your thesis, and
support your interpretation with adequate textual evidence.

Recognizing the presence of death: Interpreting "A Rose for Emily"

Upon first reading William Faulkner's "A Rose for Emily" (1931; see
Appendix B), readers might feel a little overwhelmed by some of the story's
unusual qualities, such as the span of decades covered by a plot lacking in
chronological order, the number of unanswered questions raised by the story
about which we are left to speculate, and the variety of topics—parental
cruelty, social isolation, the destructive power of gossip, conformity and
rebellion, among others—that emerge as we read.

We might not notice, therefore, that "A Rose for Emily" opens and closes with references to the death of main character Emily Grierson or that references to and images of death occur throughout the text. Indeed, the presence of death might be the one consistent thread woven through the story. Well, isn't that to be expected in a narrative about a woman who poisons her suitor and sleeps with his dead body, which she keeps hidden in her bed until her own death forty years later? Yes, Emily's murder of Homer Barron, whose body the town of Jefferson—and the reader—discover only at the end of the story, can lead us to see "A Rose for Emily" as a sort of eerie murder mystery in which an emotionally unstable woman kills the rascal who apparently planned to abandon her. Striking as this aspect of the plot may be, however, the pervasive presence of death throughout the text suggests that this topic exceeds the story of Emily's murder of Homer. For as Faulkner's story illustrates, death isn't just an event that marks the end of a life. It can be a pervasive destructive presence during the course of a life, as well. Any force that cuts us off from other people, from productive self-expression, from honest self-reflection, from meaningful occupation, from the enjoyment of living, or from any other life-affirming experience can be considered a spirit-killing force, a force of death.

With the topic of death in mind, our task is to discover the story's theme, or meaning as a whole, and to support our discovery with formal elements from the text itself. In order to fulfill this task, we must identify: (1) the central, or most important, tension operating in the story, which will guide us to the story's theme and help us lay the groundwork for our interpretation; (2) the story's theme; and (3) the formal elements in the story that support the theme we have identified, thereby showing that our interpretation of the story is valid.

The text's central tension

In order to find the text's central tension and lay our interpretive groundwork, it can help to brainstorm a list of the oppositions related to our topic and embodied in plot events; in characters' behavior, attitudes, or physical appearance; and in the text's imagery. So let's start by finding evidence in the story of the following oppositions, each of which identifies an example of the presence of death in the story and contrasts that example with its opposite.

1   The opening description of Emily's house and neighborhood as they are at the time of her death vs. the opening description of Emily's house and neighborhood as they were in the 1870s, when the house was built.
2   The description of Emily as she is seen by the aldermen who call on her concerning her taxes vs. the description of Emily as a young woman, pictured behind the figure of her angry father in the open doorway.
3   The various images of Emily sitting alone behind her window vs. the descriptions of Emily being courted by Homer Barron on Sunday afternoons.
4   Emily's purchase of arsenic, or "rat poison," for Homer Barron vs. her earlier purchase of handsome personal items, also for Homer.

5   The description of Homer Barron's dead body vs. the description of Homer when he first comes to Jefferson.
6   Signs that Emily is living in the past vs. signs of the modernization that comes to the town of Jefferson over the years.
7   The closing description of Emily's bedroom in terms of its function as a tomb vs. the closing description of Emily's bedroom in terms of its function as a bridal chamber (which we can only imagine because the bridal ornaments are decayed and covered with dust).

As you can see, these examples cluster around the opposition between the forces of life and the forces of death. Emily was once a young belle dressed in virginal white, but that life force is thwarted by her father's determination to drive off suitors. Emily once had hopes of love and marriage, but that life force is thwarted by the outcome of her relationship with Homer Barron. And while the town of Jefferson moves toward modernization over the years, Emily becomes a hermit living in the past.

The text's theme

As we have just seen, the central tension in "A Rose for Emily" is the tension, or opposition, between life and death. We will discover the text's theme by asking, Which side of this tension has a stronger presence in the story? Or does the text suggest that they are equally strong forces in Emily's life? Although we often take it for granted that life is ultimately stronger than death, the oppositions listed above show that Emily's attempts to have some connection to others, some connection to the life around her, are, in terms of her life as a whole, short-lived. They are not enough to overcome the shadow of death that remains the dominant presence in her life. In addition, these oppositions suggest that the presence of death (in the form of isolation and stagnation as well as in the form of literal death) is embodied in Emily's desire to live in the past.

In the next section, we will do a close reading of the story in search of additional formal elements supporting our *thesis* (our debatable opinion, which is the main point of our interpretation) that the text promotes an understanding of the ways in which death can be stronger than life. If we don't find such textual evidence or don't find enough of it or find conflicting textual evidence that doesn't fit our interpretation, we will have to amend our thesis to fit the textual evidence we find. However, at this point, we might reasonably argue that the text's theme can be stated as follows: *Death, as a presence that shadows and depletes the life force, can be stronger than life and is embodied in the desire to live in the past.*

Textual evidence: Formal elements that support the text's theme

Let's look again at our statement of the text's theme so that we can determine the kind of textual evidence we need to support our claim that we have correctly identified the theme. To make sure we don't miss anything, let's divide our statement of the theme into its component parts.

Components of the theme

1 Death, as a presence that shadows and depletes the life force,
2 can be stronger than life
3 and is embodied by the desire to live in the past.

Now we can formulate the questions that will serve as guidelines in our search for textual evidence to support our claim.

Questions to guide our search for textual support

1 How is death a literal presence in the text? (Which characters die over the course of the story?)
2 In what ways is Emily cut off (or in what ways does she cut herself off) from other people and, apparently, from the enjoyment of living?
3 In what ways does Emily desire to live in the past?
4 How is death a stronger metaphorical presence in the text than life? (What images show that death—in the form of isolation, stagnation, decay, and the like—is the dominant presence in Emily's life?)

If we can find the textual evidence—including such formal elements as characterization, plot events, setting, imagery, ambiguity, and so forth—that answers each of these questions, then we will be able to support our thesis. That is, we will be able to show that our statement of the story's theme is valid. So let's translate these questions into the specific textual evidence we need to find in the story.

Finding our textual evidence

1 Find textual evidence that death is a literal presence in the text. Specifically, list the five characters, all known to Emily, who die over the course of the story.
2 Find textual evidence, including the following, that Emily is cut off from (or cuts herself off from) other people and from the enjoyment of living.

  a How is the young Emily prevented from seeing suitors?
  b What becomes of Emily's relationship with Homer Barron?
  c What becomes of Emily's china-painting lessons?
  d How do we know that Emily doesn't converse with any of the townsfolk and, apparently, not even with Tobe?
  e How does the text indicate that Emily doesn't leave the house during the final decades of her life?

3 Find textual evidence, including the following, that Emily wants to live in the past.

a How does Emily react when her father dies?

b What does Emily do with Homer's dead body?

c How does Emily react to the death of Colonel Sartoris?

d How does Emily react as the town of Jefferson moves into the future, for example, when home mail-delivery comes to Jefferson and when the new sheriff and alderman try to collect her taxes?

e Ask yourself: How does living as a hermit, which is addressed above in item #2e, help Emily live in the past?

4 Find evidence that death is a stronger metaphorical presence in the text than life.

a Find all the images of life and youth that you can—for example

   i the opening description of the Grierson home and neighborhood as they were in the 1870s, when the house was built;

   ii the image of Emily as a young woman, pictured behind the figure of her angry father in the open doorway;

   iii the description of Homer Barron when he first comes to Jefferson;

   iv the descriptions of Homer courting Emily, and

   v the description of the handsome personal items Emily purchases for Homer.

b Find the passages demonstrating that images of death—in the form of isolation, stagnation, decay, and the like—are more numerous and vivid than the story's images of life and youth, thereby supporting the claim that death is the dominant presence in Emily's life. Paying attention to the language used in each passage, find, for example

   i the opening description of the Grierson home and neighborhood as they are at the time of Emily's death (note the ways in which Emily's decaying home can be seen as a metaphor for Emily herself);

   ii the description of Emily's living room as it is seen by the aldermen who call on her concerning her taxes;

   iii the description of Emily as she is seen by the aldermen who call on her concerning her taxes (note the simile comparing her to a corpse);

   iv the description of Homer Barron's dead body;

   v the descriptions of the bottle of arsenic and of a man "sowing" lime (used to neutralize the smell of death) around Emily's home;

   vi the various images of Emily sitting alone behind her window, and

   vii the description of Emily's bedroom as it is found at the story's close, in which bridal images, associated with life, are decayed and covered with dust.

c The rose in "A Rose for Emily" is an ambiguous symbol. How might it symbolize life, death, or both?

Focusing your essay

You should be able to use the textual evidence you've gathered to focus your essay on the ways in which "A Rose for Emily" illustrates the power of death to overcome the forces of life. Specifically, you should be able to support your thesis that the text's theme is as follows: Death, as a presence that shadows and depletes the life force, can be stronger than life and is embodied in the desire to live in the past. Perhaps the most memorable symbol of the intimate connection between the presence of death and the desire to live in the past occurs in the description of Homer's remains found in Emily's bed. For it is evident that his body "had apparently once lain in the attitude of an embrace," and the strand of long gray hair found on the indented pillow next to it reveals that Emily has, literally, lain in that embrace over the course of the many years since Homer's murder, thereby living in a world in which Homer is still alive and still loves her.

Indeed, Emily's desire to live in the past lays her in death's embrace figuratively, as well: in her initial refusal to accept the loss of her father and release his dead body, which foreshadows her refusal to accept the loss of Homer; in her belief that the long-dead Colonel Sartoris is still alive; and in her isolation from her fellow inhabitants of Jefferson and thus from the town's movement into the twentieth century. Even the china-painting lessons she gives to the young girls of Jefferson before she isolates herself completely suggest a desire to live in the past, for china-painting, as a sign of the accomplished young lady, is a rather old-fashioned feminine avocation even in Emily's time. In this context, the fact that Emily is the last of the Grierson line is particularly significant. The Griersons are the only family in town whose lineage goes back to wealthy, pre-Civil War plantation owners. So the death of Emily marks the death of the Grierson line and, symbolically, the death of the Old South.

Of course, you don't have to limit yourself to the analysis of the story I've offered you. You might want, instead, to see what themes are revealed when the text is explored through different topics. For example, given the emotionally conflicted relationships represented in the story, you might want to examine "A Rose for Emily" in terms of the topic of love and hate. How can we understand Emily's feelings for her father and for Homer Barron in terms of both love and hate? Might we not also examine the ambivalent feelings of the townsfolk for Emily through this lens? What does "A Rose for Emily" suggest about the conflicted relationship between these two emotions?

Rather than exploring the story thematically, you might prefer to use our New Critical concepts to analyze the first-person-plural narrator, the disembodied voice that tells the story and refers to itself as "we." For the conscientious examination of a narrator can contribute a great deal to our understanding of the text's meaning as a whole. Of course, in that case, the narrator, rather than the story's theme, would be the focus of your thesis. Nevertheless, in analyzing the narrator you would still use the same kinds of textual evidence that you would use for a thematic analysis: characterization, plot events, setting, imagery, tension, ambiguity, and so forth. Among the specific textual evidence required for an analysis of Faulkner's narrator, who is often thought to embody the town of Jefferson, you would need to examine the tensions evident in the narrator's ambivalence toward Emily. In what ways does the narrator seem to respond to her positively or feel sorry for her? In contrast, when does the narrator's attitude suggest disapproval or some other negative view of Emily's conduct? Or is the narrator non-judgmental, reporting the townsfolk's occasional envy or outrage without sharing it? And if the story's title is a clue to the narrator's feelings about Emily, what might be the symbolic meaning of the ambiguous rose? In short, what does an analysis of the narrator contribute to our appreciation and understanding of "A Rose for Emily"?

Whatever your interpretation, be sure you understand the New Critical concepts you choose to employ, compose a clear statement of your thesis, and support your interpretation with adequate textual evidence.

Understanding the power of alienation: Interpreting "The Battle Royal"

Set in 1950 in a small city in the American South, Ralph Ellison's "The Battle Royal" (1952; see Appendix C) offers a gripping representation of racist brutalization that occurs within the walls of a single room over the course of a single evening. For the "entertainment" of a group of drunken white civic leaders, ten African American young men, who have few opportunities to make money, are paid five dollars each to compete against one another in a horrifying group "boxing" match, a battle royal, and submit to other acts of physical and psychological abuse.

The story is told by an unnamed first-person narrator—the valedictorian of his high-school graduating class who participates in the battle royal before giving his graduation speech to the assembled white leaders—so we see the evening's events from his point of view. Indeed, the story consists of the narrator's personal responses to his experiences at this gathering of civic leaders, and his narrative of that evening is framed, or preceded and followed by, his reflections on himself and his family.

"The Battle Royal" is also told from a "single window" in another way: the narrator isn't just alone in his own thoughts; he's also alone in his complete lack of emotional bonds with other human beings. It is striking that his thoughts about others—including his family and the other young men who participate in the battle royal—reveal an absence of personal connectedness that leaves him profoundly isolated in his efforts to survive the racism rampant in the American South of the 1950s. However their efforts to survive and thrive don't include the sacrifice of emotional ties. Indeed, the narrator's emotional isolation from others reflects his emotional disconnectedness from himself and suggests that alienation—which might be defined as the loss of shared values and the absence of loyalty to and affection for one's fellow human beings—is an important topic in this story.

With the topic of alienation in mind, our task is to discover the story's theme, or meaning as a whole, and to support our discovery with formal elements from the text itself. In order to fulfill this task, we must identify: (1) the central, or most important tension operating in the story, which will guide us to the story's theme and help us lay the groundwork for our interpretation; (2) the story's theme; and (3) the formal elements in the story that support the theme we have identified, thereby showing that our interpretation of the story is valid.

The text's central tension

In order to find the text's central tension and lay our interpretive groundwork, it can help to brainstorm a list of the oppositions related to our topic and embodied in plot events; in characters' behavior, attitudes, or physical appearance; and in the text's imagery. So let's start by finding evidence in the story of the following oppositions, each of which identifies an example of alienation in the story and contrasts that example with its opposite.

1   The narrator's alienation from the other young men participating in the battle royal vs. the young men's bond with one another.
2   The narrator's position at the head of his graduating class due to his grades vs. Tatlock's position at the head of his group of friends due to their loyalty to him.
3   The narrator's focus on pleasing the white civic leaders vs. the other young men's focus on their collective purpose.
4   The narrator's alienation from his family vs. his family's bond with one another.
5   The narrator's belief that only the white civic leaders can understand and help him vs. the white civic leaders' belief that the narrator is merely a pawn in their plan to maintain racial dominance.
6   The narrator's alienation from himself vs. his grandfather's self-understanding.

As you can see, these examples cluster around the opposition between alienation and belonging. All of the African American characters suffer racist oppression. However, Tatlock and his friends have one another for support, and the narrator's family members have ties to both family and community. Only the narrator suffers the disadvantage of living in emotional isolation, unable to relate to anyone. And we see the chilling effects of that isolation in his tormented inner world, in which he seems unable to relate even to himself.

The text's theme

As we have just seen, the central tension in "The Battle Royal" is the tension, or opposition, between alienation and belonging. We will discover the text's theme by asking, Which side of this tension seems to have the stronger presence in the text? That is, which side of the tension does the text attempt to explore and illuminate? Or does the text seem interested in some combination of both? I think most readers will agree that the text's representations of alienation are the more sustained and vivid: The sense of belonging experienced by Tatlock and his friends as well as by the narrator's family is subtly portrayed and forms a background against which we can better appreciate the extreme nature of the narrator's alienation.

In the next section, we will do a close reading of the story in search of additional formal elements supporting our *thesis* (our debatable opinion, which is the main point of our interpretation) that the text promotes an understanding of the ways in which emotional isolation from our fellow human beings, although it might seem the only way to survive in some situations, can rob us of the very support we need for emotional survival. If we don't find such textual evidence or don't find enough of it or find conflicting textual evidence that doesn't fit our interpretation, we will have to amend our thesis to fit the textual evidence we find. However, at this point, we might reasonably argue that the text's theme can be stated as follows: *A sense of belonging can help us in the worst of times, and without it we risk becoming alienated not only from others but from ourselves, as well.*

Textual evidence: Formal elements that support the text's theme

Let's take another look at our statement of the text's theme so that we can determine the kind of textual evidence we need to support our claim that we have correctly identified the theme. To make sure we don't miss anything, let's divide our statement of the theme into its component parts.

Components of the theme

1   A sense of belonging can help us in the worst of times,
2   and without it we risk becoming alienated not only from others
3   but from ourselves, as well.

Now we can formulate the questions that will serve as guidelines in our search for textual evidence to support our claim.

Questions to guide our search for textual support

1   How does a sense of belonging help Tatlock and his friends on the evening of the battle royal?
2   What bonds are shared by the narrator's family?
3   In what ways is the narrator alienated from others?

4   In what ways is the narrator alienated from himself?
5   How does the narrator's alienation harm him?

If we can find the textual evidence—including such formal elements as char-acterization, plot events, setting, imagery, ambiguity, and so forth—that answers each of these questions, then we will be able to support our thesis. That is, we will be able to show that our statement of the story's theme is valid. So let's translate these questions into the specific textual evidence we need to find in the story.

Finding our textual evidence

1   How does a sense of belonging, including the following examples, help Tatlock and his friends on the evening of the battle royal?

   a   Where do we see the bond among Tatlock and his friends?
   b   How do they work together, by plan, during the battle royal, and how does that collective purpose help them?
   c   What image in the story do you think best represents their bond?

2   What bonds, including the following examples, are shared by the narrator's family?

   a   What are the family's shared values?
   b   What are the family's shared strategies for surviving racism?
   c   The family were deeply frightened by the grandfather's dying declaration—fearful of what might happen to them should the white community learn that the old man had considered white people the enemy and that his meekness had been just a strategy to ensure his safety.

     i   How do the family stick together in their response to the old man's last words?
     ii   What image in the story do you think best represents the family's shared response to the old man's revelation?

3   In what ways, including the following examples, is the narrator alienated from others?

   a   How is the narrator alienated from his family? That is, find textual evidence that he shares neither their values, nor their strategies for surviving racism, nor their response to his grandfather's dying words.
   b   How is the narrator alienated from Tatlock and his friends, despite the fact that they are fellow objects of the white men's brutalization and humiliation?
   c   How does the narrator feel about using the service elevator with them?
   d   What is his chief concern about participating in the battle royal?
   e   How does his exchange of words with Tatlock reveal the narrator's complete ignorance of his opponent's viewpoint and, presumably, the viewpoint of his opponent's friends?

    f What image in the story do you think best represents the narrator's alienation from others?

4 In what ways is the narrator alienated from himself?

    a Where do we see his self-alienation in terms of his relationship to the white community?

        i   What does he think are the intentions of the civic leaders toward him, and how is he wrong about them?

        ii Find the ways in which his desire to please these men, and white people in general, controls his thoughts, paralyzes him in indecision, and causes him to act against his own best interests.

        iii How do the images of thick cigar smoke and blindfolds symbolize the narrator's inability to see the truth, despite the fact that, ironically, his own blindfold gets pushed aside?

    b How does the narrator's description of the white dancer, also a fellow object of "entertainment" for the white men, reflect his own feelings of self-alienation?

        i   Note the dehumanizing elements in the narrator's description of the dancer, which resonate with the white leaders' dehumanization of the narrator.

        ii Note all the ways in which his personal response to the dancer consists of opposing impulses, which resonate with the opposing impulses in his inner world.

    c Where do we see the narrator's self-alienation in terms of his dream about his grandfather?

        i   What is this dream trying to tell him about the real motive behind the scholarship given him by the white leaders?

        ii What image from the dream do you think best reveals the dream's meaning?

        iii What does the narrator's inability to see the obvious meaning of his dream—which he must understand on some level because the dream emerges from his own sleeping mind—indicate about the degree of his self-alienation?

    d How does the fact that the narrator is unnamed contribute to our sense that he is alienated from himself?

5 Drawing on the textual data you've gathered so far, list those items that show how the narrator's alienation harms him—for example

    a how his alienation renders him less capable of understanding others,

    b how it confuses him and either leads him to make unwise decisions or renders him incapable of making any decision at all, and c how it makes him a stranger to himself, without self-knowledge or self-confidence.

Focusing your essay

At this point, the textual evidence you've collected should allow you to focus your essay on the ways in which "The Battle Royal" illustrates the destructive power of alienation. Specifically, you should be able to support your thesis that the text's theme is as follows: A sense of belonging can help us in the worst of times, and without it we risk becoming alienated not only from others but from ourselves, as well. Although the story's opening lines reveal that the narrator will, at some point in the future, look back at the events he describes and understand them, his narrative focuses on a period in his life when he has no insight into the real meaning of his experiences and no awareness of his own alienation.

It's not surprising, in representations of oppression, to find the oppressed characters alienated from their oppressors. Indeed, Tatlock and his friends seem alienated, and rightly so, from the white civic leaders bent on intimidating and humiliating them. They know that these men are not well-intentioned toward them and that the only good to be gained from this evening of abuse is the money they will earn by enduring it. And the narrator's family, if not completely alienated from their oppressors, are very much afraid of them because they know all too well the dangers they face in a society that classes them as much less important, and probably less human, than its white citizens. Indeed, Tatlock and the narrator's family offer a kind of fight-or-flight alternative for dealing with racism: Tatlock and his friends will behave as brutally as their survival requires, and the narrator's family will keep a low profile while they try to rise within the limitations set for them by white society. In both cases, however, the members of each group share emotional ties with one another. They are not alone in their efforts to overcome their oppression. The narrator, in contrast, lives in emotional isolation, outside the bonds of family and friends. And the narrator, despite his success and the recognition he's gained from both black and white communities, is alone and lost, adrift in the only desire he seems to have left: the desire to please the white people who see him as their inferior.

As you think about your essay, remember that it's not a question of which African American characters are right or wrong in their strategies for dealing with a racist society. Nor is it a question of condemning the narrator for emotionally rejecting his family and community. Rather, it's a question of understanding the narrator's alienation as a self-destructive response to the whirlwind of oppressive social forces into which he was born.

Of course, you don't have to limit yourself to the analysis of the story I've offered you. You might want, instead, to see what themes are revealed when "The Battle Royal" is explored through different topics. Given, for example, the story's vivid images of dim light, obscured vision, and bright light that fails to "illuminate," you might want to analyze the text in terms of the topic of blindness and insight. How are most or all of the characters, black and white, unable to "see," or understand, something important about themselves or others? Do any of the characters seem to have insight into the situation in which they find themselves? Or is this primarily a story about human beings' inability to adequately understand the complex social forces of which they, themselves, are a part?

Perhaps, instead, if your attention was seized by the unrelenting inhumanity depicted in the story, you might want to examine the text's representation of the corrupting influence of power. What does the civic leaders' behavior—their drunkenness, abusiveness, vulgarity, and the like—reveal concerning the effects of unrestrained power on those who possess it? And what is the impact of unrestrained power on those who are victimized by it? Specifically, how does their relative powerlessness result in a need for whatever power or superiority, real or imagined, they can get, as we see in the case of the narrator, the exotic dancer, and Tatlock? How does the text link the exercise of power with images of degradation? In short, how does "The Battle Royal" suggest that unrestrained power is, fundamentally, a power to degrade others that results in self-degradation, as well?

Whatever your interpretation, be sure you understand the New Critical concepts you choose to employ, compose a clear statement of your thesis, and support your interpretation with adequate textual evidence.

Respecting the importance of nonconformity: Interpreting "Don't Explain"

Jewelle Gomez's "Don't Explain" (1987; see Appendix E) is set in a place and time associated with strict conformity to social norms: Boston in 1959. For at that time Boston had long been known for its adherence to narrow standards of propriety. Indeed, the phrase "banned in Boston" had come to refer to novels, movies, paintings, or any other artistic productions that were slightly risqué: not indecent enough to be prohibited elsewhere but too indecent to be permitted in Boston. And, in 1959, the whole country was mired in Cold War fears of communism and distrust of anything foreign or different. Women were expected to conform to society's definition of femininity—in their physical appearance, in their chaste dependence on men, and in their single-minded purpose to become wives and mothers—because that was considered the only right and natural way for women to be. It is within this tableau that Gomez places her characters.

Delia, her cousin Terry, and their friends, however, don't conform to some of society's most imperative expectations of women at that time. They dress to please themselves, they support themselves financially, they have no romantic interest in men, and they won't become wives and mothers. They are lesbians who accept their sexual orientation, and because women were not allowed to marry other women in 1959, they have sexual relations outside of marriage. In order to enjoy the freedom to be themselves and to live the private lives they choose, these women must be willing to run some serious risks. For a woman's lack of romantic interest in men and unwillingness to marry, if known, would surely raise suspicion. In fact, should the sexual orientation of Delia, Terry, and their friends be discovered, they would be vulnerable to verbal harassment, job termination, and sexual assault, which they could not report to the police without fear of further abuse by the authorities. These are the risks that Letty, the story's main character, does not want to take.

Letty struggles to conform to society's rules against same-sex love. But while her efforts to conform have kept her physically and emotionally protected, they have left her alone and unhappy. Since she came to work at the 411 Lounge seven years ago, Letty's decision to conform has required her to forget Maxine, her former lover; to avoid having such feelings for any woman ever again; and to keep her acquaintances from getting close enough to discover that she is "different." Letty can't even listen to the music of her favorite singer, the recently deceased Billie Holiday, because Billie's music reminds Letty of Maxine and of her own sexual orientation. Clearly, the difficult choice between conformity and nonconformity, each with its risks and rewards, is an important topic in this interesting story.

With this topic in mind, our task is to discover the story's theme, or meaning as a whole, and to support our discovery with formal elements from the text itself. In order to fulfill this task, we must identify: (1) the central, or most important tension operating in the story, which will guide us to the story's theme and help us lay the groundwork for our interpretation; (2) the story's theme; and (3) the formal elements in the story that support the theme we have identified, thereby showing that our interpretation of the story is valid.

The text's central tension

As our topic suggests, the central tension operating in "Don't Explain" seems to be the tension between conformity and nonconformity. To confirm that we've correctly identified the central tension and lay our interpretive groundwork, it can help to brainstorm a list of the oppositions related to our topic and embodied in plot events; in characters' behavior, attitudes, or physical appearance; and in the text's imagery. So let's start by finding evidence in the story of the following oppositions.

1   The conformity required of Letty and Delia at the 411 Lounge vs. the individuality enjoyed among the women gathered at the home of Delia and Terry.
2   Letty's refusal to socialize with her acquaintances at the 411 for fear that they will discover her difference from them vs. Letty's acceptance of Delia's invitation to the gathering of friends at her home.

3   Letty's initial response to the realization that her new acquaintances are lesbians vs. her "spitting" out, or refusing that negative reaction.
4   Letty's unwillingness, since Billie Holiday's death, to listen to the singer's music because it brings back frightening memories of her socially forbidden love for Maxine vs. Letty's willingness to listen to "Don't Explain" with Maryalice.
5   The threat to her safety Letty feels in the presence of Tip, afraid lest he discover her lack of romantic interest in men, vs. the comfort and safety she begins to feel among her new acquaintances.
6   Letty's habit of keeping "close to the chest," of not letting others know anything about her, vs. her acceptance of the women gathered at Delia and Terry's apartment, which means letting them know, and letting herself accept, that she's a lesbian.

As expected, all of these examples cluster around the tension between Letty's conformity and her movement toward the nonconformity embodied in Delia, Terry, and their friends. In addition, these examples suggest the tension between self-negation—the rejection of one's true feelings, of one's true self—and self-acceptance. For conformity to society's dictates can require self-negation, as we see in Letty's self-negating efforts, throughout most of the story, to reject her sexual orientation—to banish all thought of it—because her sexual orientation doesn't conform to society's expectations.

The text's theme

As we have just seen, the central tension in "Don't Explain" is the tension, or opposition, between conformity and nonconformity. We will discover the text's theme by asking, Which side of this tension does the text promote, or portray more favorably? Or does the text favor some combination of both? I think most readers will agree that the text promotes nonconformity—the embracing of one's individuality—because it portrays Letty's unhappiness as the result of her conformity to the social norms of the day, a conformity that requires her self-negation. In contrast, Letty's nonconformity, and the self-acceptance that accompanies it, bring her the relief and comfort she needs.

In the next section, we will do a close reading of the story in search of additional formal elements supporting our *thesis* (our debatable opinion, which is the main point of our interpretation) that the text depicts the danger of conforming to social expectations that require self-negation and reveals the ways in which nonconformity can be the key to self-acceptance. If we don't find such textual evidence or don't find enough of it or find conflicting textual evidence that doesn't fit our interpretation, we will have to amend our thesis to fit the textual evidence we find. However, at this point, we might reasonably argue that the text's theme can be stated as follows: *When conformity requires self-negation, then self-acceptance requires nonconformity.*

Textual evidence: Formal elements that support the text's theme

Let's take another look at our statement of the text's theme so that we can determine the kind of textual evidence we need to support our claim that we have correctly identified the theme. To make sure we don't miss anything, let's divide our statement of the theme into its component parts.

Components of the theme

1   When conformity requires self-negation,
2   then self-acceptance requires nonconformity.

Now we can formulate the questions that will serve as guidelines in our search for textual evidence to support our claim.

Questions to guide our search for textual support

1   In what ways does Letty try to conform to the expectations of society?
2   In what ways does her conformity require her self-negation?
3   In what ways are Delia, Terry, and their friends nonconformists?
4   How does their nonconformity improve the quality of their lives?
5   In what ways does Letty risk herself beyond the boundaries of conformity?
6   How does Letty's nonconformity encourage her self-acceptance?
7   How does Billie Holiday symbolize the power of nonconformity in this story?

If we can find the textual evidence—including such formal elements as characterization, plot events, setting, imagery, ambiguity, and so forth—that answers each of these questions, then we will be able to support our thesis. That is, we will be able to show that our statement of the story's theme is valid. So let's translate these questions into the specific textual evidence we need to find in the story.

Finding our textual evidence

1   In what ways does Letty try to conform to society's expectations, and how does her conformity require self-negation?

    a   Find the textual evidence that reveals the price Letty must pay for her conformity.

        i   What strategies does Letty use to avoid socializing with her acquaintances at the 411 Lounge so that she doesn't risk their becoming suspicious about her "difference"?

        ii   Find the textual evidence that, in order to conform, Letty rejects her own thoughts and feelings.

    b   What image in the story do you think best represents the self-negation that Letty's conformity requires?

2   Delia, Terry, and their friends are clearly nonconformists in terms of their lesbian sexual orientation: they embrace their feelings instead of succumbing to the intense social pressure to suppress them. In what additional ways are these women all individuals, and how does their individuality benefit them?

   a   In the 1950s, most women conformed to the dictates of feminine fashion: dresses or skirts and blouses; high heels; makeup; and medium-length hair, softly waved or worn up. They also tended to conform even more closely to the clothing and hairstyles of the women with whom they regularly socialized. In what ways are Delia, Terry, and their friends individuals in terms of their clothing and hairstyles?

   b   In the 1950s, it was common for people of color to socialize not only with people of their own race, but with people of their own—lighter or darker—skin color. How do we know that Delia, Terry, and their friends don't conform to this practice?

   c   In literary representations, party guests that the reader does not get to know are rarely given names. Note how the name given to each of Delia and Terry's friends increases our sense of their individuality. (They are not presented to the reader as a group, "lumped" together, but as individuals.)

3   In what ways does the nonconformity of Delia, Terry, and their friends seem to improve the quality of their lives?

   a   One way to find this textual evidence is to note the ways in which their lives are different from Letty's life.

   b   Be sure to include Delia and Terry's openheartedness, which we see, for example, in their invitation to Letty despite the danger to them-selves: what if they are mistaken about Letty's being a lesbian? Find the passage that reveals Delia's anxiety about Letty's visit so that we can appreciate the cousins' willingness to share their good fortune.

   c   What image in the story do you think best represents the individuality of Delia, Terry, and their friends?

4   In what ways does Letty risk herself beyond the boundaries of conformity, and how does her nonconformity encourage her self-acceptance?

   a   What actions, on Letty's part, allow a subtle bond of trust to grow between herself and Delia, thereby opening herself to the risk of being known?

   b   At Delia and Terry's apartment, in what specific ways does Letty begin to reject society's strictures against same-sex love and begin to accept her own feelings?

   c   What image in the story do you think best represents the link between Letty's nonconformity and her self-acceptance?

5   How does Billie Holiday symbolize the power of nonconformity in this story?

a   In Letty's thoughts about Billie Holiday, how does the singer stand alone, literally and figuratively, and how does she triumph in the face of society's readiness to see her fail?

b   In Letty's memories of the singer's visit to the 411 Lounge, in what ways is Billie's individuality positively portrayed?

    i   Although she's a big star, where does the singer sit?

    ii   How does she reject the social requirement that women must have small appetites, especially when dining in public?

    iii   How does she treat the people "beneath her" who work at the 411?

c   Whose song is playing when Letty, finally embracing her true self, sits down with Maryalice?

Focusing your essay

At this point, the textual evidence you've collected should allow you to focus your essay on the ways in which "Don't Explain" illustrates the role nonconformity can play in the attainment of self-acceptance. Specifically, you should be able to support your thesis that the text's theme is as follows: When conformity requires self-negation, then self-acceptance requires nonconformity. For if Letty weren't finally able to reject, as her new friends have rejected, the conformity required by the society in which she lives, she might never have learned to accept herself, and self-acceptance is her first step to a more meaningful life, a life that includes real friendship and, possibly, love. Perhaps the most powerful reward Letty receives for venturing beyond the boundaries of conformity is the freeing of her inner world, of her thoughts and feelings. She no longer needs continually to monitor herself in an effort to erase memories that should be precious, not poisonous, and hopes that should gladden her heart, not strike it with fear.

Of course, you don't have to limit yourself to the analysis of the story I've offered you. You might want, instead, to see what themes are revealed when "Don't Explain" is explored through different topics. Perhaps, for example, you are interested in the unequal power relations depicted in "Don't Explain." In that case, you might want to examine the various kinds of power dynamics operating among the characters in the story: those between employer and employees at the 411 Lounge, which is based both on the financial difference between owner and workers and on racial difference; those between men and women; and those between heterosexuals and lesbians. In short, how does "Don't Explain" explore the inequities of unequal power relations as well as the strategies people employ to deal with them? Or maybe, instead, you are struck by the images of isolation and loneliness that dot the commonplace, workaday landscape of this story: for example, the image of Letty alone in her booth at the 411 and, again, alone at night in her apartment; of Ari alone at the end of the bar, sitting in his own special seat; of Tip, in his sharkskin suit, eating dinner alone; of Maryalice alone at a gathering of friends; and of Billie

Holiday, as Letty thinks of her, alone onstage before an unfriendly audience. What do these images suggest about the loneliness of everyday living? Does the story offer a remedy? Or does the strength of these images, taken together, suggest that loneliness must play a role in every life? Whatever your interpretation, be sure you understand the New Critical concepts you choose to employ, compose a clear statement of your thesis, and support your interpretation with adequate textural evidence.

Responding to the challenge of the unknown: Interpreting "I started Early—Took my Dog"

The first thing most readers are able to say, with some degree of certainty, about Emily Dickinson's "I started Early—Took my Dog" (c. 1862; see Appendix A) is that the poem depicts a young woman, the poem's speaker, who walks down to the sea and then, with the sea in close pursuit, runs back to the safety of the "Solid Town." From what is she really running and why? That is, what frightening force does the sea symbolize in this poem, and how does the speaker feel about it? This question is usually a source of disagreement among readers because the meaning of the text as a whole—a text that clearly represents a fantasy, a product of the speaker's vivid imagination—rests largely on the symbolic meaning of the sea. Yet the poem's portrayal of the sea is ambiguous: it has more than one possible meaning. Readers might reasonably regard Dickinson's sea as a symbol of, for example, life, death, emotion, or sexual desire, for the sea in this poem has fundamental qualities in common with each of these elements.

If we limit ourselves to just one of these interpretive options, however, we will probably neglect some important dimension of the poem's meaning as a whole. So let's see what happens if we seek a broader symbolic meaning for the sea, and for the poem as a whole, that will account for the sea's ambiguity, for the speaker's response to the sea, and for the rest of the poem's formal elements. Specifically, what do the various possible meanings of the sea— which, in Dickinson's poem, both attracts and frightens the speaker—have in common? I think most readers will agree that, in each case, the sea is both inviting and frightening because it symbolizes the unknown, whether we think of the unknown in terms of the mysteries of life, of death, of the human heart, of sexual desire, or of any other area of complex human experience.

With the unknown as our topic, then, our task is to discover the poem's theme, or meaning as a whole, and to support our discovery with formal elements from the text itself. In order to fulfill this task, we must identify: (1) the central, or most important tension operating in the poem, which will guide us to the poem's theme and help us lay the groundwork for our interpretation; (2) the poem's theme; and (3) the formal elements in the poem that support the theme we have identified, thereby showing that our interpretation of the poem is valid.

The text's central tension

In order to discover the text's central tension and lay our interpretive groundwork, it can help to brainstorm a list of the oppositions related to our topic and embodied in the text's formal elements. Because the text we're attempting to interpret is a poem, we will consider such formal elements as the behavior, attitude, and physical appearance of the speaker (the voice that "tells" the poem) and of other characters that may be in the poem; the events that occur in the poem; the poem's imagery; and the nature of the poem's rhyme and meter. Given that our topic is the unknown, we could list these oppositions in terms of the unknown and the known, thereby contrasting the sea with the town, the mermaids with the fully clothed speaker, and so forth. However, the poem as a whole is focused on the relationship between the speaker and the sea—that is, on the speaker's response to the unknown, a response that changes over the course of the poem. So let's start by finding evidence in the poem of the following oppositions, each of which reveals some aspect of the speaker's conflicted response to the unknown.

1   The speaker's desire to be alone with the sea vs. her desire for protection from it (her voluntary visit to the sea at a time—early morning—when no one else is likely to be there vs. the presence of her dog, an emblem of domesticity and protection).

2   The exotic appeal of the sea vs. the comfort and safety of the speaker's ordinary life (the appeal of exotic lands and the adventure of sea voyages suggested by the appearance of mermaids and frigates—wooden sailing ships—with extended hempen ropes that invite the speaker to climb aboard vs. the speaker's everyday clothing and the "Solid Town" to which she flees).

3   The speaker's fear of the sea vs. her sensitivity to its beauty and majesty (her terror of the enormity of the sea, which she feels is about to consume her as if she were as small as a drop of dew upon the petal of a dandelion vs. her references to "silver" and "pearl" in her description of the pursuing tide of sea foam as well as her description of the sea as a stern but majestic gentleman "bowing—with a Mighty look" as he takes leave of her).

4   The use of images that are ambiguous in ways that reflect the speaker's conflicted feelings, for example, the image of mermaids (lovely creatures that betoken exotic lands vs. dangerous creatures that lure sailors to their deaths), the image of ropes (helpful devices for climbing aboard frigates vs. deadly devices used to bind or hang people), and the image of the "Solid Town" (a safe, reliable refuge vs. a place of unchanging, confining customs).

5   The sudden changes in the action of the poem vs. the consistent quality of the poem's meter, or rhythm, and rhyme (sudden changes in the behavior of the sea and of the speaker vs. the poem's steady meter and regular rhyme scheme).

As expected, all of these examples cluster around the tension between the speaker's attraction to and fear of the unknown. She begins with a "visi[t]" to the sea—perhaps to become acquainted, or better acquainted, with it, as the word *visit* implies—but ends by fleeing from the sea in terror. And throughout the poem, the speaker's descriptions of the sea include images of the fear it inspires in her as well as images of its beauty.

The text's theme

As we have just seen, the central tension in "I started Early—Took my Dog" is the tension, or opposition, between attraction to and fear of the unknown. We will discover the text's theme by asking, Which side of this tension has the strongest, or most vivid presence in the poem? Or does the text favor some combination of both? I think most readers will agree that the text's representation of the sea suggests that both attraction and fear contribute to the speaker's response to the unknown. Indeed, perhaps the sea would not seem so dangerous to her if she didn't find it so inviting: it's the speaker's attraction to the sea's awesome power that makes her feel so vulnerable to it.

In the next section, we will do a close reading of the poem in search of additional formal elements supporting our *thesis* (our debatable opinion, which is the main point of our interpretation) that the text depicts the complex nature of human beings' response to the unknown, which we find simultaneously inviting and terrifying. If we don't find such textual evidence or don't find enough of it or find conflicting textual evidence that doesn't fit our interpretation, we will have to amend our thesis to fit the textual evidence we find. However, at this point, we might reasonably argue that the text's theme can be stated as follows: *We fear the unknown largely because we are attracted to it, for our attraction to the unknown makes us feel our vulnerability to it.*

Textual evidence: Formal elements that support the text's theme

Let's take another look at our statement of the poem's theme so that we can determine the kind of textual evidence we need to support our claim that we have correctly identified the theme. To make sure we don't miss anything, let's divide our statement of the theme into its component parts.

Components of the theme

1 We fear the unknown
2 largely because we are attracted to it,
3 for our attraction to the unknown makes us feel our vulnerability to it.

Now we can formulate the questions that will serve as guidelines in our search for textual evidence to support our claim.

Questions to guide our search for textual support

1   In what ways does the speaker reveal her fear of the unknown?
2   In what ways does the speaker reveal her attraction to the unknown?
3   How, specifically, does the speaker communicate her feeling of vulnerability?
4   What ambiguous images can you find that, because they can be interpreted in both positive and negative terms, reflect the speaker's conflicted response to the unknown?
5   How do the poem's meter and rhyme contrast—or conflict—with the poem's action, thereby reflecting the speaker's conflicted response to the unknown?

If we can find the textual evidence—including such formal elements as the portrayal of the speaker and of other characters that may be present in the poem, the events that occur in the poem, the poem's imagery, and the nature of the poem's rhyme and meter—that answers each of these questions, then we will be able to support our thesis. That is, we will be able to show that our statement of the poem's theme is valid. So let's translate these questions into the specific textual evidence we need to find in the poem.

Finding our textual evidence

1   In what ways, including the following examples, does the speaker reveal her fear of the unknown?

   a   What source of protection does she bring with her when she visits the sea?
   b   How do her detailed descriptions of the sea's behavior toward her reveal her fear? Be specific.
   c   What does the speaker do in response to the sea's behavior toward her, and why is it significant that she seeks refuge in the town?

2   In what ways, including the following examples, does the speaker reveal her attraction to the unknown?

   a   At what time of day does she visit the sea? How might this choice reveal her attraction to the sea?
   b   What images in the poem suggest the appeal of exotic lands and the adventure of sea voyages?
   c   What makes her feel she is being invited aboard the frigates?
   d   Even as she flees the pursuing sea in terror, what beautiful images does she use to describe it?
   e   At the poem's end, how does her description of the sea suggest that she imagines it in rather intriguing, perhaps even somewhat appealing terms?

3   In addition to fleeing from the sea, how, specifically, does the speaker communicate her feeling of vulnerability?

a   How does her small size, in contrast to the sea's enormity, reveal her feeling of vulnerability? For example, to what two very small things does the speaker compare herself?

b   How do the word *aground* and the disappearance of the speaker's dog after the poem's opening line indicate her feeling of vulnerability?

c   How does her description of her clothing suggest her feeling of vulnerability?

4   Explain how the following images, because of their ambiguity, reflect the speaker's conflicted response to the unknown. Specifically, note the opposing—positive and negative—meanings that can be associated with

a   The mermaids.

b   The ropes (the frigates' "Hempen Hands").

c   The "Solid Town" (note the opposing meanings associated with *solid*).

d   The tide's "Silver Heel" (note the positive meaning of *silver* vs. the negative meaning of *heel* as a part of the shoe used for its power to crush or kick).

e   Additional ambiguous images you find in the poem that reflect the speaker's conflicted response to the unknown.

5   How does the consistent quality of the poem's steady meter and regular rhyme scheme contrast—or conflict—with the unpredictable nature of the sea and thus reflect the speaker's conflicted response to the unknown?

a   Find textual evidence that the poem's meter, in each stanza, has the following pattern: 8–6–8–6, which means that the first and third lines each have eight beats, while the second and fourth lines each have six beats. (Note that the word *basement* in the first stanza can be considered to have three syllables.)

b   Find textual evidence that the poem's rhyme scheme, in each stanza, is A-B-C-B, which means that the second and fourth lines rhyme.

c   Note that the consistent pattern of meter and rhyme operates like a steady drumbeat, reliable as a metronome.

d   Observe the contrast—or conflict—between, on the one hand, the consistent drumbeat of the poem's meter and rhyme and, on the other hand, the sudden changes in the behavior of the sea. Note that this contrast reflects the speaker's conflicted response to the unknown.

Focusing your essay

At this point, the textual evidence you've collected should allow you to focus your essay on the ways in which "I started Early—Took my Dog" illustrates human beings' conflicted response to the unknown, which we find both inviting and frightening. Specifically, you should be able to support your thesis that the text's theme is as follows: We fear the unknown largely because we are attracted to it, for our attraction to the unknown makes us feel our vulnerability to it. Indeed, it seems that the speaker's attraction to the unknown is what makes her feel so extremely vulnerable to it, for she imagines the sea as a dangerous adversary, even as a predator, at the same time that she imagines it as a source of beauty and adventure. It is interesting to note that the sea's ambiguity is the source both of the interpretive problem posed by the poem and of the poem's richness. For it is difficult to be insensitive to the various possible symbolic meanings of Dickinson's sea even as we pursue our own interpretation. Although an awareness of alternative interpretations can be, at times, unsettling, it can also give us an appreciation for the complexity of a literary work that, at first glance, might seem disarmingly simple.

Of course, you don't have to limit yourself to the analysis of the poem I've offered you. You might want, instead, to see what themes are revealed when "I started Early—Took my Dog" is explored through different topics. Let's take a look, for example, at two of the topics mentioned in the opening of this interpretation exercise: life and death. If we regarded the sea in this poem as a symbol of life—for it sustains the existence of the myriad life forms within it and of the earth as a whole—then we would examine the speaker's actions throughout the poem in terms of her feelings about life. Does she begin and end the poem with both her everyday clothing and her reliance on the "Solid Town" intact because she fears life, because she fears to venture out on her own? How does the poem's imagery, especially, support this interpretation? Analogously, if we viewed the sea as a symbol of death—a force of nature that has taken millions of human lives—then we would examine the speaker's actions throughout the poem in terms of her feelings about death. Is her fear of the sea actually a fear of death, a fear of being overwhelmed by death, a fear of having her body become nothing more than a dispersal of atoms like the dewdrops dispersed atop dandelions? Is her fear of death such that she can't face it directly but must express it only in symbolic terms? Whatever your interpretation, be sure you understand the New Critical concepts you choose to employ, compose a clear statement of your thesis, and support your interpretation with adequate textual evidence.

Food For further thought

Thinking it over

If you've worked through all of the interpretation exercises offered in this chapter, you should feel quite familiar with the basic approaches to understanding literature provided by concepts from New Critical theory. We've seen how New Critical concepts can be used to interpret a literary text by determining its theme, or meaning as a whole, and examining how the text's formal elements support that theme. Specifically, we've seen how New Critical concepts can be used to interpret:

1   literary texts that address the topic of tradition and change (our example: "Everyday Use"; the text's theme: the adoption of new ideas about cultural heritage should not result in the abandonment of family traditions, for these traditions keep us connected to our family history and contribute to the emotional bond among family members),

2   literary texts that address the topic of death (our example: "A Rose for Emily"; the text's theme: Death, as a presence that shadows and depletes the life force, can be stronger than life and is embodied in the desire to live in the past),

3   literary texts that address the topic of alienation (our example: "The Battle Royal"; the text's theme: A sense of belonging can help us in the worst of times, and without it we risk becoming alienated not only from others but from ourselves, as well),

4   literary texts that address the topic of conformity and nonconformity (our example: "Don't Explain"; the text's theme: When conformity requires self-negation, then self-acceptance requires nonconformity), and

5   literary texts that address the topic of the unknown (our example: "I started Early—Took my Dog"; the text's theme: We fear the unknown largely because we are attracted to it, for our attraction to the unknown makes us feel our vulnerability to it).

You might notice that, in keeping with a New Critical approach, all of the topics and themes listed above are rather general in nature, of the sort that might be considered, as New Criticism puts it, "universal," or applicable to all humankind. For those are the kinds of topics and themes that New Critics valued and believed to be present in great literature. Thus, whereas Marxist concepts might help us understand the role of consumerism and the American dream in "Everyday Use," and psychoanalytic concepts might help us understand the psychological conflicts of the main character in "Don't Explain," New Criticism explores what it considers more general topics, seeks what it considers more general themes, and focuses on the text's formal properties rather than on its social or psychological dimension.

Sometimes, however, a literary text can compel our emotional attention so effectively—as we see, for example, in the vivid and horrifying details provided by the narrator of "The Battle Royal"—that it may be difficult to think about themes, formal elements, or anything else associated with New Critical theory. Indeed, New Criticism's interest in how the formal elements of a text work together to support its theme might seem too far removed from the realities portrayed in the text to be meaningful. For although a New Critical analysis wouldn't ignore a literary text's representation of, for example, social oppression or psychological dysfunction, a New Critical analysis would "thematize" these aspects of human experience. That is, a literary representation of social oppression or psychological dysfunction would be seen only in terms of its role in producing the text's larger, more inclusive theme. Thus, the social and psychological issues represented in, for instance, "A Rose for Emily" became, in our New Critical reading of the text, the aspects of setting, characterization, and imagery we examined in order to understand the text's representation of death.

Nevertheless, New Criticism's attention to formal elements can contribute a good deal to our understanding even of a literary work we choose to interpret through a Marxist, African American, or any other theoretical lens. As you'll see in the following chapters, whatever approach we take to interpret a literary work, a convincing interpretation will have strong textual support, and a good deal of that support will rely on our ability to notice and interpret the text's formal elements. So an understanding of New Critical concepts can help us to not only read literature through a New Critical lens, but to gather valid evidence to support other kinds of interpretations, as well.

The more we learn about formal elements, then, the better. And there certainly are many more kinds of formal elements in literature than those that have gotten us started here. Your instructor may choose to introduce you to such additional formal elements as, for example, foreshadowing, flashback, stream of consciousness, irony, alliteration, authorial intrusion, and dozens more. We don't need to be acquainted with each and every one, but the more we increase our literary vocabulary, the more we will be able to recognize, analyze, and enjoy in our reading of literature.

New Critical theory and cultural criticism

We can also use concepts from New Critical theory to help us analyze cultural productions other than literature, including such productions of "high" culture as opera, painting, and sculpture and such productions of popular culture as movies, song lyrics, and television ads. For New Critical concepts can be used to help us interpret any cultural production whose overall meaning we want to explore in relation to its formal elements: for example, in relation to its arrangement of words, musical notes, brush strokes, camera angles, colors, or shapes. However, New Critical concepts cannot be used by themselves to practice cultural criticism. Even if used to interpret a production of popular culture, which is cultural criticism's primary area of interest, New Criticism's purpose in doing so would be to analyze the relationship between the meaning of that production and its formal elements whereas cultural criticism, in contrast, wants to discover the relationship between the meaning of that production and the specific culture that created it.

Consider, for example, the television commercial for Hallmark greeting cards—"Brother of the Bride" (directed by Joe Pytka, 2008)[1]—which we examined for the purposes of cultural criticism using concepts from reader-response theory (see Chapter 2). In this ad, as you may recall, we see a young man, probably in his early twenties, at his sister's wedding reception. It is immediately evident that Brother—rather pudgy, sweet-looking but not classically handsome— has a gift for saying the wrong thing. First, he offends a young woman he's trying to compliment when he tells her, "You look like you've lost a ton of weight!" Next, his attempt at a little male bonding fails miserably when he remarks that a good-looking young woman across the room is "high maintenance," and the young man to whom he is speaking answers resentfully, "That's my fiancée." Finally, Brother's effort to exchange a friendly greeting with Barbara, his father's third wife, backfires when he addresses her as Kate, which is the name of Dad's second wife. So when our blundering protagonist stands up at the bride's table to toast his sister, many of the wedding guests, as well as the bride and groom, clearly expect the worst. However, the toast is perfectly worded and quite moving. Everyone can now see Brother's good heart, and their smiling faces bespeak their warm approval. The camera zooms in to show us that Brother has read his toast from a Hallmark card as he finishes up by saying, "I didn't actually write those words, but I do mean them." The bride hugs Brother as the wedding guests applaud. Now that the guests have seen this side of Brother, their goodwill towards him does not diminish as the commercial closes on his final gaffe: "Eat up, everyone. My mom paid, like, two grand for that cake."

Using my personal reader-response to "Brother of the Bride" as a first step in my cultural analysis of the commercial in the previous chapter, I hypothesized that the ad sends, whether deliberately or not, the following cultural message. *People will overlook our shortcomings but only if we can find the right words to show them that our good qualities make up for our failings. So the right words are essential to social success, even if we have to get those words from a greeting card. Indeed, unless we're really sure of ourselves, it's probably prudent to have some mistrust of our own words.* With this hypothesis as my starting point, I knew I would be able to use the concepts from psychoanalytic and Marxist theories provided in Chapters 4 and 5 to analyze the ways in which this commercial encourages social anxiety in the viewer in order to sell greeting cards, which the commercial suggests is a safer, more effective, and easier way to express my feelings than trying to express them in my own words.

A New Critical approach to the commercial, in contrast, would seek a more objective interpretation, and it would start by establishing the commercial's theme, or overall meaning. Given that Brother's good heart, which is clearly revealed during the commercial's closing scene, remains hidden, until then, behind his off-putting attempts at conversation, we might argue that the commercial's theme is *Don't judge a book by its cover*. And we could find support for this theme by noting, among others, the following formal elements, which show the contrast between Brother's "cover," or exterior, and his "book," or interior: the contrast between the unfortunate results of his brief interactions with three different wedding guests and his good intentions in initiating these interactions; the contrast between the superficiality of his social blunders and the heartfelt quality of his toast to the bride; and the contrast between Brother's somewhat nerd-like physical appearance and his gallant heart.

If we were to claim, however, that the commercial's cultural message is simply its New Critical theme—*Don't judge a book by its cover*—we would, in effect, be ignoring the psychological and ideological complexity of the cultural work performed by the ad. For New Critical concepts would not incline us to question the psychological motives of the wedding guests, or the ideological motives of the commercial itself, unless those motives could be used as evidence to support the commercial's theme. And even if we try to sidestep this problem by choosing a theme that includes the commercial's psychological and ideological aspects—for example, *Fears about our own self-image often keep us from revealing our own, or perceiving another's, true self*—our New Critical purpose in so doing would be only to find the formal elements supporting that theme, not to examine the cultural work the theme performs.

Nevertheless, though we can't employ concepts from New Critical theory alone for the purposes of cultural criticism, we should remember that the attention to formal details New Criticism teaches us can strengthen our interpretations of popular culture—just as it can strengthen our interpretations of literary works—even when we rely on concepts from other critical theories to guide our analyses. And perhaps most important, New Critical concepts are invaluable for reminding us that no cultural production, of any sort, can be fully appreciated without valuing the ways in which its meaning is related to its form, to the arrangement of the elements of which it is made.

★ ★ ★

Remember, it's natural to feel a little uncertain when we encounter a new theory of literary interpretation, even if the concepts from that theory are somewhat familiar to us, as the concepts from New Critical theory may be. Uncertainty is an unavoidable part of learning and growing. Keep in mind, too, that others may disagree with your opinions. Readers often disagree in their interpretations of literature, even when drawing upon the same New Critical concepts for their analyses. The keys to a good interpretation—besides intellectual curiosity and an open mind—are a clear understanding of the New Critical concepts you've chosen to use and strong textual evidence to support your analysis.

Taking the next step

Questions for further practice

1   The many differences between Miss Oceola Jones and Mrs. Dora Ellsworth in Langston Hughes' short story "The Blues I'm Playing" (1934) suggest that the story's central tension lies in some important difference between the attitudes, values, or beliefs embodied in the two characters. For example, find textual evidence that the story's central tension is that between Mrs. Ellsworth's beliefs and those of Oceola concerning the role of art in the life of an artist. Which beliefs does the text support by portraying them,

and the character who holds them, more favorably? What, then, do you think is the story's theme?

2   Kate Chopin's *The Awakening* (1899) can be viewed as the story of pro-tagonist Edna Pontellier's efforts to escape the narrow confines of conventional society in order to find personal freedom. We might therefore argue that the novel's central tension is the tension between freedom and entrapment, which is reflected in the novel's vivid nature imagery: among other images, the caged birds that open the novel, the tall Kentucky grass through which Edna wanders as a girl, the numerous images of the sea, the bird with a broken wing, and the smell of flowers at the novel's end. Find as many nature images relevant to the topic of freedom and entrapment as you can, note where these images occur in the novel, and explain how they help us interpret the text in terms of this topic. Based on your findings, what do you think is the novel's theme?

3   The topic of Arthur Miller's *Death of a Salesman* (1949) seems to be the plight of the "common man" in an increasingly fast-paced and impersonal society. How does the setting contribute to the play's development of this topic? As the play opens, for example, how do the colored lighting, the sounds the audience hears, and the size and location of the Loman home suggest that Willy Loman is the victim of a harsh and overwhelming modern world? In addition to other uses of setting, how is the Loman home employed to alert us to the changes in time-period that occur during Willy's recurring flashbacks to happier days? Given its topic and use of setting, what do you think is the play's theme?

4   Louise Erdrich's "Dear John Wayne" (1984) conveys its topic—profound loss—by means of a number of different formal elements that build in intensity over the course of the poem. Consider, for example, the description of the mosquitoes in the first stanza; the reference to sunset in the second stanza; the comparison of the enlarged, big-screen image of John Wayne's face, in the fourth stanza, with the face of the land that was stolen from Native Americans; the actions of the Native American viewers who fall and slip in the fifth stanza; and the vivid, implied reference, in the poem's final two lines, to the cancer that took John Wayne's life. How does each of these elements convey the poem's topic? Using these formal elements to guide your interpretation of the poem as a whole, what do you think is the poem's theme?

5   As we saw earlier in this chapter, New Critical concepts cannot be used alone to engage in cultural criticism. However, you can use New Critical concepts to do New Critical readings of narratives that occur in productions of popular culture—for example, in movies—as long as the production in question has an important theme, a theme that contributes to our understanding of what it means to be human. For example, do you have a favorite movie—whether it's comedy, drama, action/adventure, science fiction, horror, or a movie intended for family viewing—that

seems to you to have an important theme? Using the same New Critical method we used to analyze literary works, what do you think is the film's central tension, main topic, and theme? Use formal elements from the movie to support your thesis concerning its theme. Include elements of characterization, plot, setting, dialogue, imagery, camera angles, use of lighting, musical score, and any other formal elements you think will help support your thesis.

Suggestions for further reading

Brooks, Cleanth. *The Well-Wrought Urn: Studies in the Structure of Poetry*. New York: Harcourt, Brace and World, 1947. (See, especially, "What Does Poetry Communicate?," 67–79.)

Brooks, Cleanth, and Robert Penn Warren. *Understanding Fiction*. 1943. 2nd ed. New York: Appleton-Century-Crofts, 1959. (See, especially, "How Plot Reveals," 77–187; "What Character Reveals," 168–271; and "What Theme Reveals," 272–393.)

——. *Understanding Poetry*. 1938. 4th ed. New York: Holt, Rinehart, and Winston, 1976. (See, especially, "Description: Images, Mood, and Attitudes," 68–95; "Analogical Language," 196–219; and "Theme, Meaning, and Dramatic Structure," 266–312.)

Davis, Garrick, ed. *Praising It New: The Best of the New Criticism*. Athens, Ohio: Swallow Press/ Ohio University Press, 2008. (See, especially, Allen Tate's "Miss Emily and the Bibliographer," 39–48; Ivor Winters' "Preliminary Problems," 75–84; Cleanth Brooks' "The Formalist Critics," 84–91; T.S. Eliot's "Hamlet and His Problems," 138–42; and Randall Jarrell's "Texts from Housman," 161–69.)

Tyson, Lois. "New Criticism." *Critical Theory Today: A User-Friendly Guide*. 2nd ed. New York: Routledge, 2006. 135–67.

Wimsatt, Jr., W.K. *The Verbal Icon: Studies in the Meaning of Poetry*. Lexington: University of Kentucky Press, 1954. (See, especially, "The Intentional Fallacy," with Monroe C. Beardsley, 3–18; and "The Affective Fallacy," with Monroe C. Beardsley, 21–39.)

Note

1 "Brother of the Bride" is available online at http://www.youtube.com/watch?v=7 ZdIjnkDpMo.

Chapter 4

Using concepts from psychoanalytic theory to understand literature

Why should we learn about psychoanalytic theory?

Life is filled with emotional ups and downs, and our hard times as well as our happy times play an important role in our personal growth. As psychoanalytic theory tells us, we all encounter life-events, as we grow up, that shape our psychological development, and these early experiences tend to play out in our adult lives. Most of us have experienced, for example, recurring episodes of sibling rivalry or other kinds of jealousy, of self-doubt or insecurity, or of loneliness or isolation. In other words, we all experience some sorts of psychological problems over the course of our lives. We can see the signs of those problems from time to time in what psychoanalytic theory calls dysfunctional behavior: for example, all those little (or big) ways in which we put ourselves unnecessarily at risk, get ourselves into trouble, or hurt the ones we love. While psychological problems are a natural and unavoidable part of being human, it is important to try to identify and understand them because, according to psychoanalytic theory, that's how we can begin to heal those problems.

In fact, our lack of awareness of our own psychological problems is what makes us so vulnerable to them. For the less we know about our problems, the more we tend to "play them out" on other people without even realizing that we're doing so. And it's this playing out that can make trouble for ourselves and others. For example, have you ever had a co-worker who always seemed to feel slighted by others; who was convinced, without reason, that he was not receiving the recognition he deserved; or who took offense at things that were not at all intended to offend him? Have you ever had a roommate who habitually forgot to give you your telephone messages, who turned into a super-flirt whenever a date came by to pick you up, or who frequently borrowed your possessions and forgot to return them, or returned them soiled or broken? Have you ever had a friend whose romantic relationships always seemed to be with partners who were bad for her, partners who drank too much or cheated on her, or routinely stood her up to go out with the guys? Psychoanalytic theory would suggest that these individuals were playing out psychological problems that they probably didn't know they had, problems that were, nevertheless, the key to understanding their dysfunctional behavior.

You're probably familiar with the idea that we destructively play out on ourselves and others such unresolved psychological problems as low self-esteem and fear of commitment. And no doubt you've had the experience of realizing that a family member or friend was in denial concerning a painful reality in his or her life. For these and other psychoanalytic concepts have come more and more into common use over the last several decades. Common use, however, usually includes some degree of misconception and is too incomplete to give us the full benefit of psychoanalytic theory. So I think you will find this chapter useful even if you've already encountered much of the psychoanalytic vocabulary used here. The concepts provided in this chapter come from the pioneering work of Sigmund Freud (1856–1939), whose ideas about human behavior are still very influential today in the field of psychoanalytic clinical practice and in the analysis of literature. His work is based on the recurring patterns of dysfunctional human behavior he observed during the many years he spent treating patients with emotional problems.

It seems logical, then, that we can start to use psychoanalytic theory to understand literature by asking the following question about any literary work we want to interpret: Do any of the characters exhibit what might be considered dysfunctional behavior, and if so, what are the psychological motives behind it? In other words, what emotional problems do the characters exhibit, and how are their emotional problems responsible for what the characters do? For a good deal of literature attempts to represent some aspect of human experience—especially its darker, more tragic dimension—and psychoanalytic theory, with its focus on the dysfunctional side of human behavior, seems a likely way to help us analyze literary works.

So let's start with a brief look at psychoanalytic theory's most basic principles. Although it's important that you read through the "Basic concepts" section that follows, don't be too concerned if you don't feel you thoroughly understand every concept listed. You'll begin to understand these concepts much better when we use them, later in this chapter, to help us interpret the literary texts that appear at the end of this book. And you'll see that these fundamental psychoanalytic concepts can help us understand other works of literature, as well.

Remember, too, that I'm offering you my own literary analyses in the interpretation exercises provided later in this chapter. You might use the same psychoanalytic concepts I use but come up with different interpretations of your own. If you disagree with any of the analyses I offer in these exercises, don't be afraid to look in the literary work in question for evidence that will support your viewpoint. A literary work can often support a number of different interpretations, even when readers are using concepts from the same theory.

Basic concepts

The family

For psychoanalytic theory, our adult personality is the result of the emotional experiences we had while growing up. And the family (which can be anything from the traditional two-parent family to the experience of group-living in an orphanage) is the most important source of our early emotional experiences—both those that affirm our being and those that harm us psychologically—because it is in the family that our sense of self and our way of relating to others are first established. However, psychoanalytic theory is more interested in understanding the origin of psychological problems rather than the origin of psychological strengths because this theory wants to offer ways of overcoming psychological problems. And it is important to remember that, for psychoanalytic theory, we all have psychological problems of some sort because we have all had some harmful emotional experiences growing up, regardless of how loving our family might be. In other words, having psychological problems is part of being human.

Repression and the unconscious

We might not know the specific source of our emotional problems—we might not even know we have such problems—because we tend to repress our most distressing experiences, push them into the unconscious, which is the psychological storehouse of painful experiences we don't want to remember. Put simply, we all tend to push out of sight those experiences we feel we can't handle. The clearest sign that an emotional problem is being repressed is the repetition of a self-destructive behavior, such as choosing unhealthy friends or romantic partners, displaying inappropriate social behavior (for example, habitually dominating conversations or throwing temper tantrums in response to disagreements), engaging in unwarranted violent behavior, engaging in substance abuse, and the like. Most of these destructive behaviors show up in the way we relate to others, for psychoanalytic theory holds that we enact, or play out, our psychological problems with other people. The recurrence of a disturbing dream might also be a clue to the existence of an unconscious problem, as might a tendency to behave in a defensive manner when certain topics come up in conversation.

The defenses

The defenses are the means by which we keep ourselves from becoming conscious of the experiences we've repressed. Many of our defenses develop during our childhood as ways of protecting ourselves emotionally. However, as we grow older our defenses become more destructive than helpful because they keep us from understanding—and therefore from healing—our own psychological wounds. The most common defenses include the following.

Denial—We are in denial when we believe that an emotionally painful situation doesn't exist or an emotionally painful event never occurred.

Avoidance—We are practicing avoidance when we stay away from people, places, or situations that might stir up the memory of repressed experiences.

Displacement—We are displacing when we take out our negative feelings about one person on someone else so that we can relieve our pain or anger without becoming aware of the real cause of our repressed feelings.

Projection—We are projecting when we believe, without real cause, that someone else feels the same way we feel, specifically that someone else has the problem we want to deny that we, ourselves, have. Once we project our problem onto someone else, we can then attack that person (in thought, word, or deed) for having the problem in order to prove to ourselves that we don't have it.

Core issues

Whether or not we realize it, we all have at least one core issue (also called *core conflict*). A core issue is a psychological problem that is the underlying cause of some sort of recurring self-destructive behavior, whether that behavior is something as seemingly mild as being habitually late for important appointments (for example, job interviews!) or something as serious as being habitually involved with abusive romantic partners. While most of us have experienced, on occasion, the problems listed below, they are considered core issues only if they are responsible for most or all of the emotional difficulties we have as adults. Examples of core issues include, among others, the following.

Low self-esteem—Low self-esteem is the unwarranted belief that we are less worthy than other human beings and, therefore, don't deserve attention, love, or any other form of life's rewards. In fact, we often believe we deserve to be punished by life in some way.

Insecure or unstable sense of self—Our sense of self is insecure or unstable if we are unable to sustain a feeling of personal identity, unable to sustain a sense of knowing ourselves. This core issue makes us very vulnerable to the influence—for good or ill—of other people, and we may have a tendency to repeatedly change the way we look (our clothing, hairstyle, and the like) or behave as we become involved with different individuals or groups.

Fear of abandonment—Fear of abandonment is the unwarranted nagging belief that our friends and loved ones are going to desert us (physical abandonment) or don't really care about us (emotional abandonment). Sometimes fear of abandonment expresses itself as *fear of betrayal*, the unwarranted nagging belief that our friends and loved ones can't be trusted: for example, can't be trusted not to laugh at us behind our backs or not to lie to us, or, in the case of romantic partners, can't be trusted not to cheat on us by dating others.

Fear of intimacy—Fear of intimacy is the unwarranted but unshakeable and overpowering feeling that emotional closeness will seriously damage or destroy us and that we must, therefore, protect ourselves by remaining at an emotional distance from others. Fear of intimacy will probably not keep us from making friends or falling in love, but it will keep us from enjoying the kind of friendship and love that comes with the ability to trust our own, and another's, feelings.

Oedipal fixation—We all pass through a natural period of oedipal attachment to a parent of the opposite sex during youth, but it is outgrown as we mature emotionally. An oedipal *fixation* (or *complex*) is a dysfunctional bond with a parent of the opposite sex that we don't outgrow and that doesn't permit us to mature into adult relationships with others.

Dream symbolism

Unlike most other critical theories, psychoanalytic theory has its own system of symbols that can be of use especially if we are interpreting a literary work as if it were a dream (which we will do later in this chapter when we interpret Emily Dickinson's poem "I started Early—Took my Dog"). For psychoanalytic theory, certain objects tend to have symbolic meaning for most human beings, whether we are aware of this meaning or not, and these symbols often show up in our dreams. The most common symbols include the following.

Water—Water can symbolize the unconscious, the emotions, and/or sexuality (which may or may not include reproduction)—all of which are, like water, fluid (without fixed form), often unpredictable, and frequently deeper than we may realize.

Buildings—Usually, buildings symbolize the self, as if our body were the "building" in which we lived.

Basements—Because buildings usually symbolize the self, basements are often associated with the unconscious as the place where we repress unpleasant memories. (Both basements and the unconscious keep things below the surface.)

Attics—Analogously, attics are often associated with the intellect or the conscious mind, though in some dreams (especially dreams in which there are no basements), attics can, themselves, symbolize the unconscious as the place where we repress unpleasant memories. (We store things out of sight in attics just as we keep them below the surface in basements, in other words, just as we repress unpleasant memories in the unconscious.)

Male imagery—Male imagery consists primarily of *phallic symbols*, for example, towers, guns, serpents, swords, or anything that can be associated with the penis. (If it stands upright, goes off, or has a serpentine form, it might be a phallic symbol.)

Female imagery—Most frequently, female imagery consists of anything that can be associated with the womb, for example, caves, walled-in gardens, or containers.

Of course, there are so many factors affecting our emotional development at any given point in our youth that different individuals can respond to similar family situations in very different ways. Nevertheless, for psychoanalytic theory the relationship among the basic concepts discussed earlier can be expressed in a formula that goes something like this.

1   A distressing event or situation that occurs in our youth is *repressed* into our *unconscious* because we don't feel we can face it consciously.
2   We keep that repressed experience buried in our unconscious through the use of the *defenses*.
3   If the experience buried in our unconscious affects us powerfully enough, it will become a *core issue*—that is, a fundamental part of our personality that determines many of our feelings and a good deal of our behavior.
4   Core issues, especially when we remain unaware of them, result in the repetition of certain *self-destructive behaviors* and may show up in the recurrence of *disturbing dreams*.

Let's begin our interpretation exercises by analyzing a story that illustrates very well the basic concepts just outlined: Alice Walker's "Everyday Use" (1973; see Appendix D). This story is especially helpful, at this point, because it includes a good deal of information about the family relationships and early experiences of its main characters, information that we don't get in every literary work.

Interpretation exercises

Analyzing characters' dysfunctional behavior: Interpreting "Everyday Use"

Let's go back to our opening psychoanalytic question and apply it to the main characters in Alice Walker's "Everyday Use": Does Maggie, Dee (also called Wangero), or Mama exhibit what might be considered dysfunctional behavior and, if so, what are the psychological motives behind it? To help us answer that question, we should look in the story for evidence of these characters' core issues, as psychoanalytic theory tells us that dysfunctional behavior is usually the result of a core issue. Remember, however, that according to this theory we all have core issues, so our examining these characters from this perspective does not necessarily mean that we are judging them negatively. Rather, we are trying to understand them in order to understand an important psychological dimension of the story.

It is also important to keep in mind that our psychoanalytic focus on the family as the source of the Johnsons' psychological problems does not mean that the family is the only source of these problems. Obviously, given the story's setting (a poverty-level, African American community in the rural South during the late 1960s and early 1970s), and the fact that Mama grew up in the same location during the 1920s, the characters' race, class, and gender are major factors (as they would be even today) in forming their personalities and creating their psychological problems. Nevertheless, psychoanalytic theory asks us to focus on the family by assuming that such cultural factors as race, class, and gender operate differently in each family, depending on the family's psychological dynamic—that is, on the role each member plays in relation to other family members.

To sum up, then, we'll try to understand the story's main characters by understanding the motivation for what psychoanalysis would call their dysfunctional behavior. And we'll accomplish this task by identifying: (1) their core issues; (2) the defenses they use to keep their core issues repressed; and (3) the ways in which the family is the source of their psychological problems.

Analyzing Maggie

1   *Maggie's core issues*—I think many readers would agree that Maggie's primary core issue seems to be low self-esteem, which is evident in most of her behavior until the very end of the story. Find all the evidence in the story you can to support this claim. Note, for example,

   a   Maggie's body language,
   b   Maggie's interactions with others, and
   c   any additional information Mama gives us about Maggie.

2   *Maggie's defenses*—Maggie's primary defense seems to be avoidance: she goes to great lengths to avoid people and situations that bring out her low self-esteem. What evidence in the story supports this idea?

3   *Maggie and her family*—Like Maggie's race, class, and gender, the house-fire that scarred her body and damaged her eyesight is surely one of the sources of Maggie's core issue. But the key question for psychoanalytic theory is this: What part does her family play in her low self-esteem? For the ways in which we respond to traumatic events are influenced by the role we play in the family dynamic. The part played by the family in Maggie's low self-esteem might be found in the following areas. See what textual evidence you can find to support these ideas. (You may have collected above some of the evidence you'll need here.)

   a   Maggie probably feels inferior to her sister in many ways, a feeling that can easily create low self-esteem.
   b   Maggie may feel that Mama has always given Dee preferential treatment while Maggie has gotten the short end of the stick, a situation that would make Maggie believe she's inferior to Dee in Mama's eyes

as well as in her own. And this is a situation that doesn't change until the very end of the story when Mama insists on reserving the quilts for Maggie.

c If the story allows us to establish that Maggie feels personally inferior to Dee and second-fiddle in terms of Mama's efforts to help her daughters, then we can argue that Maggie feels she's on the losing side of a sibling rivalry for Mama's love, which would also contribute to her low self-esteem.

Analyzing Dee

1 *Dee's core issues*—Dee's core issue seems to be fear of intimacy, which we can see throughout her life in her emotionally distant relationships with both family and friends and which I think is related, in her case, to fear of abandonment. (Fear of abandonment often causes fear of intimacy: if we feel somehow emotionally abandoned by our family and therefore fear abandonment from others, we are liable to have trouble letting anyone get too close to us emotionally. For if we're not emotionally close to others, we feel we have less to lose when they leave us.)

a Find textual evidence that Dee suffers from fear of intimacy. (Note all the ways in which she keeps friends and family at an emotional distance.)

b Find textual evidence that Dee suffers from fear of abandonment. (Note all the ways in which she may feel excluded from the things Mama and Maggie have shared in the past and share now.)

2 *Dee's defenses*—Dee seems to have two primary defenses: avoidance (she stays away from her family for long periods of time and avoids close relationships with friends and family; indeed she uses her superior attitude to drive people away) and denial (Dee's superior attitude—which she seems almost obsessed with maintaining through the achievement of a fashionable lifestyle—also helps her deny that she needs close relationships with others).

a Find textual evidence that Dee practices avoidance.

b Find textual evidence that Dee is in denial.

3 *Dee and her family*—What role does her family play in Dee's fear of intimacy and fear of abandonment? Find textual evidence to support the following answers to that question. (You may have collected above some of the evidence you'll need here.)

a Dee probably feels excluded from the bond that has always existed between Mama and Maggie, and such exclusion, even if Dee wanted to separate herself from her family, is liable to create feelings of abandonment.

i List all the things Mama and Maggie have in common with each other and not with Dee.

    ii   List all the activities Mama and Maggie have always shared in which Dee has not been included.

  b The absence of a father—whether through death, divorce, or desertion—could also have contributed to Dee's feeling of abandonment and, in turn, fear of intimacy. Does the story mention that a father was ever present in the household?

  c Dee probably feels excluded, too, from the emotional tie created by Mama's saving Maggie from the fire. Find the specific images of Dee's isolation and of Mama's bond with Maggie in that scene.

  d If the story allows us to establish that Dee feels emotionally excluded by her family, then we can argue that Dee feels she's on the losing side of a sibling rivalry for Mama's love, which would also contribute to her fear of abandonment and, in turn, her fear of intimacy.

Analyzing Mama

1 *Mama's core issues*—Despite her many abilities and impressive physical strength, Mama's primary core issue seems to be low self-esteem. Can you find the numerous examples the text offers of Mama's self-doubts and low self-image? Include, among other things,

  a Mama's mixed feelings about her physical appearance,

  b the insights we gain into Mama through her recurring dream, and

  c the amount of formal education Mama received and how this could affect her self-esteem.

2 *Mama's defenses*—Mama's primary defense might be hard for you to see on your own, but I think there's a good deal of textual evidence to suggest that it's projection. Specifically, Mama projects her low self-esteem onto each daughter in a different way.

  a Find textual evidence that Mama projects onto Dee her own desire for recognition, approval, and all the opportunities that were denied her due to her race, class, and gender.

    i   What do we learn from Mama's recurring dream?

    ii Find all the textual evidence you can that shows Mama's pride in Dee, despite the negative things Mama says about this daughter.

  b Find textual evidence that Mama projects onto Maggie her own insecurities and vulnerabilities.

    i   How do Mama and Maggie resemble each other?

    ii Why might Mama see Maggie as a version of herself?

    iii Can you find any ways in which Mama may be unconsciously holding Maggie back?

3   *Mama and her family*—Of course, a good deal of this strong, capable woman's low self-esteem surely comes from being a poor, dark-skinned, big-boned, African American woman with a second-grade education living in a country that values wealthy, educated, slender, white women. But what part does her family play in Mama's low self-esteem? Find textual evidence to support the following answers to that question. (You may have collected above some of the evidence you'll need here.)

  a   Mama *might* have felt somewhat inferior to her own sister Dee, whose name is short for the name Dicie, a Johnson family name. (Look at Mama's explanation of the familial origin of her daughter Dee's name and the reference to Mama's sister during the brief discussion of the Johnson family history. What did Mama's sister have that Mama didn't have?)
  b   In terms of Mama's relationship to her daughter Dee, that child's light skin, good figure, and quick mind might explain Mama's projection of her own desire for recognition and approval onto Dee, which might have been one reason Mama managed to obtain for Dee the opportunities she wishes she'd had for herself.
  c   In terms of Mama's relationship to her daughter Maggie, that child's dark skin, unfashionable figure, and apparently slower mind might explain Mama's projection of her own insecurities and vulnerabilities onto Maggie, which might be one reason she wants to keep Maggie at home, or near home, safe from an inhospitable world.

Focusing your essay

So what do we do with all of these psychoanalytic insights into "Everyday Use"? How do we make them hang together in a coherent essay? Well, you'll probably be relieved to hear that you don't have to use all of them. You might choose to write a paper analyzing just one of these three characters, in which case you'd limit yourself to the kinds of claims made earlier about that character and the textual evidence you found to support those claims. Given the information the story provides about the family, even an analysis of one of the sisters would automatically involve you in an explanation of that character in terms of her relationship to her sister and mother. However, your focus would be narrower and your paper probably shorter than if you chose to analyze, instead, both sisters or the family as a whole. If you choose to analyze both Maggie and Dee, you might organize your data in terms of their sibling rivalry. Or if you choose to analyze the family as a whole, which would involve using all the information gathered above, you might organize your findings in terms of the ways in which parents' core issues can help form the core issues of their children, in Mama's case by living vicariously, though in different ways, through both of her daughters.

   This last approach would give you the most complete psychoanalytic interpretation of the story. Specifically, you would argue that Mama projects

her own low self-esteem onto Maggie, thus holding Maggie back and contributing to Maggie's low self-esteem. Analogously, Mama projects her own
unfulfilled desire for success onto Dee, thus pushing Dee away from the nest
and contributing to Dee's fear of intimacy and fear of abandonment. Such a
view of Mama doesn't mean that she doesn't love her children or that she isn't
a good mother. It just means that she's human.

Remember, too, that you don't have to limit yourself to the character
analyses I've offered you. For example, you might believe that Dee's underlying
core issue is low self-esteem, not fear of abandonment. After all, Dee tries so
hard to impress people that she seems to be trying continually to boost her
own ego, which she wouldn't need to do if she had enough self-esteem. Or
you might think that Maggie suffers from fear of intimacy as well as low self-
esteem. Do you think you can find adequate textual evidence to show that
Maggie is afraid of being hurt if she gets too close to others? Whatever
your interpretation, be sure you understand the psychoanalytic concepts you
choose to employ, compose a clear statement of your thesis, and support your
interpretation with adequate textual evidence.

Exploring a character's insanity: Interpreting "A Rose for Emily"

The story of a woman who murders her suitor and sleeps with his corpse in
her bed, as Miss Emily Grierson does in William Faulkner's "A Rose for
Emily" (1931; see Appendix B), seems a likely candidate for psychoanalytic
theory. For it would be an understatement to say that Emily, the story's main
character, exhibits dysfunctional behavior. Indeed, Faulkner's tale offers us a
portrait of a woman who goes insane. And Emily's insanity, when contrasted
with the psychological problems of the Johnson family in Alice Walker's
"Everyday Use," discussed earlier, shows us that the difference between mental
health and mental illness is often a matter of degree. As we'll see shortly, some
of the same core issues and defenses that appear in the characterization of the
Johnson women, whose relationships with one another have a good deal in
common with the relationships found in many average American families, also
appear in the characterization of Emily Grierson. However, Emily has these
core issues and defenses to a much more extreme degree and, therefore,
manifests them in much more extreme and unhealthy ways.

The first question many readers ask, once they realize that Emily poisons
Homer Barron with the arsenic she purchases from the druggist, is *why* Emily
commits this murder. And the answer many readers give is that Emily kills
Homer because he plans to leave her. She expects him to marry her—that's
why she buys him the monogrammed, silver toilet articles (personal grooming
articles, such as hairbrushes) and arranges her bedroom like a bridal suite—so
it's reasonable to conclude that he must have refused to marry her. Fine. That
explanation works. But what does it really tell us about Emily? Many people
have disappointments like hers without resorting to murder. And how do we

explain her keeping Homer's body in her bed and, over the years, sleeping with the corpse, as indicated in the closing description of Emily's gray hair on the indented pillow next to Homer's head? Finally, how do we explain her other unhealthy behavior, such as her determination to completely isolate herself from the community and her desire to live in the past, a desire evident in her reference to the long-dead Colonel Sartoris as if he were still alive and in her refusal to allow her house to be numbered for home mail-delivery? Again, there is a simple answer: Emily is crazy. After all, her great-aunt Wyatt was crazy, and perhaps insanity runs in the Grierson family. But, again, that answer tells us very little about Emily.

To understand Emily—her experience, her feelings, the reasons for all of her unhealthy behavior—we need to understand the psychological motives that drive her to commit murder, to sleep with the dead body, to isolate herself from the entire community, and to live in the past. And psychoanalytic concepts can help us understand those motives. While "A Rose for Emily" doesn't provide the kind of detailed information about family dynamics that we get in "Everyday Use," Faulkner's story gives us ample clues to Emily's psychological experience in its descriptions of Emily's behavior over the course of her life and in the few hints the story offers about her relationship to her father. We don't need information about a character's childhood or family relationships in order to use psychoanalytic concepts to analyze that character. All we need is adequate evidence of dysfunctional behavior. However, when the text offers us information about a character's family, no matter how little, we should not ignore it.

Okay, so where do we start? Well, as we did earlier (in our interpretation of "Everyday Use"), we can try to identify Emily's core issue, which psycho-analytic theory tells us is the source of dysfunctional behavior, and her defenses, which keep her from facing her problems and thus keep her from dealing with them in a healthy manner. The examples of core issues listed in the "Basic concepts" section of this chapter include low self-esteem, an insecure or unstable sense of self, fear of abandonment, fear of intimacy, and oedipal fixation. Do any of these seem to you to belong to Emily Grierson? It seems to me we could argue that Emily has any one of, at least, these last three core issues. In fact, I think we could argue that she has all three. And I think we could show how these issues are the source of all of her dysfunctional behavior. So let's collect the textual evidence that reveals: (1) Emily's core issues; (2) the defenses she uses to keep her core issues repressed; and (3) the family dynamics responsible for Emily's developing these core issues in the first place.

Emily's core issues

1 *Fear of abandonment*—What happens to Emily that could give her such an extreme fear of abandonment that she murders Homer and keeps his body? Well, in addition to the fact that Emily apparently lost her mother

at a young age, her father keeps her isolated (which must feel like being abandoned by the whole town), and then he abandons her, himself, by dying.

a   Find the evidence in the story that shows how Mr. Grierson keeps Emily from forming ties

   i   with other family members,
   ii   with members of the community, and
   iii with young men.

b   Find the evidence in the story that shows how Emily's fear of abandonment manifests itself right after her father's death. What does she do when the townsfolk come to take his body?
c   Find the evidence in the story that shows how Emily's fear of abandonment manifests itself during the year after her father's death. Consider, for example,

   i   her long illness,
   ii   her subsequent haircut, which makes her look like a little girl, and
   iii the "crayon [chalk] portrait" of her father (where does she keep it?).

2   *Fear of intimacy*—Emily may or may not want to go out and mix with the community while her father is alive, but it is clear that, after his death, she doesn't want to be with anyone except Homer Barron. In other words, once her father's death deprives her of the only person she knows, she so fears abandonment that she is afraid to get close to anyone else for fear that she will be abandoned again. This means that her fear of abandonment contributes to her fear of intimacy.

a   How does the story show us Emily's fear of intimacy? List as many examples as you can.
b   How does Emily's choice of Homer Barron also show that she fears intimacy? How is Homer characterized as a person who avoids emotional intimacy?

3   *Oedipal fixation*—How is Homer a stand-in for Emily's father? Despite their differences, the two men have a good deal in common that could make them seem similar in Emily's eyes.

a   Find every example you can of the traits the two men share.
b   Remember, too, that Emily doesn't want the community to bury her father; she wants to keep his body in the house with her. So how is Homer, even after his death, a stand-in for her father?

Emily's defenses

The defenses listed in the "Basic concepts" section of this chapter include denial, avoidance, displacement, and projection. Which defenses do you see operating in Emily? It seems to me that her primary defenses are denial and avoidance.

1   *Denial*—Find in the story all the ways in which Emily is in denial, all the ways in which she just says no to reality. Include, among other evidence,

    a   Emily's refusal to release her father's body,
    b   the ways in which Emily's personality becomes a good deal like her father's because resembling her dead father is one way of keeping him "alive," of denying that he is dead, and
    c   Emily's apparent refusal to see any difference between her social class and that of Homer Barron.

2   *Avoidance*—Find in the story all the ways in which Emily practices avoidance—that is, all the ways she finds to stay away from people, places, and situations that might remind her of experiences she wants to forget. Include all the ways in which Emily seems to be trying to live in the past after her father is buried and after Homer's death. For living in the past helps Emily avoid an awareness of whatever current situation she doesn't want to face.

Emily and her family

By this point in our discussion of the story, the role of Emily's father in the creation of her core issues is probably fairly obvious to you. Find all the textual evidence you can to support the following claims, each of which relates to all three of Emily's core issues. (You may have collected above some of the evidence you'll need here.)

1   Emily's father does everything he can to isolate her from everyone in her family and in her community.
2   Mr. Grierson puts Emily on a pedestal (no one is good enough for her) and behaves toward her in an overprotective, even jealous manner.
3   Because Emily has no one but her father, she cannot handle his death. She experiences his death as an overwhelming abandonment.
4   Mr. Grierson appears to have a selfish, authoritarian, violent disposition. Textual evidence to support this claim will allow us to speculate that his relationship with his daughter is neither warm nor open and that she therefore feels emotionally abandoned by him even while he is alive.

Focusing your essay

Given the textual evidence you've collected, I think you might focus your essay on the ways in which "A Rose for Emily" illustrates the following well-known psychoanalytic premise: adults tend to model their romantic relationships on the relationship they had with a parent of the opposite sex. (You've heard that old song about men wanting to marry women that remind them of their mothers, haven't you? It begins, "I want a girl just like the girl that married dear old Dad.") But disastrous results can ensue when that parent–child relationship is seriously disordered, as is the relationship between Emily and her father. From this perspective, you might argue that Emily's oedipal attachment to her father, which Mr. Grierson creates by putting his daughter on a pedestal and making himself the only man in her life, is the underlying cause of a fear of abandonment and of intimacy that become intense enough to drive Emily to commit murder.

Remember, as always, that you don't have to limit yourself to the analysis of Emily I've offered you. For example, you might argue that Emily chooses Homer not because he reminds her of her father but because he is the kind of man her father would say isn't good enough for her. From this point of view, she goes out with Homer not because she has an oedipal fixation and needs Homer as a stand-in for Dad, but because she is angry at her dead father for ruining the first thirty years of her life and wants to punish him.

In contrast, if you think that Emily's oedipal fixation on her father is strong enough, you might argue that Emily doesn't kill Homer because he is going to leave her but because he wants to marry her. Does this idea surprise you? Just think about it for a minute. If Emily's oedipal attachment to her father is strong enough, she might feel that marrying Homer would be a betrayal of her love for her father. In other words, if she unconsciously feels "married" to Dad, then sleeping with Homer would be like cheating on her father. But neither could she refuse Homer's marriage proposal and risk losing him: her fear of abandonment is too great for that. And as Homer is an emotional stand-in for her father, losing him would be like losing her father all over again. Killing Homer and sharing her virginal bed with his dead body is thus the perfect solution. She gets to keep Homer (which is like keeping her father) without having to marry him (which means she can remain loyal to her father).

Don't be overwhelmed by all the possible interpretations this story offers. If you like, focus on only one or two main ideas from among all those offered, and develop those one or two ideas as fully as you can. For example, focus just on Emily's fear of abandonment, or focus just on her oedipal fixation. Whatever your interpretation, be sure you understand the psychoanalytic concepts you choose to employ, compose a clear statement of your thesis, and support your interpretation with adequate textual evidence.

Understanding dream images in literature: Interpreting "I started Early—Took my Dog"

As you may recall, I suggested at the beginning of this chapter that you can bring psychoanalytic concepts to your understanding of a literary work by first asking this question: Do any of the characters exhibit what might be considered dysfunctional behavior, and if so, what are the psychological motives behind it? I hope our psychoanalytic explorations of "Everyday Use" and "A Rose for Emily" illustrate for you how well this question often works in developing your psychoanalytic understanding of literature. This is a good question to start with because literature is filled with characters whose personal problems are of a psychological nature, and those problems are usually responsible for a good deal of what happens in a story, poem, or play. For it is often the dark side of human experience that authors are trying to understand.

What should we do, however, if a text doesn't seem to provide any illustrations of dysfunctional behavior? Does that mean the text does not have a psychoanalytic dimension for us to explore? Not necessarily. Even in the absence of self-destructive characters, a text often has an important psychoanalytic component, as we can see in Emily Dickinson's Poem 520, "I started Early—Took my Dog" (c. 1862; see Appendix A). For like a good deal of poetry—as well as poetic passages in stories and plays—Dickinson's poem can be analyzed as if it were a dream because of the dream-like, unreal quality of many of its images, such as the mermaids emerging from beneath the sea to look at the poem's speaker, the ships along the shore beckoning to her, and the sea pursuing her all the way to town. As we noted in the "Basic concepts" section of this chapter, dreams can tell us a good deal about the dreamer's repressed fears, needs, and conflicts. So we can use the dream elements of Dickinson's poem to explore its psychoanalytic content. When we want to read a literary work as if it were a dream, it often helps to take the following steps: (1) summarize the work as if it were a dream; (2) use your summary to help you draw some general conclusions about the meaning of the work viewed as a dream; and (3) analyze the dream imagery to make your interpretation more specific.

Summarizing the "dream"

As poetic language can sometimes be difficult to follow, especially for beginners, your instructor might allow you to summarize the poem-as-dream in your own words, in as much detail as you can provide, to be sure that you've understood the events it describes. If a poem is written in simple, modern English and is easy to follow, this step may be unnecessary. Our Dickinson poem is easy to follow at some points but difficult at others, so why don't you summarize as much of the poem as you can? Then see if the following summary agrees with yours.

Summary of Poem 520: The speaker, presumably a young woman, takes her dog for an early morning walk by the sea when no one else is there. As she arrives at the shore, mermaids come up from the "Basement" (l. 3)—that is, from beneath the sea—to look at her. She also sees frigates, or wooden ships, towering above her. The hemp ropes that secure these ships to land seem to her to be long hands inviting her to climb aboard the way mice used to climb along such ropes to get aboard wooden ships. But no one disturbs her—indeed, she is apparently the only human being present—until the tide suddenly rises so high that it covers her body, right up to her neck. In fact, the sea, which is clearly male, rises so quickly that he seems about to swallow her as if she were no larger than a drop of dew on the petal of a dandelion. The prospect of being consumed by the sea seems to frighten her greatly, for she flees the shore and runs toward town. However, the sea pursues her so closely that she feels the edge of the tide (his "Silver Heel," l. 18) upon her ankle, and the bubbling foam of the sea (the "Pearl," l. 20) overflows into her shoes as she runs. This close pursuit continues until she reaches town, with which the sea is unacquainted. Here, the sea ends his pursuit. He bows to her, gives her a powerful look, and goes back from whence he came.

Drawing some general conclusions from your summary

Using your summary to guide you, go back to the poem and list what you think are the most important things the "dream" tells us about the speaker. The following five points are examples of the kinds of general conclusions you can draw. Find all the evidence in the poem you can to support these conclusions. If you've drawn different conclusions, find evidence that supports your conclusions.

1   The speaker is extremely frightened by the sea.
2   The speaker also seems attracted to the sea, at least at some points in the poem.
3   The speaker runs to town to escape the sea.
4   All of these conclusions suggest that the speaker has a conflicted relationship to the sea. That is, she has directly opposed feelings about the sea. Make sure you have found all the evidence the poem offers to support this claim.
5   Especially in the first two stanzas, the speaker feels self-conscious: she feels that she is an object of curiosity and that judgments of some sort are being made about her. Given our claim that the speaker is both attracted to and frightened by the sea—that is, she is attracted to something that frightens her—her self-consciousness may mean she has some desire about which she feels guilty, for we often imagine we are being watched or judged when we want something we feel we shouldn't want.

Analyzing the poem's dream symbolism

In order to turn our general conclusions into an interpretation of the poem as a dream, we need to interpret the dream imagery in a way that makes sense in context of the poem as a whole. For example, earlier in this chapter, the "Dream symbolism" section of "Basic concepts" told us that water—in this case, the sea—can symbolize the unconscious, the emotions, and/or sexuality.

How can we determine which interpretation is most applicable here? Well, we can look at how the sea behaves. Does this poem's representation of the sea seem as sexual to you as it does to me? If you think we can argue that the speaker's conflicted attitude toward the sea implies a conflicted attitude toward sex (sex both attracts and frightens her), find all the textual evidence you can to support the following claims about the poem's dream symbolism. Keep in mind that we're not making the kind of unwarranted "symbolic leap" described in Chapter 2: "Using concepts from reader–response theory to understand our own interpretations." For psychoanalytic theory provides us with the dream symbols we're using. However, we must be careful to use them in a way that makes sense in terms of our interpretation of the poem as a whole.

1   *The Sea*—The sea seems to symbolize sex, specifically the sexual pursuit of a woman by a man. (This sea is chasing her for a reason!)

2   *The "Pearl"* (l. 20)—If the sea symbolizes sex, then the "Pearl," which is literally sea-foam, works as a symbolic stand-in for semen. That is, the sea, here, emits sexual fluid. Or, at the very least, we can say that the sea is overflowing with sexuality.

3   *The "Basement"* (l. 3)—The "Basement," which is, ordinarily, an underground storage space and refers in the poem to the deeper water below the sea's surface, seems to symbolize the speaker's unconscious, which contains her own repressed sexuality. For this "Basement" is inhabited by mermaids, and mermaids are at home in the sea (sexuality) and are often portrayed as very sexually attractive to human males.

4   *The Mermaids* (l. 3)—Given the preceding discussion of the "Basement," it follows that the Mermaids symbolize the speaker's own sexual desire.

5   *The Frigates* (l. 4)—Because the Frigates inhabit the "Upper Floor" (and because the "Basement" has already taken the role of the unconscious), the Frigates which float upon the surface of the sea probably symbolize the speaker's conscious mind. In that case, she must see herself, as the Frigates do, as a helpless creature, like a mouse, in need of protection from the sea.

6   *The Town*—Given that the speaker flees to the "Solid Town" (l. 21) to escape from the sea, the town must represent something directly opposite the sexual freedom of the sea. In addition, any location in which a community of people live in an orderly fashion and obey common laws is generally associated with the repression of individual desire. Thus, the town can be taken to symbolize the restraints placed on sexuality by laws and customs.

Focusing Your essay

I think the work we've done on the poem suggests that you might focus your paper on the topic of sexual repression. You might argue, for example, that the speaker represses her sexual desire because she is afraid of its power.

Because we're reading the poem as a dream, however, it may occur to you to wonder whose dream it is. Is it the author's? Well, it may or may not be the author's dream, but we can't make such a claim unless we're prepared to back it up with evidence from Dickinson's life, letters, and other poems, a task that few of us are prepared to undertake. So it's best to argue simply that the poem, read as a dream, represents the conflicted attitude human beings often have toward their own sexual desire. Or you might make the equally valid and perhaps more interesting claim that the poem, read as a dream, reflects the kind of conflicted attitude toward sex that was prevalent during the nineteenth century, when the poem was written.

Remember, too, that you don't have to limit yourself to the analysis of the poem I've offered you. For example, you might feel, instead, that this poem, read as a dream, implies a fear of rape or the trauma of a woman who has been raped, which is how some of my students have viewed the poem. After all, there is a symbolic emission of semen (the overflowing "Pearl," l. 20). And at the end of the poem, the sea, "with a Mighty look" (l. 23)—implying a threatening power—"withdrew" (l. 24), which in a sexual context can imply the withdrawal of the penis after intercourse. In other words, the speaker may flee to the town for safety, but she doesn't arrive there in time to escape the sexual aggression that threatened her.

In contrast, you might feel that this poem, read as a dream, implies the indulgence of a guilty desire on the part of the speaker, as other of my students have suggested. In this case, you would argue that symbolic sexual intercourse does take place but that it does so with the guilt-ridden consent of the speaker. In other words, the speaker believes that sex is wrong and tries to avoid it but is overwhelmed by her own sexual desire. After the sexual act occurs and her desire is satisfied, she feels the full force of her guilt. Thus, the speaker describes the town as "Solid" (l. 21), not because it represents a safe refuge but because it represents all the solid social institutions of the nineteenth century that condemned sexual pleasure. Whatever your interpretation, be sure you understand the psychoanalytic concepts you choose to employ, compose a clear statement of your thesis, and support your interpretation with adequate textual evidence.

Recognizing a character's self-healing: Interpreting "Don't Explain"

Perhaps the most obvious and surely the most important psychological dimension of Jewelle Gomez's "Don't Explain" (1987; see Appendix E) is the story's depiction of the negative effects on the main character's emotional health of feeling isolated as a lesbian in a heterosexual world. Of course, this aspect of Letty's emotional life is included in the story to help us understand lesbian experience. Therefore, you'll find it discussed in the interpretation of "Don't Explain" offered in Chapter 7, "Using concepts from lesbian, gay, and queer theories to understand literature." Similarly, the chapters on Marxist, Feminist, African American, and postcolonial theory include interpretations of

Gomez's story that discuss, among other things, the ways in which Letty's class, gender, race, and cultural identity, respectively, affect her psychological relationship to herself and her world.

So let's focus here on a different dimension of Letty's psychological makeup: her feelings about the late Billie Holiday, one of America's most famous jazz singers, known especially for her moving renditions of songs about the pain of being in love and the pain of losing love. As the story progresses, Letty's thoughts return again and again to Billie Holiday, whose famous recording of the song "Don't Explain" provides the story's title. I'm not suggesting that Letty's feelings about Billie Holiday have nothing to do with the main character's class, gender, race, sexual orientation, or cultural identity. Of course these factors play a large role in her emotional relationship to Billie. However, Letty also feels a bond with Billie because of what she sees as the singer's loneliness and insecurity. And surely, loneliness and insecurity are relevant to the psychological experience of us all, regardless of the social categories by which we are defined.

Because this focus on Letty's emotional relationship with Billie Holiday is so specific, it might produce a briefer analysis than did the previous psycho-analytic discussions of literary works. But this narrower focus is nevertheless valuable because it allows us to explore another aspect of literature to which we can bring psychoanalytic tools: representations of emotional self-healing. Although literary representations of self-destructive characters certainly seem much more numerous than literary works that illustrate healthy forms of coping with life's problems, "Don't Explain" is an excellent example of this kind of literary text.

Over the course of the story we learn that Billie Holiday, also known as Lady Day, has recently died. And since Billie's death, Letty has not been able to bring herself to play any of the singer's records on the juke-box, which Letty had been in the habit of doing during her breaks at the 411 Lounge where she has worked for the past seven years. The depth of Letty's mourning for Billie Holiday, whom she has met only once, reveals the very important and very personal meaning this singer holds for Letty. Our first task, then, is to understand the bond Letty feels with Billie and how that bond helps heal the main character's psychological wounds, a healing process that begins to occur at the end of the story when Letty is finally able to listen to a Billie Holiday record. Even more impressive is the fact that Letty is able to share this moment with another person: she is beginning to emerge from her shell. Because we are arguing here that Letty has psychological wounds which her bond with Billie Holiday helps to begin to heal, we must do three things: (1) discover Letty's psychological wounds; (2) determine why Letty identifies with Billie Holiday (determine what Letty believes she has in common with Lady Day, which convinces Letty that she knows how the singer feels); and (3) determine why Letty admires Billie Holiday, an admiration that ultimately helps Letty feel that she, herself, can begin to take the emotional risk of living a fuller life than she has allowed herself to live so far.

Letty's psychological wounds

1 *Letty's lost love*—Letty has lost someone she loves—Maxine—and she can't stop thinking about her. (We are not told exactly how Letty lost Maxine. Evidently, they were a couple and then broke up. In any event, it is Letty's sense of loss that is important for our analysis.)

   a Find the textual evidence showing that Letty tries to block the memory of Maxine out of her mind because thinking about her makes Letty very sad.
   b Find the textual evidence showing that the reason Letty has recently stopped listening to Billie Holiday records is that her sadness over Billie's death makes Letty feel more lonely for Maxine.

2 *Letty's fear of intimacy*—Because of the pain Letty suffered over losing Maxine, she has put herself in a shell. For Letty, fear of intimacy may or may not be a core issue, but at least since the loss of Maxine seven years ago, Letty has been afraid of putting her heart at risk again. (If it's a core issue—a permanent part of her personality due to unresolved psychological wounds—then Letty will continue to fear intimacy even as she allows herself to make new friends and even if she falls in love. We don't know what happens after the story ends, but we do know that Letty exhibits fear of intimacy during most of the story.)

   a Find the textual evidence showing that, until the very end of the story, Letty doesn't let herself get close to anyone.
   b Find the textual evidence showing that Letty's fear of intimacy is due to her fear of getting hurt again.

Letty's identification with Billie Holiday

Letty believes that she and Billie have a great deal in common and that she therefore knows how Billie feels. Find textual evidence to support the following claims, and see if you can find evidence of any other qualities Letty believes she and Billie have in common.

1 Letty believes that she and Billie have the same kind of loneliness.
2 Letty believes that she and Billie have many of the same insecurities.
3 Letty believes that, like her, Billie loves a woman and is keeping her love a secret.
4 Though Letty may or may not realize it, she has many strengths in common with Billie. For example, like Billie, Letty

   a is very good at her job,
   b has a generous spirit, and
   c is kind to others.

Letty's admiration of Billie Holiday

1   List all the things that Letty seems to admire about Billie Holiday.
2   Note, too, that Letty admires the singer not just because of Billie's good qualities, but because Letty sees that Billie has achieved success—has become extremely good at her music and has become famous—*despite* her setbacks and insecurities. In other words, Letty admires Billie's strength in the face of adversity. Find all the textual evidence you can to support this claim.

Letty's self-healing

"Hey, Billie is insecure just like I am! But she went out on stage even when her audience knew she had a drug problem and came just to watch her fail. And she didn't fail—she sang so well that she won them over. If she can take a risk like that, then so can I!"

1   Letty doesn't say these words out loud, but how does the text show us that something like this is what she must be feeling? In other words, what risks does Letty's admiration for Billie Holiday finally help her to take?
2   How do we know that Letty is feeling better at the end of the story? Find as many lines as you can that show the improvement in Letty's spirits.

Focusing your essay

As we've seen throughout our exploration of "Don't Explain," the story illustrates how an individual can find a source of psychological strength in an emotional identification with another person, even if that other person is a relative stranger. For Letty doesn't really know Billie Holiday: they've met only once. And though that one meeting reinforced all of Letty's positive feelings about the singer, Letty's real bond with Billie Holiday comes from her emotional response to Billie's music and from the public knowledge available about Billie's career and personal problems. So you might focus your essay on the ways in which "Don't Explain" illustrates the potential healing power of the kind of positive emotional identification Letty has with Billie Holiday. Or to put the matter another way, you might argue that we can't fully understand Letty if we don't understand the psychological role Billie Holiday plays in her life.

Remember, you don't have to limit yourself to the analysis of Letty I've offered you. For example, you might feel, instead, that Letty's emotional relationship with Billie Holiday, as we've described it here, is too narrow a focus to give us an understanding of the main character's healing process, in which case you might want to combine what you've learned here with the insights into Letty's emotional experience offered in one or more subsequent chapters. For as we noted when we began our psychoanalytic interpretation of "Don't Explain," although each of the other theories we will study has its own unique focus on a particular aspect of human experience, those theories can also draw on psychoanalytic concepts to help us understand our psychological experience in terms of our social class, gender, sexual orientation, race, and cultural identity.

Or perhaps, instead, your instructor might allow you to do some research on Billie Holiday's life in order to write an essay that compares, more thoroughly than we have done, the singer's experiences and problems with those of Letty. Such an essay should also allow you to speculate about the accuracy of Letty's intuitions about Billie. A biography that you might find especially useful for this purpose is Stuart Nicholson's *Billie Holiday* (Northeastern University Press, 1995), which includes a good deal of information about the singer's early years, her career, her success, the racial discrimination she suffered, and her sexual orientation. Whatever your interpretation, be sure you understand the psychoanalytic concepts you choose to employ, compose a clear statement of your thesis, and support your interpretation with adequate textual evidence.

Using psychoanalytic concepts in service of other theories: Interpreting "The Battle Royal"

As we saw in the opening and closing paragraphs of our discussion of "Don't Explain," psychoanalytic concepts can be used to develop Marxist; feminist; gay, lesbian, and queer; African American, and postcolonial readings of a literary work because these theories include attention to the ways in which psychological damage is done to people who are oppressed for reasons of, respectively, class, gender, sexual orientation, race, and cultural identity. "The Battle Royal," the first chapter of Ralph Ellison's novel *Invisible Man* (1952; see Appendix C), provides another excellent example of how theories can overlap, how one theory can be used "in service" of another theory. For in reading "The Battle Royal" we can use psychoanalytic concepts to develop Marxist, feminist, gay, African American, and postcolonial interpretations of the story. In fact, we have little choice, as the source of all the psychological content of "The Battle Royal"—the characters' dysfunctional or self-destructive behavior—is clearly the enormous imbalance of power between the story's middle-class white Americans and working-class African Americans and, as a kind of subplot, between the story's middle-class white men and the white female exotic dancer. Buried even deeper in the story—"in the closet," we might say—there is also a psychological dimension of the story related to the white male characters' attitude toward black male sexuality that can be developed in a gay reading of the story.

There is, however, no psychological experience represented in "The Battle Royal" that can be viewed independently of the characters' class, gender, sexual orientation, race, or cultural identity. The only reference to any character's emotional experience within the family is a description of the intense fear, prevalent in the narrator's family, of the absolute power of whites. But the story's description of that fear does not include a description of the family's psychological dynamics, in contrast to "Everyday Use," for which we can generate a separate psychoanalytic interpretation *in addition to* our Marxist, feminist, gay, African American, and postcolonial readings of Walker's story. Neither does "The Battle Royal" illustrate a psychological experience that can be explored as a kind of "universal" experience—one that can happen to anyone from any background—like the emotional self-healing discussed in our interpretation of "Don't Explain."

Obviously, when a literary work clearly ties the psychological experience of its characters to the social categories by which their world defines them, we must tie our interpretation of the characters' psychological experience to those same social categories. Therefore, the psychological dimension of "The Battle Royal" appears in the interpretations of this story offered in subsequent chapters. As we're not going to develop a separate psychoanalytic reading of the story here, let me just list for you the various uses to which psychoanalytic concepts are put in those interpretations.

Our Marxist interpretation—Our Marxist interpretation of "The Battle Royal" explores, among other things, the *psychological* effects of the protagonist's misplaced belief in the American Dream.

Our feminist interpretation—Our feminist reading of Ellison's story implies that the white civic leaders have *psychological* motives in treating the exotic dancer as a sex object and that their behavior toward her has negative *psychological* effects, both on the dancer and on the African American youths forced to watch her.

Our gay interpretation—In our gay interpretation of "The Battle Royal," we examine the *psychology* of homophobia.

Our African American interpretation—Among other things, our African American interpretation explores the *psychological* effects of racism.

Our postcolonial interpretation—Our postcolonial reading of this story analyzes, among other things, the *psychological* oppression of the African American characters and of the white exotic dancer, all of whom are treated as inferiors, as outsiders, by the wealthy white dominant culture.

However you decide to use psychoanalytic concepts in developing your interpretation of "The Battle Royal," be sure you understand the theoretical concepts you choose to employ, compose a clear statement of your thesis, and support your interpretation with adequate textual evidence.

Food for further thought

Thinking it over

If you've worked through all of the interpretation exercises offered in this chapter, you should feel quite familiar with the basic approaches to understanding literature provided by concepts from psychoanalytic theory. Specifically, we've seen how psychoanalytic concepts can be used to interpret

1   literary works that illustrate the kind of "everyday" dysfunctional behavior found, to varying degrees, in most families (our example: "Everyday Use"),
2   literary works that illustrate insanity (our example: "A Rose for Emily"),
3   literary works that consist largely of dream imagery (our example: "I started Early—Took my Dog"),
4   literary works that illustrate psychological self-healing (our example: "Don't Explain"), and
5   literary works whose representations of psychological experience should not be analyzed using psychoanalytic theory alone (our example: "The Battle Royal").

We also saw, in our discussions of "Don't Explain" and "The Battle Royal," that psychoanalytic concepts can be employed in reading literature from Marxist, feminist, gay and lesbian, African American, and postcolonial perspectives. The reason is fairly simple. Among other things, all the theories you'll read about in subsequent chapters oppose some form of oppression: oppression due to social class, gender, sexual orientation, race, or culture, respectively. And all of these forms of oppression include psychological oppression. Individuals who belong to the "wrong," or devalued, group in a given culture are usually treated as if they were inferior human beings and, therefore, often come to believe that they *are* inferior human beings. In other words, oppression frequently creates low self-esteem and other forms of insecurity in those who are oppressed, and when this happens it is called psychological oppression. So while psychoanalytic concepts can help us understand the ways in which our personalities are formed within the dynamics of the family in which we were raised, they can also help us understand the ways in which our personalities are formed within the everyday dynamics of the community in which we live.

Whatever our analysis of a given psychological problem—whether it's a problem exhibited by a literary character or one of our own—most students new to psychoanalytic concepts want to know if such problems can ever be overcome. If, for example, low self-esteem is one of my core issues, can I ever be rid of it? The bad news is that, according to psychoanalytic theory, I can never be completely rid of a core issue. Because I've developed aspects of my personality in response to that issue, it will always be, in some way, a part of me. However, the good news is that I can change my relationship to a core issue. The more I learn about a given problem I have, the more I can develop new ways to deal with it, to not let it push me into behavior that is destructive to myself or to others. And I also have the benefit of knowing that, when I backslide, when an old problem suddenly shows up again, I'm not back where I first started. The recurrence of an old problem from time to time is natural, unavoidable, because it's "built into" my past and therefore "built into" me. So occasional backsliding doesn't mean I haven't made good progress. And we all, of course, have psychological problems simply because we're human beings. According to psychoanalytic theory, our psychological problems are part of the hand we're dealt by our life experience. It's how we play that hand that matters.

Psychoanalytic theory and cultural criticism

We can also use concepts from psychoanalytic theory for the purposes of cultural criticism. That is, we can use psychoanalytic concepts to help us analyze the cultural messages sent, whether deliberately or not, by the everyday productions of the culture in which we live, such as movies, games, television shows, song lyrics, toys, and other productions of popular culture discussed in Chapter 1. In fact, any cultural production that in some way represents human behavior—that has characters and a plot—can be analyzed using concepts from psychoanalytic theory just as we use those concepts to analyze literary works. For example, an understanding of core issues and defenses can offer us insights into the classic film romance *Pretty Woman* (directed by Garry Marshall, 1990), in which good-hearted prostitute Vivian Ward (Julia Roberts) and lonely, self-made corporate raider Edward Lewis (Richard Gere) find true love and a happy future together.

Too busy to give adequate time and attention to his romantic relationships— the most recent of which has just ended badly—Edward decides to hire the lovely, free-spirited Vivian to be his "beck-and-call-girl" for one week in order to ensure himself a trouble-free companion for the various social events he must attend in pursuit of his latest corporate takeover. Over the course of the film, Vivian gets Edward to loosen up, slow down, and smell the roses. Instead of destroying his latest corporate target, the fatherly Mr. Morse (Ralph Bellamy), Edward saves the man's company and goes into business with him. Analogously, Edward gets Vivian to broaden her horizons and have faith in her ability to achieve a better life. By the end of the film, Vivian has decided to quit her life on the street—she has even rejected Edward's offer to keep her as his mistress—and get her high-school-equivalency diploma. Luckily, Edward catches up with Vivian before she leaves town and offers her the "happily ever after" they both want.

As interesting and entertaining as *Pretty Woman* is at face value, it can become even more so if we are familiar with psychoanalytic concepts. How can we understand, for instance, Vivian's self-destructive behavior in terms of low self-esteem and denial? For example, how do we know that Vivian thinks she doesn't deserve much out of life? And how does Vivian reveal her state of denial, during the film's opening scenes, by her insistence that she's doing fine just as she is? Analogously, how can we understand Edward's self-destructive behavior—his inability to sustain a romantic relationship and his heartless business practices—in terms of fear of intimacy? Specifically, how does he reveal his deep-seated fear of getting close to anyone at all? And how do we know that his choice of business and his drive to succeed in that business are really the displacement of his negative feelings toward his father onto other corporate tycoons? This kind of analysis can help us understand the lives led by Vivian and Edward before they meet early in the movie and thus show us why they are drawn to each other for reasons beyond Vivian's beauty and Edward's money. And such an analysis, while interesting and worthwhile in itself, can serve as a first step to answering a question of particular importance for psychoanalytic cultural criticism: How does a given production of popular culture seem to define emotional health or normality? In the case of *Pretty Woman*, in what ways do Vivian and Edward become emotionally healthy by the end of the movie? In short, how does the film suggest that, as the old sayings go, "Love cures all," and "All you need is love"?

I believe most viewers would agree that *Pretty Woman* is a charming movie with an engaging story, very sympathetic leading characters, and a satisfyingly happy ending. That's why so many of us, I think, take away such pleasant feelings when the movie is over. But do we also take away—perhaps without quite realizing it—something else? By suggesting that true love can heal, over the course of one week, the kinds of psychological wounds that both Vivian and Edward carry from their youth, *Pretty Woman* seems to overlook or even trivialize the importance of the kind of psychological self-knowledge that requires much more time and work. I'm not suggesting that the plot should be changed to have Vivian and Edward sign up for pre-marital counseling. Personally, I wouldn't change the movie at all. I am suggesting that, from the perspective of psychoanalytic cultural criticism, *Pretty Woman* sends a specific cultural message, or as cultural critics would put it, *Pretty Woman* performs specific cultural work. Whether or not it intends to do so, the movie reinforces tendencies within American culture to favor "quick fixes" over sustained effort and to believe that "love conquers all." In particular, *Pretty Woman* gives us permission, so to speak, to deny the importance of dealing with our own psychological issues. In other words, part of our enjoyment of the movie is a kind of indefinable feeling of freedom, a sense of relief, a reinforcement of our desire to believe that any unhappiness we have can be turned around at any moment by the good fortune, or happy fate, of falling in love with the right person.

★★★

Remember, it's natural to feel a bit uncertain when we encounter a new theory—a new way of looking at ourselves and our world—that may call into question many of the beliefs that have been pressed upon us, and that we've accepted uncritically, for most of our lives. Uncertainty is an unavoidable part of learning and growing. Keep in mind, too, that others may disagree with your opinions. Individuals often disagree in their interpretations of literature, popular culture, or everyday experiences, even when drawing upon the same psychoanalytic concepts for their analyses. The keys to a good interpretation—besides intellectual curiosity and an open mind—are a clear understanding of the psychoanalytic concepts you've chosen to use and strong evidence to support your analysis.

Taking the next step

Questions for further practice

1   In Langston Hughes' short story "The Blues I'm Playing" (1934), we see a strong contrast between the psychological well-being of Miss Oceola Jones and the psychological problems of Mrs. Dora Ellsworth. What attitudes and behaviors does Oceola exhibit that show her psychological health? In contrast, where do we see evidence that Mrs. Ellsworth lives vicariously through her protégés in an attempt to fill the emotional void in her own life; that she tries to control every aspect of her life in order to avoid her own emotions (does Mrs. Ellsworth suffer from fear of intimacy?); that she projects onto Oceola her own unhappy experience of marriage; and that she is in denial about her psychological problems?

2   Edna Pontellier, the protagonist in Kate Chopin's novel *The Awakening* (1899), goes through many changes over the course of her short life. One consistent pattern of behavior, however, can be found in her relationships with men. Edna is attracted to unattainable men: in addition to Robert Lebrun, consider the unattainable men she falls for during her girlhood in Kentucky. In addition, she doesn't love the two men she does attain: her husband Léonce and her lover Alcée Arobin. This pattern suggests that Edna has a fear of intimacy. Find all the textual evidence you can to support this claim, including her early experiences with her mother, father, and sisters. (Were her early family experiences likely to create a strong capacity for emotional intimacy?)

3   In many ways, Arthur Miller's *Death of a Salesman* (1949) can be seen as a psychological play about the emotional breakdown of protagonist Willy Loman. Find as much textual evidence as you can to show that Willy's low self-esteem and fear of abandonment are responsible for most of his self-destructive behavior. For example, how can we see his low self-esteem in the lies he tells his wife, his sons, and others? Note, too, the effects on Willy of being abandoned, as a young boy, by both his father and his older brother. Or you might consider how *Death of a Salesman* can be seen as a play about the power of denial. Gather all the textual evidence you can showing the ways in which all four members of the Loman family are in denial throughout the play.

4   In Janice Mirikitani's "Breaking Tradition" (1978), the speaker's mother taught her to repress and deny her feelings, desires, and painful memories; to never show defiance or passion; and to limit herself to a confining world of housekeeping and childrearing. In short, the speaker was taught

to be silent and to stay "in her room"—that is, within her self. How does the poem illustrate the harmful effects of such behavior? Although the speaker wants to communicate with her daughter as her own mother never did with her, how do we see that this communication has not yet occurred? And while the speaker wants a different life for her daughter, in what ways is her daughter repressing her own feelings, remaining in her own "room," in her own state of denial?

5   Use concepts from psychoanalytic theory to help you interpret some aspect of a movie, television show, song lyric, cartoon, video game, or any other production of popular culture that you find interesting and that seems to have a psychoanalytic dimension. For example, how are human emotions and human relations represented? Are core issues or psychological defenses represented in some way? What information, if any, is provided concerning family relationships, romantic relationships, or friendships that might be useful from a psychoanalytic perspective? Based on your observations, what cultural work does your chosen cultural production do relevant to psychoanalytic theory? Specifically, what definitions of normality or psychological well-being does it imply? Be sure to offer evidence from your chosen production to support your ideas.

Suggestions for further reading

Berg, Henk de. *Freud's Theory and Its Use in Literary and Cultural Studies: An Introduction.* Rochester, New York: Camden House, 2003. (See, especially, "The Psychoanalysis of Literature," 73–108.)

Davis, Walter A. "The Drama of the Psychoanalytic Subject." *Inwardness and Existence: Subjectivity in/and Hegel, Heidegger, Marx, and Freud.* Madison: University of Wisconsin Press, 1989. 232–313. (See, especially, "The Familial Genesis of the Psyche," 242–50; "Identity and Sexuality," 296–307; and "Love Stories," 307–13.)

Fanon, Frantz. "The Negro and Psychopathology." *Black Skin, White Masks.* 1952. Trans. Charles Lam Markman. New York: Grove Press, 1967. 141–209.

Gay, Peter, (ed.) *The Freud Reader.* 1989. New York: W. W. Norton, 1995. (See, especially, "On Dreams," 142–72; "Creative Writers and Daydreaming," 436–43; "The Theme of the Three Caskets," 514–22; "Mourning and Melancholia," 584–89; and "Civilization and Its Discontents," 722–72.)

Loomba, Ania. "Psychoanalysis and Colonial Subjects." *Colonialism/Postcolonialism.* 2nd ed. New York: Routledge, 2005. 115–28.

Tyson, Lois. "Psychoanalytic Criticism." *Critical Theory Today: A User-Friendly Guide.* 2nd ed. New York: Routledge, 2006. 11–52.

Wright, Elizabeth. *Psychoanalytic Criticism: A Reappraisal.* 2nd ed. New York: Routledge, 1998. (See, especially, "Classical Psychoanalysis: Freud," 9–32, and "Classical Freudian Criticism: Id-Psychology," 33–47.)

Chapter 5

Using concepts from Marxist theory to understand literature

Why should we learn about Marxist theory?

Most of us realize that a country's socioeconomic system determines who has the most power in that country. For example, in medieval Europe's feudal system, the most power belonged to those who controlled the most land, and a powerful class system developed that kept the descendants of those land-owning families in power. In the capitalist systems operating in most Western nations today, the most power belongs to those who control the most money—the word *capital* means *money*—and that control may or may not change hands at any given time.

For Marxist theory, however, the socioeconomic system in which we live does much more than determine who has the most power. It also determines, among other things, how we are educated, and it influences our religious beliefs, which together control to a great degree how we perceive ourselves and our world. For if a socioeconomic system is to survive, the people who live within it must be convinced that it is the right system. For a rigid class system to survive, then, its people must be convinced of the natural superiority of those born into the upper class. Analogously, for American capitalism's American Dream to survive, Americans must be convinced of the natural superiority of those who manage to rise from the bottom to the top of the financial heap. And it is our education and our religious beliefs that do much of the convincing by determining how we perceive ourselves and our world.

Let me develop this point further. To understand the kind of influence a socioeconomic system exerts over its members, let's take a minute to look a bit more closely at the ways in which those of us born and bred in the United States have been influenced by ours. To succeed in the US, we must compete against other Americans for financial prosperity. So we must believe in the virtues of both competition and financial prosperity. Now consider that the American educational system teaches us, from the earliest grades, to compete, each of us alone against the rest of the class, for prizes in spelling bees, essay contests, talent contests, and the like. Consider, too, that Puritan culture in colonial North America, from which much of our national culture developed, included the belief that certain individuals are "elected" before birth to be among God's chosen and that the signs of one's "election" included financial prosperity. Thus, in the United States, financial success became associated with moral virtue. This belief persists today in the American Dream, which celebrates as a virtue the individual's rise to the highest plateau of financial achievement of which he or she is capable. In other words, both America's educational philosophy and religious history foster the spirit of individual competition and the desire for financial prosperity that are the basis of its capitalist socioeconomic system. This is just one example of the ways in which a nation's socioeconomic system influences how its members perceive themselves and their world. Marxism, therefore, is concerned with how the socioeconomic system in which we live shapes our personal identity.

The goal of Marxism is to achieve a worldwide classless society by exposing the oppressive ideologies (belief systems) that keep the nations of this planet bound within socioeconomic systems in which a relatively small number of people are extremely wealthy while most people are struggling, or even failing to get by. For example, while the top executive officers of international corporations often have *personal* financial holdings in the hundred millions, the vast majority of people on this planet are lucky if they can feed, clothe, and shelter themselves and their children, let alone afford such "luxuries" as adequate healthcare and educational opportunities. And too many families—even in such a prosperous country as the United States—are unable to do that. So we can start to use Marxist theory to understand literature by asking the following two questions about any literary work we want to interpret. (1) What oppressive socioeconomic ideologies influence the characters' behavior? (2) Does the literary work combat those ideologies by clearly illustrating the damage they do? If the literary text does *not* combat those ideologies, then, for Marxist theory, that text is considered part of the problem—because it blinds us to the problem—rather than part of the solution. The most common oppressive socioeconomic ideologies are defined in the "Basic concepts" section that follows. Although it's important that you read through this list of concepts, don't be too concerned if you don't feel you thoroughly understand every one. You'll begin to understand these concepts much better when we use them, later on in this chapter, to help us interpret the literary texts that appear at the end of this book. And you'll see that these fundamental Marxist concepts can help us understand other works of literature, as well.

Remember, too, that I'm offering you my own literary analyses in the interpretation exercises provided later in this chapter. You might use the same Marxist concepts I use but come up with different interpretations of your own. If you disagree with any of the analyses I offer in these exercises, don't be afraid to look in the literary work in question for evidence that will support your viewpoint. A literary work can often support a number of different interpretations, even when readers are using concepts from the same theory.

Basic concepts

Note that the basic concepts listed below are all examples of socioeconomic ideologies that have existed for centuries and in which many people believe today. Marxism didn't invent these ideologies. Rather, Marxism opposes them. For according to Marxist theory, each of these ideologies fosters a socioeconomic hierarchy that grants enormous wealth and power to a relatively small number of people at the top of the socioeconomic ladder, prevents a large number of people from escaping the poverty in which they are trapped at the bottom of the ladder, and keeps those on the middle rungs—if there are any middle rungs—at the financial mercy of such unpredictable occurrences as increased taxes and the rising costs of heathcare, education, and housing. Therefore, the definition of each socioeconomic ideology listed below is followed by a Marxist description of that ideology's flaws.

You'll notice many references to the United States in the following paragraphs because American culture, I think, illustrates with particular clarity the ability of socioeconomic ideologies in general, and of capitalist ideologies in particular, to customize themselves to fit the self-image of any society in which they have taken hold. Indeed, two of the capitalist ideologies defined below—the American Dream and rugged individualism—have American origins, though they now exert their influence globally.

Classism

Classism is the belief that our value as human beings is directly related to the social class to which we belong: the higher our social class, the higher our natural, or inborn superiority. It is only right and proper, classists believe, that those in the highest class should assume leadership roles, for they are, by birth, more intelligent, honorable, energetic, and dependable than those beneath them on the social scale. Analogously, classist ideology tells us that people born into the lowest class have, by birth, a greater tendency to be slow-witted, dishonorable, lazy, and undependable. In traditional classist societies, social class is determined by birth and cannot be changed by the accumulation or loss of wealth because class superiority or inferiority is believed to be "in the blood"—that is, determined by the class to which our parents belong.

Marxist theory, in contrast, rejects the idea that the social class into which we are born determines our superiority or inferiority as human beings. All our class standing determines is whether we'll be socially advantaged or disadvantaged. In other words, Marxist theory considers classism unfair and unwise because it grants privileges to a small segment of the population and withholds privileges from a large segment of the population without regard for individual merit. And unfortunately, classist ideology is hard to defeat.

The United States, for example, tried to eliminate classism by creating a society in which one's social class can change with the accumulation or loss of wealth. This method, it was thought, would allow individuals of merit to rise to the top. However, Marxist theory points out that the accumulation of wealth, especially of enormous wealth, isn't necessarily a sign of merit. All too often it's a sign of questionable ethics. Indeed, as history has shown us, the accumulation of great wealth, or even the maintenance of great inherited wealth, depends upon such unethical practices as the exploitation of cheap labor, the production and sale of such dubious commodities as alcohol and drugs, the exorbitant pricing of such necessities as healthcare and prescription drugs, and the destruction of the environment. In addition, classism exists in the United States, despite the fact that Americans can change the social class into which they were born, because those who occupy the upper class at any given point in time usually expect to be treated, and usually are treated, as if they were superior to those below them on the socioeconomic ladder. And members of the American upper class usually have the same kind of political clout as upper-class people in traditional classist societies. Analogously, those who get trapped in the lower class in the US, due to limited educational and occupational opportunities, are treated as if they were inferior, as if it were their fault that there aren't enough high-paying jobs to go around.

Capitalism

As we saw earlier, the word *capital* means *money*. So capitalism is a system in which everything—every object, every activity, every person—can be defined in terms of its worth in money, its "going rate" on a specific market. Because the market (the availability of and demand for a given product) is considered the best regulator of a product's monetary worth, capitalist governments tend to avoid regulating business profits. Industries are therefore left in private hands.

Marxist theory suggests, however, that unregulated business profits tend to promote what might be called an ethics of greed, according to which the only virtue, or the only virtue anyone really wants to cultivate, is the virtue of making the most money. For only an ethics of greed could permit the kinds of huge profits enjoyed, for example, by the large American pharmaceutical companies, which have resulted in the inability of most Americans who become ill, especially who become chronically ill, to pay for their medication without prescription insurance, which most Americans don't yet have. Marxist theory can point to many examples of the destructive nature of capitalism's promotion of greed, including the squeezing out, by large chain-stores, of the small, independent businesses that used to be so numerous in the United States and the rapidly rising cost of many necessities, in addition to prescription drugs, beyond the easy reach of many people in the United States and throughout the world: hospitalization and other healthcare services and products; decent housing; education; safe, accessible transportation; and even adequate food.

Despite its flaws, however, it seems to many of us who live in capitalist societies that capitalism is, if not perfect, unavoidable. After all, isn't it human nature to want more money? That's the kind of ideology capitalism promotes in order to keep us from questioning it. And that's why, to give you just one striking example, Americans have long believed the myth that the island of Manhattan, on which New York City is now located, was sold to white settlers for beads and trinkets valued at about twenty-four dollars. The fact is that the island of Manhattan was not for sale. The Native Americans who allegedly "sold" it didn't believe that land could be bought and sold (just as air can't be bought and sold). The island was so rich in wildlife that all Native Americans, even tribes engaged in hostilities, were allowed to hunt there in peace. When the white settlers offered beads and trinkets to the locals, the native hunters simply believed it was an offering of friendship made in gratitude for being allowed to hunt on the island! Clearly, it is not human nature to want more money because not all human cultures share this desire. Nevertheless, the settlers moved in and defended their new "purchase" with guns, believing, or choosing to believe, that the island now belonged to them.

Capitalist ideologies

Competition—Capitalism believes that competition among individuals— competition for jobs, for pay raises, for customers, for loans, for awards, and so forth—is the best way to promote a strong society because competition ensures that the most capable, most intelligent people will rise to the top.

In contrast, Marxist theory suggests that unrestrained competition is oppressive because it tends to ensure that the most selfish, unethical people will rise to the top, as they're the ones willing to do whatever it takes to win. The result is that the needs of the community as a whole are usually overlooked, and the needs of those least willing or able to compete are usually sacrificed entirely. That is, competition emphasizes the importance of the individual—"me, me, me"—instead of the group. In addition, it's difficult to confine the spirit of competition to the school or the workplace. We tend to bring it home with us and become competitive in our personal lives, as well, getting unduly upset if we don't win the Scrabble game or if our child doesn't win the spelling contest or if our furniture isn't as new as our neighbor's.

Commodification—A commodity is anything that has a price tag. Because capitalism defines everything in terms of its monetary worth, it encourages commodification. That is, it encourages us to relate to things and people as commodities. We *commodify* something when we relate to it in terms of how much money it's worth, or put another way, how much money it can be exchanged for (its *exchange value*). When we buy something with a high price tag, we acquire social status, so we also commodify something when we relate to it in terms of the social status its ownership gives us (its *sign-exchange value*). For example, I commodify the man I'm dating if I go out with him because he spends a great deal of money on me, in which case

I'm dating him for his exchange value. Also, I commodify him if I go out with him to impress my friends, in which case I'm dating him for his sign-exchange value.

You probably don't need Marxist theory to show you the dangers involved in this capitalist ideology. We all know that it's not good to date someone for shallow, selfish reasons. However, we see this kind of behavior so often that it seems almost "natural," and it seems to many of us, even if we don't admire it, relatively harmless. So let me offer you a more striking, though less visible example. The commodification of human beings is such an accepted part of big business in the United States that the price-tag placed on human life is frequently the chief motive determining whether or not a given airline company will upgrade its airplanes for safety. The cost of the upgrade is weighed against the cost—for example, the cost in terms of lawsuits and bad publicity—of however many lives are liable to be lost, according to statistical analysis, if the upgrade is not done. If the cost of the upgrade is sufficiently higher than the cost of the loss of human life, the upgrade is not done.

The American Dream—The American Dream is a capitalist ideology associated specifically with American history and culture. According to the ideology of the American Dream, anyone who has the determination to work hard enough and the persistence to work long enough can rise from "rags to riches" because America is the land of equal opportunity for all.

Marxist theory points out, however, that our belief in the American Dream blinds us to the reality that a vast number of people have not had and do not have equal opportunity in education, employment, or housing due to such factors as, for example, their gender, race, religion, sexual orientation, and socioeconomic class. And worse, the American Dream leads us to believe that poor people who are unable to significantly improve their financial status must be shiftless and lazy or in some other way undeserving of decent living conditions. After all, the American Dream tells us that all it takes to make it in America is hard work and determination, and that those who don't make it have only themselves to blame.

Rugged individualism—The American Dream has fostered the ideology of rugged individualism, which holds up for our admiration the example of the individual who strikes out alone in pursuit of a goal not easily achieved, for example, the goal of undertaking an untried, high-risk line of business, in which attempt one could lose all one's money, or rushing for gold on the American frontier, in which attempt one could lose one's life.

Marxist theory suggests, however, that the rugged individualist has been greatly romanticized by American folklore while, in reality, rugged individualism generally requires putting self-interest above the needs of the community and a commitment to the belief that "nice guys finish last." The rugged individualist—who generally believes that his first duty is to himself and his first goal is to win whatever competition he's entered—isn't the person most likely to stop and share his canteen of water with a thirsty straggler who has lost his way to the gold-fields.

The role of religion

For many people, religion is a source of spiritual strength and moral guidance. And Martin Luther King has shown us that the church can function as a powerful force against political oppression when parishioners organize for that purpose.

Marxist theory observes, however, that religion too often plays a role in oppressing the poor. One of the best-known Marxist sayings is that "religion is the opiate of the masses." This means that religion acts as a kind of drug that keeps poor people quiet. Belief in God is not the issue here. Rather, the issue is what is done in the name of organized religion to keep the poor oppressed. For example, white plantation owners in the pre-Civil-War American south used the Bible to justify slavery. And religious belief has long been used to keep poor people satisfied in the knowledge that they'll get their reward in heaven, thus keeping the poor from rebelling against those who oppress them.

There are, of course, additional oppressive ideologies that Marxism opposes, but these are enough to get us started using Marxist theory to interpret literature. Let's begin our interpretation exercises by analyzing a story that illustrates very well several of the concepts just outlined: Alice Walker's "Everyday Use."

Interpretation exercises

Understanding the operations of capitalism: Interpreting "Everyday Use"

Alice Walker's "Everyday Use" (1973; see Appendix D) is set in the rural south of the late 1960s and early 1970s and tells the story of the Johnsons, an African American family consisting of a mother and her two grown daughters. Although the college-educated Dee Johnson has escaped the poverty into which she was born, Mama and Maggie Johnson have not. And it is the story's portrayal of the economically successful Dee, especially when con-trasted with its portrayal of Mama and Maggie, that makes "Everyday Use" a promising candidate for a Marxist interpretation. Indeed, the depiction of Dee illustrates the operations of all the capitalist ideologies listed in the "Basic concepts" section of this chapter: (1) competition; (2) commodification; (3) the American Dream; and (4) rugged individualism. So let's take a look at each of these capitalist values in turn and try to see the role it plays in Walker's tale. To the extent that these ideologies play a positive role in the characters' lives, the story is pro-capitalist—it shows capitalism in a good light—which means, in Marxist terms, that the story promotes capitalist oppression. To the extent that these ideologies play a negative role in the characters' lives, the story is anti-capitalist—it reveals the evils of capitalism—which means, in Marxist terms, that the story combats capitalist oppression. Of course, from a Marxist perspective, a story that combats capitalist oppression performs a very important task.

Competition

I think most readers would agree that Dee is the most competitive character in the story. From the time we see her as a young girl to her current visit with Mama and Maggie, almost everything she does reveals her need to compete with other people: to show that she is more intelligent, wittier, better dressed, more successful, and more sophisticated than anyone else. She even competes with her mother and sister as she has done with her friends, despite the fact that Mama and Maggie don't compete with her at all.

1   Find all the evidence you can that Dee has internalized this capitalist ideology.
2   How has competition damaged her relationships with other people?

Commodification

One thing you probably noticed right away is that Dee's first priority is social status. She commodifies almost everything and everyone. Specifically, she relates to the ownership of objects and to relationships with people in terms of the social status they give her (in terms of their sign-exchange value). Even the Black Pride Movement seems important to this character mainly for its sign-exchange value. As a result, she relates to the people and things in her life in a superficial manner.

1   Find the numerous examples offered in the story that Dee has internalized this capitalist ideology.
2   How has commodification damaged her relationships with other people?
3   How does Mama's decision about the quilts, at the end of the story, reveal her opinion of Dee's value system?

The American Dream

1   *Dee*—Dee seems to view herself as an American-Dream success story. She was born into poverty in the rural south, a poverty made more difficult to escape, we can assume, by the sub-standard schooling available in the working-class community in which she grew up as well as by her race and gender. Yet through determination and many years of hard school work, Dee has raised herself to a successful, urban, middle-class lifestyle. And she blames Mama and Maggie for not having achieved what she has achieved, as if anyone could do what she did if they just had enough get-up-and-go. In other words, she has bought into the ideology of the American Dream.

   a Find evidence in the story that Dee has the kind of determination
      associated with the attainment of the American Dream and that she has,
      in fact, achieved that Dream: that she has achieved a level of financial
      success and social status much higher than that into which she was born.
   b Find evidence in the story that Dee's belief in the ideology of the
      American Dream has damaged her relationship with her family.

2 *Mama and Maggie*—Mama's failure to get her piece of the American pie
   reveals that the American Dream does not offer equal opportunity to
   everyone. Mama has worked hard her whole life and shown a good deal
   of determination in raising her daughters alone, supporting her family
   alone, and finding the financial help she needed to send Dee to college.
   Despite her extraordinary efforts, however, Mama has not achieved the
   American Dream. She and Maggie still live in relative poverty. Mama's
   fantasy about being on television shows that she would like to have
   succeeded more, but she was unable to do so. Maggie has always been a
   hard worker, too, but it seems highly unlikely that she will be able to raise
   herself beyond the poverty level, even after she marries John Thomas.

   a Find the textual evidence that shows the many ways in which Mama
      and Maggie work hard.
   b Find all the textual evidence you can to show that the American
      Dream is not available to Mama and Maggie, though it claims to be
      available to everyone.

      i   How are Mama and Maggie held back by the limited availability
          of educational opportunities for people of color, poor people, and
          disabled people (note Maggie's impaired vision)?
      ii Given the story's setting, why is it safe to assume that Mama and
          Maggie have limited job opportunities?

3 In addition to the data you just collected about Mama and Maggie, find
   all the textual evidence you can to show that the story portrays these two
   characters positively, in other words, that the text wants us to like Mama
   and Maggie and not blame them for their poverty, as Dee does.

Rugged individualism

Dee seems to have forgotten that she wouldn't have had the chance to
become financially successful without the help of Mama and her community.
She acts as if she did it all on her own. And she doesn't seem inclined to lift a
finger now to help Mama and Maggie improve their lot.

1 Find evidence in the story that supports these claims about Dee's selfish
   attitude.
2 Explain how Dee's ingratitude toward and neglect of her family is
   encouraged by the ideology of rugged individualism.

Focusing your essay

As we've just seen, all of the capitalist ideologies represented in the story damage the character who embraces them: Dee. And the story portrays Dee in a way that makes it difficult for most readers to like her. In contrast, the characters who seem to reject capitalist ideology—Mama and Maggie—are sympathetically portrayed. So it seems reasonable to focus your essay on the ways in which "Everyday Use" is anticapitalist, the ways in which the story invites us to reject the capitalist ideologies it illustrates, which, from a Marxist perspective, is a very good thing for a story to do.

As always, remember that you don't have to limit yourself to the analysis of the story I've offered you. For example, while you might agree that the story's portrayal of Dee shows the damaging effects of capitalism on personal values and family solidarity, you might argue that Mama and Maggie's situation doesn't offer us an inviting alternative to capitalism. If the choice of lifestyle offered in "Everyday Use" is between that afforded by Dee's financial stability and the undereducated poverty of Mama and Maggie, many readers, at least unconsciously, will probably be drawn to Dee's capitalist lifestyle despite whatever personal dislike they might feel for her. From a Marxist perspective, this would be a flaw in the story.

You might also argue that the story's Marxist critique of capitalism isn't as thorough as it might be. For Marxist theory doesn't want the poor to be content with their poverty, as Mama and Maggie seem to be. Rather, Marxism wants the poor to work against their own victimization, for example, by joining together in community, state, national, and international groups to organize efforts to change laws and policies that discriminate against the poor. Whatever your interpretation, be sure you understand the Marxist concepts you choose to employ, compose a clear statement of your thesis, and support your interpretation with adequate textual evidence.

Recognizing the operations of the American Dream: Interpreting "The Battle Royal"

Sometimes a literary work illustrates the operations of one capitalist ideology in particular, as we see in Ralph Ellison's "The Battle Royal" (1952; see Appendix C). In this story, the nameless narrator takes us back to his youth. As a young man who has just graduated from high school, the narrator seems fixed on one idea: he wants to "get ahead." Through hard work and determination, he wants to become a financial success and raise himself out of the poverty in which most of the members of his African American community are stuck. In other words, he wants to achieve the American Dream. And because he knows that the local white civic leaders hold the key to his success, the narrator knows he must please them if he is to have any chance at all of achieving that Dream. In fact, he is so focused on his own desire for success that he is unable to understand the meaning of the bizarre events that occur in the hotel ballroom on the evening he is to give a speech before the town's leading white men. For his attention to the scene around him is repeatedly interrupted by his concern over what the white civic leaders might be thinking about him.

So there's our start: the story portrays a young man's belief in the American Dream. Now in order to determine whether the story is defending or attacking this capitalist ideology, we must examine whether the American Dream is portrayed positively or negatively. In other words, are the effects of the narrator's devotion to the American Dream positive or negative? To answer that question, note what is going on in the story each time the young man's thoughts dart to his concern about the civic leaders' opinion of him, a concern that often takes the form of worrying about his speech. I think you'll observe that each time this happens, the narrator's desire to know what the white men are thinking—which is a desire for his own success, for his own chance at the American Dream—blinds him to the reality of what is going on in that hotel ballroom and in his life. Specifically, I think you'll find that the narrator's belief in the American Dream blinds him to five important things: (1) the real intentions of the white civic leaders he tries so hard to please; (2) the significance of his alienation from the other young men from his community; (3) the significance of the white exotic dancer the civic leaders parade before the young black men; (4) the meaning of the battle royal in which the narrator participates; and (5) the meaning of the narrator's dream about his grandfather. Let's take a look at each one in turn.

The real intentions of the white civic leaders

The white civic leaders have invited the narrator to their smoker to give a speech, a speech the young man believes will open for him the path to the American Dream. And the narrator does, in fact, give a speech, after which he is presented with a briefcase and a scholarship to a state college for black youth. Nevertheless, it seems rather clear that these leaders—who represent such public institutions as the government, the church, and the schools—do not intend that the narrator will do anything more in the future than serve the white power structure by helping to keep his people "in their place." These men have no intention of helping him achieve the American Dream, unless it is in the form of an unofficial pay-off for services rendered: the narrator may be permitted to achieve a slightly higher degree of financial success than the rest of the black community, but that success will come at the cost of helping the white power structure keep his people down. Yet this black youth is unable to see how these powerful white men feel about him.

1   Find all the evidence in the story you can to show the real intentions of the white civic leaders toward the narrator.

a Find the lines that show why the white men like the narrator's graduation speech.

b Find the lines that reveal why the white men are sending the narrator to college.

2 Find the textual evidence that shows how the narrator's focus on the American Dream keeps him from seeing the white men's intentions, and keeps him in denial about the realities of his situation.

a In the narrator's opinion, who are the only people capable of judging his worth?

b What does the narrator hope his speech will do for him?

The narrator's alienation from his community

The narrator's negative reaction to the young men with whom he is to participate in the battle royal might be considered an example of classism: he feels he doesn't belong with them because he believes himself socially superior to them. However, notice that he is mainly concerned that the white civic leaders will associate him with these less successful and presumably less deserving young men and that this will lessen his chance of being aided by the white community in his quest to achieve the American Dream.

1 Find the textual evidence that shows us how the narrator's devotion to the American Dream alienates him from the young men in his own community.

a Find the lines that show how the narrator feels about the other black youths.

b Find the lines that show how these black youths feel about the narrator.

2 Find the textual evidence showing that the narrator isn't even able to fully realize how the other young men feel about him. (His encounter, in the ring, with Tatlock is especially revealing.)

The significance of the exotic dancer

From the perspective of Marxist theory, the exotic dancer is a commodity for the white men who have hired her, a token of their social status, and their social status is the source and mirror of their social power. In fact, as a sign of white men's prestige and power, the exotic dancer represents white women in general. Such tokens have little meaning if they are not displayed for others to see. This is why the civic leaders insist on displaying her before the young black men. They want these young men to desire her. The white men are telling the black youths, in effect, "You want white women, but you can't have them because they are our property, a sign of our social status, a sign that we are superior to you."

1   Find all the evidence in the story you can to support this claim.
2   Find the textual evidence that shows the narrator's inability to see this aspect of the white men's relationship to the exotic dancer.

    a   Does it ever occur to the narrator that the white men are displaying their power in this scene?
    b   Instead of getting angry at the white men, where does the narrator direct his anger?

The meaning of the battle royal

Of course, the battle royal is a chilling example of racist brutality, and it is the degradation of young black males in their prime that the white men apparently find so "entertaining." However, from the perspective of Marxist theory, the battle royal also mirrors one of the ways in which the socioeconomically oppressed are kept down by those in power. They are kept fighting among themselves, forced to compete with one another for the limited amount of money thrown their way. In the story, the young men must compete for the limited amount of money thrown on the electrified rug. In the real world, the socioeconomically oppressed must compete for the limited number of jobs available to them. Do you see the parallel? And as long as the oppressed are kept battling one another, they won't join forces and turn against their oppressors. In fact, this is why the white men want the narrator to participate in the battle: he, too, must be kept down where he "belongs."

1   Find the evidence the story provides to support the claim that the battle royal represents this kind of keep-them-fighting-among-themselves strategy.

    a   What do the white men say to the fighters before the battle?
    b   What do the white men yell at the fighters during the battle?
    c   What do the white men do when they think that a fighter is trying to escape from the ring?

2   Find the textual evidence that shows us how the narrator's focus on the American Dream blinds him to this meaning of the battle royal.

    a   Note how often the narrator's thoughts drift to his speech, on which he has pinned his hopes of future success.
    b   Note exactly what is happening each time the narrator's thoughts drift to his speech.

3   In this context, explain the significance of the fact that the fighters in the battle royal are blindfolded.

The meaning of the narrator's dream about his grandfather

Toward the end of the story, the narrator is finally allowed to give his speech, and he receives a scholarship to the state college for black youth. That night he dreams about his grandfather, who horrified the family years ago by telling them, on his death bed, that his life of meekness and humility had been just a disguise to fool white folks, whom he considered the enemy of his people. Look closely at this dream. As we learned in the previous chapter on psychoanalytic theory, dreams sometimes reveal a truth that we have buried in our unconscious—that is, a truth we are afraid to face because we fear we can't handle it.

1   What truth is revealed in the narrator's dream about his grandfather? In other words, what does the narrator unconsciously know about his position as a black person in a racist society dominated by whites?
2   How does the American Dream help him close his eyes to this truth?

Focusing your essay

It should be a fairly simple task to focus your essay based on the evidence you've collected above because all of that data point to one idea: the story suggests that the American Dream is not only a false ideology—it doesn't keep its promise—but a dangerous ideology. The narrator is so blinded by his belief in the American Dream that he can't see the obvious reality of his own situation. And if he can't see the problem, then he can't even begin to try to solve it. In the same way that religion is referred to by Marxist theory as "the opiate of the masses," Ellison's tale shows us how the American Dream can operate as a drug in its own right. For the narrator, the American Dream is a religion, and his unquestioning belief in it blinds him to the reality that surrounds him, keeping all his hopes and all his attention focused on some indefinite future when he believes he will be rewarded for proper conduct by being allowed to achieve his piece of the American pie. However, the narrator's hard work and determination, not to mention the chilling sacrifices of personal safety and dignity he makes to please the white civic leaders portrayed in the story, do not ensure that he will be offered his rightful opportunity to attain the American Dream. Rather, it is quite clear that he will be kept running in pursuit of an American Dream he will never be allowed to earn. And he will be kept running because his belief in the Dream doesn't permit him to realize how completely the deck is stacked against him.

It's probably easier to see why people who have succeeded in climbing the socioeconomic ladder believe in the American Dream than to understand why those whom it excludes remain committed to it. But an essay based on the evidence you've collected above will show the power of the American Dream to blind even the poorest Americans to the fact that the Dream is not equally accessible to all. You may be thinking, "Well, it's still good for the poor to have something to hope for even if they can't get it." But a hope that blinds you to the reality of your circumstances is dangerous because, without a clear understanding of the situation you're in, you can't help but be victimized by it. In such a case, your hope is like the hope of a person addicted to gambling: because addicted gamblers believe they can win—that is, they have hope—they can't quit gambling. As long as the narrator in "The Battle Royal" clings to the American Dream, which is a dream of coming out on top, of beating the competition, he will not be able to realize what Marxist theory would have him realize: that his only real hope lies in uniting with other oppressed people and working to change the laws and attitudes that created and sustain socioeconomic oppression.

Of course, you don't have to limit yourself to the analysis of the story I've offered you. For example, you might focus, instead, on the ways in which the white civic leaders commodify everyone in the story: the narrator, the group of young black men they bring in for the battle royal, and the exotic dancer. For these white men relate to those beneath them on the socioeconomic ladder as tokens of their own sign-exchange value, of their own social status. Such an analysis would include a discussion of the negative effects of commodification on the white men's moral character. In other words, you'd be showing how "The Battle Royal" reveals the harmful effects of capitalist ideology even on those it privileges.

If you would prefer, instead, to focus your essay on the ways in which the story illustrates the damaging effects of classism, keep one thing in mind. The classist behavior you see in the story—the white men's belief in their class superiority and the narrator's belief that he "outclasses" the young men from his community—is based on skin color. The underlying assumption is that white people are superior to black people and that light-skinned blacks are superior to those with darker skin. So in "The Battle Royal," classism is based on racism, a subject explored in depth in Chapter 8, "Using concepts from African American theory to understand literature." Whatever your interpretation of this story, be sure you understand the Marxist concepts you choose to employ, compose a clear statement of your thesis, and support your interpretation with adequate textual evidence.

Analyzing the operations of classism: Interpreting "A Rose for Emily"

America was founded on the belief that human beings should not be bound by a class system that keeps sons and daughters chained to the same profession, and therefore the same socioeconomic class, as their parents. Nevertheless, at different times and places in American history, the traditional class system—according to which one's family name, one's ancestry, is one's defining characteristic—has been the factor that determines one's social class and therefore one's social standing in the community. We see the remnants of this kind of traditional class system operating in William Faulkner's "A Rose for Emily" (1931; see Appendix B). The death of Mr. Grierson reveals that he has lost his fortune and that his daughter Emily, the story's main character, will not inherit the money the family once had. Nevertheless, the town of Jefferson still considers Emily a member of the upper class because, as a Grierson, she can trace her lineage back to one of the big plantation families who ruled the South before the Civil War. In order to determine how the story wants us to respond to the classism it portrays—in order to determine if the story promotes or attacks classist ideology—we must determine the story's attitude toward that ideology. So: (1) let's take a look at each example of classist behavior portrayed in the story and see whether the effects of that behavior are positive or negative; and (2) given that classism is an ideology that promotes the belief in the superiority of members of the upper class, we will also check to see if the text paints a positive or negative portrait of its upper-class characters.

Examples of classist behavior

1   *Mr. Grierson's classism*—The Grierson family belongs to the upper stratum of southern society occupied by the wealthy plantation owners before the Civil War, from whom they are descended. In contrast, the rest of the town belongs to the middle and lower classes. Mr. Grierson's classism is visible in his refusal to let Emily mingle with those he considers her social inferiors: because the only young people available are "beneath her," he doesn't allow her to have boyfriends or friends of any kind. Also, it is logical to assume that another reason for his keeping Emily isolated is that he doesn't want anyone to know that he has lost his fortune. If Emily mixed in the social life of the town, she would need a wardrobe befitting her station. If she married, a dowry and wedding finery would be required. Mr. Grierson cannot afford such expenditures, but his classism has fostered a personal pride that won't let him reveal the truth of his circumstance to those beneath him. Because he believes in the superiority of the upper class, he needs to maintain the illusion that he still has the fortune appropriate to his rank in society.

    a   Find the evidence in the story that reveals Mr. Grierson's classism.
    b   Find the textual evidence that shows all the harmful effects his classism has on his daughter.

2   *Colonel Sartoris's classism*—After Mr. Grierson's death, Colonel Sartoris, the mayor of Jefferson, keeps Emily from losing her home and protects her pride by making up a story to justify her not having to pay municipal taxes. Surely, there are many needy people in town. Why does Colonel Sartoris go to such lengths to protect Emily Grierson, an adult, able-bodied woman? It's reasonable to assume that he does so because he's a classist. Presumably, Sartoris was an officer in the Confederate Army during the Civil War. Therefore, it is highly probable that he shares his peers' classist belief in the superiority of the plantation owners and that his own social rank is not far below that of the Griersons. So it is his job to protect a "lady," a woman of rank, in distress.

a   Find all the textual evidence you can of Colonel Sartoris's classism.

b   Find textual evidence that the Colonel's classism is part and parcel of his racism, that he equates what he sees as inferiority of race with inferiority of class.

3   *Emily's classism*—As the young Emily is growing up, she may or may not share her father's belief that she is too good for the town. By the time he dies, however, it seems clear that she has internalized his classist ideology.

a   Find all the evidence you can in the story to illustrate Emily's classism. Include, for example,

   i   the ways in which she acts like a member of a "superior" class (for instance, "china-painting"—painting designs on china dishes— was considered a pastime of refined young ladies), and

   ii   her snobbish contempt for almost everyone in town, including the town's leading citizens.

b   Why would a classist like Emily allow Homer Barron, a man from a lower social class, to court her? Might she think that her social rank requires an escort and, having no social experience whatsoever, might Emily feel more comfortable with a man to whom she feels superior? The text doesn't give us explicit evidence with which to answer this question. Can you come up with a reasonable speculation related to social class that doesn't contradict textual data?

c   What evidence is there in the story that Emily believes she can give Homer the appearance of being from a higher class than the one to which he belongs?

d   If Emily thought Homer was going to leave her, how would her classism motivate her to murder him?

4   *Homer Barron's classism*—Homer is not a one-woman man. He is described as the fun-loving, rough-and-ready type. He is probably capable of courting Emily for her money or her beauty, but everyone knows she doesn't have much of either. How can we, then, account for his choice of Emily? It's reasonable to argue that her social rank is the attraction because it's apparently the only attraction she has. As a man who likes to be the center of attention, and having no social rank of his own because he's a northerner and a laborer, it stands to reason that he doesn't like being considered inferior to the town's middle-class population. Thus, it is likely that Homer wants to raise his social status by associating with a woman from the upper class. In other words, Homer is a classist: he believes in the importance of social rank.

a   Find all the evidence in the story you can to show that Homer is motivated by classist ideology. For example, how is he trying to fit into Emily's class? Note, for instance:

     i   any mention of his appearance when he is with Emily,
     ii the principal activity in which they publicly engage, and
     iii the quality of the horse and buggy Homer rents.

  b If elevating his class status were Homer's only goal in courting Emily, how might his classism contribute to the couple's unhappiness if they married?

  c How might Emily's classism also contribute to the couple's unhappiness if they married?

5 *The community's classism*—The white community in which Emily lives apparently consists of middle-class and working-class people. Their attitude toward Emily is conflicted: at times they respect her social rank or sympathize with her situation; at times they seem jealous and are glad to see her brought down a peg or two. But both their favorable and unfavorable feelings about Emily result from their classism, from their belief that she is somehow superior to them because she is a member of the upper class.

  a Find all the evidence in the story you can to illustrate the community's classism.

  b Find textual evidence to show that their classist attitude, though based on a belief in the Griersons' social superiority, actually does Emily harm.

The portrayal of the upper class

A story that gives us Mr. Grierson, Emily Grierson, Emily's cousins from Alabama, and old lady Wyatt and her heirs as its only representatives of the upper class is not painting an attractive portrait of that class. These very negative characterizations—which make the ordinary townsfolk seem fairly harmless by comparison—insure that the story is not endorsing the classism it illustrates. List all the negative traits "A Rose for Emily" ascribes to the following upper-class characters:

1 Mr. Grierson,
2 Emily Grierson,
3 Emily's cousins from Alabama, and
4 old lady Wyatt and her heirs.

Focusing your essay

Based on the work we've done so far, I think you might safely focus your essay on the ways in which "A Rose for Emily" illustrates the damaging effects of classism. For it seems we can reasonably argue that classist ideology harms all of the story's main characters. Classism isolates both Mr. Grierson and Emily from the rest of the community. Classism deprives Emily of the chance to develop the interpersonal skills she needs to make a life for herself after her father's death. In fact, we might say that, given the extreme degree of Emily's isolation, classism helps drive her mad. Classism very probably plays a role in Homer Barron's death, both because it is probably his classist attitude toward social rank that inspired him to court her and because Emily's classist pride is probably a factor in her decision to kill him rather than let him humiliate her by deserting her.

Remember, as always, that you don't have to limit yourself to the analysis of the story I've offered you. For example, you might feel that Emily's classism is responsible for Homer's murder in a different way. Perhaps it isn't Homer's desertion she can't face but, rather, his desire to marry her. That is, when push comes to shove, maybe she can't bring herself to marry beneath her rank. Yet if she doesn't marry Homer he will leave her. The solution: she murders him and keeps his body in her bed so that she can still be with him without degrading herself by "marrying down." Or perhaps you might want to focus your essay, instead, on the community as a whole, in which case you might try to map the changes that occur over the course of the many decades during which the story unfolds. Does there seem to be less classism in Jefferson as time goes on, or does classism merely take different forms with the passage of time? Whatever your interpretation, be sure you understand the Marxist concepts you choose to employ, compose a clear statement of your thesis, and support your interpretation with adequate textual evidence.

Resisting classism: Interpreting "Don't Explain"

Jewelle Gomez's "Don't Explain" (1987; see Appendix E) is set in Boston in 1959, a period of relative prosperity for the white middle and upper classes, but a period of continued struggle for the working class, especially for working-class people of color, who worked hard for low wages and with little hope of finding better paying jobs. They are represented in the story by Letty, Delia, and the other African American women who work at the 411 Lounge, and by Terry and her friends, who clean office buildings at night.

We determined that the stories discussed earlier in this chapter are anti-capitalist or anticlassist because they show the evils of capitalism or classism and thereby encourage readers to reject those oppressive ideologies. "Don't Explain" encourages readers to reject classism, but you might have noticed that it does so in a different way. Instead of portraying the evils of classism, the story illustrates the virtues of an anticlassist attitude. Specifically, the tale: (1) gives us positive images of the oppressed, positive portrayals that work against stereotypes of the lower classes as lazy, undependable, unintelligent, and dishonorable; (2) gives us a main character, Letty, who herself displays anticlassist behavior, which serves as a positive model for us to follow; and (3) illustrates the importance of solidarity—of unity and mutual support—among members of the working class. Let's look at each of these elements in turn.

Positive portrayals of the working class

1   *Letty*—List all the textual evidence you can find that Letty has, among others, the following positive qualities.

    a   She is a very capable worker and knows her job very well.
    b   She is intelligent, as evidenced by her insights into her customers and the people with whom she works.
    c   She is kind-hearted and caring.

2   *Delia*—List all the textual evidence you can find that Delia has, among others, the following positive qualities.

    a   Although she has worked at the 411 Lounge for just a year, she has learned how to handle her job very well.
    b   There are potential dangers in working at the 411, but she has learned how to avoid them.
    c   She is sensitive to others and doesn't want to make anyone feel uncomfortable or hurt anyone's feelings.

3   *Terry*—List all the textual evidence you can find that Terry has, among others, the following positive qualities.

    a   She is kind-hearted.
    b   She is sensitive to the needs of others.

4   *Billie Holiday*—Billie Holiday grew up in an economically impoverished African American neighborhood. Despite her rise to fame and fortune, she was often treated as a second-class citizen because of her race. For example, in segregated areas of the country, Billie wasn't allowed to stay in the same hotels, eat in the same restaurants, or use the same public facilities as her white band members. As Letty recalls, however, neither Billie's fame nor the personal insecurity created by her painful experiences made the great singer deny her working-class roots.

    a   Find textual evidence that Billie still identifies with the working class.
    b   Find evidence that the story invites us to like this aspect of her personality.

Letty's anticlassist behavior

Because Letty is near the bottom of the socioeconomic ladder, we might expect that she would be tempted to look down on those who could be considered below her in some way, for example, the pimps and prostitutes (or "business" girls, as they're called in the story) who frequent the 411 Lounge. It is not unusual for the members of any socioeconomic class to try to boost their own self-importance by believing themselves superior to those they feel are below them. We might even say that classism feeds on people's need to feel superior. But Letty does not seem to have this need. She thinks well or ill of people based on their personal qualities, not on their social rank.

1   Find all the evidence in the story you can to support this claim.
2   Find textual evidence that the story invites us to share Letty's anticlassist attitude by portraying this attitude in a positive light.

The importance of working-class solidarity

One of the reasons why Marxist theory wants us to reject socioeconomic ideologies that pit individual against individual is that people at the bottom of the socioeconomic ladder suffer the most damage from those ideologies. The bank accounts of the very wealthy are not endangered by capitalist ideologies that emphasize the importance of "me" instead of "us," as competition, commodification, the American Dream, and rugged individualism do. Neither are the bank accounts of the very wealthy endangered by classism, even when it excludes from the "best" society those who've acquired a large bank balance only recently. Rather, it is the lower classes who are harmed by socio-economic ideologies that work against their members uniting together in a common cause. For any ideology that tells the lower classes it is right and natural to compete against one another for limited jobs and limited opportu-nities, any ideology that tells them to look down on those who fall slightly below them in social rank, is an ideology that helps keep the lower classes from working together to change the system and make it more just and equitable for those at the bottom.

From a Marxist perspective, then, the depiction of working-class solidarity in "Don't Explain" is an important part of the tale. Find the passages in the story that describe the following examples of working-class solidarity (some of which you may already have found in gathering textual evidence required earlier), and explain how the story encourages us to see these images of working-class solidarity in a positive light:

1   Letty's efforts to help Delia, rather than compete with her,
2   the respect and kindness Delia returns to Letty,
3   Letty's anticlassist attitude toward customers that some people would look down upon,
4   Billie Holiday's warmth toward the employees of the 411 Lounge,
5   Terry's desire to include Letty in her group, and
6   the gathering of working-class women at the home of Terry and Delia at the end of the story.

Focusing your essay

As we've seen throughout our exploration of "Don't Explain," the story rejects classist ideology and invites readers to do the same. If you draw on the textual evidence you've gathered above, you can focus your essay on the ways in which the story accomplishes this task. And the practice you gain here will help you recognize this kind of anticlassist text when you encounter it elsewhere.

Remember, as always, that you don't have to limit yourself to the analysis of the story I've offered you. For example, you might want to expand your argument to include a discussion of the attitude of Ari (Aristotle), the owner of the 411 Lounge, toward his employees; the vulnerability of the waitresses (who don't want to lose their jobs) to customers like Tip; and any other aspect of the story relevant to the waitresses' grace under pressure. For any element of "Don't Explain" that invites us to sympathize with its working-class characters or appreciate their positive qualities is part of the story's rejection of classist ideology. Whatever your interpretation, be sure you understand the Marxist concepts you choose to employ, compose a clear statement of your thesis, and support your interpretation with adequate textual evidence.

Learning when not to use Marxist concepts: Resisting the temptation to interpret "I started Early—Took my Dog"

Recognizing the absence of illustrations of capitalism

Emily Dickinson's "I started Early—Took my Dog" (c. 1862; see Appendix A) seems to offer us very little material that lends itself to a Marxist interpretation. We don't see any illustrations of capitalist ideology in the poem: there are no representations of competition, consumerism, or commodification, and no one seems to be pursing the American Dream. We might be inclined to say that the poem illustrates rugged individualism because the speaker is somewhat adventuresome. She's a woman alone who goes to a deserted spot with no protection beyond a dog that disappears from the poem after the first line, and she survives what seems to be a dangerous encounter with nature. However, I think the speaker's visit to the sea is better defined as an example of nonconformity, which is not the same as rugged individualism. For one thing, although she deliberately walks the beach alone, her dangerous encounter with nature is accidental and not goal-oriented. As we saw in the "Basic concepts" section of this chapter, to qualify as rugged individualism, one's nonconformity has to involve the deliberate pursuit of a goal not easily achieved, such as undertaking an untried, high-risk line of business or the rush for gold on the American frontier. If Dickinson's speaker has a goal in mind, she is certainly not conscious of it.

Recognizing the absence of illustrations of classism

Just as there are no illustrations of capitalism in Dickinson's poem, there do not seem to be any illustrations of classism either. In fact, we can't even be sure to what socioeconomic class the speaker belongs. That she's wearing an apron and a "simple Shoe" (l. 10) and is walking out of doors without an escort might indicate, in a literary work written in the mid-nineteenth century as this one was, that the speaker is not a member of the upper class. First, she's wearing common, unadorned clothing. Second, during this period it was deemed inappropriate, at the very least, for a lady of high social rank to venture out-side to a lonely spot without a proper companion, such as a female friend, a relative, a friend of the family, or some other chaperone. (Her dog would not have been considered an adequate chaperone!) Yet we can't build an inter-pretation of the poem simply on the likelihood that the speaker is not a member of the upper class. For none of the action of the poem seems directly related to her socioeconomic class, whatever that class might be.

Resisting the temptation of large/small or high/low imagery

Despite the absence of capitalist and classist illustrations in "I started Early—Took my Dog," many students want to use Marxist concepts to read the poem as an illustration of the upper class's oppression of the lower class. And they derive this interpretation from the fact that the frigates in the poem, which are described as occupying "the Upper Floor" (l. 5), tower over the speaker, whom the frigates "[p]resum[e] … to be a Mouse" (l. 7)—that is, a much smaller, dependent creature who is located low to the ground. Did you have that impulse, too? It's a common response among students new to Marxist theory to view the juxtaposition of a large object with a small object, or an object raised up high with an object placed down low, as a symbolic representation of the relationship between the upper class and the lower class.

However, unless there's something specific in the poem, or in the theory we're using, to justify such a symbolic interpretation, we're making a symbolic leap, an unjustified symbolic connection, which we discussed in Chapter 2, "Using concepts from reader-response theory to understand our own literary interpretations." That is, we're arguing for a symbolic interpretation without enough evidence that the symbolic connection we think exists actually does exist. I can just as easily argue, for example, that the big ships and the little mouse symbolize the triumph of good (the ships) over evil (the mouse), the triumph of the country girl (the mouse) in resisting the temptations of the big city (the ships), the eternal David-and-Goliath battle between the underdog (the mouse) and the odds-on winner (the ships), or any other big/little, high/low symbolic opposition that occurs to me. In short, there is nothing in the poem or in our Marxist concepts to justify choosing one of these symbolic interpretations of the frigates and the mouse over another, which means we are not justified in choosing any of them.

Choosing a different poem

If you want to use Marxist concepts to interpret a Dickinson poem, you'll have to find a poem that allows you to do so. If you want to examine the attitudes about class and social rank that are clearly expressed elsewhere in Dickinson's work, you might analyze Poem 401, "What soft Cherubic Creatures" (c. 1862). This poem criticizes the hypocrisy and superficiality of the high-ranking gentlewomen of Dickinson's time and thus lends itself well to a Marxist interpretation. Or you might analyze Poem 457. "Sweet—safe—Houses" (c. 1862), which criticizes wealthy people who use their money to insulate themselves from life's most fundamental realities. Or instead, you might analyze what seems to be the anticapitalist attitude expressed in Poem 709, "Publication—is the Auction" (c. 1863). This poem can be read as an argument against commodification, which is a fundamental capitalist ideology. Whatever Dickinson poem you interpret, be sure you understand the Marxist concepts you choose to employ, compose a clear statement of your thesis, and support your interpretation with adequate textual evidence.

Food for further thought

Thinking it over

If you've worked through all of the interpretation exercises offered in this chapter, you should feel quite familiar with the basic approaches to understanding literature provided by concepts from Marxist theory. Specifically, we've seen how Marxist concepts can be used to analyze

1   literary works that are anticapitalist in that they illustrate the harmful effects of capitalist ideologies (our example: "Everyday Use"),
2   literary works that are anticapitalist in that they illustrate the harmful effects of one particular capitalist ideology, for example, the American Dream (our example: "The Battle Royal"),
3   literary works that are anticlassist in that they illustrate the harmful effects of classism (our example: "A Rose for Emily"),
4   literary works that are anticlassist in that they provide positive images of working-class people, images that operate against lower-class stereotypes, and/or admirable characters who, themselves, display anticlassist behavior (our example: "Don't Explain"), and
5   literary works whose juxtaposition of large/small or high/low images will tempt us to misinterpret them by imposing a Marxist framework that the literary work does not justify (our example: "I started Early—Took my Dog").

At this point, you may be wondering if some literary works illustrate capitalist or classist ideologies *without* revealing their harmful effects. In other words, don't some literary works reinforce capitalist or classist ideologies by depicting them as harmless or even beneficial? Yes, there are literary works that, whether they intend to or not, reinforce capitalist or classist ideologies in just this way. And in such cases, we would use concepts from Marxist theory to expose this flaw in the work in question, for from a Marxist perspective this aspect of the literary text would be a flaw.

The promotion of capitalist or classist ideologies in a literary work, however, is often rather difficult to spot because, in these cases, the socioeconomic system depicted usually forms little more than a distant backdrop to give historical color to a tale of action or romance or tragedy. For example, in Mary Shelley's novel *Frankenstein* (1818), the tragic experiences of protagonist Victor Frankenstein, the young scientist who creates the monster, occur against the backdrop of a class system that the novel reinforces by depicting the upper-class characters as intelligent, honorable, and generous. Characters from classes beneath them are portrayed in a positive light only to the extent that they believe in the class system and admire those above them. However, many readers don't even notice the classism the novel reinforces because their attention is so taken by Victor's personal trials and tribulations.

Perhaps an additional example will help. Given the emphasis Marxist theory places on our being able to see when oppressive socioeconomic ideologies are operating in a literary work, we might argue that Faulkner's "A Rose for Emily" is also flawed, though to a much lesser degree than *Frankenstein*. Certainly, "A Rose for Emily" doesn't hide the classism it illustrates. The characters' classism does not merely form a backdrop to the story but is clearly responsible for most of the story's action. Nevertheless, we might argue that this dimension of the tale is overshadowed by the drama of Emily's descent into madness and the mystery of Homer's disappearance. And for a student of Marxist theory, anything that seriously interferes with readers' perceptions of the oppressive socioeconomic ideologies illustrated in a literary work is a flaw in that work.

Generally speaking, then, at least in the case of literature that was written in the last few hundred years and that we're likely to find in most classrooms, when a literary work seems to deliberately draw our attention to capitalist or classist ideologies, its purpose is usually to show how these ideologies harm the characters portrayed. In other words, one of the purposes of such a literary text is to criticize the oppressive socioeconomic ideologies it represents. And only in texts like these is it relatively easy for students new to Marxist theory to spot these ideologies at work. That's why our study of Marxist concepts in this book focuses on literature in which the socioeconomic ideologies represented are not buried in the background.

Finally, Marxist concepts can be used in service of the theoretical approaches discussed in the following chapters of this book. For example, Marxist concepts can be helpful when we want to understand how classism, the American Dream, or any of the other ideologies described in this chapter oppresses members of a particular group—a political minority—by denying them equal access to education, employment, housing, and other sources of socioeconomic power. So a Marxist understanding of socioeconomic oppression can be helpful even when our primary goal is to use feminist; lesbian, gay, or queer; African American; or postcolonial concepts to understand a literary work.

Marxist theory and cultural criticism

We can also use concepts from Marxist theory for the purposes of cultural criticism. That is, we can use Marxist concepts to help us analyze the cultural messages sent, whether deliberately or not, by the everyday productions of the culture in which we live, such as movies, games, television shows, song lyrics, toys, and other productions of popular culture discussed in Chapter 1. Indeed, those cultural productions that in some way represent human behavior—that have characters and a plot—can be analyzed using concepts from Marxist theory just as we use those concepts to analyze literary works. An understanding of classism, consumerism, and the American Dream, for example, can offer us insights into the classic "rags-to-riches" film romance *Pretty Woman* (directed by Garry Marshall, 1990), in which good-hearted prostitute Vivian Ward (Julia Roberts) and lonely, self-made corporate raider Edward Lewis (Richard Gere) find true love and a happy future together.

Too busy to give adequate time and attention to his romantic relationships—the most recent of which has just ended badly—Edward decides to hire the lovely, free-spirited Vivian to be his "beck-and-call-girl" for one week in order to ensure himself a trouble-free companion for the various social events he must attend in pursuit of his latest corporate takeover. Over the course of the film, Vivian gets Edward to loosen up, slow down, and smell the roses. Instead of destroying his latest corporate target, the fatherly Mr. Morse (Ralph Bellamy), Edward saves the man's company and goes into business with him. Analogously, Edward gets Vivian to broaden her horizons and have faith in her ability to achieve a better life. By the end of the film, Vivian has decided to quit her life on the street—she has even rejected Edward's offer to keep her as his mistress—and get her high school equivalency diploma. Luckily, Edward catches up with Vivian before she leaves town and offers her the "happily ever after" they both want.

Part of the charm of this engaging movie lies in the anticlassist cultural work it performs—in this case, its negative depiction of classism—which it accomplishes largely through its negative portrayals of classist characters who get what's coming to them: for example, the two rude saleswomen who mistreat Vivian, the snobbish women at the polo match, and Edward's obnoxious lawyer, Phil Stuckey (Jason Alexander). A clear anticlassist message like this one becomes even more powerful when accompanied by the positive portrayal the movie offers of lower-class characters—specifically of Vivian and Kit De Luca (Laura San Giocomo), Vivian's roommate, best friend, and fellow prostitute—and of characters like hotel manager Mr. Thompson (Hector Elizando) and Edward himself, who become increasingly sympathetic as they become increasingly appreciative of Vivian. Equally helpful in sending an anticlassist message is, of course, Edward's willingness to ignore class lines and marry for love. It means nothing to him that others will think he has married "beneath him," and the characterization of Vivian encourages us to realize that he will *not* be marrying "beneath him" in any meaningful way. From a Marxist perspective, so far, so good.

What cultural messages does *Pretty Woman* send, however, in terms of consumerism and the American Dream, two destructive capitalist ideologies represented in the movie? Concerning consumerism, I think the answer is easy to find if you think of the movie's humorous and seductive depiction of the fun of shopping for expensive clothing with a rich man's credit card in your pocket and of the romantic purposes served by Vivian's gorgeous new designer wardrobe. Indeed, during Vivian's memorable shopping spree—which is among the most entertaining scenes in the film—consumerism appears to be an innocent good time had by all or, at worst, harmless. In fact, at the end of her shopping spree, dressed in her new makeover apparel, we see yet another pay-off of purchasing power: Vivian's face-to-face triumph over the two rude saleswomen is so satisfying that it risks making their classism seem unimportant, just a backdrop for Vivian's consumerist enjoyment.

As for the American Dream, the movie's cultural message certainly seems to be that the Dream is beneficial and equally available to everyone. Look what it did for the self-made Edward Lewis, whose business acumen and determination took him from an impoverished childhood to the lifestyle of the rich and famous. And isn't Vivian living her own version of the American Dream, a spin-off of the traditional female version of the Dream? For she will become Edward's wife as a result of her refusal to become his kept woman, as a result, that is, of her determination to hold out for, as she says, "the fairy tale." Finally, look what the American Dream does even for Kit: one shot of the Dream and Kit De Luca actively pursues vocational training as a beautician, a trade that will provide her with a reliable income, geographic mobility, and respectability.

A Marxist cultural critic might argue, then, that *Pretty Woman*'s cultural message is mixed: the movie sends an effective anticlassist message, but it also sends destructive pro-capitalist messages. And the probability that most viewers will not recognize the film's pro-capitalist messages as destructive, or even as pro-capitalist, makes those messages more harmful. For the feeling that we're being entertained, that there's nothing we need to guard against, allows *Pretty Woman* to easily reinforce, whether it intends to do so or not, what most viewers already believe: the American Dream is just wonderful, and buying "lots of stuff"—especially lots of expensive stuff—is just fun.

★★★

Remember, it's natural to feel a bit uncertain when we encounter a new theory—a new way of looking at ourselves and our world—that may call into question many of the beliefs that have been pressed upon us, and that we've accepted uncritically, for most of our lives. Uncertainty is an unavoidable part of learning and growing. Keep in mind, too, that others may disagree with your opinions. Individuals often disagree in their interpretations of literature, popular culture, or everyday experiences, even when drawing upon the same Marxist concepts for their analyses. The keys to a good interpretation—besides intellectual curiosity and an open mind—are a clear understanding of the Marxist concepts you've chosen to use and strong evidence to support your analysis.

Taking the next step

Questions for further practice

1   How might we argue that Arthur Miller's play *Death of a Salesman* (1949) is anticapitalist in that it portrays how the "little man," embodied in protagonist Willy Loman, is crushed by the destructive forces of American capitalism? For example, after working for the same firm his whole life, how is Willy mistreated by his employer? What role does the employer's unquestioning endorsement of competition and commodification play in his attitude toward Willy? How does Willy's unquestioning admiration for rugged individualism keep him from realizing that his brother Ben acquired his wealth through, almost certainly, unethical means? Especially important, how does Willy's unquestioning belief in the American Dream contribute to his failures?

2   Mrs. Dora Ellsworth, in Langston Hughes' short story "The Blues I'm Playing" (1934), has everything money can buy. The one thing she wants that she can't buy is artistic or musical talent. How does the story show that, in financially aiding Miss Oceola Jones and other young artists and musicians, Mrs. Ellsworth is really making a kind of purchase—that she is commodifying art, music, and the young people who create it? For example, how do we know that Mrs. Ellsworth wants the sign-exchange value associated with being a patroness of the arts? Indeed, how does the story suggest that her commodification of art, music, and her young protégés is related to her emotional "disconnect" from them? Or you might consider how the story is anticlassist through its positive portrayal of Oceola's anticlassist behavior and its negative portrayal of Mrs. Ellsworth's classism.

3   In Kate Chopin's novel *The Awakening* (1899), protagonist Edna Pontellier goes to great lengths to create a life for herself beyond the conventions imposed by society in general and by her husband Léonce in particular. How might we argue that Edna, though she wouldn't use these words, is seeking an alternative to capitalism? In other words, how is she seeking a less money-oriented life in which she is not commodified (can you find the ways in which Léonce commodifies her?) and in which she is not obligated by social convention to commodify possessions and people as Léonce and his circle do? Note, too, how Edna's refusal to commodify people includes a refusal to choose her friends based on their social standing, so she is also turning her back on classism.

4   How does Leslie Marmon Silko's "Lullaby" (1974) illustrate the economic exploitation of the working poor through its portrayal of Chato, Ayah, and their children? Consider, for example, the ways in which Chato has been exploited by the rancher who employs him, the abject poverty in which the family must live, and the indifference of the

authorities (among others, the officials who take Danny and Ella away from their parents) to the family's plight. In addition, consider the fact that Jimmie, the older son, lost his life fighting for a nation that allows the capitalist exploitation of families like his to persist.

5   Use concepts from Marxist theory to help you interpret some aspect of a movie, television show, song lyric, cartoon, video game, or any other production of popular culture that you find interesting and that you think might lend itself to a Marxist interpretation. For example, are stereotypes of or negative references to individuals from the lower classes included in this cultural production? Is the upper class idealized in some manner? (Both of these questions refer to ways in which your chosen cultural production might illustrate classism.) Is the American Dream, commodification, competition, rugged individualism, or any other capitalist ideology idealized in some way? Or does this cultural production seem to offer alternatives to classism and capitalism? Based on your observations, what cultural work does your chosen cultural production do relevant to Marxist theory? Specifically, does it seem to be telling us that classism is natural or acceptable? Does it seem to be telling us that destructive capitalist ideologies are natural or acceptable? Or does it seem to illustrate the harmful qualities of these values, values to which Marxism is opposed? Be sure to offer evidence from your chosen production to support your ideas.

Suggestions for further reading

Bender, Frederic L., ed. *Karl Marx: The Essential Writings.* 2nd ed. Boulder, CO: Westview Press, 1986. (See, especially, "Essentials of the Theory," 164–207; "The Commodity," 327–34; "Exchange and Money," 346–48; and "The General Formula for Capital," 349–54.)

Eagleton, Terry. *Marxism and Literary Criticism.* Berkeley: University of California Press, 1976. (See, especially, "Preface," vi–viii; and "Literature and History," 1–19.)

hooks, bell. *Where We Stand: Class Matters.* New York: Routledge, 2000.

Tyson, Lois. "Marxist Criticism." *Critical Theory Today: A User-Friendly Guide.* 2nd ed. New York: Routledge, 2006. 53–81.

Veblen, Thorstein. *The Theory of the Leisure Class: An Economic Study of Institutions.* 1899. New York: Viking, 1965. (See, especially, "Conspicuous Leisure," 35–67; "Conspicuous Consumption," 68–101; and "Dress as an Expression of the Pecuniary Culture," 167–87.)

Weber, Max. *The Protestant Ethic and the Spirit of Capitalism.* 1904–5. Trans. Talcott Parsons. New York: Charles Scribner's Sons, 1958. (See, especially, "The Spirit of Capitalism," 47–78; and "Asceticism and the Spirit of Capitalism," 155–83.)

Chapter 6

Using concepts from feminist theory to understand literature

Why should we learn about feminist theory?

As we saw in Chapter 4, psychoanalytic theory asks us to examine the ways in which our personal identity is formed by our early emotional experience within the family. In Chapter 5 we saw that Marxist theory asks us to examine the ways in which our personal identity is formed by the socioeconomic system in which we live. Feminist theory asks us to examine, instead, the ways in which our personal identity is formed by our culture's definitions of what it means to be a man or a woman. For from a feminist perspective, our experience of both the family and the socioeconomic system in which we live depends to a large extent on our sex: on the ways in which men and women are treated differently and on the way men are socialized to be masculine and women are socialized to be feminine.

Specifically, in most cultures men occupy most or all positions of power, which is why those cultures are called patriarchies or patriarchal cultures. For the word *patriarchy*, broadly defined, refers to any society in which men hold all or most of the power. In a patriarchy, women suffer varying degrees of oppression depending on, among other things, their race, ethnicity, socioeconomic class, religion, sexual orientation, and the country or region in which they live. Feminism, therefore, seeks to understand the ways in which women are oppressed—socially, economically, politically, and psychologically—in order to reduce, if not eliminate their oppression. Ideally, feminism would like to achieve a society in which women and men are encouraged to fulfill their full potential as human beings regardless of the extent to which their abilities and inclinations differ from traditional (patriarchal) definitions of femininity and masculinity.

Of course, patriarchal ideology (the patriarchal system of beliefs and assumptions) is difficult for most of us to recognize clearly and consistently because our everyday experience is so saturated with it. We have become so accustomed to patriarchal ideology that it often seems invisible. However, its invisibility makes this ideology all the more dangerous: it's easier to address a problem we can see than a problem that pretends it does not exist. In addition, the word *feminist*—which, for many years, was a target of ridicule by patriarchal leaders in politics, the media, and other social institutions—remains an unpopular term among many people today. The result is that many anti-patriarchal women and men still feel uncomfortable identifying themselves as feminists or might not even recognize that they *are* feminists. I agree

This unfortunate state of affairs should not surprise us, however, given the amount of misinformation about feminism still in circulation. To cite just one example, it is still generally assumed that feminism is directly opposed to family values. The fact is, however, that feminists continue to lead the struggle for better family policies, such as nutrition and healthcare for mothers and children; parental leave; high-quality, affordable daycare; the provision of shelters for battered women and their children; and the like. So if you need help, as many of us still do, adjusting to the idea that you're a feminist, you can start by thinking of feminism as a form of human-rights activism, which it certainly is. feminism = human rights act

We can start to use feminist theory to understand literature by asking the following question about whatever literary work we want to interpret: Do the characters conform to patriarchal gender roles? To choose the simplest example, is the role of the strong, rational protector given to a male character while the role of the submissive, emotional nurturer is given to a female character? Or to put the question another way, are the female characters depicted according to patriarchal stereotypes of women? These include, for example, virginal angels and selfless caregivers (which are patriarchal stereotypes of women who conform to traditional gender role) as well as nags, gossips, seductresses, and "bitches" (which are patriarchal stereotypes of women who violate the traditional gender role).

When a literary text portrays characters who conform to patriarchal gender roles or depicts female characters as patriarchal stereotypes, we say that the text illustrates patriarchal ideology. That is, the text shows us what patriarchal ideology "looks like," so to speak. Now, sometimes a literary text illustrates patriarchal ideology because it approves of that ideology. For example, a story or a play might positively portray characters who conform to traditional gender roles and negatively portray characters who violate those roles. Such a literary work would be considered a patriarchal text, which, from a feminist perspective, means that it promotes damaging beliefs about women and men. But keep in mind that a literary work can illustrate patriarchal ideology in order to show us what's *wrong* with that ideology. For example, a novel or a poem might show us that the characters who conform to traditional gender roles are harmed by those roles, or it might show us the negative effects of patriarchal stereotyping. In both these cases, the literary work would be considered an antipatriarchal text, which, from a feminist perspective, means that it promotes accurate perceptions of women and men. Another, though less common kind of antipatriarchal text is one that offers positive portrayals of characters who violate traditional gender roles, for example, female characters who are independent, who think and act for themselves in admirable ways, or male characters who are admirably sensitive and nurturing. Our interpretation exercises, which follow the "Basic concepts" section later, include examples of these various kinds of patriarchal and antipatriarchal texts.

It's often difficult, however, to tell for sure what a literary work wants us to think about the gender roles its characters embody. Does the text want us to admire or reject its patriarchal characters? Does the text want us to admire or reject its antipatriarchal characters? Even experienced readers often disagree about a text's attitude toward its characters' gender roles. So don't be upset if you find it difficult to figure out whether a literary work is patriarchal or antipatriarchal. At this point, you may have to be content, at times, with determining what patriarchal or antipatriarchal ideology the text illustrates, without being certain whether or not the text endorses that ideology. So let's start with a brief look at the patriarchal ideologies that feminist theory considers most fundamental to our understanding of patriarchal oppression. Although it's important that you read through the "Basic concepts" section that follows, don't be too concerned if you don't feel you thoroughly understand every one. You'll begin to understand these concepts much better when we use them, later in this chapter, to help us interpret the literary texts that appear at the end of this book. And you'll see that these fundamental feminist concepts can help us understand other works of literature as well.

Remember, too, that I'm offering you my own literary analyses in the interpretation exercises provided later in this chapter. You might use the same feminist concepts I use but come up with different interpretations of your own. If you disagree with any of the analyses I offer in these exercises, don't be afraid to look in the literary work in question for evidence that will support your viewpoint. A literary work can often support a number of different interpretations even when readers are using concepts from the same theory.

Basic concepts

Note that the basic concepts listed here are all examples of patriarchal ideologies that have existed for centuries and that are considered right and proper by many people. Feminism didn't invent these ideologies. Rather, feminism opposes them. For according to feminist theory, these ideologies are responsible for the oppression of women throughout the world and for the failure of most women and men to live up to their full human potential. Therefore, the definition of each patriarchal ideology is followed by feminist theory's argument against it.

Patriarchy

As we saw earlier, a patriarchy is any society in which men hold all or most of the power. Usually, a patriarchy gives men power by promoting traditional

[margin handwritten notes: "Sometimes diff. to understand purpose of text" and "brainwash"] gender roles. Patriarchal men and women believe that anyone who violates traditional gender roles is in some way unnatural, unhealthy, or even immoral. For example, in the United States, the patriarchal belief that assertiveness in a woman is unattractive, even unnatural, makes it difficult for many Americans to feel comfortable with women in leadership roles of any kind—from a woman taking charge of the White House to a woman asking a man out on the first date.

In contrast, feminist theory tells us that socializing women and men to conform to traditional gender roles means limiting people's options, denying them the choice to follow the path that best fulfills their potential. Therefore, patriarchal programming is unnatural, unhealthy, and unethical.

Traditional gender roles

According to traditional gender roles, men are naturally rational, strong, protective, and decisive. In contrast, traditional gender roles define women as naturally emotional (which, in a patriarchy, usually means irrational), weak, nurturing, and submissive.

Feminist theory points out, however, that these gender roles are produced by patriarchy rather than by nature. And they have been used to justify many inequities, which still occur today. For example, women today are still excluded from equal access to leadership and decision-making positions in the family as well as in the world of business and politics. Men still tend to receive higher wages than women for doing the same job. And traditional gender roles still tell women, among other things, that they are not cut out for careers in areas such as mathematics and engineering and that, regardless of the job a wife holds outside the home, she has primary responsibility for the children and for domestic chores.

The objectification of women

From a patriarchal perspective, women who adhere to traditional gender roles are considered "good girls." They are put on pedestals and *idealized* as pure, angelic creatures whose sense of self consists mainly or entirely of their usefulness to their husbands, fathers, or brothers. In contrast, women who violate traditional gender roles are thought of as "bad girls," especially if they violate the rules of sexual conduct for patriarchal women, such as dressing or behaving in a manner that could be considered sexually provocative. Patriarchal men sleep with and then discard "bad girls"—who are relegated to the role of *sex objects*—but they marry "good girls" because only a "good girl" is considered worthy of bearing a man's name and children.

Feminist theory points out, however, that both "good girls" and "bad girls" are *objectified* by patriarchy. That is, they are not viewed as independent human beings with their own goals, needs, and desires. Rather, they are evaluated only in terms of their usefulness to patriarchal men. They are viewed only as patriarchal objects. If you consider again the examples of patriarchal stereotypes listed earlier, you'll see that they all fall under the "good girl"/"bad girl" categorization of women. Virginal angels and selfless nurturers are examples of patriarchal "good girls"; nags, gossips, seductresses, and "bitches" are examples of patriarchal "bad girls." So even those patriarchal stereotypes that appear to be "positive," such as virginal angels and selfless nurturers, are damaging because they reduce women to their roles as patriarchal objects and suggest that "good" women aspire to nothing else.

Sexism

Patriarchy is based on sexism, which is the belief that women are innately (that is, by nature) inferior to men: less intelligent, less rational, less courageous, and so forth. For this reason, sexist individuals believe that traditional gender roles—which cast men as decision-makers and women as dutiful followers—are right and natural because men's innate superiority dictates that they should be in charge, not only in the family but in business, politics, and all other important social institutions. Although in everyday language the term *sexist* is usually reserved for a person who expresses his or her patriarchal beliefs with particular arrogance, self-righteousness, or anger, the term really applies to any person who holds sexist beliefs as well as to any practice, policy, or custom that disadvantages women only because they are women. Thus the terms *patriarchal* and *sexist* are more or less synonymous, although the term *sexist* is usually considered insulting while, at least for patriarchal men and women, the term *patriarchal* is not.

In order to oppose sexism, many feminist thinkers differentiate between our *sex*, which is our biological makeup as female or male (for example, our sex organs and body chemistry), and our *gender*, which is our cultural programming as feminine or masculine (for example, our behaving as "sweet little things" or "macho-men"). Feminism argues that while we may be born female or male, we are not born feminine or masculine. Rather, it is society that decides which behaviors are considered feminine, and therefore appropriate only to females, and which behaviors are considered masculine, and therefore appropriate only to males. As Simone de Beauvoir argues in her groundbreaking book, *The Second Sex* (1949), "One is not born a woman; one becomes one." In short, women wear pointy shoes with high heels not because they have pointy feet and need help reaching the top shelf of the cupboard, but because patriarchy tells them such footwear is feminine. And such footwear is considered feminine because, among other things, it makes women less mobile than men and therefore, in appearance at least, less able to compete.

The "cult of 'true womanhood'"

In the nineteenth century, Victorian patriarchy promoted the "cult of 'true womanhood,'" which idealized what it called the "true woman," a concept that still influences patriarchal thinking today. The "true woman," who fulfilled her patriarchal gender role in every way, was defined as fragile, submissive, and sexually pure. Her proper sphere was the home; she would not venture beyond that sphere because to do so would be considered unwomanly. Women who had these characteristics were idealized and considered worthy of every form of masculine protection and gallantry. Today, this feminine ideal survives in, for example, various versions of the "helpless female," whose abilities are limited to such "womanly" domains as the cultivation of personal beauty, cooking, and home fashions and who makes men feel, in contrast, capable, powerful, and in control.

As African American feminists have pointed out, however, the Victorian definition of the "true woman" excluded African American women and poor women of all races whose survival required hard physical labor and who, because their jobs took them out of the home, were vulnerable to rape and to sexual exploitation in the workplace. In other words, a woman whose racial or economic situation forced her to perform physical labor and made her the victim of sexual predators was considered unwomanly and therefore unworthy of protection from those who exploited her. Also, because the "cult of 'true womanhood'" originated as a white cultural ideal, women of color, no matter how feminine their attire or behavior, were generally devalued, if not entirely excluded from the definition, on racial grounds. Today, the survival of this kind of feminine ideal excludes poor women of all races whose survival requires them to be tough, assertive, or in any way "unfeminine." Such women are often stereotyped as loud, brassy, promiscuous, and unattractive to men except as sexual objects. And the devaluation of women of color has persisted wherever the definition of feminine beauty has been based on an Anglo-Saxon ideal.

There are, of course, additional patriarchal ideologies that feminism exposes and additional concepts that feminism offers to counteract patriarchal thinking. However, these are enough to get us started using feminist theory to interpret literature. Let's begin our interpretation exercises by analyzing Ralph Ellison's "The Battle Royal," a story that gives us a straightforward illustration of a form of patriarchal ideology that most readers find objectionable and that the story itself clearly finds objectionable as well.

Interpretation exercises

Rejecting the objectification of women: Interpreting "The Battle Royal"

Although Ralph Ellison's "The Battle Royal" (1952; see Appendix C) is concerned primarily with racial issues in the post-World-War-II south, in which the story is set, there is one passage in the text that lends itself readily to a feminist analysis: the passage that revolves around the exotic dancer hired to entertain the white civic leaders. Though brief, this passage illustrates patriarchal ideology so clearly, so negatively, and with such emotional intensity that it's well worth our attention.

Because feminist concepts help us develop the habit of noticing how characters behave in terms of traditional gender roles, you might have observed that the whole scene in the hotel ballroom is one in which the white civic leaders display symbols of their male power through their indulgence in what patriarchy calls "masculine" pleasures. It is through the story's negative portrayal of these pleasures that we can see the text's rejection of patriarchal ideology. And as the white men's enjoyment of the exotic dancer is depicted as the most objectionable of their pleasures, we can see that the patriarchal ideology most under attack in this story is the objectification of women. In order to see how "The Battle Royal" achieves this effect, we'll need to examine: (1) its representation of "masculine" pleasures in general; (2) its depiction of the white leaders' behavior toward the exotic dancer; (3) its portrayal of the dancer herself; and (4) its depiction of the reaction of the young black men to the dancer.

The portrayal of "masculine" pleasures

The party in the hotel ballroom is referred to in the story as a "smoker," which means a men-only gathering for the purpose of pursuing pleasures that wives and sweethearts wouldn't enjoy and that men wouldn't want them to see. At this particular smoker, the men indulge in a number of patriarchal-male pleasures. Find the specific textual evidence that shows us how each of the pleasures listed below is portrayed.

1   Smoking is a traditional masculine pleasure.

   a   What do the men smoke?
   b   What are the effects of the smoke on the air in the room?
   c   What kind of emotional atmosphere does the smoke create?

2   Drinking is a traditional masculine pleasure.

   a   What are the men drinking?
   b   How much are they drinking?
   c   What effect does their consumption of alcohol have on them?

3   Watching a fight is also a traditional masculine pleasure. How does the battle royal show us the darkest side possible of this form of entertainment?
4   How is each of these pleasures—including the fact that the party is held in the ballroom of the best hotel in town—a symbol of masculine power for these white men?

The white leaders' behavior toward the exotic dancer

Of all the patriarchal-male pleasures represented in the story, the one that is most often associated with a smoker—and most often associated with male power and privilege—is the exotic dancer, the stripper who, by the time the reader sees her, has already taken off every stitch of clothing and is about to begin to dance. Note that she is not even wearing the usual minimal covering associated with strippers: the "pasties" and "g-string."

1   How does the dancer's complete nudity heighten our sense of her vulnerability and the white men's sense of their own power?
2   How do most of the white men behave toward her? Find specific textual evidence.
3   How is their parading her before the young black men a form of male competition, and how does it show that they consider her a symbol of their male power?
4   How does all of this data show us that the white men have objectified the dancer, that they do not see her as a human being?
5   How does this depiction of the white leaders invite us to reject the patriarchal ideology they represent?

The portrayal of the exotic dancer

Note how the dancer is described: her hair, her makeup, her frozen smile, and the expression in her eyes as she begins to dance and later as the men toss her in the air.

1   Does the dancer like her job? How do we know that she doesn't?
2   How is she trying to insulate herself emotionally from what she is doing and from the men who have hired her? Find specific textual evidence.
3   If she doesn't like this kind of work, why might she be doing it? (Consider the limited educational and occupational opportunities available to women in the time and place in which the story is set. How might a beautiful woman in need of money be drawn into such a situation?)
4   How does this depiction of the dancer invite us to feel sorry for her rather than blame her? (Keep in mind that, even if the dancer liked her work, patriarchal ideology would still be responsible because it is patriarchal ideology that tells women their value lies in their physical beauty, as defined by patriarchy, and in their appeal to men.)

The reaction of the young black men to the exotic dancer

Look closely at the scene in which the black youths brought in for the battle royal are forced to look at the exotic dancer. Find the specific textual evidence that answers the following questions.

1   How do the young black men react to seeing this naked white woman?
2   How do we know that the young men are well aware of the danger they are in if they show their desire? In other words, how do we know that they are well aware of the dancer's role as the white men's sex object and possession?
3   In addition, note the complex reaction of the narrator when he sees the exotic dancer. Describe his conflicted response (his opposing impulses toward her).

4   Explain how the narrator's responses can be understood if we realize that he is experiencing the dancer in terms of the two reactions to women patriarchy allows men to have:

a   men are supposed to protect women, but
b   if the woman in question is a "bad girl," patriarchal ideology invites men to use her as a sex object and hold her in contempt.

Focusing your essay

Given the textual data you've collected, you should be able to focus your essay on the ways in which the story invites us to reject patriarchal ideology—that is, on the ways in which "The Battle Royal" is an antipatriarchal text. Specifically, the story attacks the patriarchal ideology that it is natural, and therefore acceptable, for men to use women as sex objects, as tokens of their male power. The dancer's numb state, followed by her fear and the obvious danger of rape; the very negative portrayal of the white men who hired her and who objectify her; and the confusion, fear, and anger of the young black men who are forced to look at her all testify to the story's rejection of the patriarchal ideology it illustrates. It's as if the text were saying, "Look at this! Isn't it terrible?" And because "The Battle Royal" does not describe the erotic dancer in a sustained sensual manner, the story does not run too great a risk of creating in its readers the very attitude it seeks to condemn, as some depictions of women as sex objects unintentionally do.

Remember, of course, that you do not have to limit yourself to the analysis of the story I've offered you. You might, for example, include a discussion of the self-contradictions in patriarchal ideology that are revealed in the story. After all, the white men are all leading citizens—doctors, lawyers, bankers, judges, teachers, and the like—in the post-World-War-II south, in which the story is set, and such men were expected to uphold the patriarchal values of hearth and home. The kinds of men these characters represent would have wives and children and would hold in their hands the welfare of the town as well as the welfare of their families. Yet the same patriarchal ideology that demands they be strong, rational decision-makers also justifies their behaving like sex-crazed brutes. For it is a patriarchal belief that men are born with more sex-drive than women and that it is acceptable to sexually exploit "bad girls" because "bad girls" don't deserve to be treated with consideration. Whatever your interpretation, be sure you understand the feminist concepts you choose to employ, compose a clear statement of your thesis, and support your interpretation with adequate textual evidence.

Resisting patriarchal ideology: Interpreting "Don't Explain"

As we just saw, "The Battle Royal" is antipatriarchal in that it illustrates patriarchal ideology in a way that invites us to reject that ideology. Jewelle

Gomez's story "Don't Explain" (1987; see Appendix E) is antipatriarchal in a different way: it illustrates *resistance* to patriarchal ideology in a manner that endorses such resistance. The story accomplishes this task by providing us with *positive* portrayals of women who do not conform to traditional gender roles and who do not fit the white patriarchal definition of the "true woman."

"Don't Explain" is set in Boston in 1959, a time when the pressure to conform to patriarchal gender roles was quite strong and few people saw anything wrong with that. It was also a time when the patriarchal feminine ideal—the 1950s' version of the "true woman"—was limited to white women who had Anglo-Saxon features and were completely fulfilled by being stay-at-home wives and mothers. Women who conformed to this ideal would never appear in public without the appropriate feminine attire of the period: a dress or skirt and blouse, stockings, feminine shoes (usually high heels), makeup, and a feminine hair-do. And of course, the "true woman" of the 1950s was married to a man who could afford to have her stay home. So strong was this feminine ideal that many women of color and poor white women tried to conform to it, despite the fact that racial bias and economic necessity would never allow them to fully "measure up" to the ideal. After all, coming as close to the ideal as possible was considered better than abandoning it altogether, and many women therefore made an effort to conform in whatever ways they could, even if they were able to make that effort only in the areas of feminine attire and feminine behavior.

So what did patriarchal America think of women whose race, socioeconomic class, and/or sexual orientation meant they had to fend for themselves in a workplace that exploited women by confining them to low-paying, insecure jobs where they were vulnerable to sexual harassment? Well, if patriarchal America thought of these women at all, it certainly didn't think of them as examples of the feminine ideal. Therefore, it was taken for granted that such women didn't merit recognition or even protection from the economic and physical abuse to which they were so vulnerable. Even when a woman's enormous talent brought her well-earned fame, as Billie Holiday's talent did, she was judged in terms of her conformity to patriarchal expectations. Patriarchal men and women might have bought Lady Day's records, but is it not likely that they were sympathetic to her unconventional lifestyle and "bad-girl" image.

"Don't Explain," then, looks back to that era and shows us the merits of those women who struggled and survived the patriarchal ideology that devalued them, women like Letty, Delia, Terry, and Terry's friends. The story encourages us to resist patriarchal ideology by encouraging us to admire characters who do not conform to its expectations. Specifically, let's explore how "Don't Explain" (1) illustrates the violation of patriarchal gender roles, including the "cult of 'true womanhood,'" and (2) provides positive portrayals of the characters who violate those roles, portrayals that combat patriarchal stereotypes of women.

The violation of patriarchal gender roles and the "cult of 'true womanhood'"

1   *Letty*

    a   Find the passages in the story that show the ways in which Letty's behavior violates patriarchal gender roles, including the "cult of 'true womanhood,'" for example,

        i   her capacity to hold down a job and perform physical labor,
        ii   her ability to handle dangerous men,
        iii her ability to survive in a work environment in which a "lady" (that is, a "true woman") wouldn't even be seen,
        iv   her emotional strength,
        v   her single lifestyle,
        vi   her lesbian orientation, and
        vii her hero-worship of "bad-girl" Billie Holiday.

    b   Find the passages that show the ways in which Letty's physical appearance violates patriarchal gender roles and the "cult of 'true womanhood,'" for example,

        i   her size,
        ii   her clothing, and
        iii her race.

2   *Delia*—Examine Delia's characterization just as you did Letty's. Find the evidence in the story that shows the ways in which Delia's behavior and physical appearance violate patriarchal gender roles and the "cult of 'true womanhood.'"

3   *Terry and her friends*—Again, find the evidence in the story that shows the ways in which the behavior and physical appearance of Terry and her friends violate patriarchal gender roles and the "cult of 'true womanhood.'"

Positive portrayals of non-patriarchal women

Now that we've examined the ways in which Letty, Delia, Terry, and Terry's friends are non-patriarchal women, let's see how the story promotes resistance to patriarchal ideology by portraying these characters positively.

1   *Letty*—Find the ways in which the story portrays Letty positively, for example, the ways in which she is

    a   loyal,
    b   protective,
    c   helpful, and
    d   generous.

2   *Delia*—Find the ways in which the story portrays Delia positively, for example, the ways in which she is

a   outgoing,
b   thoughtful,
c   sensitive, and
d   kind.

3   *Terry and her friends*

a   Find the ways in which the story portrays Terry positively, for example, the ways in which Terry is

    i   protective,
    ii   insightful, and
    iii kind.

b   Find the ways in which the text positively portrays Terry's friends, who, though guarded in their behavior toward a newcomer, are

    i   supportive of one another, and
    ii   already beginning to accept Letty's presence among them.

4   *Counteracting patriarchal stereotypes of women*—As we saw earlier in this chapter, patriarchal ideology asserts that women who violate traditional gender roles, especially by failing to conform to the ideal of the "true woman," fit some sort of unappealing stereotype: they are nags, gossips, seductresses, or "bitches." As seductresses and "bitches," they are stereo-typed as loud, brassy, promiscuous, and unattractive to men except as sexual objects. In "Don't Explain," however, the female characters who violate traditional gender roles and fail to conform to the ideal of the "true woman" fit none of these stereotypes. In fact, they represent a range of different physical and personality types. List the variety Gomez gives us in her portrayal of these characters, including the variety of

a   clothing,
b   voices,
c   physical appearance (for example, body types and complexions), and
d   personality traits.

Focusing your essay

Drawing on the textual data you've gathered, it should be a fairly simple task to focus your essay on the story's resistance to patriarchal ideology. For as we've just seen, "Don't Explain" encourages us to resist the patriarchal ideology that says women like Letty, Delia, Terry, and Terry's female friends are less important, less valuable, less deserving than women who fit more closely the feminine patriarchal ideal. In fact, "Don't Explain" challenges patriarchal definitions of femininity and masculinity by showing us that we don't have to be "feminine" to be nurturing and sensitive, and we don't have to be "masculine" to be strong and protective. We can just be whoever we are, for human beings should be judged by such qualities as kindness and generosity, not by the extent to which we fulfill patriarchal gender roles.

Remember, as always, that you don't have to limit yourself to the analysis of the story I've offered you. For example, you might extend your essay to include a discussion of the hardships patriarchy imposes on the women in the story: none of them are in positions of authority in the workplace; because they have so little power, they have to learn to avoid incurring the displeasure of Tip, an unsavory customer, and Ari, who owns the 411 Lounge in which Letty and Delia work; and because they have opted against marriage, they have little or no economic security. You might also want to include an analysis of the story's characterization of Billie Holiday, for instance, the ways in which she, too, violated patriarchal ideology and the ways in which patriarchy's oppression of women contributed to her emotional insecurity. Whatever your interpretation, be sure you understand the feminist concepts you choose to employ, compose a clear statement of your thesis, and support your interpretation with adequate textual evidence.

Recognizing a conflicted attitude toward patriarchy: Interpreting "Everyday Use"

Sometimes we'll read a literary work and find ourselves feeling, at some moments, that the text is attacking patriarchy and, at other moments, that the text is supporting patriarchy. This experience could be the result of our own uncertainty about feminist concepts, or as we discussed in the opening of this chapter, it could be caused by the text's failure to clarify its own position toward the human behavior it illustrates. Because patriarchal ideology is such a common, and often invisible force in our culture, most literary works embody some form of this ideology without knowing that they do so, and that's why it's often difficult to discern how the text feels about the patriarchal or antipatriarchal behavior of its characters.

Sometimes, however, we may have difficulty deciding if a work is patriarchal or antipatriarchal because our perception that the text both attacks and supports patriarchal ideology is a correct perception. For many literary works, though they may not realize it, do both. In such a situation we can argue that the text, itself, has a conflicted attitude toward patriarchal ideology. I think we can argue that this is the case in Alice Walker's story "Everyday Use" (1973; see Appendix D).

The story's main concern, which we'll discuss at greater length in our African American and postcolonial readings of the work, is to show the importance of solidarity to the well-being of the African American family and community during America's Black Pride Movement of the late 1960s and early 1970s. This period, during which the story was written and is set, was a time when emotionally charged disagreements—disagreements over how to define African

American heritage and achieve social equality in a country whose white majority population seemed determined to maintain its racist domination—divided black families as well as the black community as a whole. Understandably, then, "Everyday Use" wants to show the flaws in any attitude or behavior—such as the attitude and behavior of Dee toward her mother and sister—that threatens the solidarity of the African American family or community.

This praiseworthy enterprise, however, seems to result in the story's sending mixed messages about patriarchal ideology. For the tale's concern with gender issues, while significant, takes a back seat to its focus on racial issues that were of primary importance during the Black Pride Movement and that remain of great importance today. "Everyday Use" thus illustrates a problem that African American women writers, and African American women in general, frequently face: how to be true to the precepts of feminism, which is often perceived by patriarchal men and women as a threat to the black family and community, as well as to the precepts of racial equality, which seem to focus more on the rights of black men than of black women.

In order to see the conflicted attitude toward patriarchal ideology in "Everyday Use," we'll need to examine both the story's antipatriarchal and patriarchal aspects. Specifically, (1) we'll look at the tale's two primary antipatriarchal elements—its positive portrayal of Mama's violation of patriarchal gender roles and its sympathetic depiction of Mama and Maggie's victimization by patriarchy—and (2) we'll also look at the story's primary patriarchal element: its negative portrayal of Dee's violation of patriarchal gender roles.

The story's antipatriarchal elements

1 *Mama's violation of patriarchal gender roles*—Patriarchal ideology tells us that the only good woman is a patriarchal, or traditional woman. So one effective way for a story to fight against patriarchal ideology is to give us positive portrayals of non-traditional women—that is, women who do not conform to patriarchal gender roles.

   a List all the ways in which Mama violates patriarchal gender roles. Include, for example, textual evidence concerning

      i her physical strength,
      ii the type of work she does out of doors,
      iii her tolerance for cold weather and for physical activities that are supposed to revolt women,
      iv the pride she takes in her physical capabilities,
      v her courage, and
      vi her emotional strength.

   b Find textual evidence that Mama is positively portrayed, that the story invites us to like her, even to admire her. (Include the ways in which

Mama's violation of traditional gender roles does not make her a bad mother, as patriarchy would have us believe is the case for such women; on the contrary, note all the ways in which Mama is a devoted mother.)

2   *Mama and Maggie's patriarchal oppression*—Another effective way for a text to fight against patriarchal ideology is to draw attention to the ways in which sympathetic female characters are oppressed by patriarchy economically, socially, politically, and/or psychologically.

a   Find as much textual evidence as you can to show the various ways in which Mama is oppressed by patriarchy.

   i   How is Mama economically disadvantaged because she is a woman? That is, how does patriarchy limit her options?
   ii   How does her failure to fit the definition of the "true woman" result in psychological oppression through the creation of low self-esteem? (See, among other evidence, Mama's recurring dream about being on television.)
   iii Can you find additional examples of Mama's oppression by patriarchy?

b   Find as much textual evidence as you can to show the various ways in which Maggie is oppressed by patriarchy.

   i   How does Maggie fail to fit the definition of the "true woman," and how does this failure result in psychological oppression through its contribution to Maggie's low self-esteem?
   ii   Given the fact that Dee's lighter skin and more "womanly" figure surely increased her opportunities to get what she wanted out of life, how does Maggie's failure to fit the definition of the "true woman" also help limit her career options to marriage with John Thomas?
   iii Can you find additional examples of Maggie's oppression by patriarchy?

c   Find textual evidence that the plight of Mama and Maggie is sympathetically portrayed. That is, find the ways in which the text shows us that these two women are doing their best under circumstances beyond their control and thereby encourages us to sympathize with them. (Just for your own information, notice the contrast with "A Rose for Emily," which is discussed next and which seems to invite us to dislike Emily and blame her for her problems though she, too, is a victim of patriarchy.)

The story's patriarchal element

One very effective way for a story to promote patriarchal ideology, which it may do unintentionally, is to give us a negative portrayal of a woman who violates patriarchal gender roles. Such a portrayal seems to say, "See what a bad person a woman becomes when she violates traditional gender roles?"

1   *Dee's violation of patriarchal gender roles*—Find the textual evidence of Dee's numerous violations of traditional gender roles. Include, for example,

   a   her independence from her family as she was growing up,
   b   the various ways in which she has struck out on her own,
   c   her independence from her family now that she is an adult, and
   d   the independent way she relates to Hakim.

2   *Dee's negative portrayal*—Find the numerous ways in which the story portrays Dee negatively, which limits our sympathy for this character and even invites us to dislike her. Include examples of

   a   her self-centeredness,
   b   her insensitivity to the needs and feelings of her mother and sister, and
   c   her tendency to "show off" in any way she can, a tendency she has had all her life.

Focusing your essay

Given the textual data we've already collected, you should be able to focus your essay on the conflicted attitude toward patriarchal ideology evident in "Everyday Use." As we have seen, while the story gives us a strong, non-traditional woman to admire and clearly depicts the patriarchal victimization of two sympathetic female characters, it also gives us a very negative portrayal of an intelligent, assertive, self-motivated young woman. In fact, in many ways, Dee fulfills the patriarchal stereotype of the "bitch," and her characterization risks being interpreted as a kind of patriarchal warning: we mustn't let young girls ignore patriarchal gender roles or they will become selfish, self-centered, self-indulgent women who don't care what becomes of their families as long as they get what *they* want. Indeed, Dee's negative portrayal makes Maggie, who is in many ways a patriarchal "good girl," seem infinitely superior—even a better role model—in contrast. And one of the last things feminist theory would want to see is yet another example of the patriarchal "good girl" put forward as an ideal.

Keep in mind, as always, that you don't have to limit yourself to the analysis of the story I've offered you. For example, you might want to focus your essay more thoroughly, or even exclusively, on the role played in the story by the "cult of 'true womanhood.'" In that case, you would analyze the ways in which the three main characters' opportunities in life, relationships with others, and self-esteem are directly related to the extent to which they fit the definition of the "true woman." By showing that "Everyday Use" illustrates the damaging effects of this patriarchal ideal, you would be arguing that the story is, in this way, an antipatriarchal text.

Perhaps, instead, you might want to focus your essay entirely on Maggie, a character that is very sympathetically portrayed and has a good deal of emotional impact on many readers. For example, you might examine the problem her characterization poses for a feminist interpretation. Although her physical appearance and manner do not fit the definition of the "true woman," much of her behavior does: her natural sphere of activity is clearly the home, we do not see her performing hard physical labor, and she is apparently sexually "pure" (in contrast to Dee, Maggie is apparently saving herself for marriage). Analogously, although she violates traditional gender roles in at least one way—like Mama, she chews tobacco, or "snuff"—she nevertheless fulfills almost all the requirements of the patriarchal "good girl." Finally, although we can see that she is victimized by patriarchal ideology, her close bond with Mama and her marriage to John Thomas seem to offer her more happiness than Dee has found thus far in life. What should we make of all this data about Maggie? Do you think the characterization of Maggie we've just outlined combats patriarchal ideology, reinforces patriarchal ideology, or is conflicted in its attitude toward patriarchal ideology? Whatever your interpretation, be sure you understand the feminist concepts you choose to employ, compose a clear statement of your thesis, and support your interpretation with adequate textual evidence.

Analyzing a sexist text: Interpreting "A Rose for Emily"

In "The Battle Royal" we saw an example of a literary work that illustrates patriarchal ideology in a way which clearly invites us to reject that ideology. As we noted in the beginning of this chapter, however, not all texts that illustrate patriarchal ideology invite us to reject it. William Faulkner's "A Rose for Emily" (1931: see Appendix B) is a case in point. While I think that we can quickly learn to see how Faulkner's story illustrates patriarchal ideology, it is more difficult for many of us to figure out whether the story wants us to accept or reject that ideology. So let's look at "A Rose for Emily" in two separate steps: (1) we'll examine the ways in which the story illustrates patriarchal ideology; then (2) we'll take the harder step—we'll look at the ways in which the story fails to reject the patriarchal ideology it illustrates. In fact, we'll see that the story endorses the sexist attitudes it portrays. We'll see that "A Rose for Emily" is, therefore, an example of a sexist text.

Don't worry if you find this second step difficult to grasp at first. Just do your best. Collect the evidence from the story you're asked to collect. And trust that future practice using feminist concepts to interpret literature will help you know when a literary work illustrates patriarchy in order to show its flaws—as we saw so clearly in "The Battle Royal"—and when a literary work accepts the patriarchal ideology it illustrates, as we'll see in "A Rose for Emily."

How "A Rose for Emily" illustrates patriarchal ideology

"A Rose for Emily" is set in the town of Jefferson during the decades preceding and following the turn of the twentieth century, and illustrations of Emily

Grierson's victimization by patriarchy abound. For example, the patriarchal society depicted in the story dictates that the only acceptable way a young woman like Emily can escape from a selfish, domineering father is through marriage, and there is nothing the town can do about the fact that Mr. Grierson forbids Emily that escape. In fact, apparently no one in Jefferson even thinks about doing something. Because Jefferson's patriarchal culture also holds that a woman of Emily's rank must not work for a living, Emily wouldn't be able to survive financially if she left her father's house without a husband to take care of her. In addition, much of the gossip and speculation about Emily, which contributes to her isolation, reveals the town's steadfast belief that the only acceptable behavior for a woman is behavior that accords with traditional gender roles. And surely patriarchal ideology contributes to Emily's apparent desperation to have a husband, any husband, and to do anything to keep him. So you could write an essay in which you argued that "A Rose for Emily" illustrates the ways in which patriarchal gender roles victimize women, even to the point of driving them crazy. And that might be a good exercise for you to do at this point. So let's collect the kind of textual evidence described earlier, which you would need in order to write such an essay: (1) Mr. Grierson's patriarchal domination of Emily; (2) the limited options available to Emily due to patriarchal ideology; (3) the ways in which Emily is oppressed by the patriarchal attitudes of the townspeople; and (4) the patriarchal aspects of Emily's relationship with Homer Barron.

Mr. Grierson's patriarchal domination of Emily

Find every example you can of Mr. Grierson's patriarchal domination of his daughter and its negative effects on her. Keep in mind that a father's patriarchal domination of his offspring goes beyond the kind of decisions a parent must make in order to protect and educate a youngster. So you'll be looking for the ways in which Mr. Grierson's decisions about Emily are

1 motivated by his own patriarchal beliefs concerning proper behavior for a young woman,
2 motivated by his desire to maintain complete control, for a patriarchal man believes it is his right and duty to control the females in his family,
3 destructive to Emily's ability to develop social skills, and
4 destructive to Emily's emotional well-being.

Keep in mind that Mr. Grierson's domination of Emily continues well into her adulthood: she is around thirty years old when he dies.

Emily's limited options

What kinds of patriarchal limitations would probably be encountered by an impoverished upper-class white woman living in a small town in the American south during the decades preceding and following the turn of the twentieth century? Many of these limitations are illustrated or implied in the story, and these limitations would exist even if Emily were not under her father's thumb. List the ways in which Emily's options are limited in terms of the following categories:

1 Choice of vocation (ways of earning a living).
2 Choice of hobbies or leisure activities.
3 Choice of friends.
4 Marital options (the option of remaining unmarried as well as the option of choosing whatever kind of husband she wants).

The patriarchal attitudes of the townspeople

Find as many examples as you can of the townspeople's patriarchal attitudes, especially those attitudes that adversely affect Emily.

1 Find those places in the story where the townsfolk talk about Emily in terms of her marriageability (for example, her prospects of finding a husband and the reasons for her failure to find one by a "reasonable" age), which the townsfolk apparently consider a woman's most important quality.
2 Find references in the story to Emily's attitude toward housekeeping and hospitality, two other feminine domains in which she fails to fulfill her traditional role, as the townspeople are well aware.
3 Find as much evidence as you can that the townspeople seem obsessed with the ups and downs of Homer's courtship of Emily, especially with Emily's failure to conform to the traditional behavior expected of an unmarried lady, which failure includes her assumed descent to the status of "fallen woman" (a woman who has sexual relations before marriage).
4 How might the townsfolk's firm belief in traditional gender roles be responsible for their inability to see the rather obvious connection among Emily's purchase of arsenic, the unexpected disappearance of Homer, and the horrible smell coming from her house shortly thereafter?

The patriarchal aspects of Emily's relationship with Homer Barron

1 How is Homer a patriarchal man? (Don't ignore the imagery available to you.)
2 Who drives the carriage in which the couple take their Sunday drives?
3 What does Homer hold in his gloved hand?
4 What aspects of Homer's behavior can be seen as rather "macho"? (See, for example, his behavior as foreman.)
5 After Emily's death, what evidence is found that she expected Homer to marry her?
6 How, then, might Emily's relationship with Homer be seen as her attempt to fulfill her traditional gender role?

Focusing your essay

The evidence you've just collected will allow you to write an essay explaining the ways in which "A Rose for Emily" illustrates patriarchal ideology. Specifically, you can show how the story illustrates a particularly severe kind of patriarchal system operating in the small-town American south, as Faulkner envisioned it, in the decades before and after the turn of the twentieth century. In fact, the textual evidence you've gathered will allow you to argue that the story illustrates how patriarchal ideology can drive a woman insane.

Because you're studying feminist concepts, you may feel that the evils of patriarchy are obvious in this story, and you may therefore conclude that the story is antipatriarchal. However, *your* ability to see the injustice of the patriarchal ideology illustrated in the story doesn't necessarily mean that *the story* is aware of that injustice. Perhaps you are able to see the patriarchal injustice in the text because of the feminist tools you're using and not because the story is inviting you to see it. Without further analysis, we can't say whether or not this text rejects or endorses the ideology it illustrates. So let's undertake that further analysis now.

How "A Rose for Emily" endorses patriarchal ideology

As we've just seen, "A Rose for Emily" illustrates the patriarchal victimization of main character Emily Grierson. However, I don't think we can argue that the story invites us to reject the patriarchal ideology that victimizes Emily because, for one thing, the text doesn't seem consistently sympathetic toward Emily, despite its sympathetic title. On the contrary, after her father's death, Emily is portrayed as such a rude and arrogant woman that it's difficult for many readers not to be put off by her. And the closing scene makes it difficult for many of us not to be revolted by her. Some of my students, when they learn that Emily has poisoned Homer and has slept with his decaying body, say things like "Gross!" and "Oh, that's disgusting!", and even "This story is whacked out!"

The story's outrageously negative characterization of Emily thus distracts our attention from her experience of patriarchal victimization and does not invite us to sympathize with her. That is, the text does not invite us to reject the patriarchal ideology it illustrates. And when a text illustrates patriarchal ideology without rejecting it, the effect is often the same as if the text endorsed patriarchal ideology, whether or not the text is aware it is doing so. Therefore, the unsympathetic characterization of Emily Grierson—the increasingly negative portrayal of the main character in the years following her father's death—should be enough to make us wonder if "A Rose for Emily" endorses patriarchal ideology in other ways as well. For example: (1) How is Emily portrayed before her father's death? (2) If she is portrayed differently before and after Mr. Grierson's demise, what seems to be responsible for the change? (3) Are the other female characters all negatively depicted as well? (4) If so, are the male characters positively depicted (which, by providing a contrast, would reinforce the negative portrayal of the female characters)? Finally, (5) if the answers to these questions reveal a sexist bias, does that bias reflect merely the opinion of the story's narrator, or does the text share that bias? Let's address these questions one at a time and see what we learn.

The portrayal of Emily before her father's death

We can see that Emily conforms to patriarchal gender roles as long as her father is alive, which is, roughly, the first thirty years of her life.

1   Whenever she is described during this period, she is portrayed as a "good girl" and depicted in a manner that elicits our sympathy. Find all the textual evidence you can to support this claim. Note, for example,

   a   the color clothing she generally wears during this time,
   b   her bodyweight,
   c   the image of her father in the doorway and how helpless she looks standing behind him,
   d   her bond to her father right after his death, and
   e   her distress during the year that follows her father's death.

2   How do all of these textual elements encourage us to have positive feelings for Emily in her role as the patriarchal "good girl"?

The change in Emily's portrayal

About a year after Mr. Grierson's demise, during which time she has been ill, Emily starts keeping company with Homer Barron, in defiance of social tradition and public opinion. From this time forward, until the end of her life, she violates patriarchal gender roles in a variety of ways.

1   With the exception of the sympathetic image of Emily giving lessons in china-painting, a traditional feminine pastime, how is she described during this period? Find all the textual data you can. Note, for example,

   a   the severe clothing she generally wears during this period,
   b   her skin color,
   c   her bodyweight,
   d   her masculine appearance, and
   e   her behavior toward the druggist, the Baptist minister, the Aldermen, and others.

2   Take a close look at the description of the corpse, the room, and the bed in the closing scene. What details suggest that:

    a   Emily considers Homer's dead body her bridegroom,
    b   she has slept in his dead embrace, and
    c   she has shared her bed with him, not just immediately after his death, but even after she has grown to be an old woman?

3   How do all of these textual elements encourage us to have negative feelings for Emily once she ceases to be a patriarchal "good girl"?

Descriptions of the female townsfolk

From the opening description of Emily Grierson's funeral, every time the narrator mentions the women of Jefferson—the minor female characters—he says or implies something negative about them.

1   Go through the story and find as many examples as you can of the narrator's references to the female townsfolk. List the qualities he ascribes to them.
2   What patriarchal stereotypes do we see operating here? Name as many as you can.
3   Does the narrator seem to believe that these qualities are characteristic of women in general? How do you know he feels this way?

Descriptions of the male townsfolk

From the opening description of Emily Grierson's funeral, every time the narrator mentions the men of Jefferson—the minor male characters—he says or implies something positive about them. In fact, the narrator often describes the male and female characters' responses to the same situation, contrasting some positive quality in the menfolk's behavior with some negative quality in the behavior of the womenfolk.

1   Go through the story and find as many examples as you can of the narrator's references to the male townsfolk. List the qualities he ascribes to them, noting how the men's admirable characteristics make the women look even worse by comparison.
2   Does the narrator seem to believe that the qualities he ascribes to Jefferson's menfolk are characteristic of men in general? How do you know he feels this way?

The portrayal of the narrator

The narrator's biased description of Jefferson's women and men reveals his sexism. You might even feel that the narrator's sexism is also responsible for the negative portrayal of Emily once she stops conforming to patriarchal gender roles. However, a sexist narrator, by itself, wouldn't allow us to conclude that we were reading a sexist story. For the story might invite us to reject the narrator's viewpoint by showing him in a bad light, for example, by portraying him as ridiculous, vindictive, or obnoxious. "A Rose for Emily," though, doesn't offer us this invitation. On the contrary, the narrator is portrayed as intelligent, knowledgeable, well educated, and objective (not overly emotional about the events he narrates and therefore able to be impartial). Such a narrator tends to inspire trust in the reader, and that trust influences us to accept his point of view without giving it too much thought. So unless a feminist perspective prepared us to be on the watch for his negative attitude toward women, we might very well not have noticed it. We would probably have accepted the narrator's viewpoint uncritically. Because the text thus promotes our acceptance of the narrator's sexism, we can argue that the text shares that sexism. Find all the textual evidence you can to show the ways in which the narrator is portrayed in a positive manner.

1   What parts of the story, or what aspects of his language, suggest that the narrator is intelligent and well educated?
2   How do we know he is knowledgeable about the people and events he describes?
3   What textual elements give the feeling that he has maintained an objective viewpoint?

Let me pause for a moment to answer a question you might have at this point: Why do we refer to the text's sexism and not the author's? While we might be able to establish that a text has a sexist viewpoint, we can't be sure this viewpoint is shared by the author. For example, the author might have written the story to mock sexism or to vent his frustration at the sexist attitudes of others or even to "test" the sexist attitudes of his readers. We might not be able to perceive this intention, however, because the author was unwilling or unable to clarify his own viewpoint in the story or because the way we respond to the story today is different from what the author expected of his audience when he wrote it. In any event, it's best to make only those claims we can support with textual evidence, which is why, unless we've undertaken to write a study of an author's life and work, we tend to avoid referring to the author's biases and refer, instead, to those of a character, a narrator, and/or a text.

Focusing your essay

As we've just seen, "A Rose for Emily" portrays Emily Grierson in positive terms when she's a patriarchal "good girl" and in negative terms when she violates traditional gender roles. In addition, the story offers a positive portrayal of a narrator whose sexism can be seen in his biased descriptions of the female and male citizens of Jefferson. You might, therefore, focus your essay on the sexist ideology promoted by Faulkner's tale. In fact, I think we can safely go so far as to say that the characterizations of Jefferson's womenfolk are blatant examples of patriarchal stereotyping, and so is the characterization of Emily. In fact, the text seems to make a connection between Emily's gender-role violation and her descent into insanity, as if a woman's failure to conform to traditional gender roles is, itself, a form of insanity. In keeping with this idea, you might note that Emily isn't characterized as just a mentally ill person, nor even as "just" a murderess. She is portrayed as grotesque, monstrous, unnatural, as if the story were implying that when a woman violates traditional gender roles, she becomes what patriarchy fears women will become if they embrace feminism: crazed man-killers.

As always, remember that you don't have to limit yourself to the analysis of the story I've offered you, although, in this case, the evidence you've been asked to collect provides you with at least two different feminist approaches to "A Rose for Emily." (1) You can write an essay simply showing the numerous ways in which the story illustrates patriarchal ideology, even if you agree with me that this aspect of the story is overshadowed by the text's sexism. Or (2) you can write an essay showing the ways in which the story endorses the patriarchal ideology it illustrates. Of course, you or your instructor might come up with an entirely different feminist reading of the story, perhaps one which disagrees with the claim that "A Rose for Emily" is a sexist story. Whatever your interpretation, be sure you understand the feminist concepts you choose to employ, compose a clear statement of your thesis, and support your interpretation with adequate textual evidence.

Understanding patriarchy's psychological oppression of women: Interpreting "I started Early—Took my Dog"

At the beginning of this chapter I offered you a question you can ask that will help you interpret a literary work using feminist concepts: Do the characters conform to traditional gender roles? Or to put the question another way, are the female characters depicted according to patriarchal stereotypes of women? As we have seen in the literary works already analyzed, this question usually works quite well because so many texts contain characters whose experience is represented in terms of their gender roles. In other words, a great deal of literature promotes, or at least illustrates, some form of patriarchal or anti-patriarchal ideology. Given that most characters, as well as the authors who create them, live in a patriarchal society, it would be strange if this were not the case.

What can we do, however, if a literary work contains no obvious examples of patriarchal or antipatriarchal ideology, such as the kinds we see in the other literary works interpreted in this chapter, and yet we feel that *something* patriarchal is going on in the text? Subtle literary representations of the patriarchal oppression of women, which may be difficult to see at first, often take the form of psychological oppression. Now, not all literary representations of the psychological oppression of women are subtle. Some are quite clear and straightforward, for example, the low self-esteem Mrs. Johnson suffers in

"Everyday Use" because she does not fit the patriarchal ideal of feminine beauty. However, when a literary representation of patriarchal oppression *is* subtle, chances are that the oppression is psychological. And when subtle representations of psychological oppression are not accompanied by representations of other forms of patriarchal oppression, we may be at a loss for how to produce a feminist interpretation of that literary work.

So here's what we can do: we can do a psychoanalytic interpretation of the literary work in question that shows the ways in which patriarchal ideology—rather than the causes usually named by psychoanalytic theory—is responsible for the psychological problems illustrated in the work. And that's just what we will do with Emily Dickinson's poem "I started Early—Took my Dog" (c. 1862; see Appendix A). We'll (1) summarize the psychoanalytic reading we did of the poem in Chapter 4; (2) go back to the poem and examine the elements that make it a work specific to the experience of women in a patriarchy; (3) see if step 2 implies that the speaker has any psychological problems our psychoanalytic reading did not pick up; and (4) see if the poem suggests that patriarchy is responsible for the psychological experience of the speaker. This method allows us to draw on psychoanalytic concepts while still doing a feminist interpretation of the poem.

Summarizing our psychoanalytic interpretation of the poem

In Chapter 4 we followed a series of steps that allowed us to produce a psychoanalytic interpretation of "I started Early—Took my Dog" by analyzing the poem's dream imagery. Why don't you go back to that interpretation and summarize it in your own words? Then see if the following summary agrees with yours.

Summary of our psychoanalytic interpretation—Our psychoanalytic reading of the poem-as-dream suggested that the speaker is sexually repressed or has a conflicted attitude toward her own sexual desire. For the sea, which operates in the poem as a dream symbol of sexuality and, more specifically, as a dream symbol of the male sexual pursuit of the female. And the speaker flees in terror from this pursuit, which she perceives as frightening, threatening, and overpowering. Nevertheless, the speaker apparently has sexual desire, for there are "Mermaids in the Basement" (l. 3)—that is, in the speaker's unconscious—and mermaids are, traditionally, at home in the sea (sexuality) and are often portrayed as very sexually attractive to human males. Finally, in running to the "Solid Town" (l. 21) for safety, the speaker is seeking protection, from the sea and presumably from herself as well, in the restraints placed on sexuality by laws and customs.

Finding textual elements specific to the experience of women in a patriarchy

Go through the poem and find every reference you can that seems to be specific to the experience of women in a patriarchy.

1   Note the way in which the speaker is compared to an animal.

    a   Is the animal large or small?
    b   Is the animal powerful or weak?

2   Note all references to women's clothing.

    a   How is the speaker dressed?
    b   Does her clothing encourage us to think that there is anything special about her? (Does she appear to be especially powerful or intelligent or courageous? Or is she dressed like an ordinary woman who does women's chores?)

3   Note the way in which the speaker is compared to a flower.

    a   What kind of flower is this?
    b   Is it generally considered of great value or beauty?
    c   What is its role on the dinner menu of a rural home?

4   Beginning with line 3, which is the point in the poem immediately after the first appearance of the word *Sea*, note that the few verbs that relate to the speaker cast her in a passive or a reactive role: actions are performed on her, or she reacts to the actions of another, but she does not initiate action. Locate the pertinent phrases.

Finding additional psychological problems implied in the poem

In our psychoanalytic interpretation of Dickinson's poem as if it were a dream, we argued that the poem's imagery strongly implies sexual repression: the speaker's terror of the sea is, in reality, a fear of her own sexual desire, and her flight from the sea therefore means that she represses her desire. However, all the data you've just collected concerning the poem's characterization of the speaker as a woman in a patriarchal society (the attention to her female attire, the comparisons of the speaker to a mouse and to a dandelion, and the casting of the speaker in a passive or a reactive role in twenty-two of the poem's twenty-four lines) suggest an additional psychological problem. Can you identify it?

1   Does the speaker seem confident?
2   Does the imagery used to describe her suggest that she has a positive self-image?
3   How do the data you've collected indicate that the speaker has low self-esteem?

Arguing that patriarchal ideology is the cause of the speaker's psychological problems

How is patriarchal ideology the cause of the speaker's sexual repression and low self-esteem? That's the question we need to answer if we are to use the psychoanalytic data we've collected to produce a feminist interpretation of the poem. In order to answer this question, first recall that, in order to be considered a "true woman" at the time this poem was written, a female had to be sexually pure. If unmarried, she must not even think about sex. If married, she must not enjoy sex, for a woman who enjoyed sex was deemed sick, evil, or both. Indeed, a woman's sexual purity was "protected" by, among other restrictions, forbidding her to go walking without an appropriate chaperone, especially if, like the speaker in Dickinson's poem, she wanted to walk in such a lonely place as a deserted seashore. Then recall that patriarchal gender roles define women as inferior to men: much less rational, less courageous, less decisive, and not at all assertive. Now combine your recollections with the textual evidence required below.

1   How does the speaker's response to the sea illustrate the ways in which patriarchal ideology promotes women's sexual repression?
2   How does the speaker's poor self-image, suggested by the manner in which she describes herself, illustrate the ways in which patriarchal ideology promotes women's low self-esteem?

Focusing your essay

By this point, you can probably see that the evidence you've collected will allow you to focus your essay on the negative effects of patriarchal ideology on the speaker. For whether or not the poem is aware that it is doing so, through the lens of feminist theory Emily Dickinson's "I started Early—Took my Dog" illustrates the ways in which patriarchy promotes in women both sexual repression and low self-esteem.

As always, remember that you don't have to limit yourself to the analysis of the poem I've offered you. For example, you could develop feminist interpretations of the poem that draw on the alternative psychoanalytic readings of the speaker offered in Chapter 4 in the section "Focusing your essay." If you prefer the psychoanalytic reading of the poem as an illustration of the fear of rape or the trauma of a woman who has been raped, then you might develop a feminist interpretation by arguing that the poem illustrates the ways in which the speaker is symbolically violated by patriarchy's damaging effects on her sexuality and her self-esteem. Or if you prefer, instead, the psychoanalytic reading of the poem as an illustration of the indulgence of a guilty desire—that is, symbolic sexual intercourse does take place, but it does so with the guilt-ridden consent of the speaker—then you might develop a feminist interpretation by arguing that the poem illustrates the way in which patriarchy psychologically punishes women for having sexual desire. Whatever your interpretation, be sure you understand the feminist (and psychoanalytic) concepts you choose to employ, compose a clear statement of your thesis, and support your interpretation with adequate textual evidence.

Food for further thought

Thinking it over

If you've worked through all of the interpretation exercises offered in this chapter, you should feel quite familiar with the basic approaches to understanding literature provided by concepts from feminist theory. Specifically, we've seen how feminist concepts can be used to help us analyze

1   literary works that are antipatriarchal in that their negative representations of patriarchal ideology encourage us to reject that ideology (our example: "The Battle Royal"),
2   literary works that are antipatriarchal in that their positive representations of characters who violate traditional gender roles encourage us to resist patriarchal ideology (our example: "Don't Explain"),
3   literary works that have a conflicted response to patriarchy in that they both combat and promote patriarchal ideology, for instance, by providing both positive and negative images of characters who violate traditional gender roles (our example: "Everyday Use"),
4   literary works that are patriarchal in that they encourage us to accept patriarchal ideology, for instance, by providing negative images of women who violate traditional gender roles and/or patriarchal stereotypes of women (our example: "A Rose for Emily"), and
5   literary works whose psychoanalytic elements can be used to produce a feminist interpretation by illustrating patriarchy's psychological oppression of women (our example: "I started Early—Took my Dog").

In addition, an understanding of feminist concepts can help us use other theories more productively. As we saw in Chapters 4 and 5, psychoanalytic and Marxist concepts can help us understand the psychological and socioeconomic oppression suffered by the politically marginalized groups addressed in subsequent chapters: women; LGBTQ people; African Americans; and postcolonial populations, or peoples dealing with the loss of native languages and cultures due to colonialist oppression. Similarly, feminist concepts remind us that, among those who suffer discrimination due to their socioeconomic class, sexual orientation, race, or cultural affiliation, female members of those groups face the additional burden of sexism.

Perhaps of greatest importance, feminist concepts can help us see the ways in which patriarchal ideology persists today where we most need to be aware of it: in our everyday lives. Think of your own experience as a student, of your dating experience, of your experience as a spouse or a parent, or of your experience on the job market or in the workplace. You might, for example, ask yourself the following questions. Can a girl in her early teens opt to take a course in woodshop—or a boy in his early teens opt to take a course in home economics—without, at the very least, being teased about it? Is it acceptable for a man (young or old) to cry when his feelings are hurt? Is it acceptable for a woman (young or old) to ask a man out on a date? In a romantic relationship, who is expected to "make the first move"—that is, to express physical affection that could be interpreted in a sexual manner? Does a man who "sleeps around" risk creating the same kind of gossip a woman would create if she engaged in the same behavior? Generally speaking, who is expected to pay the bills when a man and a woman go out on a date? When both father and mother are employed outside the home, which parent is usually expected to be the children's primary caregiver? Which working parent is usually expected to do the lion's share of such household tasks as meal preparation, laundry, and house cleaning? Can men and women expect to be treated fairly and with respect when they seek or take jobs traditionally assigned to members of the opposite sex? You or your instructor can probably come up with other questions of this kind, but these few should help you begin to develop your own insights about the degree to which patriarchal ideology plays a role in your life and in the lives of those around you.

Feminist theory and cultural criticism

We can also use concepts from feminist theory for the purposes of cultural criticism. That is, we can use feminist concepts to help us analyze the cultural messages sent, whether deliberately or not, by the everyday productions of the culture in which we live, such as movies, games, television shows, song lyrics, toys, and other productions of popular culture discussed in Chapter 1. Indeed, those cultural productions that in some way represent human behavior—that have characters and a plot—can be analyzed using concepts from feminist theory just as we use those concepts to analyze literary works. For example, an understanding of traditional gender roles and "good-girl"/"bad-girl" ideology can offer us insights into *Pretty Woman* (directed by Garry Marshall, 1990), a classic film modernization of the Cinderella story in which kind-hearted prostitute Vivian Ward (Julia Roberts) and lonely, self-made corporate raider Edward Lewis (Richard Gere) find true love and a happy future together.

Too busy to give adequate time and attention to his romantic relationships—the most recent of which has just ended badly—Edward decides to hire the lovely, free-spirited Vivian to be his "beck-and-call-girl" for one week in order to ensure himself a trouble-free companion for the various social events he must attend in pursuit of his latest corporate takeover. Over the course of the film, Vivian gets Edward to loosen up, slow down, and smell the roses. Instead of destroying his latest corporate target, the fatherly Mr. Morse (Ralph Bellamy), Edward saves the man's company and goes into business with him. Analogously, Edward gets Vivian to broaden her horizons and have faith in her ability to achieve a better life. By the end of the film, Vivian has decided to quit her life on the street—she has even rejected Edward's offer to keep her as his mistress—and get her high school equivalency diploma. Luckily, Edward catches up with Vivian before she leaves town and offers her the "happily ever after" they both want.

Part of the charm of this engaging movie lies in what seems to be its abandonment of patriarchal gender roles in favor of a romantic relationship in which the male and female participant each has strengths and weaknesses not associated with traditional masculinity and femininity. Vivian knows a great deal about cars and handles the Lotus like a race-car driver; Edward knows nothing about cars and can't handle the Lotus at all. Edward suffers from a fear of heights; Vivian apparently has no phobias whatsoever. Because she's worked as a prostitute, Vivian is presumably more sexually experienced than Edward, and Edward doesn't mind. Both are intelligent and sexually tender. Under the other's influence, each is able to make significant changes for the better. When Edward rescues Vivian—symbolically, by climbing the fire escape to her apartment and, literally, by deciding to offer her marriage in lieu of the condo-with-expense-account arrangement that she has refused—Vivian says that a damsel rescued by a prince "rescues him right back," which indeed she has already done. Clearly, then, the cultural work performed by these aspects of *Pretty Woman* is antipatriarchal: the film suggests that we should be free to learn and grow without worrying whether or not our behavior is conventionally masculine or feminine, and a woman's patriarchal "good-girl" or "bad-girl" status tells us nothing about the kind of person she is.

What cultural message does *Pretty Woman* send, however, when we think of the movie along the following lines? Edward has the real power in this relationship. He has everything Vivian lacks: money, refinement, connections, and a broad knowledge of the world into which he brings her. Edward must overcome his emotional problems in order to sustain a relationship with Vivian, but Vivian must be made over entirely in order to sustain a relationship with Edward. Somewhat like Eliza Doolittle in the film *My Fair Lady* (directed by George Cukor, 1964), she must learn to dress differently and speak differently; she must improve her posture and her table manners; and she must learn to behave like a lady. In fact, like Eliza, over the course of the movie Vivian is transformed, by a take-control man, from an undereducated, underbred member of the underclass into a lady. And in Vivian's case, her profession— despite all her redeeming personal qualities—means that her transformation is also one from "bad girl" to "good girl." The cultural work performed by these aspects of the movie is certainly patriarchal: the man is, as patriarchy deems he should be, ultimately in control of his relationship with a woman, and a woman's patriarchal "good-girl"/"bad-girl" status is very important to the successful future of a romantic relationship.

I believe it's the combination of these two opposing strands of the movie—its reinforcement of both antipatriarchal and patriarchal ideologies—that makes *Pretty Woman* such an interesting source of debate from a feminist perspective. Indeed, a feminist cultural critic might reasonably argue that *Pretty Woman*'s cultural message opposes patriarchal thinking, that it supports patriarchal thinking, or that it confuses the two in a way that is rather difficult to untangle. I think the third option offers the most thorough and compelling understanding of the movie from a feminist perspective because it draws our attention to the ways in which antipatriarchal and patriarchal ideologies work together in this film. Specifically, *Pretty Woman*'s engaging antipatriarchal elements—the couple's complementary strengths and mutual helpfulness—run the risk of merely sugarcoating the film's patriarchal ideology, thereby making it all the more easy to swallow.

★★★

Remember, it's natural to feel a bit uncertain when we encounter a new theory—a new way of looking at ourselves and our world—that may call into question many of the beliefs that have been pressed upon us, and that we've accepted uncritically, for most of our lives. Uncertainty is an unavoidable part of learning and growing. Keep in mind, too, that others may disagree with your opinions. Individuals often disagree in their interpretations of literature, popular culture, or everyday experiences, even when drawing upon the same feminist concepts for their analyses. The keys to a good interpretation—besides intellectual curiosity and an open mind—are a clear understanding of the feminist concepts you've chosen to use and strong evidence to support your analysis.

Taking the next step

Questions for further practice

1   Find the textual evidence to show the ways in which Kate Chopin's *The Awakening* (1899) is antipatriarchal. For example, how does the novel suggest that the traditional duties of wife and mother, while fulfilling for some women, should not be the only option for all women? Also, how does the novel counter the patriarchal myth, prevalent in nineteenth-century America, that women don't require, and don't even want, fulfilling sex lives? Do you think that, in some ways, the novel falls short of its antipatriarchal project? Explain.

2   Appreciation for women's emotional strength is an important dimension of feminist thinking, and we see such appreciation in Leslie Marmon Silko's "Lullaby" (1974). Although it is a painfully moving story of unconscionable loss, "Lullaby" is also a heroic story of a woman's strength in the face of overwhelming adversity. Note all the hardships and emotional traumas Ayah has experienced during her life. Find the textual evidence showing that, even as Ayah feels the pain of these memories, she has sustained her strength through her intimate emotional bond with nature and with the Native American women's traditions of her childhood.

3   A literary text can contain both antipatriarchal and patriarchal elements. How is Langston Hughes' short story "The Blues I'm Playing" (1934) antipatriarchal in its characterization of Miss Oceola Jones? Consider, for example, her financial independence; her musical talent, which places her among the best, throughout the world, in her field; and her pre-marital living arrangements with Pete. In contrast, how is the story patriarchal on the topic of marriage and children? Consider, for example, its portrayal of Oceola's thoughts on this subject, and note how the text hints that Mrs. Dora Ellsworth's unhappiness is due largely to her childlessness. Which seems stronger to you: the text's antipatriarchal or patriarchal dimension?

4   In what ways does Arthur Miller's play *Death of a Salesman* (1949) illustrate patriarchal ideology? For example, how do Willy, Biff, and Happy Loman treat women as sex objects and tokens of male status? How is Linda Loman a patriarchal woman? Does *Death of a Salesman* seem to promote the patriarchal ideology it illustrates by means of its sympathetic portrayal of Willy and its apparent approval of Linda's support for Willy's patriarchal attitude (in which case we would say the play is patriarchal)? Or does the play, instead, invite us to criticize the patriarchal behavior it illustrates (in which case we would say that the play is antipatriarchal)? In 1949, when the play was first produced, viewers would have tended to see Willy as a sympathetic character and Linda as a good woman and a good wife. It is doubtful that ordinary viewers would have objected to the play's patriarchal ideology. From a feminist perspective today, however, how might modern viewers have some difficulty seeing these two characters in a wholly positive light?

5   Use concepts from feminist theory to help you interpret some aspect of a movie, television show, song lyric, cartoon, video game, or any other production of popular culture that you find interesting and that seems to lend itself to a feminist interpretation. For example, are patriarchal gender roles illustrated in some way? Are they idealized as the only normal, healthy roles for women and men? Do we see any "good-girl"/"bad-girl" ideology at work in this cultural production? Are women represented in a way that objectifies them? If mothering or fathering is portrayed, what does this production seem to be saying about these roles? Based on your observations, what cultural work does your chosen cultural production do relevant to feminist theory? Specifically, what definitions of femininity and masculinity does it promote, and how does it seem to define the "good" woman? Be sure to offer evidence from your chosen production to support your ideas.

Suggestions for further reading

Christian, Barbara. *New Black Feminist Criticism, 1985–2000*. Eds. Gloria Bowles, M. Giulia Fabi, and Arlene R. Keizer. Urbana: University of Chicago Press, 2007.

hooks, bell. *Feminism Is for Everybody: Passionate Politics*. Cambridge, MA: South End Press, 2000.

Oliver, Kelly, (ed.) *French Feminism Reader*. London: Rowan and Littlefield, 2000. (See, especially, Simone de Beauvoir's "Introduction to *The Second Sex*," 6–20; "The Mother," 20–27; and "The Woman in Love," 27–34.)

Robbins, Ruth. *Literary Feminisms*. New York: St. Martin's Press, 2000. (See, especially, "Images of Women Criticism," 50–69; "Psychoanalysis and/or Feminism?" 105–18; "Reading the Boys' Own Stories: *The Strange Case of Dr. Jekyll and Mr. Hyde, The Picture of Dorian Gray, and Heart of Darkness*," 217–41; "Reading the Writing on the Wall: Charlotte Perkins Gilman's 'The Yellow Wall-paper,'" 242–58; and "Afterword: The Mark on the Wall—Marking Differences, Marking Time," 259–56.)

Stavans, Ilan, ed. *Latina Writers*. Westport, CT: Greenwood Press, 2008. (See, especially, Phillipa Kafka's "Saddling La Gringa: Major Themes in the Works of Latina Writers," 3–15; and Debra A. Castillo's "Chicana Feminist Criticism," 16–37.)

Tyson, Lois. "Feminist Criticism." *Critical Theory Today: A User-Friendly Guide*. 2nd ed. New York: Routledge, 2006, 83–133.

Warhol, Robin R., and Diane Price Herndl, (eds.) *Feminisms: An Anthology of Literary Theory and Criticism*. Revised ed. New Brunswick, NJ: Rutgers University Press, 1997. (See, especially, Bonnie Zimmerman's "What Has Never Been: An Overview of Lesbian Feminist Literary Criticism," 76–96; Cordelia Chávez Candelaria's "The 'Wild Zone': Thesis as Gloss in Chicana Literary Study," 248–56; bell hooks' "Male Heroes and Female Sex Objects: Sexism in Spike Lee's *Malcolm X*," 555–58; Judith Fetterly's "Introduction: On the Politics of Literature," 564–73; Paula Gunn Allen's "Kochinnenako in Academe: Three Approaches to Interpreting a Keres Indian Tale," 746–64; and Amy Ling's "I'm Here: An Asian American Woman's Response," 776–83.)

Chapter 7

Using concepts from lesbian, gay, and queer theories to understand literature

Why should we learn about lesbian, gay, and queer theories?

How can we understand human identity without understanding human sexuality? Our capacity to be kind, generous, tender, and understanding; our capacity to experience pleasure; the ways in which we define pleasure—all of these personality traits tell us about our sexuality. And they also tell us about the kind of person we are in our everyday lives: working at our jobs, shopping for groceries, playing basketball, or watching a movie. So whether or not we are sexually active, our sexuality is part of who we are, for our sexuality is related to most or all of the other characteristics by which we define ourselves.

Yet at every level of education, classes in the humanities—that broad field of study which includes literature, history, and philosophy and which explores the various experiences by which we define our humanity—rarely discuss in any depth the topics of sex and sexuality. Even if a class is reading a literary work in which, say, an adulterous affair plays a key role in the story, the affair is usually treated as an event in the plot rather than as a dimension of the character's sexuality or a dimension of the work as a whole that requires close analysis. In fact, if we look at the degree to which the topics of sex and sexuality have been omitted from the humanities, we may reasonably wonder how an academic discipline that claims to study human experience has managed to overlook, or at least under-represent, one of the most important dimensions of that experience.

Surely, part of the reason for this marked omission is the discomfort teachers and students often experience in discussing topics related to sexuality, especially LGBTQ sexuality: lesbian, gay, bi, transgender, or queer sexuality.[1] You might be experiencing some discomfort yourself at this moment. If you are, I hope you won't let it worry you—or prevent you from reading this chapter. Keep in mind that, whatever your personal feelings about sexuality in general and LGBTQ sexuality in particular, it's not unusual to feel a bit uncomfortable, at first, discussing in a classroom setting topics that have rarely, if ever, come up in the classroom, topics that most of us have been raised to believe are strictly private, if not downright transgressive. But whether you're accustomed to the subject or not, I think you'll find this chapter interesting as well as informative because lesbian, gay, and queer theorists have not only helped draw our attention to human sexuality as a serious aspect of studies in the humanities, but they have done so in ways that are meaningful to all of us, regardless of our sexual orientation. For they raise questions that are important to any understanding of human sexuality and how it relates to human identity and culture. Let me give you a few examples.

Lesbian theorists have raised important questions about what it means to define oneself as a lesbian. For instance, if identifying oneself as a lesbian requires sexual relations with another woman, then shouldn't identifying oneself as a heterosexual woman require sexual relations with a man? If so, how can heterosexual virgins claim to be heterosexual? Furthermore, what "counts" as sexual relations? Must genital contact be involved in order for an encounter to be categorized as sexual? With these questions in mind, how should we define lesbian orientation? In fact, with these questions in mind, how should we define any sexual orientation?

Gay theorists have reminded us that definitions of heterosexuality and homosexuality can differ from culture to culture. For example, in the United States today, sexual relations with, or even sexual desire for, a same-sex partner define a man as gay. However, in white working-class American culture at the turn of the twentieth century, as well as in some South American cultures, a man who has sex with another man is still defined as a heterosexual as long as he assumes the masculine role: as long as he penetrates but is never penetrated by his partner and as long as he behaves in a dominant, aggressive, traditionally masculine manner. In contrast, citizens of ancient Athens didn't choose sexual partners based on sex or gender behavior; they chose them in terms of social caste. A male member of the Athenian elite class could have legitimate sexual relations with anyone beneath him in social rank: women and girls of any class or age, boys of his own class who were past puberty but had not yet attained the age of manhood, and all slaves and foreigners. As these examples suggest, definitions of sexual orientation and of legitimate sexual relations depend on cultural attitudes toward sexuality.

Finally, queer theory, which is an outgrowth of lesbian and gay theories, rejects definitions of sexuality that depend upon the sex of one's partner. As we'll see in the "Basic concepts" section of this chapter, queer theorists believe that the biological sex of the people to whom we are sexually drawn tells us nothing other than the biological sex of the people to whom we are sexually drawn. That is, queer theorists find human sexuality much too complex, ambiguous, and dynamic to be understood by this single biological fact: many more personal factors must be taken into account in order to begin to understand human sexuality.

Lesbian, gay, and queer theorists are also interested in questions involving issues of social justice. For example, why does the dominant culture in the United States, among other cultures around the world, tend to define LGBTQ sexuality as deviant, even dangerous, while some cultures define it as natural, even admirable? What is the best way to change American laws, practices, and attitudes that still discriminate against LGBTQ individuals, as if they were not deserving of the same civil rights other Americans enjoy, despite our growing awareness of the enormous contribution of LGBTQ people throughout American history to all areas of American life? (To cite just a few well-known literary examples, consider the work of Walt Whitman, Sarah Orne Jewett, Willa Cather, Hart Crane, Langston Hughes, Gertrude Stein, T.S. Eliot, Tennessee Williams, James Baldwin, Allen Ginsberg, Carson McCullers, Edward Albee, Adrienne Rich, Alice Walker, Audre Lorde, Mark Doty, and David Sedaris.) For discrimination against LGBTQ individuals persists in the United States, not only in the violent hate crimes that still occur, but also in the availability of jobs and housing, in the use of public facilities such as hotels and taverns, in areas of family law such as the right to retain custody of one's children, as victims of police harassment, and in AIDS-related discrimination.

Additional questions raised by lesbian, gay, and queer theorists concern the origin of our sexual orientation, as sexual orientation is traditionally defined in the West today. Is our orientation toward same-sex or opposite-sex romantic partners the result of our genes? (This view is called *biological essentialism* because it tells us that our sexual orientation is an essential, or inborn part of our biological makeup.) Or is our sexual orientation the result of our individual experience? (This view is called *social constructionism* because it tells us that our sexual orientation is constructed by our experience in society.) Or might genetics be the source of sexual orientation for some people while experience is the source of sexual orientation for others? Or might the answer lie in some combination of our genetic makeup and our experience? A related question involves the issue of choice: if LGBTQ sexuality is simply a matter of personal choice, as some people believe, then when and by what process do individuals choose to be heterosexual?

Although we won't discuss here the numerous issues addressed by lesbian, gay, and queer theorists, I think it's important to be aware of them so that you can see what an important and diverse field of inquiry lesbian, gay, and queer concepts open up for our understanding of human sexuality and its relationship to human identity and culture. And as we'll see later, in our interpretation exercises, these concepts also open up literary texts to new and interesting readings. For now, though, let's concentrate on the foundation-level understanding of lesbian, gay, and queer theories offered in the "Basic concepts" section that follows. Although it's important that you read through this list of concepts, don't be too concerned if you don't feel you thoroughly understand every one. You'll begin to understand these concepts much better when we use them, later on in this chapter, to help us interpret the literary texts that appear at the end of this book. And you'll see that these fundamental lesbian, gay, and queer concepts can help us understand other works of literature as well.

Keep in mind that I'm offering you my own literary analyses in the interpretation exercises provided later in this chapter. You might use the same concepts I use but come up with different interpretations of your own. If you disagree with any of the analyses I offer in these exercises, don't be afraid to look in the literary work in question for evidence that will support your viewpoint. A literary work can support a number of different interpretations, even when readers are using concepts from the same theory.

Basic concepts

All of the concepts defined below can be employed to produce lesbian, gay, or queer interpretations of literature, with the following qualifications. As you would expect, the concept of the *woman-identified woman* is not generally employed from a gay perspective, and the term *queer theory* signals the use of the theoretical approach by that name described below.

Heterosexism

Heterosexism is institutionalized discrimination against LGBTQ people. It is discrimination that is "built into" such social institutions as the family, education, religion, and the law enforcement system. And it is based on the belief that heterosexuality is the only right or natural sexual orientation. A heterosexist society—for example, most of heterosexual American culture—permits or encourages discrimination against LGBTQ individuals through its laws, customs, and common practices. The examples of discrimination against LGBTQ people listed earlier are thus examples of heterosexism. In fact, the pressure to be heterosexual placed on young people is so enormous that lesbian poet and theorist Adrienne Rich refers to that pressure as *compulsory heterosexuality*.[2] In other words, our heterosexist society teaches us that we must be heterosexual regardless of how we feel about it.

Homophobia

Homophobia is the intense fear and loathing of homosexuality. Psychologists tell us that *homophobes* (homophobic people) hate LGBTQ people because homophobes are uncertain about their own sexuality and are trying to prove to themselves that they are heterosexual. From this perspective, homophobia is a product of compulsory heterosexuality: if there weren't so much pressure on people to be heterosexual, they wouldn't be so terrified of the possibility that they might *not* be heterosexual. Homophobia is, of course, responsible for hate crimes against LGBTQ individuals. And I think we should also see the ways in which homophobia is responsible for heterosexism, for surely the kind of heterosexist discrimination described earlier is based on the collective, if sometimes unconscious homophobia promoted by traditional heterosexual culture, or what feminism calls patriarchy. *Internalized homophobia* refers to the self-hatred some LGBTQ people experience because, in their growth through adolescence into adulthood, they've internalized (taken into themselves, or "bought into") the homophobia pressed upon them by heterosexist culture.

Homosocial activities

Homosocial activities are simply same-sex bonding activities. Going to the movies, playing cards, fixing the car, preparing a meal, or any other shared leisure or work project is a homosocial activity if it is performed by two or more members of the same sex. The sexual orientation of the participants is irrelevant in homosocial bonding. What is important is the sharing of experiences that makes one feel closer to—"at home" with—members of one's own sex. Homosocial relationships (same-sex friendships) deserve our attention here because, although such relationships contribute to the development and main-tenance of a healthy sense of self, many of us limit or even avoid them because we (consciously or unconsciously) fear that we will be perceived as LGBTQ or that we actually are LGBTQ. In other words, homophobia shuts down homosocial bonding and thereby shuts down an important part of human experience.

The woman-identified woman

Throughout much of Western history, compulsory heterosexuality—which included barring women from opportunities to achieve financial independence so that they would have to marry to survive—has caused many women to marry who would have preferred to share their lives with women. In addition, patriarchy (any society in which men hold all or most of the power) tells us that sexual drive of any kind is much more natural in men than in women, a belief that has caused many women, especially in the past, to deny or be unable to recognize their sexual attraction to other women. For these reasons, a strict focus on what we would define today as sexual activity or sexual desire runs the risk of ignoring an important dimension of women's lives—the homosocial dimension—that might best be understood fully from a lesbian perspective. Many lesbian theorists believe, therefore, that lesbian identity is not restricted to the sexual domain but also can consist of directing the bulk of one's attention and emotional energy to other women and having other women as one's primary source of emotional sustenance and psychological support. From this perspective, a lesbian is a woman-identified woman: a woman who identifies exclusively with women and whose primary relationships (which may or may not be sexual) are with women.[3] Thus, just as a woman who has never had sexual relations with a man can still consider herself heterosexual, a woman who has never had sexual relations with a woman can still consider herself a lesbian. (In contrast, most gay male theorists today assume that gay male identity is defined by sexual activity, or even just sexual desire, between

[Margin notes, handwritten:]

repressed by homophobia

homosocial = same-sex activities

lesbian identity = sexual attraction +/- homosocial activity

woman-identified woman - exclusive identification w/ women

men.) It is also important to note that many lesbian thinkers consider woman-identification essential to a woman's development of her personhood—of a healthy sense of herself as an independent being—for every woman regardless of her sexual orientation.

essential?

Homoerotic imagery

Homoerotic imagery consists of erotic (though not necessarily overtly sexual) visual images that imply same-sex attraction or that might appeal sexually to a same-sex reader. For example, a lush, sensual depiction of a group of women helping one another undress or of nude men bathing in a beautiful pond would be considered homoerotic. We can find many homoerotic images in literature as well as in, for instance, painting, sculpture, film, and photography.

Queer theory

Taking back the word!

Some LGBT people have adopted the word *queer* to refer to themselves for a number of reasons. Referring to themselves positively with a word that has been used to insult them is a way of taking power away from heterosexist society, a way of saying "We're proud that we're different, and we're not going to be intimidated by heterosexism." In addition, the word *queer* is used positively as a broad, inclusive category that acknowledges the shared political and social experience of lesbian, gay, bisexual, transgender, and all people who consider themselves, for whatever reasons, not heterosexual. Hence, LGBT has evolved, for many, into LGBTQ. Finally, and most important for our interpretation of literature, the word *queer* is used to indicate a specific theoretical perspective—called *queer theory*—which we will use later, in our interpretation exercises, to analyze Faulkner's "A Rose for Emily."

Queer theory argues that human sexuality cannot be understood by such simple opposed categories as homosexual and heterosexual, which define our sexuality by the sex of our partner and nothing more. Human sexuality consists of a host of important factors that are not related to the sex of our partner. For example, what is our sexual "personality"? Are we kind? Cruel? Generous? Selfish? Assertive? Timid? Are we drawn to a particular physical type, or "look"? Do we tend to be drawn to older or younger partners? Do we tend to be monogamous, or do we prefer a variety of partners? Do we prefer certain sexual acts or certain kinds of locations for sexual encounters? Do we like to role play sometimes? Always? If so, what are our favorite roles? Do we prefer a particular kind of lighting? Does our sexual behavior fit traditional definitions of masculinity or femininity, or do we have traits associated with both or neither? The answers to questions like these are among the many qualities that reveal important aspects of our sexuality not revealed by the current definition of sexual orientation. Furthermore, for queer theory, our sexuality is wholly determined neither by genetics nor environment, neither by nature nor nurture, because the sources of each individual's sexuality can be many and varied. In addition, our sexuality, depending on how we choose to define it, may be different at different times during our lives or even at different times during the week. Thus, human sexuality is a dynamic, fluid force: it's always changing and growing, and its boundaries are not permanently rooted in any one rigid definition or in any single category.

Of course, there are additional concepts used to interpret literature from a lesbian, gay, or queer perspective, but these are enough to get us started. Let's begin our interpretation exercises by analyzing "Don't Explain," a story by lesbian author Jewelle Gomez that gives us positive images of lesbians and a realistic portrayal of some of the hardships they face in a heterosexist world.

Interpretation exercises

Rejecting lesbian stereotypes: Interpreting "Don't Explain"

Set in Boston in 1959, Jewelle Gomez's "Don't Explain" (1987; see Appendix E) gives us a glimpse into the lives of lesbian characters a decade before the Gay Liberation Movement, which began in 1969, initiated organized political activity to obtain civil rights for gay people in the United States. While the story thus gives us an idea of lesbian experience at a time when lesbians were afforded few or no civil rights—for example, lesbians could be beaten and raped with little if any chance of protection from the police or the judicial system—the issues the story raises are still relevant to life in America today. For American law still does not offer LGBTQ individuals the same civil rights it offers heterosexuals, such as the right to form families legally recognized as such. And even in those situations where every American's rights are protected by law—such as the right to be protected from physical assault and the right to fair housing and employment—heterosexist individuals still often deny LGBTQ people those rights without having to worry too much about the law stepping in to stop them.

"Don't Explain," then, offers us, in addition to an interesting story, an affirmative portrayal of lesbians—represented by Letty, Delia, Terry, Terry's friends, and Billie Holiday[4]—living in a heterosexist world. In order to see how Gomez's story accomplishes this task, we'll examine: (1) its depiction of lesbian isolation in a heterosexist world; (2) its positive portrayals of lesbian characters; and (3) its focus on the importance of lesbian community for the provision of emotional support.

Lesbian isolation in a heterosexist world

We see the events in the story through the eyes of Letty, the main character. Although she's been working at the 411 Lounge for seven years, she doesn't seem to have any close friends, despite the fact that she works with women she likes and with whom she has a good deal in common. Collect the following textual evidence to show that heterosexism and homophobia are responsible for Letty's isolation.

1   Find all the textual data you can to show that Letty feels conflicted about her sexual orientation, that she thinks she should not have the sexual feelings she has. In other words, find the textual evidence that Letty suffers from internalized homophobia.

2   Given Letty's internalized homophobia, she has reason to fear women she thinks might be lesbians, for they might bring to the surface her own sexual feelings, which she is trying to control. Or they might recognize her sexual orientation, which she is trying to hide. In addition, she has reason to fear straight people because they will probably reject her if they discover her secret, and she could lose her job as well. So whether Letty thinks another woman is a lesbian or a heterosexual, she has reason to be on her guard.

   a   Find all the places in the story where we see Letty's interest in:

      i   Delia
     ii   Terry, and
    iii   Billie Holiday, whom she met one night when the singer visited the 411 with her band.

   b   Find all the places in the story where we see Letty holding back, keeping to herself, keeping quiet about her feelings.

3   Given Letty's sexual orientation, her fear of Tip, the pimp who is her regular customer, takes on added weight. If he discovers Letty's secret, she'll be in danger of his physical abuse. Find the line that shows Letty's awareness that Tip likes to hurt people.

4   Given the heterosexist world in which they live, Delia and Terry have to be careful about revealing their sexual orientation. Therefore, though they evidently believe that Letty is a lesbian—that's why Terry asks Delia to invite Letty to meet their friends—they also have reason to be nervous about allowing Letty in on their secret. This is probably why they didn't invite Letty over sooner. Find the places in the story where we see Delia's nervousness about inviting Letty to the get-together she and Terry are having at their apartment.

Positive portrayals of lesbian characters

Negative myths about lesbians that used to be generally accepted as truth and that still exert some influence today include the false belief that lesbians are sick or evil or both, that they hate all men, that they look like men and want to be men, and that their chief goal in life is to prey on other women sexually. The textual data required below ask you to see how the story's portrayals of its lesbian characters—Letty, Delia, Terry, Terry's friends, and Billie Holiday— combat these stereotypes.

1   *Positive qualities of lesbian characters*—Do any of the portrayals of the story's lesbian characters imply that they are sick or evil? Or does the text, instead,

combat this stereotype by giving us lesbian characters whose positive qualities don't allow us to consider them as sick or evil? List all of the positive qualities you can find that the text ascribes to its lesbian characters, including those that we see in such areas as

a attitude toward others,
b personal interaction with others,
c attitude toward work, and
d job capability.

2 *Lesbian characters' attitudes toward men*—Except for the women's get-together at Terry and Delia's apartment at the end of the tale, most of the story's action takes place in the 411 Lounge, where we see Letty's— and to a lesser extent Delia's—interactions with and thoughts about men. Look at all of the passages that refer to men. Do Letty and Delia seem to be man-haters? Which lines in particular show us that Letty—the character about whom we learn the most—is not biased against men?

3 *Physical appearance of lesbian characters*—Look at all of the physical descriptions of the story's lesbian characters. List their personal traits in terms of body types, clothing, voices, and any other traits that can be described in terms of traditional masculinity and femininity. Do all or most of the lesbian characters look alike, as the stereotype suggests? Do they seem to want to be men? Or do we see a variety of individual differences in the way they

a look,
b dress, and
c speak?

4 *Are the lesbian characters sexual predators?*—Look again at the data you've already collected under the heading "Positive qualities of lesbian characters." Does the information you gathered under that heading, or the information available anywhere else in the story, suggest that the chief goal of these characters is to sexually prey on one another or on heterosexual women? Sexual predators are not known for their sincere acts of kindness, for their genuine sensitivity to the needs of others, or for their ability to be a good, non-manipulative friend—at least not when it comes to their potential prey. So all the acts of true kindness, sensitivity, and friendship toward women we see performed by Letty, Delia, Terry, Terry's friends, and Billie Holiday present an image of lesbians that offers a striking contrast to the image perpetrated by the myth that lesbians are sexual predators. Find as many examples as you can of these characters'

a kindness,
b sensitivity, and
c acts of friendship toward women.

The importance of lesbian community

Letty, Delia, and Terry all moved from the American south to the north, from the country to the city. (Can you find the lines in the story that tell us so?) One reason for such a move was surely the increased employment northern cities usually offered working-class women of color. Another reason was probably the women's lesbian orientation: the relative anonymity of city life would allow them to live as they chose—as long as they did so quietly—without being the object of gossip, ridicule, or worse; and the larger, more diverse population increased the possibility of finding other lesbians with whom they could be friends. Find the textual evidence required below to show the important role lesbian community plays for these characters.

1   How many women do Terry and Delia have at their home the evening that Letty joins them? How does the story let us know that these women get together often and know one another well?
2   The clearest evidence of the importance of lesbian community in "Don't Explain" is the dramatic and positive change we see in Letty once she realizes—and accepts—that all of the women in Terry and Delia's apartment are lesbians. Find all the lines that show us this change for the better in Letty.
3   Although Letty meets her only once, Billie Holiday is an important source of strength for Letty because of the emotional bond Letty feels with the singer. Although it was generally assumed, at the time, that Billie Holiday was heterosexual, Letty believes her to be a lesbian, which is why Billie can be viewed as part of Letty's lesbian community. Can you find textual evidence of Letty's belief?

   a   How does the song "Don't Explain" become an emblem of lesbian community at the end of the story?
   b   How can the lyrics of the song, provided in the story, be seen as an emblem of lesbian community?
   c   How does the song help forge a bond between two of the women at Terry and Delia's home?
   d   Given the story's focus on lesbian experience, why is it significant that "Don't Explain" is a Billie Holiday song?

Focusing your essay

Given the textual data you've just collected, you should have little trouble focusing your essay on the ways in which "Don't Explain" combats negative stereotypes of lesbians through its positive portrayals of lesbian characters. Letty, Delia, Terry, and Terry's friends have overcome great odds in order to survive and thrive. And they must continue to overcome those odds if they are to go on surviving and thriving in a world that oppresses them not just in terms of their race, class, and gender but in terms of their sexual orientation as well. Surely, the support they've found in one another as a group will continue to help them in that endeavor.

Even the character of Billie Holiday—who suffered much unhappiness in real life as in the story—has a positive impact on the other characters, both lesbian and straight. And like the other lesbian characters in "Don't Explain," Billie Holiday had an uphill struggle not just against racism, classism, and sexism, but against heterosexism as well. Yet it is the emotional strength Letty gets from Billie's music, and from seeing Billie's kindness to everyone at the 411 Lounge the night the singer stopped in with her band, that helps Letty feel less alone in the world. Indeed, as we see at the end of the story, Billie continues to help others through her music—this time Letty and her new friend Maryalice—even after the singer is dead.

Remember, of course, that you don't have to limit yourself to the analysis of the story I've offered you. For example, you might find additional ways in which "Don't Explain" illustrates the hardships faced by lesbians, offers positive images of lesbians, or corrects stereotypes. Or you might expand your discussion to include some historical research to see what you can learn about the specific forms of discrimination suffered by lesbians during the period in which the story is set so that we can better understand the characters' need both for group support and secrecy. For this purpose, you might consult a history of lesbian and gay experience in the United States, such as *The Gay and Lesbian Liberation Movement* by Margaret Cruickshank (New York: Routledge, 1992), which includes information about the kinds of discrimination practiced against gays and lesbians in the decades leading up to the movement's initiation in 1969. Whatever your interpretation of "Don't Explain," be sure you understand the concepts from gay, lesbian, or queer theory you choose to employ, compose a clear statement of your thesis, and support your interpretation with adequate textual evidence.

Analyzing homophobia: Interpreting "The Battle Royal"

Ralph Ellison's "The Battle Royal" (1952; see Appendix C) plunges readers into a dark, smoky underworld of white male privilege, power, and lust. Set in the post-World-War-II American south, Ellison's tale depicts a group of upper-middle-class white men—the town's civic leaders—abusing their power over women, in the form of a blond exotic dancer they've hired, and abusing their power over people of color, in the form of a group of African American young men they've brought in to perform in the battle royal, a bizarre and unusually violent "boxing" match. In terms of its sexual content, "The Battle Royal" is overtly, even classically, heterosexual. As one of my students said of the text's sexual dimension, "It's about a bunch of guys drooling over a naked blond and watching a fight—two things most guys like to do."

From a gay perspective, however, we can see that these white leaders, though they don't realize it, are also fascinated by the black youths, and this is one of the reasons for their violent behavior toward the young men. For in addition to the violence fueled by the white men's racial hatred, the white men's violent behavior toward the young black men is fueled by their curiosity about the sexual prowess of black males. As you may know, especially in decades past, many white people believed the racist myth that black men are better sexually endowed (have larger male organs) and more sexually promiscuous than white men. (The myth is racist because it is born of the belief that black people are animal-like.)

"Well," you may wonder, "Isn't that just jealousy? Aren't the white leaders behaving badly toward the young black men because they're jealous of them?" Yes, but as we shall see, the white men's jealousy is itself a sign of their insecurity about their own masculinity and, therefore, about their own sexuality. For heterosexist men, insecurity about one's masculinity means insecurity about one's sexuality because such men believe that heterosexual men are naturally masculine and homosexual men are naturally feminine, despite the existence of many masculine gay men.

Of course, as lesbian, gay, and queer theorists know, insecurity about one's own sexuality is at the root of homophobia, the fear and loathing of homosexuality, which often results in aggressive and even violent behavior. Thus, "The Battle Royal" illustrates the workings of homophobia: it shows us how homophobia operates within the homophobic individual as a response to his own sexual insecurity. In other words, as we see in the story, homophobia reveals the sexual psychology of the homophobe, not of the people to whom the homophobe is reacting, for the people to whom the white men in the story are reacting—the black youths—are heterosexual. To see how "The Battle Royal" accomplishes this task, we'll examine: (1) the white men's curiosity about black male sexuality; (2) the white men's treatment of the black youths as, in a sense, sex objects; and (3) the white men's sexual insecurity.

The white men's curiosity about black male sexuality

Although the white men don't admit that they are curious about black male sexuality, the story shows that they are, for this is one of the reasons they deliberately parade the exotic dancer before the young men: they want to see how the young men respond. Collect the following textual evidence to support this claim.

1 How do we know that the black youths are forced, against their will, to look at the exotic dancer? List as many examples as you can find of the young men's negative reaction to this situation.
2 How do we know that the white leaders have conflicted feelings about their own curiosity? For example, what two contradictory threats do the white men yell at the black youths as they display the exotic dancer before the youngsters?

The white men's treatment of the black youths as "sex objects"

In traditional heterosexual culture, women are often treated as sex objects for men. This means that their role is to provide sexual pleasure for men with no concern for their own feelings. Two important features of the treatment of women as sex objects are that women provide visual entertainment for men (they are "eye candy" or, to use more theoretical language, "objects of the male gaze"), and they are submissive to men. Find the textual evidence required below to support the claim that the white men's treatment of the black youths is similar to their treatment of women as sex objects.

1   How are the black youths "objects of the (white) male gaze"?

    a   How do they provide visual entertainment for the white men?

        i   What are these young men wearing?
        ii   What are they required to do?
        iii   What emotions do they feel during these activities, emotions that are clearly visible?

    b   How is this entertainment similar to the entertainment provided by the exotic dancer?

2   How do the white leaders force the young black men to be submissive to their will? List all the ways in which the white men control these youngsters. (The data you find in answering question 2 may overlap with the data you found in answering question 1 because both of these questions ask us to analyze the white men's abuse of power.)

The white men's sexual insecurity

Of course, the white men's curiosity about black male sexuality and their treatment of the black youths as "sex objects" are both signs that the white men are insecure about their own sexuality. If they were secure in their sexuality, their curiosity about the young black men wouldn't take such an aggressive form: they wouldn't need to humiliate them and render them helpless. In addition, there are other signs in the story that the white men are insecure about their own sexuality. Find the additional evidence listed below to support this claim.

1   Like their aggression toward the black youths, the white leaders' aggression toward the exotic dancer is an ego boost, an attempt to prove to themselves that they are powerful men. Find evidence of their aggression toward her.
2   Their sexual display for one another—as if to show how much they like sex—is an attempt by the white leaders to prove to themselves, by proving to others, that they are "real" men. Find the descriptions of their sexual "acting out."

Focusing your essay

Having gathered the textual data required, you should be able to write an essay showing how "The Battle Royal" provides a useful illustration of the operations of homophobia. As the story shows, the white men's insecurity about their own masculinity, which for them means insecurity about their own sexuality, is at least partly responsible for their violent hatred of the black youths. Indeed, as we have seen, the white leaders' aggression toward these young men has a good deal in common with their aggression toward the exotic dancer because they want to control both in order to feel sexually secure. They want to reassure themselves that they're "real men," which they wouldn't need to do if they weren't insecure.

Remember, of course, that you don't have to limit yourself to the analysis of the story I've offered you. For example, in addition to the argument already outlined, you might want to discuss further the parallel between the white men's treatment of the black youths and their treatment of the exotic dancer, a parallel that is sustained in the similarity between the response of the black youths and that of the exotic dancer to the white men's brutal behavior. In fact, the similarity between the white leaders' aggression toward the young men and toward the exotic dancer may lead you to consider another aspect of homophobia to which the story points: that the homophobia aimed at gay men is, at bottom, a hatred of the feminine—that is, a hatred of women. This idea would help explain why homophobes tend to characterize all gay men as feminine, despite the large number of gay men who exhibit masculine behavior, and why homophobes tend to refer to gay men with such feminine words, used disparagingly, as *fairy* and *queen*. It would also help explain why a homophobic man's insecurity about his masculinity can cause such violent acting out: he's terrified of the possibility that he might have any feminine qualities because he believes that feminine qualities are inferior to masculine qualities. Whatever your interpretation of "The Battle Royal," be sure you understand the concepts from gay, lesbian, or queer theory you choose to employ, compose a clear statement of your thesis, and support your interpretation with adequate textual evidence.

Recognizing the woman-identified woman in a heterosexual text: Interpreting "Everyday Use"

Sometimes a literary work can have a lesbian, gay, or queer dimension that is very subtle, very quiet, and barely noticeable (if noticeable at all) to a reader not acquainted with lesbian, gay, or queer theory. This dimension lies "beneath" the literary work, beneath the text, which is why it's called a subtext, but it can nevertheless have something important to tell us. Such is the case with what might be seen as the subtle lesbian dimension of Alice Walker's "Everyday Use" (1973; see Appendix D), a story of women's emotional strength and survival set in America's rural south during the Black Pride Movement of the late 1960s and early 1970s.

Clearly, "Everyday Use" is a tale about women who consider themselves heterosexual, and we have no reason to doubt them. Mrs. Johnson is apparently a widow and has two daughters, Maggie and Dee (also called Wangero). Maggie will marry John Thomas, and Dee has arrived home for a visit with Hakim, the man with whom she lives, in tow. However, despite the fact that the Johnson women confine their sexual relationships to the heterosexual domain, I think we can argue that Mama and Maggie are woman-identified women. Specifically, the story suggests that one can be a woman-identified woman even if one's sexual activities are confined to the heterosexual domain. In other words, "Everyday Use" illustrates the ways in which woman-identification is an *emotional orientation* that can play an important role in any woman's life, regardless of her sexual orientation. In the case of Mama and Maggie, this emotional orientation contributes to the inner strength that helps them live productive, satisfying lives despite the socioeconomic limitations imposed on them due to their race, class, and gender.

Just as the concept of the woman-identified woman might be considered a subtle dimension of lesbian theory—a concept that allows us to see lesbianism as an emotional orientation that may or may not involve lesbian sexual activity— so the presence of the woman-identified woman in Walker's story might be considered a subtle dimension, or a subtext, of that story. This presence may seem to you as quiet as a whisper, but if you listen you can hear the voice of the woman-identified woman speaking softly behind the story's more audible, more obvious heterosexual dimension. In order to hear what that voice has to tell us, we'll examine: (1) the lack of a fully developed, traditional masculine presence in the story; and, in contrast, the way the story portrays (2) the power of female presence; and (3) the importance of female bonding.

The lack of a fully developed, traditiontal masculine presence

Interestingly, the lack of a fully developed, traditional masculine presence in "Everyday Use" isn't due entirely to a lack of male characters. Hakim plays a role in the story, and a number of minor male characters are mentioned, though we don't actually meet them: Mr. Johnson, John Thomas, Jimmy T, Uncle Buddy, Stash, Grandpa Jarrell, and Great Grandpa Ezra. Yet, as the textual data you collect to answer the following questions will reveal, the male characters don't exert much force in the story—don't have a strong emotional presence—especially when contrasted with that of the female characters.

1   *Hakim*

   a   How much do we learn about Hakim, the one male character we actually meet in the story?
   b   Does Dee seem strongly attached to Hakim?

    c What do you think has drawn the two together?

    d How do we know that Hakim remains an emotional outsider to the three women during this visit?

    e How do Mama and Maggie react to him?

    f On whom is the bulk of Dee's attention focused?

2 *Mr. Johnson*

    a How much do we learn about Mr. Johnson, Dee and Maggie's father, whom we never meet?

    b How often does Mama mention Mr. Johnson?

    c How often do Dee and Maggie mention him?

3 *John Thomas*

    a What do we learn about John Thomas, whom we never meet?

    b How often does Maggie mention John Thomas?

    c Does anyone mention his name to Dee?

4 *The other minor male characters*—Although we don't meet them, what do we learn about each of the other minor male characters mentioned in the story?

The power of female presence

In strong contrast to the lack of a fully developed, traditional masculine presence in the story, we are given an extremely powerful female presence in the form of Mama, Dee, and Maggie. As you will see when you gather the textual data to answer the following questions, because of the Johnson women's circumstances—especially the ways in which they have had to survive on their own—all three characters have developed traits that are associated with both traditional (patriarchal) femininity and masculinity. In other words, in a very real sense, the depictions of Mama, Dee, and Maggie, taken together, provide both the feminine and the masculine presence in the story. (To see this aspect of the story clearly, be sure to collect all the textual data you can find about their physical appearance, personalities, skills, and experiences.) Even the minor female characters, whom we don't meet—Aunt Dee (also called Dice and Big Dee) and Grandma Dee—have a more solid presence in the story, because we learn more about them, than the more numerous minor male characters. The point here is that the depictions of the female characters are so powerful, and the female world those characters create is so complete, that the absence of a fully developed, traditional masculine presence seems natural. Indeed, we might say that "Everyday Use" is a woman-identified story.

1 *Mama*

    a In what ways does Mama fit the traditional definition of femininity?

    b In what ways does Mama fit the traditional definition of masculinity?

2 *Dee*

    a In what ways does Dee fit the traditional definition of femininity?
    b In what ways does Dee fit the traditional definition of masculinity?

3 *Maggie*

    a In what ways does Maggie fit the traditional definition of femininity?
    b In what ways does Maggie fit the traditional definition of masculinity?

4 *Aunt Dee and Grandma Dee*—Although we don't meet them, what do we learn about these two minor characters?

The importance of female bonding

In addition to being mother and daughter, Mama and Maggie seem, in many ways, like friends. And the importance of this kind of friendship is illustrated not only in the emotional support it provides these two characters, but in the need for emotional support evident in Dee, who does not share their bond. For the story suggests that Dee's desire for closer ties with her mother and sister is much stronger than she might realize. In fact, the homosocial bonds that structure the story exist between generations—Mama and Maggie feel strongly connected to their female forebears—as well as within the generation of women we meet in the story. And these female bonds have more emotional force, for both the three main characters and the reader, than the male–female ties portrayed. Indeed, these homosocial bonds are represented by the story's inanimate "main characters"—the quilts—which were made by women working together and passed down through the female line. To see how the story shows us the importance of homosocial bonding, collect the textual evidence required below.

1 *Mama and Maggie*—What are the various ways in which the story shows us the bond that exists between Mama and Maggie?

    a What traits do Mama and Maggie have in common? Include the two women's similarities in

        i   physical appearance,
        ii personality traits, and
        iii values.

    b What kind of work do Mama and Maggie do?
    c What other things do Mama and Maggie do together?
    d Look at the image used to describe the two when Mama saves Maggie from the fire. How is this an image of bonding?
    e What does it mean, in this context, that Mama gives Maggie the quilts at the end of the story?

2   *Dee's desire for a stronger bond with Mama and Maggie*—How does the story show us that Dee, whether she realizes it or not, wants more from her relationship with Mama and Maggie?

   a   Why has Dee come home for a visit?

      i   In what ways might she be looking for Mama and Maggie's approval?
      ii   How is she trying to impress them?

   b   Although Dee might not realize it, how can her taking the family's butter-churn dasher and lid be viewed as a desire to be closer to Mama and Maggie?

   c   How might Dee's intense desire for the quilts be viewed as a desire to be closer to Mama and Maggie and to connect, as they connect, to the family's female line?

   d   How does the story indicate that Dee lack's Mama and Maggie's emotional grounding, their emotional connection to and contentment with themselves and others?

   e   How do we know that Dee was discontented when she was in high school?

   f   How does Dee seem discontented even now that she has achieved the financial success she wanted?

   g   How did Dee relate to her mother and sister when she was in high school?

   h   How does Dee relate to her mother and sister now?

   i   How did Dee relate to the few friends she had in high school, including Jimmy T?

   j   How does Dee relate to Hakim?

3   *Male–female bonds*—How does the story indicate that the male–female bonds between characters are less important (less necessary, less emotionally sustaining) than the female–female bonds? To answer this question, you can use the data you have already collected under the headings "The lack of a fully developed, traditional masculine presence" and "The importance of female bonding."

4   *The importance of the quilts*—How do the quilts function as a symbol of female bonding in the story?

   a   Who made the quilts?

   b   To whom did those women teach the art of quilting?

   c   When she becomes a mother, to which of her children will Maggie, in turn, probably teach quilting?

   d   In the Johnson family, are the quilts passed down to subsequent generations through the male or the female line?

   e   How does quilting make the Johnson women the keepers of family history, and how does this role, itself, increase the importance of female bonding in the Johnson family?

Focusing your essay

Taken together, the textual data you've collected should allow you to focus your essay on the role of the woman-identified woman in "Everyday Use." Specifically, the story suggests that heterosexual women, as well as lesbians, can be woman-identified. For being woman-identified is an *emotional orientation* that can play an important role in any woman's life, regardless of her sexual orientation.

This argument does not mean to imply that men don't play an important role in the Johnson family or that the Johnson women don't care about their men. However, it does suggest that the emotional ties the Johnson women share with men aren't as important as their emotional ties with women, both between the generations and within the current generation. For the Johnson women receive their most important and sustaining emotional support from one another. And it is reasonable to assume that it is this support that has allowed Mama and Maggie to survive, even flourish, on their own in a world that is hostile to poor women of color.

In this context, it is not surprising that the beautiful, financially successful Dee seems less happy, less contented than the unattractive, financially unsuccessful Maggie. Dee's ties to her mother and sister—as well as her ties to Aunt Dee and Grandma Dee—are not as strong as the ties that connect Maggie to Mama and to her female forebears. Maggie, not Dee, was taught to quilt by her female relatives. Maggie, not Dee, knows the family history. Maggie, not Dee, has the homosocial support she needs. And no amount of beauty or financial success can compensate Dee for the lack of that support.

Yes, you can develop a reading like this one strictly within a heterosexual framework: emotionally supportive ties to their female family members have contributed a great deal to Mama and Maggie's inner strength and satisfying lives, while Dee's lack of such an emotional foundation has deprived her of the same kind of fulfillment. Such an interpretation, however, would risk underplaying the importance of Mama and Maggie's non-traditional gender behavior in allowing them the full emotional lives they lead. Of course, one could reasonably argue that Mama, at least, has had no choice in terms of her gender behavior: for example, she has had to do traditionally male farm chores, as well as "women's work," because she has had no man to do them for her and her daughters. However, Mrs. Johnson is very capable and proud of doing "men's work," which is the work she prefers. Although "having a man around the farm" would have lightened the load for all three main characters, a fully developed, traditional masculine presence in their lives would surely have limited the degree to which they have felt free to adopt whatever gender behavior they wished. In addition, the use of lesbian concepts encourages us to consider the interesting idea that "Everyday Use" is a woman-identified story: the emotional force of the narrative is carried by the three female main characters and their female forebears, and the story is set in a female world where the fecundity of nature is required to sustain life. Finally, interpreting the story from a lesbian perspective allows us to see more clearly that the concept of the woman-identified woman creates common ground between lesbian and straight women and thus encourages sisterhood.

As always, remember that you don't have to limit yourself to the analysis of "Everyday Use" I've offered you. For example, it might be interesting to consider Mama, Maggie, and Dee in the context of the woman-identified women portrayed in Alice Walker's other literary works. How do Mama, Maggie, and Dee compare and contrast with, for instance, Celie, Nettie, and Shug Avery in Walker's well-known novel *The Color Purple* (1982)? For Celie, Nettie, and Shug, although they all seem to be woman-identified women, each has a different sexual orientation. Whatever your interpretation, be sure you understand the concepts from gay, lesbian, or queer theory you choose to employ, compose a clear statement of your thesis, and support your interpretation with adequate textual evidence.

Using queer theory: Interpreting "A Rose for Emily"

William Faulkner's "A Rose for Emily" (1931; see Appendix B) is a story about Emily Grierson and the man she plans to marry, Homer Barron. That is, it's a tale about a heterosexual couple whose relationship ends in murder, presumably because Homer intends to desert Emily, and she decides to poison him and sleep with his dead body rather than sleep alone. Many students, when they first read Faulkner's story, believe that Homer Barron is gay, which they cite as one of the reasons he doesn't marry Emily. After all, as many readers note, the text tells us that Homer is not the marrying kind, that he likes the company of men and enjoys drinking with the younger men in the town of Jefferson. The problem with using this textual evidence to argue that Homer is gay, however, is that it is extremely unlikely that Homer could be openly gay in the location in which the story is set: a small town in the American south around the turn of the twentieth century. If the people of Jefferson knew Homer was gay, they would, at the very least, run him out of town. Therefore, we must assume that the townsfolk, including the narrator, interpret Homer's preference for male activities and his opposition to marriage as signs that he is a fun-loving womanizer, that he doesn't want to be tied down to one woman or trade his bachelor freedom for the responsibilities of a family man, which is what the description of Homer would have implied, at least to most straight readers, when the story was published in 1931. As we shall see, however, it is Homer's womanizing that, along with other textual evidence, can support the claim that Homer is gay, whether or not he is aware of it. And Homer's possible gay orientation is only one aspect of the queer dimension of "A Rose for Emily" that our reading will explore.

Our interpretation of Faulkner's tale will be queer in the inclusive sense of the term because it will analyze more than one kind of sexuality represented in the story. And our reading will be queer in the theoretical sense (it will draw on queer theory) because it will show that the story illustrates the ways in which the terms *heterosexual* and *homosexual*, the traditional categories by which our sexuality is defined, are inadequate for understanding the complexities of human sexuality. In order to understand how "A Rose for Emily" illustrates this idea, we'll examine: (1) Emily's lack of a fixed gender identity (the fact that she is described as very feminine and very masculine at different points in the story); (2) Homer Barron's ambiguous sexual orientation; and (3) Homer and Emily as, symbolically speaking, a "gay" couple.

Emily's lack of a fixed gender identity

Find all the descriptions of Emily that relate to her gender identity, to the ways in which she seems to be traditionally feminine at some points in the story and traditionally masculine at others. Remember that femininity and masculinity are defined by the society in which we live, and Emily lives in a very patriarchal southern town during the decades preceding and following the turn of the twentieth century. This is a society that expects its women, especially unmarried women from the upper class, to be "ladies": gracious; soft-spoken; gratefully dependent upon others; submissive; devoted to hearth and home; as physically attractive as possible; and attired in pleasing, ladylike clothing at all times. So her femininity or masculinity would be defined by such characteristics as her gracious behavior toward others; her melodious voice; her ladylike dependence upon others; her submission to the dictates of custom and public opinion; her engagement in traditional feminine activities in the home; her housekeeping standards; her hospitality; her physical appearance, including her clothing; and the like.

1   List all of the characteristics of physical appearance and behavior that depict Emily as traditionally feminine.
2   List all of the characteristics of physical appearance and behavior that depict Emily as traditionally masculine.

Homer's ambiguous sexual orientation

Homer has many of the characteristics of physical appearance and behavior that heterosexist culture associates with heterosexual men. However, he also has many of the characteristics often seen in men practicing macho overcompensation, in men who have the desire to prove to themselves and to others that they are "real" men—that is, staunch heterosexuals. Macho overcompensation tends to be displayed when a traditional heterosexual man is insecure about his sexuality—that is, when he's afraid he's not masculine enough and worried that there might be something "wrong" with him; when a gay man is in denial about being gay; or when a gay man who knows he is gay is trying to hide his sexual orientation from heterosexist society. Homer's characterization, then, is ambiguous in terms of sexual orientation: it raises questions about his sexuality but doesn't allow us to draw a conclusion with certainty. To see the ambiguity of this aspect of Homer's characterization, collect the textual data required below.

1   List all of the characteristics of physical appearance and behavior that depict Homer as a traditional heterosexual man.
2   List all of the ways in which Homer seems to be practicing macho overcompensation. Does the story give any indication which of the motives listed above is responsible for this behavior?

Homer and Emily as a "gay" couple

Although the text depicts Emily's gender identity, traditionally defined, as feminine at some points in the story and masculine at others, much of the aggressive, defiant behavior traditionally associated with men is ascribed to Emily during Homer's courtship of her. One implication is that Emily does not assume the traditional feminine, submissive role in her relationship with Homer. Another implication is that Homer finds her masculine behavior attractive. That is, given the possibility that Homer is either a gay man in denial or a gay man in the closet, his attraction to Emily at this point in the story carries some symbolic weight. And Emily continues, for the most part, to display traditional masculine behavior over the years during which she continues to sleep with Homer's dead body, thus increasing the evidence that she plays a masculine role in their relationship. So although Homer and Emily are a heterosexual couple in terms of their biological sex, we might argue that, in terms of traditional gender behavior, they are, symbolically speaking, a "gay" couple: both "men."

1   Find the descriptions of Emily that indicate her gender identity at the time Homer courts her. (Don't forget that Emily kills Homer, which is, to say the least, an unfeminine, aggressive act.)
2   Find the descriptions of Emily that indicate her gender identity during the years she sleeps with Homer's dead body.

Focusing your essay

At this point, the textual data you've gathered should make it fairly easy to focus your essay on the queer dimension of Faulkner's story. For as we've just seen, the characterizations of Emily and Homer cannot be fully understood in terms of the traditional definition of sexuality as either heterosexual or homosexual. Emily's physical appearance and gender behavior cross back and forth between the masculine and the feminine. Homer's sexual orientation is ambiguous, but he seems to be either a gay man in the closet or a gay man in

denial about his sexual orientation. In terms of their biological sex, Homer
and Emily are, of course, a heterosexual couple. In terms of their gender behavior,
however, they are more like a gay couple: at the time of their courtship, they
are both described in masculine terms, and Emily exhibits traditional masculine
traits both when she kills Homer and over the years that she continues to sleep
with his dead body. Thus, although "A Rose for Emily" is presumably a story
about heterosexual passion and transgression, it is also (or more so) a queer
text that reveals the limits of the traditional definition of sexual orientation.

Of course, you don't have to limit yourself to the analysis of the story
I've offered you. For example, you might, instead, examine the ways in which
"A Rose for Emily" is a homophobic text. As we saw in our interpretation of
Ralph Ellison's "The Battle Royal," a literary work can illustrate homophobia
by depicting homophobic characters through which we can learn something
about how homophobia operates. Of course, Ellison's tale doesn't endorse the
homophobia it illustrates. Indeed, its homophobic characters are portrayed so
unsympathetically that readers are not liable to approve of anything those
characters do. In contrast, "A Rose for Emily" does not depict homophobic
characters. Rather, whether it intends to do so or not, it portrays Emily's
sexuality as a form of psychological illness, and in so doing it endorses a
homophobic view of sexuality. In order to reveal this homophobic dimension
of the text, you would need to argue that the story presents Emily's gender-
bending (her masculine appearance and behavior) as one of the symptoms of
the madness that results in her murder of Homer, a madness that has its origin
in her father's barring suitors, or as the narrator puts it, "thwart[ing] her
"woman's life." Whatever your interpretation, be sure you understand the
concepts from gay, lesbian, or queer theory you choose to employ, compose a
clear statement of your thesis, and support your interpretation with adequate
textual evidence.

Drawing upon context: Interpreting "I started Early—Took my Dog"

There may be times when you read a literary work that seems to have a gay
or lesbian dimension, but that dimension emerges only in one or two images
or one or two lines. You may feel strongly that that image or those lines are
meaningful—that they're trying to tell you something—but the literary text
doesn't provide enough data for you to work with. In such a case, you might
consider taking a look at other literary works by the author, and perhaps you
might also browse through biographical materials such as letters, journals, or
biographies, in order to learn whether or not there is some justification for
your feeling that the piece you're reading has a lesbian, gay, or queer dimension. In fact, you might find that more than a single work by this author is
necessary to allow you to use concepts from gay, lesbian, or queer theory
productively. In other words, instead of doing a gay, lesbian, or queer reading
of one of the author's works, you may wind up arguing that a gay, lesbian, or

queer dimension recurs throughout the author's corpus (all of the author's literary work, taken as a whole) and that you will show how this aspect of the author's work operates in two or three different pieces. That's how we'll develop a lesbian interpretation of Emily Dickinson's "I started Early—Took my Dog" (c. 1862; see Appendix A), a short, dream-like poem about a woman who is pursued by the sea from the shoreline where she'd been walking all the way to the edge of the town to which she presumably flees for safety.

First, of course, we have to identify the elements of Dickinson's poem that suggest the possibility of a lesbian reading. Before we go any further, why don't you take a few minutes to read through the poem and see what images or lines you think might lend themselves to a lesbian interpretation? Then, as you read through the rest of this exercise, keep in mind that it offers you steps you can follow to interpret other literary works that have only a small quantity of gay, lesbian, or queer content which you nevertheless feel is significant: (1) identify what seem to you to be the work's gay, lesbian, or queer elements; (2) find the gay, lesbian, or queer elements, if there are any, in other literary works by that author; and (3) find evidence of the author's LGBTQ sexual orientation, if there is any, in biographies or in the author's letters or journals.

The poem's lesbian elements

Most readers tend to see two elements in the poem that might allow a lesbian reading: the mermaids in the first stanza and the fact that the dangerous sexual presence in the poem—the sea—is characterized as male. Let's consider the speaker's representation of the sea first because its presence is felt throughout the poem and is probably, therefore, the more important element.

1 *The Sea*—From the perspective of lesbian theory, it is significant that the male sexuality in the poem—the sea, whose "overflow" of "Pearl" in stanza five (l. 20) is a fairly apparent reference to semen—is represented as threatening, dangerous, even carnivorous (as we see in stanzas two and three, the sea apparently wants to consume the speaker entirely). And it is significant, too, that the speaker runs from it. In this way, the poem seems to reject heterosexuality. In fact, we might say that the poem "denaturalizes" the sea: it portrays the sea, a part of nature, as something unnatural, something that violates the laws of nature by rising out of the ocean floor and pursuing the speaker inland to the edge of town. Thus, the poem might also be seen as implying that heterosexuality isn't necessarily natural or isn't natural for all people.

2 *The Mermaids*—Given the rejection of heterosexuality implied by the poem's portrayal of the threatening male sea and of the speaker's negative response to it, it seems reasonable that we should give some weight to the speaker's brief mention of the only other female presence in the poem besides herself: the mermaids in the first stanza (l. 3). What are

mermaids and how might they suggest a lesbian presence in the poem? Well, mermaids are female. They apparently live with other mermaids, so they constitute a female community. And though human males consider them sexually attractive, men also consider mermaids a threat to human life—legend has it that mermaids sometimes lured sailors from their ships and to their death—just as heterosexist people believe the myth that lesbians are a threat to human life because they lure women from their proper reproductive roles as the wives of men. From the perspective of lesbian theory, it is interesting to note that the mermaids are the first creatures the speaker sees at the shore, that they have come out from their home in the ocean's depths just to look at her, and that whatever interaction she might have had with them is prevented by the aggressive sexual advances of the male sea.

Lesbian elements in other Dickinson poems

If the portrayal of the sea and the mermaids seems to you to suggest that the poem has a lesbian dimension, you might want to check other Dickinson poems for similar elements—for example, other threatening male images and other images of female sexuality—especially if you feel that, by themselves, the depictions of the sea and the mermaids don't provide enough material for you to work with.

1 *Threatening male images*—Like the aggressive, dangerous sea in "I started Early—Took my Dog," we see other male images in Dickinson's poetry that also seem to pose a sexual threat. Probably the most obvious one is found in "In Winter in my Room" (poem 1670). In this poem, the speaker is disturbed by the presence of a "Worm— / Pink, lank, and warm." "Worms presume," says the speaker, and so she doesn't feel "quite ... at home" with him. In fact, she ties him to something nearby, just to be safe. Now, if you suspect that this worm might be a phallic symbol, an image of male sexuality, your suspicion will be confirmed when the worm transforms itself into "A snake ... ringed with power." And how does the snake behave? Like the sea in "I Started early—Took my Dog," the snake is a threatening presence who "project[s]" himself toward her. And like the speaker in that poem, this speaker flees in terror, "Nor ever ceased to run / Till in a distant Town / Towns on from mine / I set me down."

2 *Erotic images of female sexuality*—As Paula Bennett observes, in an essay she wrote for *Lesbian Texts and Contexts* (New York University Press, 1990), Dickinson's poetry links female sexual imagery—specifically, images associated with the clitoris and vaginal lips—with the pleasures of paradise. These images are usually very lush and oral in nature. For example, in "All the letters I can write" (poem 334), the speaker calls upon a lover to "Play it ... / ... just sipped" her "Depths of Ruby, undrained, / Hid,

Lip, for Thee," which is an image of oral sex performed on female anatomy. And this lover is represented by the tiny form of a humming-bird—hardly a male image—whose gender is referred to, ambiguously, as "it." Similarly, "I tend my flowers for thee" (poem 339) includes such female sexual images as "My Fuchsia's Coral Seams / Rip—while the Sower—dreams" and "My Cactus—splits her Beard / To show her throat." As Bennett points out, the focus in such poems as these is on female sexuality and strongly suggests same-sex attraction.

The lesbian dimension of Dickinson's life

Biographical data about the author is not required to argue that a literary work has a lesbian, gay, or queer dimension. After all, the lesbian, gay, or queer elements in a literary work could have been placed there unconsciously by an author who was in denial about his or her sexual orientation or by an author who successfully hid his or her sexual orientation. In both these cases, biographical data might offer us little or nothing of value. However, when biographical data is available about an author's LGBTQ orientation, it can be helpful to make use of it because, in our heterosexist society, many readers still resist gay, lesbian, and queer interpretations of literature. In Dickinson's case, it seems clear that, at the very least, the poet was a woman-identified woman, that her emotional bonds were primarily with women, and that women were the primary source of her emotional support. In addition, you will find increasing acknowledgement, in biographical studies, of the probability of her lesbian orientation—of her sexual attraction to the female body—though no one knows whether that attraction ever expressed itself in a sexual relationship with another woman or remained at the level of sexual fantasy. Specific reference is often made to her lifelong friendship with Susan Gilbert, who married Dickinson's brother and lived, with her husband, next door to the poet. Dickinson's letters to Gilbert, which contain exuberant expressions of passionate love, suggest that the poet's relationship with Gilbert was the most important emotional bond in Dickinson's life.

Focusing your essay

What I've offered you above is an outline you can follow in writing about a gay, lesbian, or queer dimension of an author's writing when, as frequently happens, a single work by that author won't allow you to make a convincing argument for a gay, lesbian, or queer interpretation. If you'd like to try this method with the Dickinson poems we used, first get copies of poems 1670, 334, and 339. ("I started Early—Took my Dog" appears, of course, at the end of this book.) Poems 1670, 334, and 339 can be found in various collections of Dickinson's poetry, including *The Complete Poems of Emily Dickinson*, edited by Thomas H. Johnson (Little Brown). Having the complete poems before you will allow you to do more thorough readings of them. That is, you will be able to find more textual evidence and analyze that evidence further. I think you will be able to argue convincingly that the lesbian dimension of Dickinson's work is evident in its rejection of heterosexuality (the female speaker who flees from a threatening male sexual advance) and, more importantly, in its lush, erotic images of female sexuality. In addition, if you choose to do some research, you will find some biographical support for a lesbian interpretation of Dickinson's poetry in Chapter 3 of Judith Farr's *The Passion of Emily Dickinson* (Harvard University Press, 1992) and in Chapter 5 of Paula Bennett's *Emily Dickinson: Woman Poet* (University of Iowa Press, 1990).

Of course, you can try this approach with the work of other authors. For example, you might examine the homoerotic imagery in the poetry of T.S. Eliot; the queer dimension of Shakespeare's plays, as seen, for instance, in the frequent cross-dressing and mistaking of men for women and women for men; or the ways in which the problems encountered by Willa Cather's male, presumably heterosexual main characters mirror the problems encountered by lesbians in a heterosexist society. However you apply this method, be sure you understand the concepts from gay, lesbian, or queer theory you choose to employ, compose a clear statement of your thesis, and provide adequate textual evidence to support your interpretation.

Food for further thought

Thinking it over

If you've worked through all of the interpretation exercises offered in this chapter, you should feel quite familiar with the basic approaches to understanding literature provided by concepts from lesbian, gay, and queer theories. Specifically, we've seen how concepts from lesbian, gay, and queer theories can be used to analyze

1 literary works that provide positive images of LGBTQ people (our example: "Don't Explain"),
2 literary works that illustrate the operations of homophobia (our example: "The Battle Royal"),
3 literary works with a lesbian, gay, or queer subtext that contributes a subtle but important element to the lives of heterosexual characters (our example: "Everyday Use"),
4 literary works that illustrate the first principle of queer theory: that the opposition of the categories *heterosexual* and *homosexual* is inadequate for understanding the complexities of human sexuality (our example: "A Rose for Emily"), and
5 literary works whose lesbian, gay, or queer dimension can be understood best when analyzed in the context of other works by the author, perhaps

with some support from biographical materials (our example: "I started Early—Took my Dog").

For many students new to the concepts provided by lesbian, gay, and queer theories, the interpretation exercises in this chapter might seem vague or flimsy or even confusing. Keep in mind that any initial difficulty we might have in using these concepts will be due largely to the fact that we've been trained by heterosexist society *not* to be able to see the lesbian, gay, or queer dimension of literary works, despite the large number of LGBTQ authors in the canon of Western literature. And we've been fed so many myths about LGBTQ people for so long that we think our heterosexist biases—in our literary analyses as in other areas of our lives—are not biases but reasonable responses to accurate information.

Probably the most destructive myth about LGBTQ people, which heterosexist culture promotes in order to justify its anti-LGBTQ sentiments, is the myth that LGBTQ individuals are sick or evil. However, if some sexualities are sick or evil, surely they are those involving such behaviors as rape, the sexual abuse of children, or any other form of cruelty inflicted on an unwilling partner. Such behaviors aren't related to whether an individual is straight, lesbian, gay, bisexual, transgender, or queer. These behaviors appear in individuals regardless of their sexual orientation. Remember, then, that our sexual orientation indicates only one thing about us: it indicates whether we're romantically drawn to people of the opposite sex, people of the same sex, or people of both sexes. Our opposite-sex or same-sex orientation is not an indication of our capacity for kindness, generosity, sensitivity, honesty, or any other quality that we generally use to define human goodness or health. Nevertheless, arguments that LGBTQ people are sick or evil still abound, so I think you might find it helpful to be acquainted both with some of the assumptions on which these arguments are based and with some of the counterarguments generally offered in response. Let me summarize them for you now.

The argument that LGBTQ people are sick is based on the assumption that LGBTQ sexual activity goes against nature, that nature intended sexual relations to occur only between males and females. However, this argument ignores two important facts about nature. First, queer sexual activity occurs among healthy animals as well as among human beings. That is, multiple forms of sexual activity occur *naturally*. For example, in addition to male–female sexual activity, animals are also known to engage in same-sex sexual activity and masturbation. Second, if sexual activity in human beings were governed by nature, then human females would not have sexual desire unless they were "in heat" (ovulating), and infertile human males (for example, those with vasectomies or with low sperm counts) would not have sexual desire at all. In fact, if sexual activity in human beings were governed by nature, the current global population crisis would have produced a natural decline in heterosexual activity and, therefore, in reproduction, for a decline in heterosexual activity is one of nature's methods of avoiding overpopulation among animals. Yet Earth's human population continues to increase at an alarming rate.

The argument that LGBTQ people are evil is usually based on the assumption that the biblical ban against sodomy (anal intercourse) means that the Bible is anti-gay. However, this argument generally ignores the fact that the Bible forbids *all* forms of non-procreative sex—that is, all forms of sex that cannot result in conception. Therefore, if we believe that LGBTQ sexual activity is evil because the Bible forbids it, we must also believe that all forms of non-procreative sexual activity are evil, including, for example, masturbation, Onanism (sexual intercourse that is not completed because semen is spilled outside, rather than inside the body of the female), oral sex, and all forms of birth control, including the use of condoms. Thus the argument that homosexuality is evil because the Bible forbids it should, by rights, include an attack on such common activities as masturbation and the use of condoms, both of which practices American culture, among many others, generally deems healthy. An argument that rejects some forms of non-procreative sex but not others cannot rest on the authority of the Bible.

Lesbian, gay, and queer theories and cultural criticism

We can also use concepts from lesbian, gay, and queer theories for the purposes of cultural criticism. That is, we can use lesbian, gay, and queer concepts to help us analyze the cultural messages sent, whether deliberately or not, by the everyday productions of the culture in which we live, such as movies, games, television shows, song lyrics, toys, and other productions of popular culture discussed in Chapter 1. Indeed, those cultural productions that in some way represent human behavior—that have characters and a plot—can be analyzed using concepts from lesbian, gay, and queer theories just as we use those concepts to analyze literary works. For example, an understanding of homophobia and heterosexism can provide us with a gay perspective on the groundbreaking, star-studded Hollywood film drama *Philadelphia* (directed by Jonathan Demme, 1993), in which brilliant young legal eagle and all-American good guy Andrew Beckett (Tom Hanks) is suddenly fired on trumped-up charges of incompetence because the homophobic partners in charge of the law firm for which Andrew works—Charles Wheeler (Jason Robards) and Walter Kenton (Robert Ridgely)—have discovered that he has AIDS, for which they can't legally fire him.

The movie owes much of its great appeal to its sympathetic portrayal of Andy, whose relationships with his large family and his long-time companion Miguel (Antonio Banderas) are models of love, commitment, and unconditional support. Andy is so positively portrayed, in fact, that the film must give him a single flaw in order to humanize him: he cheated on Miguel once, several years ago, which he deeply regrets. Arrayed against Andy are the wealthy, powerful men who fired him and whom Andy courageously decides to sue for wrongful termination; a justice system that needs to be educated about the realities of gay life in a heterosexist culture; and a heterosexist public, whose homophobic comments we overhear in the neighborhood tavern, in the anti-gay protest outside the courthouse during the trial, and in other public locales. In fact, Andy is unable to find a single lawyer willing to handle his lawsuit. He must therefore handle it himself until Joe Miller (Denzel Washington), a gifted but not particularly successful lawyer, finally agrees to represent him. Joe shows the jury, and us, that the real reason for Andy's termination was neither incompetence nor AIDS; it was the partners' virulent homophobia. And it becomes evident during the trial that the partners' homophobia is the result of their insecurity about their own manhood, their own self-image.

Joe Miller functions, in many ways, as the straight audience's heterosexual guide through the complexities of their own feelings, for he himself is misinformed about gay issues and harbors anti-gay biases about which he is in denial and with which he comes to terms over the course of the film. In fact, the genuine friendship that is gradually established between Joe and Andy issues in many positive personal outcomes for Joe: he and his wife form a meaningful bond with Andy and Miguel; he forms a meaningful bond with Andy's family; and he overcomes his own homophobia in his fight to defend the rights of a gay man. The social outcomes of Joe and Andy's gutsy stand are also very positive: although Andy doesn't live to see it, Joe wins what has become a very public lawsuit, and the law firm must pay millions of dollars in fines.

From a gay perspective, the cultural messages apparent in this summary of *Philadelphia* are numerous and educational: (1) like most straight men, gay men are human beings whose happiness depends largely on a loving, committed relationship with a life partner, on family support, and on productive, satisfying work; (2) even when the law opposes discrimination on the basis of sexual orientation, that discrimination is still practiced covertly; (3) an individual can overcome his or her own homophobia; (4) heterosexism relies largely on misinformation and indifference, homophobia on willful ignorance and insecurity about one's own manhood; and last but not least, (5) AIDS has a human face—it is not just an anonymous statistic about people who have nothing to do with mainstream America. Indeed, to everyone in the audience who doesn't have a gay friend, the movie gives us one in the character of Andy Beckett. In addition, I think we can argue that the film reveals the ways in which heterosexism and homophobia, while they are defined differently, actually overlap. For how can a society's majority membership persevere, whether overtly or covertly, in groundless institutionalized anti-gay discrimination (heterosexism) without some kind of personal psychological investment, whether conscious or unconscious, against gays (homophobia)? In short, the movie performs cultural work that is anti-heterosexist, anti-homophobic, and that strongly supports gay rights.

Of course, you may notice that Andy seems almost too good to be true. Why is he so perfect: so handsome, so brilliant, so kind, so wise, so courageous, so unreservedly beloved by his family, and so committed to Miguel, whom Andy's loving family embrace so thoroughly as one of their own? Come to think of it, why are the portrayals of gay affection in the movie so brief and so chaste? Why do we see so little camp self-expression among Andy and Miguel's gay friends at their party? Evidently, the filmmakers felt they would lose their audience—or at least their straight audience—if they did otherwise. That is, the narrative choices made during the production of *Philadelphia* tell us something about the mainstream American movie-going audience in 1993: it was too homophobic to be counted on to spend money at the box office for anything less non-threatening. And given the period during which the film was produced, surely the filmmakers wanted to avoid the negative gay stereotypes that had been so common in the film industry up to that point in time, for example, the stereotype of the oversexed, promiscuous, or exhibitionist gay man. It is apparent that great care was taken in the production of *Philadelphia* in an effort to ensure that its important cultural work would not be lost.

***

Remember, it's natural to feel a bit uncertain when we encounter a new theory—a new way of looking at ourselves and our world—that may call into question many of the beliefs that have been pressed upon us, and that we've accepted uncritically, for most of our lives. Uncertainty is an unavoidable part of learning and growing. Keep in mind, too, that others may disagree with your opinions. Individuals often disagree in their interpretations of literature, popular culture, or everyday experiences, even when drawing upon the same lesbian, gay, or queer concepts. for their analyses. The keys to a good interpretation—besides intellectual curiosity and an open mind—are a clear understanding of the lesbian, gay, or queer concepts you've chosen to use and strong evidence to support your analysis.

Taking the next step

Questions for further practice

1 David Sedaris' short story "I Like Guys" (1974) offers numerous illustrations of heterosexism, homophobia, and internalized homophobia. Find as many examples of these concepts in the story as you can. How do these illustrations show us the destructive effects of such anti-gay attitudes, especially on young people? Be specific.

2 In Kitty Tsui's poem "A Chinese Banquet" (1983)[5] the speaker is eating dinner at a large family gathering to which the woman she loves is not invited. How do we know that the speaker is serious about the woman she loves and very happy with their relationship? Why did the speaker confide in her mother about this part of her life? How would you characterize the mother's response to her daughter's sexual orientation, both

when she first learned of it and now when she speaks to her daughter at the family gathering? A family banquet is, both literally and figuratively, a form of nourishing. How does the poem communicate these positive aspects of the banquet and, in contrast, the speaker's feelings of alienation from her family? How does the poem show us that heterosexism, at the level of the family, will cost the family its gay child?

3   Certainly, Kate Chopin's *The Awakening* (1899) is a novel about hetero-sexual love and marriage. Protagonist Edna Pontellier is a wife and mother; she falls in love with a man, Robert Lebrun; and she has a sexual relationship with a man, Alcée Arobin. Nevertheless, an awareness of the ways in which Edna's portrayal is not limited to the heterosexual domain can enrich our understanding of the complexity of her characterization. For example, find textual evidence showing the homoerotic dimension of Edna's response to Adèle Ratignolle's voluptuous beauty. How is a homoerotic atmosphere created by Mademoiselle Reisz's behavior toward Edna—including the way the older woman addresses the protagonist—during the latter's visits to the pianist's tiny apartment? Note, too, how descriptions of Edna's beauty give it a masculine quality, especially when contrasted with Adèle's traditional femininity. Finally, find textual evidence showing the ways in which Edna's behavior—for instance, the way she goes where she plea-ses, with or without companions; talks about race-horses; drinks brandy; and tolerates Arobin for sexual purposes only—places her beyond the rigid confines of traditional heterosexual womanhood depicted in the novel.

4   Explore the ways in which the speaker in Walt Whitman's "Song of Myself" (1855) eroticizes almost everything he sees: for example, the bodies of young men and women; the venerability of old men and women; the strength and serenity of animals; the magnificent beauty of the mountains, the sea, and other elements of nature; the bustling energy of cities; and almost every part of his own body. How does this aspect of the poem illustrate the primary premise of queer theory: that human sexuality is too complex to fit tradi-tional categories of sexual orientation—heterosexuality, homosexuality, and bisexuality—based solely on the biological sex of our partner?[6]

5   Use concepts from lesbian, gay, or queer theory to help you interpret some aspect of a movie, television show, song lyric, cartoon, video game, or any other production of popular culture that you find interesting and that seems to lend itself to a lesbian, gay, or queer interpretation. For example, do gay or lesbian stereotypes or negative references to LGBTQ individuals appear in this cultural production? Is heterosexism, homophobia, or internalized homophobia represented in some way? If so, what does this production seem to be saying about these values? Based on your obser-vations, what cultural work does your chosen cultural production do relevant to lesbian, gay, or queer theory? Specifically, what definitions of "normal" masculinity, "normal" femininity, and "normal" sexuality does it imply? Be sure to offer evidence from your chosen production to support your ideas.

Suggestions for further reading

Abelove, Henry, Michèle Aina Barale, and David M. Halperin, (eds.) *The Lesbian and Gay Studies Reader.* New York: Routledge, 1993. (See, especially, Eve Kosofsky Sedgwick's "Epistemology of the Closet," 45–61; Marilyn Frye's "Some Reflections on Separatism and Power," 91–98; Barbara Smith's "Homophobia: Why Bring It Up?," 99–102; Phillip Brian Napier's "Eloquence and Epitaph: Black Nationalism and the Homophobic Impulse in Responses to the Death of Max Robison," 159–75; Adrienne Rich's "Compulsory Heterosexuality and Lesbian Experience," 227–54; Audre Lorde's "The Uses of the Erotic: The Erotic as Power," 339–43; Henry Abelove's "Freud, Male Homosexuality, and the Americans," 381–93; and David M. Halperin's "Is There a History of Sexuality?" 416–31.)

Jay, Karla, and Joanne Glasgow, (eds.) *Lesbian Texts and Contexts: Radical Revisions.* New York: New York University Press, 1990. (See, especially, Paula Bennett's "The Pea That Duty Locks: Lesbian and Feminist-Heterosexual Readings of Emily Dickinson's Poetry," 104–25; Judith Fetterly's "*My Antonia,* Jim Burden, and the Dilemma of the Lesbian Writer," 145–63; and Diane A. Bogus' "The 'Queen B' Figure in Black Literature," 275–90.)

Lorde, Audre. *Sister Outsider: Essays and Speeches.* Freedom, CA: The Crossing Press, 1984. (See, especially, "Scratching the Surface: Some Notes on Barriers to Women and Loving," 45–52; "Uses of the Erotic: The Erotic as Power," 53–59; "An Open Letter to Mary Daly," 66–71; "Man Child: A Black Lesbian Feminist's Response," 72–80; and "The Master's Tools Will Never Dismantle the Master's House," 110–13.)

Radicalesbians. "The Woman-Identified Woman." Pittsburgh: Know, Inc., 1970. (Full text available online at http://scriptorium.lib.duke.edu/wlm/womid/)

Richardson, Diane, and Steven Seidman, (eds.) *Handbook of Lesbian and Gay Studies.* London: Sage, 2002. (See, especially, Barry D. Adam's "From Liberation to Transgression and Beyond: Gay, Lesbian, and Queer Studies at the Turn of the Twenty-first Century," 15–26; Dawne Moon's "Religious Views of Homosexuality," 313–28; and Stephen Engel's "Making a Minority: Understanding the Formation of the Gay and Lesbian Movement in the United States," 377–402.)

Tyson, Lois. "Lesbian, Gay, and Queer Criticism." *Critical Theory Today: A User-Friendly Guide.* 2nd ed. New York: Routledge, 2006. 317–57.

Woods, Gregory. *A History of Gay Literature: The Male Tradition.* New Haven, CT: Yale University Press, 1998.

Notes

1 A transgender person's gender (masculine or feminine) doesn't match his or her biological sex (male or female). For example, a transgender woman has the anatomy of a female but knows that, inside, she is a man: her biological sex is female, but her gender is masculine. Furthermore, her transgender status doesn't indicate her sexual orientation. Finally, a transgender individual who has undergone the process of sex change is no longer transgender (for sex and gender now match) but transsexual.

The word *queer,* as you'll see in the "Basic concepts" section of this chapter, can be used in different ways. For example, *queer theory* refers to a framework for understanding human sexuality that is not based on the biological sex of the people to whom we are sexually attracted. The word *queer* is also often used as a positive, inclusive term referring to LGBT (or GLBT) individuals and to anyone who is, in whatever way, not strictly heterosexual. The inclusive acronym, therefore, is LGBTQ (or GLBTQ). However, many people use the Q in *LGBTQ* to refer to the word *questioning*—that is, to refer to people who are uncertain of their sexual orientation—or to refer to both *queer* and *questioning*.

2 See Adrienne Rich's "Compulsory Heterosexuality and Lesbian Existence," *Signs* 5.4 (1980): 631–60. Rpt. in *The Lesbian and Gay Studies Reader*, eds. Henry Abelove, Michèle Aina Barale, and David M. Halperin (New York: Routledge, 1993), 227–54.

3 See "The Woman-Identified Woman," Radicalesbians (Pittsburgh: Know, Inc., 1970). Full text available online at http://scriptorium.lib.duke.edu/wlm/womid/.

4 See Stuart Nicholson's biography, *Billie Holiday* (Boston, MA: Northeastern University Press, 1995). During her lifetime, the general public assumed that Billie Holiday was a heterosexual, for outside the circle of her musician friends, she could not freely admit her bisexuality. In the context of "Don't Explain," however, Billie Holiday functions as a lesbian character because that's how Letty sees her, and it is from Letty's point of view that Billie has importance in the story.

5 Kitty Tsui's "A Chinese Banquet" is included in her collection of poetry and prose, *The Words of a Woman Who Breathes Fire* (Iowa City: Women's Press, 1983), 12–13.

6 For a similar approach to "Song of Myself," see Lois Tyson's "Lesbian, Gay, and Queer Criticism," *Critical Theory Today: A User-Friendly Guide*, 2nd ed. (New York: Routledge, 2006), 337–38.

Chapter 8

Using concepts from African American theory to understand literature

Why should we learn about African American theory?

Having seen, in previous chapters, how a knowledge of issues concerning class, gender, and sexual orientation can help deepen our understanding of literary works, it should not be surprising to learn that an understanding of racial issues can also increase our ability to appreciate and analyze literature. Indeed, like many nations, the United States consists of people of many different races, all of whom have contributed to our country's literary production as well as to its history. However, Americans of African descent, whose presence in the New World is as old as the presence of the first European settlers, have developed not only a very large body of internationally acclaimed literature but, as the title of this chapter indicates, a collection of widely used critical tools with which to analyze literature, as well. It makes sense, then, to use an African American perspective as our source, in this chapter, of concepts concerning race.

Despite, however, the enormous role played by African Americans in the history and cultural development of the United States, my recurring experience in the classroom has been one of surprise and alarm at how few opportunities my students have had in school to learn about African American history, culture, and literature or to learn to recognize and understand the enormous gulf that still separates white and black Americans.

For example, I've had many fine students, of all races, who have never heard of or are only slightly aware of the important role played by black Americans in such areas as the development of American art, film, literature, science, education, philosophy, law, medicine, theater, dance, and music. Have you ever seen a film by pioneer filmmaker Oscar Michaux? Are you aware of the role played in the history of American theater, music, and politics by Paul Robeson? What do you know about Harriet Tubman and the Underground Railroad or about the work of Sojourner Truth in the struggle for racial and gender equality? How familiar are you with the philosophical debate between Booker T. Washington and W.E.B. DuBois concerning the relationship between education and the attainment of political equality? How much do you know about the outpouring of African American literature, art, and music during the Harlem Renaissance of the 1920s or during the Black Arts movement of the 1960s? Are you aware of the number and importance of the pioneering advances made both in agricultural science and in industrial uses for agricultural products by scientist and inventor George Washington Carver? Have you heard of the work of political activist and journalist Ida B. Wells? Are you familiar with the painting and collage of Romare Bearden? The influential work of countless black Americans such as these has helped produce the American life we live today. Their efforts have contributed both to the development of African American culture and to the development of our national culture. Yet these Americans are too often overlooked or underrepresented in our classrooms, and students have few if any opportunities to get a real sense of just how beautifully black are many of the deepest roots of American culture.

Similarly, I've known many fine white students who were so ill-informed concerning the realities of race in America that they believed racism ended with the Civil War—or at least with the turn of the twentieth century—or that the only racists left in the United States today are the members of the Ku Klux Klan. So when we read William Faulkner's story "That Evening Sun" (1931), which portrays the racist attitudes that separate a white family from the black people who work in their home during a period several decades after the Civil War, a number of students nevertheless assumed that the black characters are slaves. "After all," these students said, "the kind of economic oppression and racial prejudice we see depicted in the story occurred only during slavery." Because they themselves hadn't observed—or perhaps more accurately, hadn't recognized—racial prejudice, they assumed that racism was, for the most part, a thing of the past.

Unfortunately, though, the evils of slavery are still with us today in a heritage of racial bias that is so thoroughly built into American law, politics, and social behavior that many white Americans are unable to see it. To cite just one striking example, until President Obama signed the Fair Sentencing Act in August 2010, possession of only five grams of crack cocaine (used predominantly by black Americans) triggered a mandatory prison sentence of five years, while the possession of five hundred grams of powder cocaine (used predominantly by white Americans) was required to trigger the same five-year mandatory prison sentence. And even now, though lessened, there is still a marked sentencing disparity for users of these two forms of cocaine: although now the possession of twenty-eight grams of crack cocaine is required to trigger the minimum five-year mandatory prison sentence, the mandatory trigger for powder cocaine remains five hundred grams.[1] Such discriminatory laws spotlight drug activity in poor black neighborhoods and have resulted in increased police surveillance in these areas, while drug activity in middle- and upper-class white neighborhoods is largely ignored. In fact, although the majority of drug users of all kinds in the United States are white, the majority of inmates serving prison sentences for drug-related offenses are black. As a result of this kind of racial bias, our prisons contain a disproportionate number of African American inmates, which perpetuates the racist myth that black Americans are "born criminals." That myth, in turn, justifies the laws that disproportionately target and penalize African Americans. Do you see why this is called a "circular" problem? Here's the circle.

Point 1—Racist beliefs tell us that black Americans are inferior to white Americans.

Point 2—These beliefs *put* black Americans in situations that *are* inferior to those of white Americans (for example, inferior housing, inferior schools, inferior jobs, and as we just saw, inferior legal status).

Point 1 (again)—The inferior situations of black Americans are used to justify racist beliefs.

To be sure that you have a firm grasp of "circular" thinking, let's briefly examine one more specific example of the "circular logic" (or more accurately, "circular illogic") of racist beliefs: the practice of denying job opportunities to African Americans and then arguing that the absence of black Americans in certain occupations is evidence of their inferiority. As recently as the 1950s, the only work readily available to people of color in the United States was menial labor. African Americans were hired as farm hands in rural areas, and in the cities they worked as maids, custodians, waiters, cooks, baggage handlers, and in other "service" occupations. In other words, the only jobs that were easily obtainable were similar to the work people of color performed under slavery. Then, because the majority of African Americans performed menial labor, it was argued that they were incapable of any other kind of work. The fact that other occupations were closed to them wasn't recognized as the cause of the problem but was seen, instead, as the result of the "limited capacity" of people of color.

Even when the judicial system protects people of color, as does the equal-opportunity law that now prohibits racial discrimination in the workplace, discrimination still occurs. For example, many white employers still discriminate against African Americans by hiring the minimum number of African Americans possible and by denying them access to leadership positions or meaningful promotions of any kind. Similarly, although the fair-housing law now prohibits racial discrimination in the sale and rental of dwellings, white real-estate agents and landlords often ignore the law and lie to prospective black clients about the availability of housing in order to keep them out of white neighborhoods. While there are many additional examples I could offer of the persistence of racism in the United States today, my point is simply that the failure of our educational system to acknowledge these realities has left many non-black students ignorant of the kinds of racial injustice that still exist in the United States.

Of course, a single, introductory-level chapter on African American critical theory can't even begin to fill in the gaps in your knowledge left by our educational system. However, it can at least alert you to the existence of those gaps and try to interest you in filling them in yourself. You can begin to accomplish this task by reading books and watching television programs that focus on African American history and culture. Perhaps Denise Dennis's *Black History for Beginners* (Writers and Readers Publishing, 1984); James and Lois Horton's *A History of the African American People* (Wayne State University Press, 1995); and the television series *Africans in America* (Public Broadcasting System, 2000), with its accompanying book of the same title, might be a good place to start. You can also learn a good deal by reading literary works by and about black Americans, for a culture's literary production is also a kind of historical record in that it represents the lived experience of its people. Finally, if you're lucky, you'll be able to take courses in African American literature, culture, and history at your college.

In any event, this chapter can help you understand some of the key concepts you'll need in order to get the most out of these educational resources, and it can give you some practice in using concepts from African American theory to interpret works of African American literature. In addition, because many literary works by white authors have African American characters or represent racial issues in some way, these concepts can be used to interpret works by white writers as well. And while the histories and cultures of all ethnic American political minority groups are unique—as are the specific kinds of racism leveled against them—I think you'll find that many of the concepts from African American theory offered in this chapter will provide a useful starting point for the appreciation of literary works by, for example, Native American, Latino/a, and Asian American writers.

Although it's important that you read through the "Basic concepts" section that follows, don't be too concerned if you don't feel you thoroughly understand every one. You'll begin to understand these concepts much better when we use them, later in this chapter, to help us interpret the literary texts that appear at the end of this book. Keep in mind, too, that I'm offering you my own literary analyses in our "Interpretation exercises." You might use the same African American concepts I use but come up with different interpretations of your own. If you disagree with any of the analyses I offer in these exercises, don't be afraid to look in the literary work in question for evidence that will support your viewpoint. A literary work can often support a number of different interpretations, even when readers are using concepts from the same theory.

Basic concepts

African American culture and literature

African American culture is rich and varied and grows, of course, out of black American history and experience. African American culture includes, among many other characteristics, the following elements:

1   oral history (the passing down of knowledge about personal family, and community life by word of mouth), which has contributed to the importance, in African American literature, of
2   orality (the sound of the spoken voice produced by the printed word, often achieved by writing in African American Vernacular English, AAVE, which is also called Black Vernacular English, BVE),
3   African American music, specifically jazz, blues, gospel, and hip hop
4   African American cuisine,
5   folk crafts, such as quilting and woodcarving,
6   the importance of people's names and nicknames as a means of connecting them to their culture and to the past, and
7   a value system that emphasizes the importance of the family, community, and church in the effort: (a) to survive the harsh realities of racism; (b) to seek the positive, often spiritual, aspects of life; and (c) to insure that every black American has the opportunity to achieve his or her full human potential.

These elements of black American culture are often represented in African American literature and have created an *African American literary tradition* that you'll come to recognize as you increase your reading of African American authors. Of course, many aspects of African American culture have influenced American culture as a whole, the best-known examples of which are probably jazz, blues, and hip hop music.

Given that some form of racial discrimination is a daily experience for most African Americans, racial issues have greatly influenced African American culture. Therefore, racial issues—for example, the economic, social, and psychological problems caused by racism; the difficulties faced by biracial individuals in America, including the temptation to pass for white; and the attempt to reclaim the African past of lost ancestors—are frequently portrayed in African American literature. African American authors have also focused a good deal of attention on such historical topics as the horrors of the Middle Passage (the transportation of captive Africans across the Atlantic from the west coast of Africa to the east coast of the United States, South America, and the Caribbean Islands), the horrific ordeal of slavery, the struggle for emancipation, the Civil War, life in the segregated south, and the attempt to find a better life in the north.

Of course, white authors have created African American characters and written about issues of race, too, and we can use concepts from African American theory to analyze their work, as well. However, it's important to keep in mind that, while some white authors have been actively antiracist in their portrayals of African Americans and their depictions of racial issues, many other white authors have reinforced racist stereotypes and racist thinking, whether or not they realized they were doing so. In other words, it's not the portrayal of African American characters or the depiction of racial issues that makes a literary text racist or antiracist. A text's *racial politics* (whether the text reinforces racism or attacks racism) depends on the way in which it portrays those characters and depicts those issues.

Racism is an unpleasant topic, to say the least. As you can see, however, it's an important topic, too, and is central to an understanding of African American theory. So let's take a closer look at racism and the various forms racism takes.

Racism

Racism is the economic, political, social, or psychological oppression of individuals or groups based on their race. Racism is fueled by the myth that the oppressed race is inferior to the "dominant" race—that is, to the race holding the power in a given society. For example, white racism is fueled by the myths that people of color are less intelligent, less "civilized," less moral, and even less attractive than white people. *Racist stereotypes* about African Americans include, among others, the following clusters of characteristics: lazy, unambitious, slow-moving, and dim-witted; violent, brutal, and criminally inclined; and sexually promiscuous, hard-drinking, and fond of drugs of any kind. Consider the following example of how racist stereotypes limit our perceptions of our fellow human beings in our everyday lives. A white shopper, having been given poor service by a white sales clerk, thinks, "What a lazy person that sales clerk is!" That same white shopper, having been given poor service by a black sales clerk, thinks, "Black people are so lazy!" Only in the second case is the white shopper stereotyping along racial lines, or ascribing a trait observed in one person to all people of the same race.

While the damaging effects of these negative stereotypes are obvious, even "positive" racial stereotypes are damaging: for example, the stereotypes that African Americans are "born" athletes, "naturally" good dancers (because they have "natural" rhythm), and devoted servants to white families. These so-called "positive" stereotypes are damaging because, like negative stereotypes, they suggest that all African Americans are alike and have no important individual qualities beyond the stereotype to which they "belong." In addition, both negative and "positive" stereotypes serve a racist desire to view African Americans only in ways that boost white importance. Negative stereotypes depict people of color as clearly inferior to whites, and racist thinking links such "positive" stereotypes as the "born" athlete or the "natural" dancer to what it sees as a "primitive," tribal heritage, while it links such "positive" stereotypes as the devoted servant to black Americans' "rightful" sense of their own inferiority to whites. In short, all stereotypes deprive stereotyped persons of their individuality and, too often, of their humanity.

Forms of racism

Institutionalized racism—In order for racism to have any real force in a society, it must be supported in some way by that society's institutions, for example, by the educational system, the judicial system, the entertainment and fashion industries, law enforcement policies, labor practices (such as the accepted attitudes that govern hiring new employees, determining their salaries, and promoting or firing them), and housing regulations. Three examples of institutionalized racism were described earlier: the enormous difference between mandatory prison sentences for users of crack cocaine (who are predominantly black) and users of powder cocaine (who are predominantly white), the persistence of racial discrimination in the workplace, and the frequent tendency of real-estate agents and landlords to successfully sidestep the fair-housing law. We also discussed earlier the failure of most American schools to include adequate coverage of the historically significant work of African Americans in all fields of endeavor, thereby blinding students to the fact that American history and culture have significant black roots as well as white roots, and this failure is also an example of institutionalized racism. Other examples of institutionalized racism include, for instance, the inadequate resources available to public schools in black neighborhoods; the continued use of racially biased textbooks and achievement tests; the inadequate representation of African American authors (who now hold top international honors) on college syllabi in American literature courses; the inadequate response of national agencies to African American health problems; the disproportionate number of municipal incinerators in black neighborhoods, which pose a serious health threat to local residents; and even such relatively routine occurrences as the disproportionate number of black motorists pulled over by law enforcement officers.

Internalized racism—Some people of color suffer from varying degrees of internalized racism, which is the acceptance of the belief pressed upon them by racist America that they are inferior to whites, less worthy, less capable, less intelligent, or less attractive. Victims of internalized racism often wish they were white or that they looked more white. Obviously, internalized racism is very damaging to self-esteem: it is difficult to maintain a positive self-image when one has been programmed to believe that one is inferior simply because of one's race.

Intraracial racism—Internalized racism often results in intraracial racism. Intraracial racism is discrimination, within the black community, against those with darker skin and more African features, such as hair texture and the shape of the lips and nose. Intraracial racism is operating when African Americans believe, for example, that light-skinned black people are more beautiful or more intelligent than darker skinned black Americans. Of course, a person who suffers from internalized racism will probably practice intraracial racism because both forms of racism "buy into" the white racist attitude summed up in the frightening old saying, "If you're white, you're alright; if you're brown, stick around; if your black, get back!" Finally, when a literary work depicts intraracial racism or internalized racism, we can assume that institutionalized racism is implied as well—perhaps as part of the current reality in which the characters live, perhaps as part of the history of the society in which they live, or perhaps as both—even if it is not depicted. For as we have already seen, institutionalized racism is the force behind the persistence of all forms of racism.

Double consciousness

Double consciousness, first described by W.E.B. DuBois in *The Souls of Black Folk* (1903), is the awareness of belonging to two conflicting cultures: the black culture, which grew from African roots and developed in response to a history of racist oppression, and the European culture imposed by white America. For many African Americans, double consciousness results from living in two very different worlds—the world at home and the white-dominated world outside the home, such as the school, the workplace, and even the shopping mall— where two different sets of expectations, or cultural "rules," are operating, and sometimes two different languages are spoken.

There are, of course, additional concepts offered by African American theory, but these are enough to get us started using this theory to interpret literature. Let's begin our interpretation exercises by analyzing Ralph Ellison's "The Battle Royal," a story that is unmistakably antiracist because of the great clarity with which it illustrates the horrors of racism, specifically, the institutionalized racism of the segregated south at a time when the judicial system offered black Americans little or no protection from the excesses of white power.

Interpretation exercises

Analyzing the overt operations of institutionalized racism: Interpreting "The Battle Royal"

One of the first things to which many of my students react when they read Ralph Ellison's "The Battle Royal" (1952; see Appendix C) is the horrifying behavior of the white men at the "smoker," the private party held by the town's leading citizens for the purpose, it would seem, of abusing their power. Unlike other examples of racist behavior we might see in the news today, this is not a gang of white teenaged boys gathered in some out-of-the-way place where they can beat up a black youth without being caught by the police. Neither is this a meeting of hooded white men concealing themselves beneath sheets so that they can threaten and harm black Americans without revealing their identities to the forces of law and order. Rather, this is a gathering of civic leaders at the town's best hotel. Although these white men engage in physically violent, racist behavior toward a group of low-income black youths paid to endure their abuse, these white leaders feel no need to hide their evening's "entertainment" from the law. Indeed, representatives of the judicial system— lawyers and judges—are present. Present, also, are other leading citizens—doctors, teachers, bankers, fire chiefs, merchants, the local superintendent of schools, and even a pastor—whom we would expect to condemn the very behavior in which they themselves are engaged.

These white men seem to have little or no sense that what they are doing is wrong, and apparently little or no fear of discovery, because their racist activities are condoned by the institutions these characters represent. That is, in the place and time in which "The Battle Royal" is set, the American south of the late 1940s, racism is widely institutionalized: it is practiced or tolerated by white institutions such as the law, the educational system, the medical profession, the banking profession, local businesses, civic organizations, and the white church as a way of keeping African Americans "in their place." In this context, the battle royal in which the black youths engage is considered a harmless entertainment justified by the monetary rewards offered to the young men in return for their participation. The events that occur in Ellison's story are thus examples of the overt—the open and flagrant—operations of institutionalized racism, which, because it is built into the laws and practices by which a society operates, offers white Americans unrestrained power over black Americans.

As a depiction of the overt operations of institutionalized racism, "The Battle Royal" provides insight into the dehumanizing effects of systematic oppression both on the white characters who wield racial power and, especially, on the black characters trying to survive the overwhelming injustice institutionalized racism forces upon them. In other words, among other things, Ellison's tale addresses two important questions about the history of institutionalized racism in the United States: (1) What happens to people who have unrestrained power over the lives of other human beings?; and (2) How do human beings victimized by that unrestrained power attempt to survive? Let's see how the story answers these questions.

The effects of unrestrained power on the white civic leaders

Because the white men in "The Battle Royal" are civic leaders and hold important professional positions, we know that they are very well educated and enjoy the privileges of wealth and social position. Given their financial and social status, they probably have wives and children, too. So it is a testimonial to the corrupting influence of unrestrained power that men with so much going for them, with so many sources of pride and fulfillment, should degrade themselves the way they do at the smoker. For their treatment of those over whom they hold power degrades themselves even more than it degrades their victims. Collect the following textual evidence to show how corrupted by power the white men at the smoker are.

1   Find all the negative images of the white leaders you can. Given that almost everything they do in the story involves their abuse of power, all negative images of these characters will serve as evidence that they have been corrupted by power. Include, for example, descriptions of the white men's

   a   cruel behavior,
   b   physical appearance, and
   c   drunkenness.

2   List all of the racist language used by the white men—the language they
    use to address or refer to the narrator and the other black youths—for
    this language reminds us both that racism is, itself, an attempt to wield
    power over others by asserting one's own racial "superiority" and that
    racism can be enacted through language.
3   Find as many examples as you can of the white men's racist stereotyping
    of African Americans. Like racist language, racist stereotyping is an attempt
    to wield power over others by asserting one's own racial "superiority."

   a   Find the lines revealing that the white men stereotype black Americans
       as unintelligent (for example, the lines that portray the men's amusement
       at the narrator's large vocabulary).
   b   Find the passage revealing that the white men stereotype black men as
       uncontrollably sexually drawn to white women.
   c   How do we know that the white men stereotype black men as
       less-than-human brutes, as "animals" or "savages"?

The black characters' survival strategies

Given that institutionalized racism gives free rein to white citizens' overt
abuses of racial power, the story's black characters have little, if anything, to
protect them from white domination and persecution. The day-to-day terror
of living under such conditions produces, on the part of the story's African
American characters, a variety of survival strategies: attitudes toward life that
individuals develop in order to survive an intolerable situation with the spirit, as
well as the body, intact. Of course, no attitude, no way of being, can guarantee a
person's physical or emotional safety. And the variety of strategies illustrated in
the story, by spotlighting this unfortunate fact, increase our awareness of the
horrors of institutionalized racism. Let's examine those survival strategies now.

1   *The narrator's family*—The narrator's family are obviously terrified that some
    harm will come to them from the racist world in which they live.

   a   What are the family's hopes?
   b   What are their fears?
   c   What do they believe they have to do to survive?

2   *The narrator's grandfather*—The narrator's grandfather lived a long life and
    headed a large family that has never gotten in trouble with the white
    power structure.

   a   What did the grandfather do to survive racism?

b   Although his behavior was apparently similar to that of the rest of his family, how was the grandfather's attitude different?

c   In what ways was he right to compare the race relations of his time and place to a war in which white folks were the enemy?

3   *The narrator*—In *Invisible Man*, the novel from which "The Battle Royal" is taken, the unnamed narrator grows up to learn that his grandfather was right and that, in terms of race relations, too little has changed since his grandfather's time. The events of "The Battle Royal" take place, however, when the narrator has just graduated from high school, and he has yet to learn all he needs to learn about race relations in the United States. How does he believe he can survive racism and even prosper, despite his position as a black man in a country dominated by whites? Be sure to examine the following elements:

a   his recurring thoughts about the white men's approval,

b   his recurring thoughts about his speech,

c   his attitude toward the black youths from his community with whom he fights the battle royal, and

d   his feelings when he receives the briefcase and the scholarship he finds inside it.

4   *The black youths*—What attitudes and behaviors have the black youths developed in order to survive the racist world in which they live? Find the passages in the story that reveal, at least, the following survival strategies:

a   sticking with, and sticking up for, their own small group of friends,

b   physical and emotional endurance,

c   taking whatever opportunities to earn money the white men offer them because they have few or no other options, and

d   guarding their behavior around white women (history tells us, and the black youths certainly know, that black males have been lynched for looking at or speaking to a white woman).

Focusing your essay

Given the textual data you've just gathered, it should be a fairly simple task to write an essay explaining the antiracist project of "The Battle Royal," the ways in which the story illustrates the evils of institutionalized racism. As the story shows, institutionalized racism creates an environment in which unrestrained power reduces the white characters to little more than brutes and forces the black characters to scramble for any means of survival they can find, even when those survival strategies provide no guarantee of safety and are personally degrading. For one of the most chilling effects of institutionalized racism on the story's black characters is the negative effect on their emotional or psychological well-being. For example, the narrator's family were so nerve-wracked by their understandable fear of white retribution should Grandfather's death bed statement become known outside the family that they were more upset by the old man's dying words than they were by his death. Similarly, the narrator is so focused on pleasing the white community that he seems to have little or no sense of himself or feeling for his own family or community.

Although "The Battle Royal" is set many decades in the past, I hope you'll be able to see that the story is still relevant to Americans today. As we saw in the opening paragraphs of this chapter, though institutionalized racism has been reduced in the United States, it has not been eliminated. And many of the racist attitudes that still persist today have their roots in the racism that ruled American thinking when racial segregation and discrimination were legal, though they're now against the law.

Of course, you don't have to limit yourself to the analysis of the story I've offered you. For example, you might want to provide some historical context for the argument already outlined by including some historical data about institutionalized racism in the time and place in which "The Battle Royal" is set. Or you might want to write a research paper focused entirely on the historical realities of institutionalized racism on which the story draws. For example, you might research the laws governing such areas as interracial marriage, racial discrimination in jobs and housing, or racial segregation in such public facilities as schools, hotels, restaurants, movie houses, and even drinking fountains.

Perhaps, instead, you might want to focus your essay exclusively on an analysis of the narrator because he's the point-of-view character and the one about whom we learn the most. In that case, in addition to the textual data you've already collected about this character, you might want to analyze the narrator's attitude toward his grandfather and toward the rest of his family (do you think it's significant that he tells us so little about them?) as well as the narrator's relationship to himself. For example, how would you describe the narrator's self-image? Does he seem to have a healthy self-esteem? How in touch does he seem to be with the "racial reality" around him, for instance, with the white men's attitude toward him or with Tatlock's reasons for hating him? In what ways is the racism the narrator has been subjected to all his life responsible for his behavior in the story? Whatever your interpretation of "The Battle Royal," be sure you understand the concepts from African America theory you choose to employ, compose a clear statement of your thesis, and support your interpretation with adequate textual evidence.

Recognizing the "less visible" operations of institutionalized racism: Interpreting "Don't Explain"

In 1959, the year in which Jewelle Gomez's "Don't Explain" (1987; see Appendix E) is set, the Civil Rights Movement, led by Dr. Martin Luther King, was in progress. However, racial discrimination was still condoned by law and common practice, and racist beliefs and attitudes were generally accepted among white Americans in the north as well as in the south. Just as in every other American city and town, Boston, the city in which the story takes place, permitted racial discrimination even in such fundamental areas of human existence as the kind of work African Americans were allowed to do (job discrimination) and the neighborhoods in which African Americans were allowed to live (housing discrimination). This is the environment in which the characters of "Don't Explain" live and work. Unlike the black youths in Ellison's "The Battle Royal," however, Gomez's Letty, Delia, and Terry are steadily employed at jobs that provide them with enough money to support themselves. Although their race, class, gender, and sexual orientation make these African American women vulnerable to violent attack, with little hope of protection from the judicial system, the story doesn't focus on this aspect of their experience as women of color.

Instead, "Don't Explain" finds another way to attack racial bigotry by showing us that institutionalized racism isn't limited to the kind of violent behavior we see portrayed in "The Battle Royal." It also operates in "less visible" ways that, while they usually go unnoticed by white Americans who don't have to deal with them, are a part of daily reality for the people of color who populate Gomez's story. In addition, "Don't Explain" is antiracist in its positive characterizations of African Americans who survive these "less visible" operations of institutionalized racism, characterizations that counteract racist stereotypes. We'll see how the story accomplishes its antiracist project by examining: (1) its subtle depiction of the "less visible" operations of institutionalized racism that the main characters deal with on a daily basis; and (2) its positive, antistereotypical portrayals of African American characters.

"Less visible" operations of institutionalized racism

Although the "less visible" operations of institutionalized racism are only a backdrop—a kind of stage setting—in "Don't Explain," they are nevertheless important because they help us understand and appreciate the main characters. Find the textual evidence the story offers to support the following statements.

1   Racial discrimination in housing is a factor in the lives of the story's African American characters.
2   Racial discrimination in the job market is a factor in the lives of these characters.

    a   What do Letty and Delia do for a living?
    b   Is the place where they work a safe environment, given that a character like Tip is welcome there? Is it reasonable to assume that Letty and Delia would have better jobs—or at least work in safer restaurants—if those jobs were available to them?
    c   What do Terry and her friends do for a living? Is it reasonable to assume that they would have better jobs if those jobs were available to them?

d What do we know about attitudes toward race in the 1950s—the period in which the story is set—that allows us to assume that racial discrimination limits these characters' job opportunities, even if the story doesn't say so directly?

3 Racial discrimination in the workplace is a factor in the lives of these characters.

a What is the race of the employees and customers at the 411 Lounge?
b What is the ethnic origin of the food sold at the 411 Lounge and of the music on its juke-box?
c What is the race of the owner of the 411?
d What is the attitude of the Lounge owner—and, in Letty's experience, of all white employers—toward black employees?

4 The portrayal of Billie Holiday contributes to the story's depiction of the "less visible" operations of institutionalized racism. If you are unfamiliar with her history, you can consult any biography of the singer (including television biographies) to see how her presence in the tale functions as a reminder of the constant emotional pressure exerted by institutionalized racism. You will find that this character brings to the story, for example, the following facts.

a Billie Holiday grew up in a segregated, economically disadvantaged, African American neighborhood.
b Despite her rise to fame and fortune, she was frequently discriminated against because of her race. For example, in segregated areas of the United States, Billie wasn't allowed to stay in the same hotels, eat in the same restaurants, or use the same public facilities as white musicians or as the white people for whom she performed.
c When Billie sang with Arty Shaw's band (the first white band to employ a black singer), a white woman named Helen Forest took Billie's place when the band played in certain white clubs that would not permit black artists to perform.

Positive portrayals of African American characters

Against this relatively subtle backdrop of institutionalized racism, Gomez gives us positively portrayed African American characters who survive the forces of racial discrimination—Letty, Delia, Terry, and Terry's friends—and a moving evocation of Billie Holiday, whose original interpretations of jazz have had a major influence on the history of American music. In addition, the main characters—and even the prostitutes, who are described by Letty—are portrayed in ways that counteract racist stereotypes of black women.

Racist stereotypes of African American women—promoted by such institutions as the film and television industries—generally fall into two categories: (1) the "mammy"; and (2) the oversexed "bad girl," or "Jezebel." The "mammy" stereotype—which is based on a misunderstanding of the complex position occupied by the slave woman who ran the master's household—casts black women as motherly servants, loyally devoted to the white families that employ them. "Mammy" always "knows her place," takes excellent care of the white home, and loves looking after white children, whom she prefers to her own children, because she knows that white people are the superior race. The black "Jezebel" stereotype casts African American women as oversexed temptresses who lure white men into immoral relationships, have violent tempers, and carry knives or razor blades, which they don't hesitate to use. Both stereotypes reveal the racist need to claim white female superiority. And the black "Jezebel" stereotype—which originally arose from the slave-masters' desire to justify the rape of female slaves—attempts to justify the mistreatment of black women. Collect the following textual evidence to see how Gomez's portrayal of the story's African American characters serves the text's antiracist project.

1   *The main characters*—Letty, Delia, Terry, and Terry's friends hold jobs typical of the jobs permitted to black women: Letty and Delia serve food at, and clean, the 411 Lounge; Terry and her friends clean business offices. And given the period in which the story is set, the people who run the business offices are undoubtedly white, just as the owner of the 411 Lounge is white. In other words, these characters do the work associated with the "mammy" stereotype, the work of servants who take good care of white people's possessions. However, while Letty, Delia, Terry, and Terry's friends are certainly too kind, quiet, and "low profile" to be considered "Jezebels," collect the following textual evidence to show that neither are they stereotyped as "mammies."

   a   Are these characters devoted to their white employers? For example, is Letty so devoted to Ari that she wouldn't leave the 411 Lounge if a better job came along? What does Letty think of Ari?
   b   Is there any indication in the story that these characters believe in white superiority or suffer from low self-esteem because they're black? How does the story suggest that these characters do *not* judge a person's value in terms of skin color?
   c   Do the emotional lives of these characters in any way revolve around the lives of white families? In contrast to the need for white approval associated with the "mammy" stereotype, how does the story suggest that Delia, Terry, and Terry's friends have formed a kind of independent social community? How does Letty's behavior at the end of the story indicate the positive quality of this group, to which, presumably, Letty will soon belong?

2   *The prostitutes*—Although prostitutes are generally thought of as "bad girls" because they make their living selling sex, the prostitutes in "Don't Explain" do not fit the black "Jezebel" stereotype. Letty's opinion of the

prostitutes and her reference to them as "business girls" lends these characters respect and works against this negative stereotype. Find the lines in the story that imply the following positive elements in the characterization of the prostitutes who frequent the 411 Lounge. The prostitutes are

a   generous,
b   fun-loving, and
c   friendly with the employees at the 411 Lounge without motives of gain (that is, their friendliness isn't based on an effort to secure more customers for themselves).

3   *Billie Holiday*—The depiction of Billie Holiday contributes to the story's positive portrayals of African Americans. If you are unfamiliar with her history, you can consult any biography of the singer (including television biographies) to see how her presence in the story functions as a reminder of the enormous contribution of African Americans to American culture. For the presence of this character in the story reminds readers, for example, that African Americans invented jazz, to which Billie Holiday gave her own unique expression and helped popularize. In addition, find the textual evidence that reveals the following positive elements in her characterization. Billie Holiday is

a   generous,
b   friendly, and
c   courageous.

Focusing your essay

You should be able to use the textual evidence you've gathered to focus your essay on the antiracist project of "Don't Explain": its subtle illustration of the "less visible" operations of institutionalized racism in American society and its positive portrayals of the characters who must contend with these racist forces in their daily lives. In case you're wondering how to deal with Tip, the only negatively portrayed African American character in the story, you can think of him as one of the harsh realities with which Letty and Delia wouldn't *have* to deal if racial discrimination didn't limit their job opportunities. Even if they stayed in their current occupations as waitresses, the removal of racial barriers in the job market would give them the opportunity to work in safer environments, in restaurants where overtly dangerous customers like Tip would not be welcome. Furthermore, the presence of Tip's undesirable character does not sabotage the story's antiracist project because the reader is encouraged to see him as just one person and not as a representative of all African American men.

Although "Don't Explain" is set in 1959, I hope you can see that the story is relevant today because the "less visible" operations of institutionalized racism it depicts are not entirely a thing of the past. Racial discrimination is now against the law, and that is a monumental step forward for the United States.

However, as we saw in the opening pages of this chapter, institutionalized racism is still a widespread problem in this country, and much work remains to be done if we are to significantly reduce its influence.

Remember, of course, that you do not have to limit yourself to the analysis of the story I've offered you here. For example, you might want to examine additional ways in which Gomez's characters do not fit racist stereotypes of African Americans. In that case, you might examine, for instance, the ways in which the characterizations of Letty, Delia, and Terry work against the myth that black Americans are less intelligent, less capable, and less hardworking than white Americans. And you might note, too, the large size of Terry and Delia's apartment and other signs that they are financially responsible; in other words, that they know how to earn, save, and wisely spend money. Or you might want to provide additional historical context for your essay by researching the racial climate in America in the 1940s and 1950s to learn, for example, some of the reasons why Letty, Delia, Terry, and Tip—like so many African Americans of that period—left their homes and families in the south to relocate up north. Or you might research the legal status of black Americans in the 1950s to get a more concrete, vivid idea of the kinds of legalized racial discrimination faced by the characters in "Don't Explain." Whatever your interpretation of the story, be sure you understand the concepts from African American theory you choose to employ, compose a clear statement of your thesis, and support your interpretation with adequate textual evidence.

Understanding the operations of internalized racism: Interpreting "Everyday Use"

The Black Pride Movement was a prominent force in African American culture during the late 1960s and early 1970s, and its positive effects can still be seen today in Americans' growing recognition of the importance of African American history and the creativity of African American culture. As an outgrowth of the Civil Rights Movement of the 1950s and 1960s, the Black Pride Movement rejected the racist belief that people of color are less intelligent, capable, hardworking, or attractive than whites. Because the forces of white racism in America had long denied black Americans full participation as American citizens and full recognition as human beings, the Black Pride Movement encouraged black Americans to look to African cultures to define their heritage and their identity.

Like many of her generation who participated in the Black Pride Movement, Dee Johnson, in Alice Walker's "Everyday Use" (1973; see Appendix D), rejects her given name, the origin of which is a slave name, and adopts an African name to replace it. Dee Johnson is now Wangero Leewanika Kemanjo. She and her boyfriend Hakim-a-barber, who has presumably changed his name for the same reason, have also adopted African-style clothing and phrases, and Hakim has adopted some practices and phrases from the Muslim religion, a religion not associated with white America. However, despite the importance of the Black Pride Movement as a social, political, and personal path to African American self assertion and self-esteem, "Everyday Use" suggests that followers of the Black Pride Movement allowed their belief in the importance of their African roots to blind them to the importance of their family's strategies for surviving lifelong racism. For as the story shows, family heritage is a vital source of personal strength that should not be belittled.

"Everyday Use," then, can be seen as a kind of debate between two different dimensions of African American culture, one of which glamorizes the African origins of black American culture, the other of which promotes its American, or family, tradition. And it's a debate that, in the opinion of many readers, Mama and Maggie apparently win. For Mrs. Johnson and Maggie, who, in contrast to Wangero, draw their strength from their family tradition, seem in many ways stronger and more contented than Wangero. In addition, Mama and Maggie are more sympathetically portrayed than the self-centered Wangero, whom many readers dislike. Drawing on concepts from African American theory, however, we can see that, despite their obvious differences, Mama and Maggie share an important characteristic with Wangero that they might not realize they share, and it's a characteristic that has helped form the identities of all three women: internalized racism, or the belief that they are inferior because of their race. Ironically, though internalized racism is something the Johnson women share, it's also something that has helped drive Wangero away from her mother and sister. For as we'll see in the textual evidence we collect later, all three women have followed the paths they have followed in part in an attempt to struggle against the personal insecurities to which internalized racism has greatly contributed. In order to see the role played by internalized racism in "Everyday Use," let's examine the role it plays in the characterizations of the story's three main characters: (1) Mama; (2) Maggie; and (3) Wangero.

Mama's internalized racism

Mama has many sources of pride in her life. Yet she doesn't seem to have quite the self-esteem that she has surely earned, a situation that is due, in large part, to her internalized racism, to the low self-image pressed upon her by racist ideology. Explain this aspect of Mama's characterization by collecting the following textual data.

1   *Mama's sources of pride*—List as many reasons as you can why Mama should be proud of herself. Include, for example, her accomplishments as a single mother who raised two daughters on a small income and her accomplishments as the head of a rural homestead that requires of her a great deal of farming knowledge and physical strength.

    a   What has Mama done for Maggie? What has she done for Wangero? List as many examples as you can.

    b   List Mama's skills and abilities as the head of a rural homestead.

2   *Mama's low self-image*—Despite Mama's many sources of pride, she still
    has the kind of low self-image that is a sign of internalized racism and
    that is surely related, in large part, to the treatment she's received over the
    course of her life as a black woman.

    a   How was race a factor in Mama's being deprived of an education?
    b   Given what we know about racism, explain how we can safely
        assume that the racist world in which Mama grew up also limited her
        job opportunities and gave her the message that she was not attractive,
        though the text does not directly tell us so.
    c   Where in the story do we see Mama's rather low estimate of her
        intelligence?
    d   Describe Mama's dissatisfaction with her physical appearance. How is
        this dissatisfaction related to race?

3   *Mama's intraracial racism*—As we saw in the "Basic concepts" section of this
    chapter, internalized racism often results in intraracial racism, discrimination
    within the black community against black Americans with darker skin
    and more African features. We see this attitude in the way Mama con-
    trasts Wangero's and Maggie's looks, a contrast that is based not just on
    Maggie's scars from the fire and her thin figure, but on differences in the
    sisters' physical appearance that are related solely to racial characteristics.

    a   How does Mama contrast her daughters in terms of skin color?
    b   How does Mama contrast her daughters in terms of their hair? (Keep
        in mind that the phrase "nicer hair," spoken by a woman of Mama's
        generation, usually meant longer, softer, straighter hair that could be
        more easily styled the way white women styled their hair.)

4   *Mama's attempt to resist internalized racism*—Mama's attempt to resist inter-
    nalized racism, to take pride in herself and in her heritage, seems to gain a
    good deal of strength from the bond she feels with her family members,
    both from her own generation and from preceding generations.

    a   Why does Mama give her first-born daughter the name *Dee*?
    b   How far back through the generations of her family is Mama able to
        trace this name?
    c   What else does Mama know about her family history?
    d   Mama has always let Wangero have her way. Mama says "no" to her
        for the first time when she gives the quilts Wangero wants to Maggie.
        How does this act show Mama's commitment to family heritage?

Maggie's internalized racism

Although Maggie's world is limited in terms of location and occupation—
she'll probably never move far away from her mother, and she'll probably
never work outside the home, even after she's married—Maggie has sources

of pride and contentment that Wangero may never have. Nevertheless, while it's understandable that Maggie's scars make her self-conscious, her low self-image seems to have its source not only in the fire that damaged her appearance, but in internalized racism as well. Explain this aspect of Maggie's characterization by collecting the following textual data.

1 *Maggie's sources of pride*—List as many reasons as you can why Maggie should be proud of herself, including the following examples.

  a What experience and skills does Maggie have that will make her an excellent homemaker?
  b What knowledge does Maggie have, which apparently surpasses even that of her mother?
  c What family craft was passed down to Maggie rather than to Wangero?
  d It seems that Maggie's shyness is not so overpowering as to prevent her from finding a boyfriend. What big event is she looking forward to in the near future?
  e Maggie is a good daughter, and it shows in the bond she shares with her mother. Describe this bond as thoroughly as you can, being sure to include the ways in which Maggie is helpful to and thoughtful of Mama.

2 *Maggie's low self-image*—As we mentioned earlier, some of the reasons for Maggie's low self-image are not related to race. However, Mama's belief that Wangero is more attractive than Maggie because she has lighter skin and nicer (that is, less stubbornly African) hair reflects the racist standard of beauty that dominated America and that the Black Pride Movement tried to overthrow. It would be next to impossible for Maggie not to have internalized the racism that dominated the world in which she grew up. To be sure you have a full sense of Maggie's low self-image, list as many examples as you can of Maggie's self-conscious, self-effacing (trying to avoid drawing attention to herself) behavior, including

  a her posture,
  b her shyness in the presence of Wangero and Hakim,
  c the infrequency with which she speaks, and
  d the softness of her speaking voice.

3 *Maggie's attempt to resist internalized racism*—Like Mama, Maggie tries to overcome internalized racism through the strength she gets from her knowledge of and pride in her family heritage. The few times she speaks during the story is to share some fact about the Johnson family history.

  a List as many examples as you can find of Maggie's knowledge of family history.
  b Although Maggie would like to have the quilts that Wangero wants to take, why does Maggie feel that she does not need to have them?

Wangero's internalized racism

At first glance, Wangero seems too confident to suffer from internalized racism. Many readers assume that her physical appearance and all her accomplishments mean that she must feel sure of herself, secure in the self-esteem that made her determined to overcome any obstacle in her path in order to get an education and move up in the world. Yet Wangero's many achievements don't seem to have eliminated the need to overcompensate—to act as if she has something to prove—that has been with her all her life. To explain this aspect of Wangero's characterization, collect the following textual evidence.

1   *Wangero's sources of pride*—List the numerous reasons Wangero has to be proud of herself, including evidence of

   a   her intelligence and education,
   b   her financial success,
   c   her attractive appearance, and
   d   her current social success.

2   *Wangero's low self-image*—Evidence that Wangero's racial self-image is not as secure as it may appear can be found in the way she seems to look down upon her mother and sister (who are darker skinned and would be considered inferior by much of white America) and in the ways in which she has always seemed to be trying too hard to prove herself superior to her family origins, to be popular, and to be accepted by the fashionable world beyond the black community in which she grew up.

   a   Find all the textual evidence you can to show that, when Wangero was growing up, she looked down upon Mama and Maggie and that she still looks down upon them now that she is an adult and living on her own.
   b   Find all the textual evidence you can to show that Wangero has always tried too hard to prove herself superior to her family origins, both as a young girl and even now that she is a successful woman.

3   *Wangero's attempt to resist internalized racism*—While Mama and Maggie embrace their family roots to increase their sense of security and belonging, Wangero does just the opposite. Apparently, she associates her family heritage with poverty, racial victimization, and the enslavement of her ancestors. She has sought a way out of the negative self-image pressed upon her by racism by trying to be as different from her family as possible.

   a   List as many examples as you can of the ways in which Wangero tried to be different from her family when she was a young girl living at home.
   b   List as many examples as you can of the ways in which Wangero is trying to be different from her family now that she is an adult.
   c   Wangero's desire to escape internalized racism, to rid herself of the negative self-image pressed upon her by racist ideology, is surely one of the reasons she is attracted to the Black Pride Movement: she is seeking a

sense of self-worth in African values and heritage. Yet it seems that the internalized racism the Black Pride Movement intended to eliminate is too deeply embedded in Wangero to allow her to fully appreciate the meaning of that Movement. List the ways in which Wangero's response to the Black Pride Movement seems rather superficial, more like an attempt to fit into a new fashionable world than a commitment to an organized effort to help herself and her people feel the pride they deserve to feel.

Focusing your essay

Given the textual data you've collected, you should be able to focus your essay on the antiracist project of "Everyday Use." For the story attacks racism in two effective ways. It illustrates the positive qualities of black women who, in different ways, accomplish a great deal despite the obstacles placed in their path by the racist world in which they live. In addition, the story illustrates the negative effects of internalized racism both on individual self-esteem and on family unity. For as we have seen, internalized racism is, in large part, responsible for the low self-image with which all three Johnson women struggle as well as for Wangero's alienation from her family and from family history and heritage. The fact that internalized racism can be a force in the lives of characters who have so many sources of self-esteem demonstrates its power to invade the self-image even of successful African Americans who are still devalued, because of their race, by the nation they call home.

As always, remember that you don't have to limit yourself to the analysis of the story I've offered you here. You might, for example, research the Black Pride Movement and write an essay in which you argue that Wangero is a poor representative of the Movement because she seems to see it as a fashion trend, or as a means of bettering her own socioeconomic status, and doesn't seem aware of its potential as a political movement.

In contrast, your research on the Black Pride Movement might lead you to write an essay in which you argue that Wangero is a fairly typical representative of the Movement's exclusive concern with its people's African roots, a concern that neglected the importance of reclaiming the *American* history of African Americans. For in the late 1960s and early 1970s, most Americans, black and white alike, were still unaware of the many sources of pride in the history of Africans in America, such as those listed at the beginning of this chapter. And slavery was still viewed as a history of humiliation for black Americans because little, if any, information was readily available concerning the remarkable achievements of American slaves: for example, the networks of communication, methods of resistance, and organized means of escape they devised right under their masters' noses.

Finally, you might prefer, instead, to write an essay about the ways in which "Everyday Use" participates in the African American literary tradition. In that case, you would focus on the story's illustration of, among other things, such themes as the importance of the family, church, and community in surviving the harsh realities of racism; the attempt to reclaim the African past of lost ancestors; and the importance of remaining connected to the past through oral history, folk crafts, and the naming of children. Whatever your interpretation, be sure you understand the concepts from African American theory you choose to employ, compose a clear statement of your thesis, and support your interpretation with adequate textual evidence.

Exploring the function of black characters in white literature: Interpreting "A Rose for Emily"

Although the primary purpose of African American theory is to help us analyze the enormous body of literature written by African Americans, this theory can also help us interpret literary works written by white authors because it enables us to see the racial dimension of white literature that we otherwise might have overlooked. For example, African American author and Nobel Prize winner Toni Morrison analyzes white literature from an African American perspective by examining, among other things, the various ways in which white authors have often created black characters whose sole purpose is to make their white protagonists look good. In Ernest Hemingway's *To Have and Have Not* (1937), for instance, Morrison argues that the black character Wesley, a crewman on the fishing boat of white captain Harry Morgan, is portrayed as silent, submissive, and cowardly in order to make Morgan appear, by contrast, more manly and courageous (*Playing in the Dark: Whiteness and the Literary Imagination*, Vintage, 1993). Whether or not Hemingway had this purpose consciously in mind when he created Wesley, that is how this character functions in the novel.

Of course, not all black characters are used in such an overtly racist fashion in white literature. In fact, the work of many white authors is antiracist. William Faulkner, for example, frequently depicted the evils of racism. And he created some African American characters who play major roles in his fiction and whose dignity and integrity far surpass those qualities in many of his white characters. Whatever the role of black characters in a white literary work, however, an analysis of their function in the text offers us a starting point for viewing the work of white writers from an African American perspective because such an analysis can often help us see the racial aspects of the work's setting, or historical context, and help us determine the text's attitude toward racial issues.

We can see how this approach can open a white literary work to an African American interpretation by using it to analyze William Faulkner's "A Rose for Emily" (1931; see Appendix B). "A Rose for Emily" is the story of a white woman, Miss Emily Grierson, who lives in the southern town of Jefferson during the decades preceding and following the turn of the twentieth century. Principal among the story's minor black characters, of course, is Tobe, an African American man employed as Emily's domestic servant. Although we're not told exactly when Tobe came to live and work in the Grierson home, we know that he is taking care of household duties when Emily, at about thirty years of age, is left on her own by the death of her father. Although almost nothing is left of the former Grierson fortune, Tobe remains with Emily—cooking, gardening, shopping, and running errands, as Miss Grierson almost never leaves the house—throughout the rest of Emily's life. At the story's close, Tobe, an old man now, finally leaves the Grierson home, and presumably flees the town of Jefferson as well, when Emily dies.

Certainly, an analysis of Tobe wouldn't suggest that this character is negatively portrayed in order to make Emily, or any other white character, look good by contrast. On the contrary, the characterization of Emily Grierson as a snobbish recluse who poisons her suitor and sleeps with his dead body tends to make other characters, including Tobe, look good by contrast. Rather, I think we can use an African American lens to examine the ways in which the characterization of Tobe, and of the other minor black characters in the story, reveals an antiracist dimension of the tale by drawing our attention to the evils of racism in the time and place in which "A Rose for Emily" is set. Thus, although the main focus of "A Rose for Emily" is white experience, I think our analysis can help us see the text's antiracist message. In addition, attention to the story's portrayal of its African American characters can also help us see some of the ways in which the tale's antiracist project doesn't completely succeed. In order to understand these aspects of "A Rose for Emily," we'll examine: (1) how the portrayal of Tobe reveals the evils of racism; (2) how the portrayal of the story's other minor black characters reveals the evils of racism; and (3) how "A Rose for Emily" doesn't fully accomplish its antiracist project.

How the portrayal of Tobe reveals the evils of racism

Various aspects of Tobe's behavior throughout the story raise questions that can be answered only by considering the racist world in which he lives. In other words, Tobe's main function in the story is quietly to make us aware of the historical realities of racism. To see how the characterization of Tobe works in this way, consider the fact that the text offers us no data at all to explain what appears to be rather illogical, even bizarre, behavior on Tobe's part, thus forcing us to remember the dangers faced by a black man living in a racist white world, as the following questions and answers illustrate. To check your own awareness of racist attitudes, you might try coming up with your own answers to the following questions and then see if you agree with the ones I offer you.

1   *Questions*

    a   Why don't the prudish citizens of Jefferson, who are always on the lookout for juicy gossip, object to Emily's living alone in the house with a male servant?

    b   Why does Tobe remain in Emily's employ, given that she can't be paying him much, if any money, and that, apparently, she rarely, if ever speaks to him?

c Why doesn't Tobe report the death of Homer Barron, of which there can be no doubt that he knows?

d Why does Tobe disappear immediately upon the entrance of Emily's neighbors after her death?

2 *Answers*

a During the period in which the story is set, racist stereotypes of African American men characterized them as either: (1) "Sambos," loyal, rather sexless individuals whose capacity for devotion to white people made them good servants despite their tendency to be rather slow-moving and dim-witted; or (2) sex-crazed "savages" who would rape white women at will if it weren't for the vigilance of white men. Both stereotypes deprive African American men of their dignity and humanity, which we see in the narrator's failure to refer to Tobe by name. Only Emily calls him Tobe; the narrator refers to him as "the Negro" or "the Negro man." Apparently, the citizens of Jefferson have stereotyped Tobe as a "Sambo": he isn't considered a threat to Emily because he isn't considered a "real" man. (Note that these black male stereotypes correspond to the "mammy" and "Jezebel" racist stereotypes of African American women discussed in our analysis of "Don't Explain.")

b Employment options were few for black men at that time—menial labor was the best that most could expect—and unprovoked physical attack by whites was always a danger. Short of moving to the north, which involved its own difficulties for people of color with no money or connections, staying with Emily is presumably Tobe's best choice. As her servant, he is physically "under her protection"—safe from physical assault, a safety that is further insured by his quiet demeanor—and he is also assured of room and board.

c Especially given the south's idealization of white womanhood at that point in time, Tobe would be in danger of being lynched for the murder of Homer Barron if the town learned of Homer's death, even if the white citizens of Jefferson secretly suspected Emily of the murder.

d Again, even if the townsfolk didn't accuse Tobe of killing Emily, they might accuse him of killing Homer, whose body, Tobe knows, they are now bound to find in Emily's bedroom. The danger of being lynched was too real for black men at that time, so Tobe probably feels that his best bet is to take up residence elsewhere.

How the portrayal of other minor black characters reveals the evils of racism

Other than Tobe, black characters are mentioned in the story only three times: the druggist's "Negro delivery boy," as he's called in the story; the African American laborers who have been hired to pave the sidewalks of Jefferson; and the black women (whom we don't actually meet in the story) referred to by Mayor Sartoris when he makes the rule that no black woman would be allowed on the streets of Jefferson without an apron. To see how these characters function in the story, consider the following historical realities of which these characters remind us, and collect the textual data requested.

1 *The "delivery boy"*—Although the term *delivery boy* would be used to designate any youngster hired to make deliveries, this character, like the other black characters in the story, reminds us of the limited job opportunities available to black men in towns like Jefferson. In fact, readers aware of African American history would be reminded of the common racist use of the word *boy* to refer to adult black males as well as to male youngsters and might therefore wonder whether or not we can know that the "Negro delivery boy" is, in fact, a boy.

2 *The African American laborers*—Again, the black men hired to pave Jefferson's sidewalks provide an illustration of the limited jobs available to black men at that time in American history. In addition, the description of the paving of the sidewalks offers other reminders of the overt racism common during that period.

   a What degrading word is used to refer to the black men hired by the construction company?
   b The laborers are black men, but what is the race of the man in charge, the foreman?
   c How does the foreman treat the laborers?
   d In addition to the black laborers, what other two "items" are we told the construction company brought with it to Jefferson? What is implied about the African American laborers by including them on a list with animals (especially this kind of animal) and machines?

3 *The black women of Jefferson*—We don't meet any African American women in "A Rose for Emily," so they're not really characters in the usual sense of the word. However, black women characters are evoked—are called into the reader's imagination—by the text's reference to Mayor Sartoris' rule that no black woman be seen in the streets of Jefferson without an apron. And this single line in the story reveals a good deal about the racial atmosphere in the town.

   a In what role does the wearing of an apron cast black women?
   b What does it tell us, then, that the Mayor of Jefferson enacts a town law that no black woman be seen without one?
   c Evidently, the white citizens of Jefferson see nothing wrong with this racist law, as they apparently do nothing to oppose it. In other words, the white townsfolk share the Mayor's extreme need to keep black folks "in their place." What does this attitude suggest about the white population of Jefferson?

The story's failure to fully accomplish Its antiracist project

As we have just seen, the function of the story's black characters is quietly to make us aware of the historical realities of racism. This is certainly a praiseworthy antiracist effort on the text's part. However, it may nevertheless be frustrating for readers, especially for African American readers, to encounter yet another white story that, even if it has a black character or two, tells us little or nothing about them beyond what serves our knowledge of the text's white characters, in this case our knowledge of the white characters' racism. This use of black characters reduces them to historical "pointers," or "signs," and does not permit us to experience them as human beings in their own right. The problem is increased by the fact that the few descriptions we do get of Tobe, the black character of whom we see the most, are given primarily to reveal something about Emily's experience and behavior. Finally, the story's attitude toward the racism it represents is not always clear. These three problems detract from the story's antiracist message. To be sure you understand them, collect the following textual data.

1   *The lack of information about black characters*—What *personal* information (for example, information about physical appearance, family background, or personal history), if any, are we given about the following characters? Why would it be accurate to say that they are hardly characters at all but, instead, part of the story's setting? Consider

   a   Tobe,
   b   the druggist's delivery boy,
   c   the black laborers, and
   d   the black women of Jefferson.

2   *How Tobe is used to reveal Emily's experience and behavior*—Except for relatively short periods of time (for example, when she is courted by Homer Barron) Emily is a recluse.

   a   How does the description of Tobe, leaving and entering the Grierson home with his basket to perform various household errands, add to our awareness of Emily's self-imposed seclusion?
   b   On the rare occasion that Tobe is heard to speak, what does the rusty sound of his voice tell the townsfolk, and the reader, about the thoroughness with which Emily has cut herself off from all human contact?

3   *The story's attitude toward the racism it represents*—As we saw earlier, the story uses its African American characters to remind us of the evils of racism. However, some readers might feel that the tale falls short of this antiracist project in its portrayal of the white narrator. In general, the narrator is positively portrayed, which encourages readers to like him and to trust his judgment. Yet he uses the word *nigger* to refer to the black

laborers paving Jefferson's sidewalks. And the narrator's continual reference to Tobe as "the Negro" or "the Negro man" (the narrator calls him
Tobe only once, when quoting Emily's calling her servant by name)
shows that he sees Tobe only in terms of his race, not as a human being
first and foremost. First, to be sure you can see the ways in which the
story positively portrays the narrator, find the textual evidence you need
to answer the questions posed below about that character. Then choose
one of the two explanations offered subsequently for the text's positive
depiction of its apparently racist narrator.

a What parts of the story, or what aspects of his language, suggest that
   the narrator is intelligent and well educated?
b How do we know that the narrator is knowledgeable about the
   people and events he describes?
c What textual elements give the feeling that the narrator has maintained an objective viewpoint (that he is not overly emotional about
   the events he narrates and therefore able to be impartial)?
d Which of the following two explanations do you find the most convincing? Why? Or do you think that both explanations are valid
   because each explains a different aspect of the story? Discuss.

   i   The story is showing us that even the best-intentioned white
       people harbor racist attitudes because racism is so ingrained in the
       culture in which they live. This aspect of the text is thus consistent
       with its antiracist message.
   ii Even if the story has the antiracist intention just described, the use
       of racist language by a character who is portrayed as intelligent,
       well educated, knowledgeable, and objective risks reinforcing
       readers' racist attitudes, especially in 1931, when the story was
       published and the acceptance of overt racism was widespread.

Focusing your essay

You should be able to use the textual data you've gathered to write an essay
explaining how the African American characters in "A Rose for Emily" promote
the story's antiracist message by reminding us of the evils of racism. And
I hope you will also be able to show that even the best literary intentions can
fall short of their mark: because the story uses its African American characters
as "pointers," so to speak, to draw our attention to the racism of the world
in which they live, the tale fails to give us any meaningful sense of their
personhood, of their individual humanity. In other words, in its effort to show
how America has deprived African Americans of their humanity, the story
inadvertently deprives its African American characters of their own humanity.

As always, you don't have to limit yourself to the analysis of the story I've
offered you. For example, you might write an essay in which you argue that

the story's antiracist message fails completely, not just because it falls short of its mark in the ways outlined earlier, but because that message is delivered much too quietly. In this case, you would probably argue that the text's antiracist elements form a backdrop that most readers won't notice in a story with such a dramatic and suspenseful plot as this one has. In contrast, you might want to write an essay in which you argue that "A Rose for Emily" doesn't fall short of its antiracist project at all. In this case, you might argue that the use of undeveloped minor black characters is a small price to pay to expose the evils of racism in a story about white experience.

Of course, you might prefer, instead, to research the history of African Americans in the south during the period in which the story is set, a period in which the enormous numbers of black Americans living in the south were, for different reasons, a source of concern both for white supremacists and for advocates of racial justice. Such an essay might address, among other things, how we are to interpret the under-representation of black characters in a story like "A Rose for Emily." Is it a sign of the text's own racist desire to ignore the existence of African Americans? Or is the story, in contrast, merely representing the racist desire of its white characters to ignore the existence of African Americans? Other stories about the south by William Faulkner—for example, "That Evening Sun" (1931), "Dry September" (1931), and "Barn Burning" (1939)—might offer you food for further thought on this topic.

Finally, you might consider comparing and contrasting "A Rose for Emily" with "That Evening Sun"—or with any other story by a white writer that you and your instructor consider appropriate—in terms of the racial issues addressed in the two stories and in terms of their portrayals of black characters. Whatever your interpretation of "A Rose for Emily," be sure you understand the concepts from African American theory you choose to employ, compose a clear statement of your thesis, and support your interpretation with adequate textual evidence.

Learning when not to use African American concepts: Resisting the temptation to interpret "I started Early—Took my Dog"

Recognizing the absence of illustrations of race or racial issues

Emily Dickinson's "I started Early—Took my Dog" (c. 1862; see Appendix A) seems to offer us very little, if any, material that lends itself to an African American interpretation. It contains no representations of African American experience or culture. We see no illustrations of racism or of other racial issues. And there are no references to African American history. In fact, though the race of the female speaker is not directly stated, the fact that the poem was written by a white woman and that it includes no references to race or racial issues leads most readers reasonably to assume that the speaker is white.

Resisting the temptation of large/small or high/low imagery

Despite the absence of material relevant to African American theory, however, students sometimes want to interpret the poem as an illustration of racial oppression. And they do so for the same reason that students using Marxist concepts want to read the poem as an illustration of class oppression.

As we saw in Chapter 5, "Using concepts from Marxist theory to understand literature," students are often tempted to interpret "I started Early—Took my Dog" as an illustration of upper-class oppression of the lower class because the frigates in the poem, which are described as occupying "the Upper Floor" (l. 5), tower over the speaker, whom the frigates "[p]resum[e] … to be a Mouse" (l. 7)—that is, a much smaller, dependent creature who is located close to the ground. In other words, because one of the characters in the poem might be seen as an underdog, students using Marxist concepts are tempted to argue that that character represents the lower class.

Similarly, students using concepts from African American theory are sometimes tempted to argue that the frigates in the poem represent racism or white society, while the speaker represents African Americans victimized by racism. Or students new to African American theory might feel that the sea symbolizes racism because it is portrayed as an aggressive entity that chases and threatens the speaker, who would again be seen to symbolize African Americans. Once you decide that the frigates, the sea, and the speaker are racial symbols, you might even be tempted, given that this work was written in the mid-nineteenth century, to interpret the poem as a symbolic representation of the flight of an escaped slave to freedom in the north, which you would argue is symbolized by the "Solid Town" (l. 21) in which the speaker finds a safe haven.

However, just as we saw in Chapter 5, unless there's something specific in the poem, or in the theory we're using, to justify such a symbolic interpretation, we're making a "symbolic leap," an unjustified symbolic connection, which we discussed in Chapter 2, "Using concepts from reader-response theory to understand our own literary interpretations." That is, we're arguing for a symbolic interpretation without enough evidence that the symbolic connection we think exists actually does exist. I can just as easily argue, for example, that the large ships and the small mouse symbolize the triumph of good (the ships) over evil (the mouse). Or I can argue that the big sea and the small speaker (after all, she's much smaller than the sea) symbolize the triumph of the country girl (the speaker) in resisting the temptations of the big city (the sea). In other words, I can argue that the image of the frigates vs. the mouse or the sea vs. the speaker symbolizes any large/small or high/low opposition that occurs to me. In short, there is nothing in the poem or in our African American concepts to justify choosing one of these symbolic interpretations over another, which means we are not justified in choosing any of them.

Choosing a different African American approach to Dickinson

If you want to use African American concepts to interpret a Dickinson poem, the logical thing to do is to find a Dickinson poem that allows you to do so: a Dickinson poem that addresses African American experience, culture, or history or a poem that addresses racism or other racial issues. Given the period in which Dickinson lived (1830 to 1886), you might certainly expect to find a poem or two about slavery. Other nineteenth-century white writers addressed racial issues, including slavery; for example, Walt Whitman, Herman Melville, and Harriet Beecher Stowe. Stories about life under slavery written by escaped or freed slaves, including such notable examples as Frederick Douglass' *Narrative of the Life of Frederick Douglass, an American Slave* (1845), were well known in the north. And New England, the region in which Dickinson was born and lived her entire life, was a hotbed of abolitionist activity. Abolitionists, who were opposed to slavery on moral grounds, aided escaped slaves, gave antislavery speeches, wrote antislavery tracts, and lobbied to have the institution of slavery abolished. In short, slavery was one of the big topics of the day and a source of endless debate among intellectuals and common folk alike.

Dickinson, a well-educated, extremely well-read, brilliant young woman, knew first-hand about the evils of oppression because she was oppressed as a woman under nineteenth-century law and gender bias. And she was very familiar with the work of, among other abolitionists, Ralph Waldo Emerson. Indeed, her friend of many years, Thomas Wentworth Higginson, was not only a co-conspirator with John Brown (who was hung for attempting to organize an armed rebellion against slavery in 1859) but also commanded the first black regiment of soldiers to fight for the north in the Civil War. Surely, Dickinson heard the evils of slavery discussed many times, as well as the question of racial injustice that continued to be a source of concern after the Civil War was over and the slaves were released.

Yet Dickinson evidently wrote no poems related to slavery. Although most of her poetry focuses on philosophical and psychological topics, Dickinson occasionally wrote poems about social issues in a general way, but these poems are related to issues of class, religion, and gender, not race. Of course, we must keep in mind that virtually none of Dickinson's poetry includes clear references to specific political issues of the day. So might some of her poems address the evils of slavery in disguised forms—perhaps through references to some sort of bondage, images of hunted or wounded animals, or references to hope and despair—that could symbolically invoke the plight of Africans held in slavery but that readers today might miss? Some of her poems do, in fact, include such elements, but their symbolic meaning is "universalized." That is, the poems apply in some way to all people, including the speaker, rather than to any specific group of people: Aren't we all in some sort of bondage, perhaps to social restrictions or to the conflicts of our own heart? Aren't we all "hunted" by the keepers of custom and tradition who would confine us to a limited sphere of activity or by regrets we thought we had expunged from our minds? Aren't we all wounded by love or by loss? Don't we all have times of hope and despair or times when we've gotten so used to despair that hope is almost painful? Yes, you could analyze what might be taken as symbolic references to slavery in Dickinson's poetry if you did so in the context of her life experience and the intellectual and political climate of the time in which she lived. For example, do her letters reveal her feelings about the racial issues of her time? What can be learned from biographies? Obviously, such an analysis of Dickinson's poetry would be difficult and would involve a good deal of research. Generally speaking, then, I wouldn't recommend that a student new to the study of literature or new to the study of African American theory attempt such an essay. Nevertheless, I hope you will think about the question raised here concerning Dickinson's apparent poetic silence on racial issues.

I also hope you will keep in mind, for future reference, that this question can be raised about other white writers as well. I'm not suggesting that white writers should be expected to address racial issues or that white writers who don't do so are racist. However, it's reasonable to ask why a particular white writer—for example, a white writer who lived or worked among African Americans, who wrote about the jazz-age culture of the 1920s or about the American jazz culture of subsequent decades, or who, like Dickinson, occupied an intellectual community inspired by the racial issues of its time—excluded African American characters or racial issues from their writing.

Food for further thought

Thinking it over

If you've worked through all of the interpretation exercises offered in this chapter, you should feel quite familiar with the basic approaches to understanding literature provided by concepts from African American theory. Specifically, we've seen how concepts from African American theory can be used to analyze

1   literary works that are antiracist in that they illustrate the harmful effects of overt operations of institutionalized racism (our example: "The Battle Royal"),

2   literary works that are antiracist in that they provide positive images of African Americans—images that work against racist stereotypes—who survive "less visible" operations of institutionalized racism (our example: "Don't Explain"),

3   literary works that are antiracist in that they illustrate the harmful effects of internalized racism (our example: "Everyday Use"),

4   literary works by white authors writing about white experience whose portrayal of black characters may be antiracist and/or racist in nature (our example: "A Rose for Emily"), and

5   literary works whose juxtaposition of large/small or high/low images will
    tempt us to misinterpret them by imposing an African American framework
    that the literary work does not justify (our example: "I started Early—Took
    my Dog").

Although many students new to concepts from African American theory find
them interesting and useful, discussions of racial issues can still be awkward.
The need felt by many white students to defend themselves—"I'm not racist!"—
and the feeling that it is unpatriotic to believe that America is still racist—
"Racism is a thing of the past!"—often combine to make learning and talking
about race in America difficult for white students. And while most African
American students are well aware that racism is *not* a thing of the past, some
want to believe it is in order to avoid a reality that is just too painful to live with on
a daily basis. In addition, the fact that most African American students know that
racism is alive and well in America today does not mean that they feel comfortable
talking about it with white students, especially if the class is predominantly
white and they are viewed as if they were speaking for their entire race.

So let's start with one thing we probably all have in common: most of us,
whatever the color of our skin, don't want to believe that we have prejudices
against our fellow human beings. We don't want to believe that our thinking
is wrong and our behavior unfair. Our desire *not* to be prejudiced can thus
lead us to deny the possibility that we might be prejudiced in ways we can't
see. And that denial, by blinding us to our own unexamined assumptions,
insures that we will not be able to change whatever racist views we've
unknowingly "inherited" from our families, from our school system, from the
movies, and so forth. Ironically, then, our desire not to be racist can result in
our being racist without our realizing it. This idea might sound a bit strange at
first, but if you think about it, it will probably make sense to you. I've found a
way to address this problem in my own life that seems to work for many of
my students, too. So let me pass it on to you. I hope my personal approach to
the problem of racism will make you more comfortable about discussing racial
issues, and it should at least give you some food for thought.

If I don't want to be racist, then presumably I've eliminated in myself any
racially biased attitudes and behaviors *of which I am aware*. But what about the
racist attitudes and behaviors I might have of which I am *not* aware? We live
in a racist world, so we're programmed, to varying degrees, to have racial
biases. We're not responsible for that programming. The question is not "Am
I a racist?" I assume I am a racist in ways of which I'm unaware. The question
is "What am I going to do about it?" So I consider myself antiracist, not
because I'm certain that I don't have any racial biases—I can't be certain of
that—but because I'm committed to being open to learning new ways in
which I might be unintentionally racist. That way of viewing myself lets
me learn and grow without feeling that I continually have to defend myself.
My job, then, isn't to prove that I'm not a racist but to commit myself to

antiracism by remaining open to all I can learn about the operations of racism and other racial issues.

Furthermore, to my mind at least, it's not unpatriotic to say that American culture is racist. It's not unpatriotic to want our country to be even better than it is. On the contrary, it's unpatriotic to accept systematic injustice toward any Americans, let alone toward such a large group of Americans who are an integral part of American history and American culture. The United States has a long, embedded history of racism, as do most countries, and that is not an easy problem to eliminate, though many people, of all colors, have worked hard and sacrificed much to try to eliminate it. We've made progress, but continued progress depends upon our recognizing that we still have a long road to travel. And African American theory—as an educational vehicle that acknowledges a history of injustice, celebrates the human capacity to overcome any obstacle, and pays tribute to the Americans on whose bloody shoulders we, all of us, stand today—can help us make that journey.

African American theory and cultural criticism

We can also use concepts from African American theory for the purposes of cultural criticism. That is, we can use African American concepts to help us analyze the cultural messages sent, whether deliberately or not, by the everyday productions of the culture in which we live, such as movies, games, television shows, song lyrics, toys and other productions of popular culture discussed in Chapter 1. Indeed, those cultural productions that in some way represent human behavior—that have characters and a plot—can be analyzed using concepts from African American theory just as we use those concepts to analyze literary works. For example, an awareness of African American culture, racist stereotypes, and internalized racism can offer us insights into the hit film romance *Waiting to Exhale* (directed by Forest Whitaker, 1995), in which we follow the diverse experiences of four thirty-something African American women through a single year of their close friendship.

It's a year of change for each of the four main characters. Career-minded Savannah Jackson (Whitney Houston) has a new job producing television. Full-time wife and mother Bernadine Harris (Angela Bassett) is being divorced by her enormously wealthy husband. Beauty salon owner and single mother Gloria Matthews (Loretta Devine) is dealing with her independent, sexually active, seventeen-year-old son Tarik (Donald Adeosun Faison). And insurance underwriter Robin Stokes (Lela Rochon) has once again ended her on-again/off-again longtime affair with her unreliable married boyfriend. These women aren't perfect, but their problems make them engagingly human.

Indeed, it's a shared problem that makes their emotional bond especially strong: their relationships with men. Savannah and Robin keep trying to find the "right" man but keep dating the wrong ones. Bernadine, in order to hold a husband who has never reciprocated her willingness to make sacrifices for him, has spent the last eleven years putting John's financial welfare and personal convenience first, against her own best interests and those of her children. And Gloria, who has raised a fine son, has used the responsibilities and rewards of motherhood to avoid dating altogether. Nevertheless, through the strength of their collective emotional support, each woman is able, over the course of the movie, to grow beyond whatever self-destructive romantic fantasy has led her to the romantic dead-end in which she finds herself as the film opens. As the film closes, each is able to place herself, with or without a man by her side, firmly on the path to her own fulfillment.

Part of the charm of this groundbreaking movie lies in the African American world in which it is set. Yes, the movie portrays familiar scenes from middle- and upper-class American life at home, at work, and at play. However, from the perspective of cultural criticism, it is noteworthy that these scenes include specific representations of African American culture and are populated by African American people. The art on the walls of Savannah's and Gloria's homes is African American. Robin's large and varied doll collection is African American. Gloria's beauty salon specializes in hairstyles for African American women. We hear mention of such popular African American magazines as *Upscale, Jet, Essence*, and *Ebony* and of such popular African American television shows as *Good Times* and *Oprah*. The music that issues from the radio, the tape-deck, and the church choir is African American, and the people enjoying some of that music during happy-hour at a local nightclub or at church on Sunday are predominantly African American. I think it's reasonable to speculate that most African American viewers are familiar with this setting while most American viewers of other races are not. In any case, because this world is underrepresented on the big screen, seeing it there in *Waiting to Exhale* offers a positive experience for all viewers.

Moreover, *Waiting to Exhale* combats a racist stereotype that has often appeared in popular American movies by portraying four beautiful black women who are *not* all light-skinned with European facial features and willowy figures. Savannah, Bernadine, Gloria, and Robin are all beautiful, but they're all beautiful in different ways, with different skin colors, facial features, and body types. And none of the four friends wishes for lighter skin or a more European-looking face or body. Clearly, internalized racism is not the focal point of the main characters' psychological experience. Neither is intraracial racism among their emotional baggage: the four women don't relate to one another—neither do they relate to the men they date—in terms of physical characteristics associated with race.

There is, however, one character in the movie for whom internalized racism is the major psychological focal point: Bernadine's husband John (Michael Beach). *Waiting to Exhale* reveals the destructive power of this problem by showing its negative effects, both on John personally and on his family. Like his enormous, neutral-colored, conservative wardrobe, John doesn't have much originality or personality. His attempts to repress his emotions make him seem, at times, like a robot. By John's choice, the Harris family live in a mansion-like home in a predominantly white, extremely wealthy neighborhood—for John's internalized racism seems inseparable from his desire for money and class status—and in contrast to the homes of Savannah, Gloria, and Robin, the only art displayed in the Harris household is European. In addition, the two Harris children, despite Bernadine's objections, attend a private school at which they are two of the four black students enrolled, and John's thirteen employees, including his divorce lawyer, are all white. Finally, John has left his wife and children for a white woman. Bernadine doesn't use the words *internalized racism*, but she knows it when she sees it: John tries to get rid of whatever he can that reminds him he is black and adopt whatever he can—especially in terms of wealthy white definitions of class status—that makes him feel he is white.

Waiting to Exhale, then, sends a number of antiracist cultural messages. While we're being entertained we're also being reminded that the African American population includes large middle and upper classes; that black women are as capable and deserving of professional success, and of self-determination, as men; that internalized racism is both self-destructive and destructive to one's family; and that feminine beauty is not limited to a European ideal.

Some viewers may wonder, however, what cultural message *Waiting to Exhale* sends in terms of its portrayal of African American men. Does the film succumb to the use of racist stereotypes for its black male characters? Six of the ten male characters with whom Savannah, Bernadine, Gloria, and Robin are in some way involved have negative qualities that frequently appear when African American men are stereotyped: Troy (Mykelti Williamson) chronically abuses cocaine and alcohol; apparently neither Troy nor Lionel (Jeffrey D. Sams) is interested in gainful employment; Russell (Leon) lies to Robin, just as Kenneth (Dennis Haysbert) lies to Savannah, about intending to leave his wife; Gloria's ex-husband David (Giancarlo Esposito) is an absentee father who isn't willing to put forth much effort to reconnect with his son; and as we've seen, John has left Bernadine and their children for a white woman. On the other hand, Kenneth seems genuinely to love his daughter and, like John and David, is financially successful and drug-free. Furthermore, the other four black male characters in the film are positively portrayed. Marvin King (Gregory Hines) is fatherly toward Tarik, generous with his time and labor, an excellent friend to Gloria, with whom he is in love, and financially independent. James Wheeler is a successful civil rights attorney; faithful to his dying wife, whom he dearly loves; and honest with Bernadine, with whom he has fallen in love. And even Michael (Wendell Pierce), whose blissfully selfish behavior as a lover makes him a comedic character early on in the movie, is marriage minded and has a successful career. Finally, Tarik, though he has the problems typical of a teenaged boy, clearly promises to be a good man.

It seems to me, then, that the cultural work performed by *Waiting to Exhale* is ideologically mixed. The film sends a strong antiracist message—about African American culture, African American women, and the destructiveness of internalized racism—but its message concerning African American men includes racist stereotypes as well as very positive portrayals. Perhaps the most important aspect of the film's ambiguous depiction of African American men, however, is the debate this issue invites, a debate that offers viewers much useful food for thought about our own cultural experience, our own cultural biases, and our own capacity for cultural insight.

★★★

Remember, it's natural to feel a bit uncertain when we encounter a new theory—a new way of looking at ourselves and our world—that may call into question many of the beliefs that have been pressed upon us, and that we've accepted uncritically, for most of our lives. Uncertainty is an unavoidable part of learning and growing. Keep in mind, too, that others may disagree with your opinions. Individuals often disagree in their interpretations of literature, popular culture, or everyday experiences, even when drawing upon the same African American concepts for their analyses. The keys to a good interpretation— besides intellectual curiosity and an open mind—are a clear understanding of the African American concepts you've chosen to use and strong evidence to support your analysis.

Taking the next step

Questions for further practice

1   How does Langston Hughes' short story "The Blues I'm Playing" (1934) illustrate and celebrate African American culture through its Harlem-Renaissance setting, its characterization of Miss Oceola Jones, its descriptions of jazz and blues, and its use of AAVE? In addition, how does the story promote antiracism through its positive portrayal of Oceola's antiracist attitude and its negative portrayal of Mrs. Dora Ellsworth's racism?

2   Audre Lorde's "Power" (1978) was written in response to actual events. How does the poem explain racial violence as a self-perpetuating cycle that begins in institutionalized racism? Specifically, what is the connection between: (a) the policeman's being acquitted of his racially motivated murder of a child; and (b) the eventual murder of an eighty-five-year-old white woman? How is institutionalized racism involved in the black juror's capitulation to the verdict desired by her eleven white fellow jurors? Finally, how does the poem's intense and vivid imagery help convey the speaker's outrage? Be specific.

3   August Wilson's The Piano Lesson (1987) dramatizes the experiences of an African American family during the Great Depression. How does the play illustrate the ways in which institutionalized racism increases the

difficulty of financial survival for African Americans during periods of economic crisis? Note, too, how the play portrays the challenges produced by internalized racism in its depiction of the relationship between Berniece and her daughter Maretha. How, specifically, does *The Piano Lesson* illustrate the importance of family—including the continuity of family over generations—in meeting these challenges?

4   Although the African American presence in Kate Chopin's *The Awakening* (1899) is small, it illustrates the view of race held by the novel's white characters, particularly by its upper-class Creoles (privileged descendants of the original French and Spanish settlers of Louisiana) living in New Orleans at the end of the nineteenth century, such as Léonce Pontellier and his circle. Find, for example, the passages referring to "the quadroon" who takes care of the Pontellier children, the "mulatto" family from whom Mademoiselle Reisz rents her room, the "black woman" who works in the Lebrun household in New Orleans, the "mulatresse" who runs the tiny eatery Edna visits on her walks around the suburbs of New Orleans, the "Griffe" who attends Adèle Ratignolle during the birth of her latest child, and the "little black girl" who works in Mrs. Lebrun's household on Grande Isle. In order to flesh out this important though barely visible aspect of *The Awakening*, write a research paper in which you explain the racial hierarchy operating in the novel, which is based on the degree of an individual's African ancestry. Be sure to define the racial terminology used in the novel and any additional racial terminology you find during your research. You might also include research concerning the history of people of color living in New Orleans at the end of the nineteenth century. What cultural groups of color were present at that time? Where did they come from, and how and when did they arrive in New Orleans? What kinds of work did they do? What were their cultural beliefs, customs, and practices? Do they have descendants living in New Orleans today?

5   Use concepts from African American theory to help you interpret some aspect of a movie, television show, song lyric, cartoon, video game, or any other production of popular culture that you find interesting and that seems to lend itself to an African American interpretation. For example, are people of color realistically portrayed in your chosen cultural production? Are elements of black American culture accurately represented and respected? Are racist stereotypes or negative references to people of color involved in this production? Do white standards of beauty seem to be operating in some way? Based on your observations, what cultural work does your chosen cultural production do relevant to African American theory? Specifically, what roles are played by race and racial issues in this cultural production? Does it seem to have racist elements, antiracist elements, or both? Be sure to offer evidence from your chosen production to support your ideas.

Suggestions for further reading

Delgado, Richard, and Jean Stefancic, (eds.) *Critical Race Theory: An Introduction.* New York: New York University Press, 2001. (See, especially, "Introduction," 1–14; "Hallmark Critical Race Theory Themes," 15–35; and "Power and the Shape of Knowledge," 67–86.)

DuBois, W.E.B., *The Souls of Black Folk.* 1903. New York: Penguin, 1989. (See, especially, "Of Our Spiritual Strivings," 3–12; and "Of Mr. Booker T. Washington and Others," 36–50.)

Gates, Henry Louis, Jr., and K.A. Appiah, (eds.) *Toni Morrison: Critical Perspectives Past and Present.* New York: Amistad, 1993. (See, especially, Barbara Christian's "The Contemporary Fables of Toni Morrison", 59–99; Roberta Rubenstein's "Pariah's and Community," 126–58; and Susan Willis's "Eruptions of Funk: Historicizing Toni Morrison," 308–29.)

hooks, bell. *Talking Back: Thinking Feminist, Thinking Black.* Boston, MA: South End Press, 1989.

Morrison, Toni. *Playing in the Dark: Whiteness and the Literary Imagination.* New York: Vintage, 1993. (See, especially, Morrison's definition of *American Africanism,* 6–17; and "Disturbing Nurses and the Kindness of Sharks," 61–91.)

Napier, Winston, (ed.) *African American Literary Theory: A Reader.* New York: New York University Press, 2000. (See, especially, W.E.B. DuBois' "Criteria of Negro Art," 17–23; Zora Neale Hurston's "What White Publishers Won't Print," 54–57; Stephen E. Henderson's "Inside the Funk Shop: A Word on Black Words," 97–101; and Barbara Smith's "Toward a Black Feminist Criticism," 132–46.)

Tyson, Lois. "African American Criticism." *Critical Theory Today: A User-Friendly Guide.* 2nd ed. New York: Routledge. 2006. 359–415.

Note

1 A full discussion of this issue is available online at *The Sentencing Project,* http://sentencing project/CRACKREFORM/.

Chapter 9

Using concepts from postcolonial theory to understand literature

Why should we learn about postcolonial theory?

If you've read the preceding five chapters, you've seen some of the ways in which concepts from psychoanalytic, Marxist, feminist, LGBTQ, and African American theories focus our attention on different aspects of human experience. Specifically, you've seen some of the ways in which our relationship to ourselves and our world is formed by our psychological wounds, by the socioeconomic class into which we were born and to which we now belong, by the capitalist system within which we were raised, by traditional gender roles, by our sexual orientation, and by our race. As we'll see, postcolonial theory gives us tools to explore how all of these factors—as well as ethnicity, religion, and other cultural factors that influence human experience—work together in creating the ways in which we view ourselves and our world. Thus, concepts from postcolonial theory can help us understand human experience as a combination of complex cultural forces operating in each of us.

Postcolonial theory developed the concepts we'll study in this chapter because, as its name implies, this theory emerged in an attempt to understand people from different cultures in terms of an important experience they all had in common: colonial domination by a superior European military force. Europe's invasions of non-European peoples began at the end of the fifteenth century with the military competition among England, France, Spain, Portugal, and the Netherlands to find new sources of wealth around the globe. By the end of the nineteenth century, England had the largest colonial empire, which covered a quarter of the earth's surface and included India, Australia, New Zealand, Canada, and Ireland, as well as significant holdings in Africa, the West Indies, South America, the Middle East, and Southeast Asia. Probably the most damaging effects of colonial domination were experienced by non-white populations, whose own cultures were completely or almost completely destroyed as British government officials and British settlers imposed their own language, religion, government, education, codes of behavior, and definitions of intelligence and beauty on the conquered peoples.

The British Empire is called a colonial empire because it gained new territories by the establishment of settler colonies—the sending of British settlers to set up communities in the territories Britain wished to control—or invader colonies, which were created by the colonization of the native populations conquered by British military force. Even when colonization occurred without the aid of military conquest, the white settlers themselves, in their desire to expand their ownership of land and natural resources, eventually killed off, drove away, or colonized the native peoples who stood in their way. The colonization of native peoples was achieved by imposing English language, religion, dress, and other cultural practices upon them and by forbidding them their own native cultural practices.

Britain began to lose its colonial holdings after World War II, and British military rule of territories outside the United Kingdom is, for the most part, at an end. Nevertheless, the attempts of formerly colonized peoples to regain their own cultures, re-establish their own language, run their own political affairs, and develop a sense of national self-esteem have been difficult because so much of their pre-colonial history, language, and culture were lost after a century or more of British domination. In other words, the colonizers picked up their guns and went home, but the devastating effects of their colonial rule remain behind. Because conquered peoples were affected by British control from the first moment British rule began, the word *postcolonial* refers to the experience of conquered peoples from the initial point of British contact to the present. Postcolonial concepts, therefore, are intended to help us analyze the experience of being colonized, the experience of living under colonial rule, and the experience of adjusting to national independence after colonial rule has ended.

British postcolonial populations include not only those that had been conquered by the British military and ruled by British officials—such as the populations of India and those of much of the West Indies, Africa, the Middle East, and Southeast Asia—but also those native populations subjugated by white settlers and governed today by the majority culture that surrounds them, such as Australian Aboriginal peoples and Native Americans in the United States and Canada. Finally, many postcolonial theorists believe that postcolonial populations also include non-white peoples who have minority status in Britain, Europe, and the United States—for example, in the US, African Americans, Latinos/as, and Asian Americans—because, like colonized populations, these peoples have been deprived of much or all of the culture, language, and status they enjoyed in their homelands or have experienced the loss of cultural traditions due to powerful socioeconomic pressures to conform to the dominant culture.

Postcolonial concepts can also help us explore the ways in which multiple forms of oppression—for example, classism, sexism, heterosexism, and racism—can combine in the daily experience of members of political minorities; the ways in which members of these groups have overcome these kinds of oppressive forces and worked together to build better lives for themselves and their communities; and the ways in which such struggles are represented in literature. Postcolonial concepts will thus enable you to combine and expand what you've learned from the critical theories you've used in preceding chapters. Don't be surprised, then, if you notice that some of the postcolonial interpretation exercises we do later overlap with some of our interpretation exercises from previous chapters. Although postcolonial concepts will often help us see a literary work from a perspective quite different from the perspectives offered by the other theories we've studied, postcolonial concepts will sometimes combine the insights offered by other theories in an effort to show us, for example, all of the cultural factors influencing characters' behavior or plot events.

The term *postcolonial literature* refers to literary works written both by members of colonized or formerly colonized populations—for example, the works of Salman Rushdie (India), Jamaica Kincaid (Antigua, West Indies), Chinua Achebe (Nigeria), and Ngugi wa Thiong'o (Kenya)—and by members of the colonizing (white) culture in colonized or formerly colonized nations, such as the fiction of South Africa's Nadine Gordimer, Andre Brink, and J. M. Coetzee. And as we noted earlier, because the experience of such ethnic political minorities as Native Americans, African Americans, Latinos/as, and Asian Americans has much in common with the experience of formerly colonized populations, postcolonial concepts can often help us interpret the work of these writers, too. Finally, given that the primary purpose of postcolonial concepts is to help us understand the complex experiences of being colonized by a culture other than our own native culture and of resisting that colonization, we can use postcolonial concepts to analyze the works of any author— regardless of her or his time and place of birth—that we feel can help us understand something about those experiences. For as we'll see in the "Basic concepts" section later in the chapter, our consciousness—our sense of self, our sense of our own culture—can be colonized, can be "taken over," by a new culture without a single shot being fired. And the culture that colonizes our consciousness doesn't have to come from a foreign country. It can exist right within the borders of our own nation.

Remember, although it's important that you read through the following list of concepts, don't be too concerned if you don't feel you thoroughly understand every one. You'll begin to understand these concepts much better when we use them, later in this chapter, to help us interpret the literary texts that appear at the end of this book. Remember, too, that I'm offering you my own literary analyses in the interpretation exercises provided later in this chapter. You might use the same postcolonial concepts I use but come up with different interpretations of your own. If you disagree with any of the analyses I offer in these exercises, don't be afraid to look in the literary work in question for evidence that will support your viewpoint. A literary work can often support a number of different interpretations, even when readers are using concepts from the same theory.

Basic concepts

Colonialist ideology

Colonialist ideology is based on the colonizers' belief in their own superiority over the colonized, who were usually the original inhabitants of the lands the colonizers settled in or invaded. According to colonialist ideology, the colonizers were civilized; the colonized were savages. Because their technology was more highly advanced, the colonizers believed that their entire culture was more highly advanced, and they ignored or swept aside the religions, customs, and codes of behavior of the peoples they subjugated, often forbidding them to speak their own language or to teach it to their children. Children in colonized nations were taught the language, customs, and beliefs of the colonizers in schools set up for that purpose. While colonization by military force is generally a thing of the past, *cultural colonization*, often called *cultural imperialism*, has taken its place in many countries around the globe. For example, American fashions, movies, music, sports, fast food, and consumerism (or "shop-'til-you-dropism") have dwarfed other nations' own cultural practices or turned them into little more than tourist attractions, as is evident, for example, in parts of the Philippines, Japan, and Mexico.

We can also see colonialist ideology operating within the borders of a single country. In the United States, for example, many white middle- and upper-class Americans believe the myth that people living in Appalachia are not only poor but stupid, dirty, and untrustworthy; that the homeless are lazy and lack willpower; and that Native Americans prefer welfare and petty thievery to gainful employment.

Othering—One of the clearest symptoms of colonialist ideology is the practice of othering: judging those who are different as inferior, as somehow less than human. For example, the colonizers saw themselves as the embodiment of what a human being should be, the proper "self"; the peoples they conquered were different, "other," and therefore inferior, subhuman. Othering divides the world between "us"—the civilized, the moral, the intelligent—and "them": the "savages," the immoral, the unintelligent. The "savage" is usually considered evil (the *demonic other*). But sometimes the "savage" is perceived as possessing a "primitive" beauty or nobility born of a closeness to nature (the *exotic other*). In either case, however, the "savage" is *othered* and, therefore, not considered fully human.

Within the borders of the United States, for example, African American men are often treated as demonic others, who might "turn violent" without much provocation. Similarly, gay men are often othered as unscrupulous sexual predators. Americans who are sometimes treated as exotic others include, for instance, beautiful Asian American women.

Subaltern—Colonialist ideology always creates a social hierarchy—a system of social status—in which members of the colonizing culture occupy the top rungs of the ladder. Subalterns are those persons who occupy the bottom rungs of the colonialist social ladder, whether their inferior status is based on race, class, gender, religion, sexual orientation, ethnicity, or any other cultural factor. The word *subaltern* thus gives us a way to refer to any person at the bottom of a society's status system. Subalterns are othered by members of the colonizing culture and are deprived both of equal opportunities to better their lives and of equal justice under the law.

Subalterns include, for example, individuals othered by racism, classism, sexism, heterosexism, and/or religious discrimination (such as anti-Semitism, or the hatred of Jews, and Islamophobia, or the pathological fear and loathing of Muslims). Among the most visible examples of subalterns in the United States are the homeless of any race, Native Americans, and economically distressed people of color.

The colonial subject

Because there is enormous pressure on subalterns to believe that they are inferior, it should not be surprising that many of them wind up believing just that. Subalterns who internalize, or "buy into" the colonialist belief that those different from a society's dominant culture are inferior are called *colonial subjects*—they have a *colonized consciousness*—whether the dominant culture in question is that of a foreign power or that of their own country. Examples of the latter include women who believe they are, by nature, less intelligent or capable than their male compatriots; people from any non-white race who believe their race makes them less attractive, intelligent, or worthy than their white compatriots; LGBTQ people who believe their sexual orientation means they are sick or evil in ways their heterosexual compatriots are not; and poor people who believe, no matter how hard they work or how ethical they are, that their poverty means they are less worthy as human beings than their financially successful compatriots.

One can be oppressed by colonialist ideology economically, politically, and socially without being a colonial subject as long as one maintains an awareness that colonialist ideology is unjust and that people who belong to the dominant culture are not naturally superior. In other words, one is a colonial subject only when one's consciousness is colonized. Colonial subjects usually practice *mimicry* and experience *unhomeliness*.

Mimicry—Mimicry is the imitation, by a subaltern, of the dress, speech, behavior, or lifestyle of members of the dominant culture. Mimicry is not intended to mock members of the dominant culture. On the contrary, it reveals a subaltern's desire to belong to that culture. Mimicry thus results from having a colonized consciousness, from believing that one is inferior because one does not belong to the dominant culture. For example, during Britain's control of India, some Indians adopted British attire, hairstyles, and the like because they wanted to be considered "as good as" their British oppressors. Analogously, working-class and middle-class people in the United States sometimes make purchases that endanger their financial security because they want to resemble the upper-class members of their own country, whom they consider superior to themselves. In contrast, if one imitates members of the dominant culture without believing that one's own culture is inferior—for example, in order to keep one's job—then one is not practicing mimicry in the postcolonial sense of the word. Sadly, mimicry often includes othering members of one's own culture. That is, in order to feel that one belongs to or has the approval of the dominant culture, one adopts that culture's prejudices against the members of one's own culture.

Unhomeliness—Unhomeliness is the feeling of having no stable cultural identity—no real home in any culture—that occurs to people who do not belong to the dominant culture and have rejected their own culture as inferior. Thus, unhomeliness, too, results from having a colonized consciousness. Being *unhomed* is not the same as being homeless. Unhomeliness is an emotional state: unhomed people don't feel at home even in their own homes because they don't feel at home in any culture and, therefore, don't feel at home in themselves.

For example, unhomeliness can be experienced by individuals who feel torn between the culture into which they were born and the culture in which they live as adults. A person born in poverty who has become wealthy may feel uncomfortable both with his wealthy friends and with his parents, of whom he's now ashamed, because he doesn't feel he fits in either world. Similar experiences of being unhomed can occur to individuals who grew up in communities of working-class ethnic minorities—for example, in Asian American, African American, or Chicano communities—but who now live in, say, a suburban community most of whose members are upper-class or upwardly mobile middle-class white people of Western European ancestry.

Anticolonialist resistance

Anticolonialist resistance—the effort to rid one's land and/or one's culture of colonial domination—can take many forms. Anticolonialist resistance includes such activities as the formation of underground (secret) groups who might engage in armed raids, perform acts of sabotage, rescue individuals unjustly imprisoned by the colonialist regime, attempt to gain the support of neutral foreign powers, or raise international awareness of colonialist abuses. Of course, anticolonialist resistance can take the form of an organized, armed rebellion against a colonialist regime, such as occurred in Cuba when followers of Fidel Castro ousted US-backed Fulgencio Batista in 1959. Or it can take the form of organized, non-violent resistance to colonialist oppression, such as occurred in India when followers of Mohandas (Mahatma) Gandhi ousted the British in 1947. However, even when political resistance is, for the most part, impossible because the forces of colonialist oppression are so overwhelming, anticolonialist resistance can occur on the psychological level. That is, even when colonized peoples have been completely subjugated to a foreign power over the course of many generations and no longer have access to their own language or their own cultural past, many oppressed individuals manage to keep their minds free of the colonialist ideology that tells them they are inferior. This kind of anti-colonialist resistance, which exists on the psychological level alone and might be termed *psychological resistance*, is perhaps the most important kind of resistance, for without it it is unlikely that other kinds of resistance would ever occur.

Examples of anticolonialist resistance in the United States are numerous. To cite just a few, there have been the Underground Railroad, which helped slaves escape to the north before they were freed by the American Civil War; the Women's Suffrage Movement, which got women the vote in 1920; the Civil Rights Movement of the 1950s and 1960s; the efforts of Cesar Chavez and the Farm Workers Organizing Committee to help Mexican American migrant laborers; the AIDS Coalition to Unleash Power (ACT UP), which fought the federal government's refusal to fund AIDS research; and the American Indian Movement (AIM), begun in 1968 to obtain civil rights and legal justice for Native Americans.

There are, of course, additional postcolonial concepts, but these are enough to get us started using this theory to interpret literature. Let's begin our interpretation exercises by analyzing a story that illustrates the evils of colonialist ideology in chilling detail: Ralph Ellison's "The Battle Royal."

Interpretation exercises

Understanding colonialist ideology: Interpreting "The Battle Royal"

If you heard someone use the words *colonialist oppression*, probably the first thought that would come to your mind would be that the speaker was talking about a relationship between two countries. For colonialist oppression usually occurs when a wealthier, technologically developed nation exploits a poorer, technologically underdeveloped nation, justifying its aggression with the claim that its culture—its laws, customs, beliefs, and so forth—is superior to that of the exploited nation. Ralph Ellison's "The Battle Royal" (1952; see Appendix C), however, illustrates the ways in which colonialist oppression can occur within the borders of a single country when the wealthier, more powerful segment of the population exploits those with little money and limited power, those whom it considers inferior due to race, class, gender, ethnicity, religion, or some other cultural category. In other words, Ellison's story shows us that the relationship between America's dominant culture and its subalterns (those with the least political power) is much like the relationship between a colonialist country and the peoples it subjugates on foreign shores.

Set in the post-World-War-II American south, "The Battle Royal" portrays a group of leading citizens—the town's wealthy white men, who are privileged in terms of their race, class, and gender—gathered for an evening's entertainment. These men obviously represent the dominant culture—that is, the segment of the population whose political, social, and economic power allows them to "run the show," so to speak. Indeed, the nature of the "show" they've arranged for themselves on this particular evening makes it very clear that they hold the power in this society and that they want those "beneath" them to know it. For it seems that the desire to display their power is the men's primary purpose in engaging the services of the white exotic dancer; the African American youths who fight in the battle royal; and the African American narrator, who gives a speech after participating in the battle royal. Clearly, the white men's behavior during each of these "entertainments" is aggressive, hostile, and intended to degrade the subaltern "entertainers," whom these leading citizens consider inferior to themselves. Ellison's tale is thus anticolonialist: it offers us an extremely negative portrait of colonialist ideology and suggests that such ideology is operating against subaltern American citizens within the borders of their own nation. We might even say that "The Battle Royal" depicts a kind of colonialist microcosm (miniature world) the occupants of which illustrate, as we'll see, both the ways in which colonialist ideology operates and some of the possibilities for anticolonialist resistance. To understand how the story accomplishes this task, we'll examine how Ellison's tale portrays: (1) the colonialist ideology of the dominant culture; (2) the subjugation of that culture's subalterns; and (3) the possibilities for anticolonialist resistance.

The colonialist ideology of the dominant culture

Although the civic leaders in "The Battle Royal" probably never heard the phrase *colonialist ideology*, it is this ideology that influences most of their behavior in the story. For the white men behave as if it were their right, as members of the "superior" culture, to exploit subalterns in whatever ways serve their purpose. And they try to justify their behavior by othering the subalterns they abuse: the white men treat the "performers" they've hired as if they were less than human and therefore not deserving of the respect and consideration afforded "full" human beings. To see how the civic leaders' colonialist ideology operates in the story, find the textual evidence required to answer the following questions.

1   How do we know the white men belong to the dominant culture? That is, what are the signs of their cultural privilege?

   a   What occupations do they hold?
   b   How do we know they have a good deal of money?
   c   How do we know they have power in the community—for example, that they can do more or less what they please without fear of punishment?

2   In what ways do the civic leaders other those relegated to the category of subaltern?

   a   How do they other the narrator (a subaltern in terms of race and class)?
   b   How do they other Tatlock and his friends (subalterns in terms of race and class), the young men brought in to fight the battle royal?
   c   How do they other the exotic dancer (a subaltern in terms of class and gender)?

The subjugation of subalterns

As we have seen, the subalterns in "The Battle Royal" consist of the narrator, Tatlock and his friends, and the white exotic dancer. Other subalterns in the story include, of course, the narrator's grandfather and the rest of his family. In order to understand the ways in which the story illustrates the various kinds of subjugation imposed upon subalterns by the dominant culture, find the textual evidence required to answer the following questions.

1   How do we know that the subalterns in the story are economically oppressed?

   a   How do we know that Tatlock and his friends are desperately in need of money?
   b   Why is it reasonable to assume that the white exotic dancer, like the black youths forced to watch her, also has limited means of earning a living? (How do we know that she does not like her line of work?)
   c   How do we know that the narrator's family can't afford to send him to college?
   d   How do we know that the narrator's family have been economically oppressed since their arrival, generations ago, in America?

2   How do we know that the subalterns in the story are socially oppressed?

   a   How do we know that, in the time and place in which the story is set, the races are segregated?

      i   What college will the narrator's scholarship allow him to attend?
      ii Why is it safe to assume that the high school from which the narrator has just graduated is for African American students only? (Were high schools integrated in this place and time? Given the story's setting, would he have been allowed to give a graduation speech in any but an all-black high school?)
      iii Why is it safe to assume that the narrator lives in a segregated community of African Americans?

   b   How do we know that the society represented in the story is segregated according to class?

     i What kind of elevator do the narrator and his schoolmates use in the hotel at which the white men's smoker is held?

     ii How does the narrator feel about having to use this elevator?

     iii Why is it safe to assume that none of the white men at the smoker would marry, openly date, or even befriend the exotic dancer?

3 How do we know that the subalterns in the story are psychologically oppressed?

  a How do we know that the narrator's family, with the exception of his grandfather, are terrified of white people?

  b How do we know that the exotic dancer is terrified of the white men at the smoker?

  c How is Tatlock's response to the narrator in the final round of the battle royal an example of the dominant culture's success in emotionally dividing members of the African American community from one another?

  d How do we know that the narrator is unhomed, that he doesn't feel he belongs either to his community's African American culture or to the culture of the white men he is so eager to please?

     i Does the narrator feel at home with the other young men from his community? Explain.

     ii Does the narrator feel at home with his family? Explain.

     iii Does the narrator feel at home with the white men whose approval he desires? Explain.

  e In what ways does the narrator practice mimicry, or attempt to resemble the dominant culture in order to be accepted by it? In other words, in what ways does the narrator "buy into" the colonialist ideology of the dominant culture that rejects him?

     i Why does the narrator feel uncomfortable riding in the servants' elevator with Tatlock and his friends? (In other words, how does he respond to members of his own community in the same way that the white men respond to them?)

     ii In the narrator's opinion, who are the only people truly capable of judging his worth? Explain.

     iii What are the narrator's emotions upon receiving the briefcase from the white men? Be specific.

The possibilities for anticolonialist resistance

For subalterns to practice anticolonialist resistance they must, first and foremost, reject the colonialist ideology that tells them they are born inferior because they were not born into the dominant culture. In other words, they must know that their oppressors, though more politically and socially powerful, are not superior to them as human beings. In short, subalterns who are likely to be capable of anticolonialist resistance do not admire their oppressors, though they might have to pretend to admire them in order to survive. Although anticolonialist resistance can include respect for the colonialist rulers as fellow human beings, as Mahatma Gandhi and Martin Luther King taught, "The Battle Royal" seems to suggest, in contrast, that the seeds of anticolonialist resistance lie in the subalterns' ability to see that colonialist oppressors forfeit the right to be respected. To understand this aspect of the story, collect the textual evidence required below to show that the possibilities for anticolonialist resistance lie in the negative feelings about the dominant culture secretly harbored by the exotic dancer, the narrator, and the narrator's grandfather.

1   *The exotic dancer*

    a   How does the exotic dancer feel about the white men at the smoker?
    b   How does she try to remain emotionally detached from the men who hire her? (Include attention to her makeup and her facial expression.)

2   *The narrator*—As we saw earlier, in some ways the narrator is already becoming a colonial subject: he sometimes practices mimicry, and he's unhomed. On the other hand, he still has the capacity for anticolonialist resistance because, in large part, the motive behind his behavior is economic survival. At least some of the time, he sees the white men not as superior human beings, but as his only source of financial aid.

    a   When is the narrator's apparent mimicry not really mimicry? That is, when is he deliberately faking compliance with white expectations in order to get ahead rather than because he believes that the dominant culture is superior?
    b   Find as many examples as you can of the narrator's negative feelings about the white men at the smoker.
    c   How does the narrator's dream, at the end of the story, indicate that, at least unconsciously, he is thoroughly aware of the dominant white culture's determination to completely subjugate him?

3   *The narrator's grandfather*—The narrator tells us that his grandfather lived his life very quietly. He never got into trouble with the colonialist power structure within which he was a subaltern due to his race and class. And until his dying moments, he never spoke against that power structure. At the very end of his life, however, he revealed his real feelings about his oppressors and the motives for his meek behavior, requesting that the truth be told to the children.

    a   Why did the narrator's grandfather have to pretend to be meek throughout his life? In other words, why was psychological resistance—which he calls fighting "the good fight"—the primary form of anticolonialist resistance available to him?

b In what ways is the grandfather correct in believing that the dominant culture represented in "The Battle Royal" is "at war" against its subalterns?

c How do we know that the grandfather succeeded in passing on his anticolonialist resistance to at least one descendant: the narrator?

Focusing your essay

The textual data you've already gathered should allow you to focus your essay on the ways in which "The Battle Royal" depicts a kind of colonialist microcosm, or a colonialist world in miniature. Although Ellison's story is set in a single town—in fact, most of the action of the story occurs in a single room—the tale nevertheless offers a thorough portrayal of the operations of colonialist ideology as well as some of the psychological possibilities for anticolonialist resistance. For Ellison's story shows us how American society mirrors, within the confines of its own borders and against its own citizens, the kind of colonialist subjugation usually associated with the colonial conquest of one country by another. Because "The Battle Royal" provides such a negative depiction of colonialist ideology, we can say that it is an anticolonialist story.

In your essay, you should probably pay particular attention to your analysis of the narrator because, as we've seen, this character illustrates the complex ways in which an individual can both resist colonialist ideology and "buy into" that ideology. For while the narrator, in some ways, rejects the colonialist injustice with which the dominant culture subjugates subalterns in America, he also greatly desires the approval of the dominant culture. In short, he knows that the white civic leaders are wrong to consider him inferior, yet he wants the approval of these men because he believes that only they are capable of judging his true ability! This is precisely the kind of psychological contradiction that colonialist ideology frequently creates.

Of course, one important reason why the narrator finds it difficult to resist colonialist ideology is that, when colonialist oppression is as thorough as it is in "The Battle Royal," resistance seems useless. Indeed, the narrator's grandfather, who practices the most anticolonialist resistance we see in the story, practices that resistance almost exclusively on the psychological level: he is a rebel only within himself. To modern readers, this may seem like a rather small accomplishment. Yet the grandfather, too, is worthy of particular attention in your essay, for his psychological resistance is not a small achievement. In order to appreciate this character's accomplishment, however, the grandfather has to be viewed in historical context—that is, in terms of the time and place in which he lived. In the story's setting, colonialist ideology offers subalterns two options: they are expected either to (1) believe the colonialist ideology that tells them they're inferior; or (2) openly reject that ideology, in which case the dominant culture will more or less eliminate them—for example, by jailing them or lynching them. The grandfather, however, did neither. Instead, as many African American slaves had done, he pretended to accept colonialist ideology while secretly rejecting it completely. He therefore survived with his sense of self and his awareness of injustice intact, and he tried to pass on the kind of resistance he practiced to his descendants, hoping that they will, perhaps, have a better opportunity to carry that resistance further than he was able to do.

Remember that you don't have to limit yourself to the analysis of the story I've offered you. For example, you might want to include in your essay a discussion of the ways in which the white men's colonialist ideology results from their own insecurity. For colonialist ideology creates a social ladder with so many rungs that even members of the dominant culture are in danger of finding themselves falling to a lower level in one way or another: "Am I wealthy enough?" "Do I live in the 'right' neighborhood?" "Did I graduate from the 'right' school?" "Are my children enrolled in the 'right' schools?" "Are my parents from the 'right' social class?" "Am I attractive and fashionable enough?" "Is my spouse attractive and fashionable enough?" "Is my last name too ethnic-sounding?" "Do I belong to the 'right' religious faith?" "Is my occupation prestigious enough?" "Do I belong to *all* the 'right' social organizations?" "Am I a member of the 'right' political party?"

Obviously, the white men at the smoker can't all be at the top of the social ladder in every cultural category imaginable. Yet colonialist ideology tells them that whatever ways in which they fall short of the top are the ways in which they are inferior as human beings. Colonialist ideology thus breeds constant insecurity. And people frequently try to hide their insecurity by abusing their power in an attempt to convince themselves and others that they are superior. You may have heard this behavior referred to as *overcompensation*, and I think it's clear that the extreme display of power by the white men in the story qualifies as overcompensation. Whatever your interpretation, be sure you understand the postcolonial concepts you choose to employ, compose a clear statement of your thesis, and support your interpretation with adequate textual evidence.

Analyzing the colonial subject: Interpreting "Everyday Use"

Alice Walker's "Everyday Use" (1973; see Appendix D) raises a question of great interest for postcolonial theory: How do individuals find a culture they can call their own when the dominant culture of their nation defines them as outsiders? In other words, how do human beings handle the cultural rejection of being categorized as subalterns? Walker's story is set in the rural south during the late 1960s and early 1970s, and this is precisely the problem that each of the story's three main characters—Mama, Maggie, and Dee Johnson—has to face. For Mama and Maggie are subalterns in terms of their race, class, and gender. And although Dee has moved away from the Johnson family homestead, obtained a college degree, and advanced a few rungs up the ladder of social class, she is still a subaltern in terms of her race and gender.

Mama and Maggie's subaltern status is responsible for their economic limitations and certainly contributes to their low self-image. But the two women
nevertheless have a fulfilling cultural identity and a strong sense of belonging
because they embrace a cultural heritage other than that of the dominant culture
which rejects them. They have the culture provided by their family heritage.
However, this is the culture that Dee has, from her youth, rejected. And it is Dee
who is of primary interest to us here because she illustrates one of the story's most
chilling postcolonial insights: that the experience of being a colonial subject,
which Dee became as a young girl, can be the kind of traumatic experience from
which people have great difficulty recovering. For colonial subjects are people who
believe in the superiority of the colonialist culture that defines them as subaltern—that is, they want the approval of the very group that considers them
inferior. By accepting the colonialist ideology that others them, they, in effect,
other themselves. And, surely, the dominant white culture during the period
in which "Everyday Use" is set is a colonialist culture because it defines itself
as the superior culture and judges other Americans "inferior" according to its
own biased definitions of such qualities as intelligence, success, and beauty.

Even when a new culture—the Black Pride Movement that emerged in the
late 1960s—offers Dee the opportunity to embrace a new cultural identity, a new
cultural home built on the foundation of her African origins, she is unable to
fully embrace this new identity. That is, although Dee has changed her name
to the African name *Wangero*, she relates to African culture the same way
she related to the white culture that categorized her as subaltern: she adopts
the "look," the opinions, and the possessions that will allow her to feel that
she "fits in" with the cultural group to which she aspires to belong. For her,
the Black Pride Movement consists of fashion statements and status symbols,
which she acquires just as she had acquired the organdy dress, the black pumps,
and the other articles of clothing required by fashionable white culture when
she was in high school. And just as she was ashamed of her family for not
conforming to white cultural norms when she was in high school, she's disappointed in them now for not taking an interest in their African origins.
Similarly, although she now wants the family artifacts she once scorned—for
example, the homemade butter-churn dasher and quilts—she wants these
items for the purposes of display. It has become fashionable, among Wangero's
set, to own such family antiques, but it's clear that she does not value these
items because she wants to embrace her family heritage or cares to learn, as
Maggie has done, the traditional family crafts. For Wangero has as little faith
now in the usefulness of her family heritage to help her succeed in life as she
had when she was in high school, a situation which, "Everyday Use" implies,
the Black Pride Movement does little to improve.

In short, it seems that Dee may be a permanent colonial subject. She may
be forever unhomed. She will remain an outsider to all cultures as long as she
continues to define culture—as she learned to define it when she was a young
girl—as something material to be displayed rather than something within

herself to be lived. If such remains her attitude, her behavior will remain a form of mimicry. Whatever clothes she wears, whatever language she speaks, and whatever name she calls herself will be an attempt to imitate the group whose approval she desires—the group she believes can help her improve her socioeconomic status—rather than a genuine expression of her membership in a culture. For as "Everyday Use" illustrates, a culture consists of a way of viewing the world and defining one's place within it, a way of relating to oneself and others, and a set of values that gives one a sense of self. Unfortunately, this is the kind of cultural belonging it seems that Dee will never experience. In order to see how Walker's story illustrates the importance of having a sense of cultural belonging and, conversely, the personal cost of being a colonial subject, we'll examine how the story portrays: (1) the ways in which the Johnson family heritage provides Mama and Maggie with an alternative to the values of the dominant white culture of the time; (2) the ways in which Dee has remained a colonial subject despite her participation in the Black Pride Movement; and (3) the ways in which the Black Pride Movement, itself, may have failed to provide an adequate alternative to the dominant white culture whose colonialist ideology it sought to expose and expunge.

The Johnson family heritage

1   In order to see how the Johnson family heritage provides an alternative to the values of the dominant white culture of the time, we need to see examples of that culture's values. How does the story show, through Dee's early adoption of those values, that the dominant culture esteems, among other things

  a   financial success,
  b   the acquisition of material possessions,
  c   fashionable home furnishings,
  d   fashionable clothing and hairstyles, and
  e   self-confidence and assertiveness?

2   In contrast to the values you've already listed, what does the Johnson family traditionally value? That is, of what does the Johnson family heritage consist? Be sure to include specific examples of the following values:

  a   a broad knowledge of family history,
  b   the use of a family name through successive generations,
  c   the knowledge and skills required by traditional family crafts,
  d   farming knowledge and skills,
  e   the ability to prepare traditional African American cuisine, and
  f   a love of country life.

3   How does her family heritage give Mama a sense of cultural belonging?

  a   What abilities does Mama seem most proud to have?
  b   How far back can Mama trace the family name Dee?

    c How do we know that Mama is a good traditional cook?

    d How do we know that Mama enjoys her rural lifestyle?

4 How does her family heritage give Maggie a sense of cultural belonging?

    a At what traditional family craft is Maggie adept?

    b From whom did she learn this craft, and to whom is she likely to pass it on?

    c How knowledgeable is Maggie about Johnson family history? Give specific examples. How do we know that Maggie, though very shy and retiring, takes pride in her knowledge?

    d How do we know that Maggie enjoys her rural lifestyle?

Dee as colonial subject

1 *Dee's unhomeliness*

    a As a youngster, how was Dee unhomed?

        i   How did she feel about the family home?

        ii   Did she want the homemade quilts Mama offered her when she went away to college? Why not?

        iii How did she feel about her mother and sister at that time? Did Dee share a close bond with them? Was she critical of them? Why?

        iv   Did Dee have any real friends among the members of her community?

    b As an adult, how is Wangero unhomed?

        i   How does the story suggest that Wangero relates to the family home (of which she takes photos), and to the items she takes from home, as items for display rather than as mementoes with emotional value?

        ii   How does Wangero feel about her mother and sister now? Does she have much in common with them? Does she seem to have a close bond with them? Is she sensitive to their needs?

        iii Does Wangero seem to have a close relationship with Hakim?

        iv   Does she talk about African culture at all or seem in any way seriously interested in it beyond her admiration of African-style dress, hairstyles, and the like?

2 *Dee's mimicry*

    a As a youngster, how did Dee practice mimicry?

        i   What fashion trends did Dee follow in high school, and how important was fashion to her?

        ii   In addition to her clothing and physical appearance, how did she try to impress her schoolmates?

    iii   What kinds of books does the story imply that Dee read to Mama and Maggie? Given what we now know about the omission of black history from American history books, the omission of black literature from American literature classes, and so forth, what might Mama have meant when she said that Dee read them "lies" and "other folks' habits"? (Note that this is an example of the dominant culture's use of the educational system to promote its own biased viewpoints.)

    iv   How did Dee other Mama and Maggie? (Othering Mama and Maggie because they didn't conform to the norms of the dominant culture is a form of mimicry because Dee othered her mother and sister in the same way that the dominant culture othered them.)

b As an adult, how does Wangero practice mimicry?

    i   In what way is Wangero's African style nothing more than style?

    ii   How does the story suggest that Hakim is Wangero's fashionable "trophy" boyfriend?

    iii   What suggests that Wangero still shares the dominant culture's values in believing that financial success and the attainment of material possessions are more important than anything else, including family?

    iv   How does the story imply that Wangero's pride is not so much pride in her African origins as pride in her new class status?

    v   How does Wangero other Mama and Maggie now? (As we noted earlier, othering one's own people is a form of mimicry in that one is copying the biases of the dominant culture.)

The Black Pride Movement

At the time in which "Everyday Use" is set, the dominant white culture in America had been treating African Americans as subalterns rather than as full American citizens and full human beings for over three hundred years. The Black Pride Movement, therefore, encouraged black Americans to look to Africa for their cultural origins. Interest grew in African history, religions, art, and music. The adoption of African names, African-style clothing and hairstyles, African forms of greeting, and African motifs in home décor became popular among African Americans who wanted to reclaim their connection to African civilizations that white colonialist ideology told them were worthless. And "black is beautiful!" was certainly a welcome change from the white colonialist belief that non-white peoples are less than human and therefore physically unattractive.

However, some African Americans believe that the Black Pride Movement suffered from a tendency to focus too heavily on the superficial aspects of African culture—such as clothing and hairstyles—and to overlook too readily the sources of black pride right here in America. White colonialist history of the United States—which was virtually the only US history readily available then—omitted or distorted the story of Africans in America, implying that their past consisted of the humiliation of slavery followed by a history of underachievement. As a result, members of the Black Pride Movement often tended to reject a good deal of the history of Africans on American soil as little more than a history of victimization. In so doing, it rejected a heritage of which, in fact, black Americans had a right to be proud. But few Americans, black or white, were aware at that time of the rich history of black courage and achievement that dated back to the earliest African presence on American soil and that included the history of African American enslavement. For even under slavery, African Americans maintained their African tradition of oral history, their knowledge of African agricultural and medical practices, their African customs, and their African folk tales. At the risk of life and limb, they secretly taught one another to read and write and developed networks of secret communication by means of which they organized several rebellions and countless escapes to freedom. And many escaped slaves and free blacks, risking Confederate retaliation, worked with the abolitionist movement in the north and fought with the Union Army during the Civil War.

In order to get a sense of the mixed attitude toward the Black Pride Movement implied in "Everyday Use," collect the following textual evidence.

1   *Wangero and Hakim*—Wangero and Hakim are the only representatives of the Black Pride Movement the story provides. Therefore, it's reasonable to speculate that the strengths and shortcomings of these two characters reveal the story's view of some of the strengths and shortcomings of the Black Pride Movement.

   a   What are Wangero's and Hakim's strengths?

      i   What have Wangero and Hakim accomplished in terms of their education?
      ii   What have they accomplished in terms of financial success?
      iii   What have they accomplished in terms of developing their self-confidence?

   b   What are Wangero's and Hakim's shortcomings?

      i   How do Wangero and Hakim show disrespect for or insensitivity to Mama or Maggie during their visit?
      ii   Do they attempt to educate Mama and Maggie about the Black Pride Movement or to help them in any way?
      iii   Do they ever mention any interest in helping other African Americans better their living conditions or go to college as Wangero has done?
      iv   How does the story suggest that the display of their financial and social success might be one of the purposes of their visit to Wangero's family?

2   *Mama's Muslim neighbors*—A mile and a half down the road from Mama's home live a family of African Americans who have apparently joined the Black Muslims, an American religious organization derived from the Muslim religion but adapted to meet the needs of African Americans. The little we learn of this family's lifestyle provides a contrast to the apparent superficiality of Wangero and Hakim's lifestyle. For the Black Muslim family have apparently embraced a religion and a culture, not as a fashion statement but as a way of life, and this has given them the strength to succeed against great odds.

a   What do Mama's Muslim neighbors do for a living?
b   How does the story let us know that they are successful?
c   How do we know that their success is resented, presumably by local racist forces, and what does the family do to protect itself?
d   How do we know that Mama—who, as narrator, greatly influences the reader's opinion—probably admires these neighbors?

Focusing your essay

The textual evidence you've gathered should allow you to focus your essay on the ways in which "Everyday Use" illustrates the importance of cultural belonging and the personal cost of becoming a colonial subject. Certainly, Mama and Maggie have internalized, or "bought into," some colonialist ideology: both have the kind of low self-esteem in terms of their physical appearance and their intelligence that colonialist ideology tells them subalterns deserve. Nevertheless, I think you can argue that the Johnson family heritage provides Mama and Maggie with a fulfilling cultural identity and a strong sense of belonging that makes the life they lead—without needing to be fashionable or to compete for material success—a form of anticolonialist resistance. In a very real sense, Mama and Maggie's lifestyle is a rejection of the dominant white culture.

In contrast, it seems unlikely that Dee's mindset as a colonial subject will ever change. It seems that she will always be trying, through mimicry, to win the approval of whatever group has a cultural status to which she aspires. In a sense, then, Dee's good fortune in having the kind of physical appearance defined as attractive by the dominant white culture isn't good fortune at all. For as a youngster, the approval she surely received from white people due to her lighter skin, "nicer" hair, and more fashionable figure was probably responsible for the temptation to accept the colonialist ideology that originally unhomed her. And the Black Pride Movement, though it's associated in the story with self-confidence and financial success, is also represented as an inadequate alternative to the dominant white culture it tried to replace. Because Walker's tale positively portrays the anticolonialist resistance of Mama and Maggie and shows us the negative effects of colonialist ideology—especially in terms of the losses suffered by the colonial subject—we can conclude that "Everyday Use" is an anticolonialist story.

Of course, you don't have to limit yourself to the analysis of the story I've offered you. For example, you might want to argue that Mama and Maggie are more conflicted in their relationship to colonialist ideology than our interpretation suggests. Perhaps you feel that the low self-image produced by their vulnerability to colonialist ideology is an important factor in their lives and deserves more attention than we have given it. And even if you agree that Dee is a colonial subject, you might feel she deserves more sympathy than many readers allow her. Therefore, you might want to focus more attention on the multiple forces that thrust colonialist ideology upon her. You might argue, for example, that, given the combined forces of racism, classism, and sexism to which women of color are vulnerable, it is no wonder that Dee should be tempted to use any means available to her to try to escape these forms of oppression, to try to rise to a socioeconomic position in which she would wield at least some of the power that has been wielded against her. Finally, you might want, instead, to write an essay in which you compare and contrast Dee with the narrator in "The Battle Royal" in terms of their behavior as colonial subjects; and you might want to compare and contrast, as well, the two stories' representations of the possibilities for anticolonialist resistance. Whatever your interpretation, be sure you understand the postcolonial concepts you choose to employ, compose a clear statement of your thesis, and support your interpretation with adequate textual evidence.

Exploring the influence of cultural categories: Interpreting "A Rose for Emily"

As we saw in the opening paragraphs of this chapter, one of the tasks postcolonial concepts help us perform is to analyze the ways in which human experience results from a combination of cultural factors that are not easy to separate. For example, as we saw in Chapter 6, "Using concepts from feminist theory to understand literature," traditional gender roles can influence men's and women's lives in various ways, depending on, for instance, their race, class, sexual orientation, religion, and ethnicity. For our personalities develop in response to a variety of cultural influences that interact together. It's important to understand how such cultural factors operate in helping to form us because our cultural background strongly influences what we think and how we behave. And an understanding of cultural influences in our lives helps us see how complex individual identity is.

Too often, however, we forget the importance of understanding the complexities of individual identity and tend to view people largely according to the cultural categories by which society defines them. In other words, we must remain aware of the complexity of individuals' cultural makeup and be careful not to start seeing people only as cultural categories—for example, "poor white male factory worker," "wealthy black male musician," "unmarried Chicana inner-city schoolteacher," "black female fundamentalist preacher," "middle-class white housewife," and the like—*rather than* as human beings. William Faulkner's "A Rose for Emily" (1931; see Appendix B) illustrates just how thoroughly, and how negatively, an over-reliance on cultural categories can influence human relations.

Set in the southern town of Jefferson during the decades before and after the turn of the twentieth century, Faulkner's tale tells the story of Emily Grierson. Born to an upper-class white family and isolated from the rest of the town by a dominating father, Emily learns, upon her father's death, that most of the family fortune has been lost. Although fallen into relative poverty, she still keeps a black manservant and maintains her disdain for those beneath her family's social class. The one exception to her refusal to mix with "common" folk is northerner Homer Barron, foreman of the work crew hired to pave Jefferson's sidewalks, whom Emily allows to court her. Presumably because Homer refuses to marry her (the reader never really learns what goes wrong between the couple), Emily poisons him and sleeps with his dead body, the remains of which are discovered by the town only after Emily's death.

Even this basic plot summary of "A Rose for Emily" indicates that cultural categories play an important role in the story. As we'll see in the text that follows, without the cultural classifications upon which all of the characters depend in deciding what to think and how to behave, we wouldn't have a story at all. Specifically, Faulkner's tale illustrates the harmful effects of basing our treatment of people on the cultural categories in which society places them, which is why "A Rose for Emily" can be considered an anticolonialist story. For colonialist ideology determines people's worth based entirely on the cultural categories by which the dominant culture defines human beings. To see how the story accomplishes this task, we'll examine the role played by cultural categories: (1) in the treatment of Emily by her father, by Homer Barron, and by the town of Jefferson; (2) in Emily's perception of herself and others; and (3) in the town's response to its African American citizens.

The role of cultural categories in the treatment of Emily

Is young Emily afraid of her father? Would she like to date some of the boys from Jefferson? Is the aging Emily lonely? Why does she allow Homer Barron, a man whose lifestyle is so alien to her own, to court her? Apparently, questions like these—questions about Emily's thoughts, feelings, and hopes—do not greatly influence people's treatment of her. That is, Emily the human being is not as important to the people of Jefferson as Emily the cultural category: an unmarried upper-class white female who has lost her financial standing but retains her status as the last representative of Jefferson's "aristocracy," the last of those Jefferson families who had been wealthy plantation owners before the Civil War. To see the influence of this cultural category on people's treatment of Emily, collect the textual evidence required to respond to the following questions.

1   *Mr. Grierson's treatment of Emily*

    a   How is Emily's sex responsible for Mr. Grierson's treatment of Emily?

        i   How is Emily's virginity an issue in a way that it wouldn't be if she were a boy?

        ii   Why would it be easier for Emily to run away from home or stand up to Mr. Grierson if she were a boy?

        iii   Who would have to provide a dowry and probably pay for the wedding if Emily were to marry (problems that would not arise if Emily were a boy)?

    b   How is the Griersons' social class responsible for Mr. Grierson's treatment of Emily?

2   *Homer Barron's treatment of Emily*

    a   Why is Emily's social class probably an attraction for Homer Barron, who is treated as a social inferior by many of Jefferson's middle-class citizens? (And Emily apparently has little else to offer him besides her social class.)

    b   How does the fact that the Grierson fortune no longer exists probably lead Homer to believe that Emily might accept his attentions?

3   *The townsfolk's treatment of Emily*

    a   How are Mr. Grierson's race, class, and gender responsible for the townsfolk's failure to intervene in the slightest way in what they believe is his mistreatment of Emily? (Apparently, no one says a word to Mr. Grierson; not even the minister offers a hint that perhaps such complete isolation of a young girl is not good for her.)

    b   How are Emily's race, class, and gender responsible for Colonel Sartoris' decision to remit her taxes? Would he do the same for a white man, a white working-class woman, or a man or woman of color?

    c   How is Emily's social class responsible both for the permissive treatment she receives in Jefferson (think, for example, of the druggist's response to her) and for the townsfolk's resentment of her?

    d   How do the townsfolk's objection to Homer's courtship of Emily reveal that they define the couple solely in terms of their cultural categories: northern working-class man and southern upper-class woman?

The role of cultural categories in Emily's perceptions of herself and others

Although we can't be certain how Emily feels as a young girl about her father's isolating her from contact with the socially "inferior" town of Jefferson, by the time Mr. Grierson dies, thirty-year-old Emily seems to share his contempt for those beneath her social class. Despite her greatly reduced financial circumstances, she's still a Grierson, and to her that means she is owed the respect due a white woman of her birth and breeding. To understand how thoroughly Emily's definition of her own cultural category isolates her from other people, collect the textual evidence needed to respond to the following questions. Note that the people she treats with contempt are those who do not show her the special respect she believes is her due. The only two individuals to whom she grants any respect are presumably the only two who treat her in the manner she requires: Colonel Sartoris and Homer Barron.

1   How does Emily treat the Aldermen who come to her home to tell her she owes taxes to the town of Jefferson?
2   How does she refer to the sheriff who sent her the notice that she owes taxes?
3   How does she treat the minister who comes to her home to counsel her against continuing her relationship with Homer Barron?
4   How does she treat the druggist who questions her about her purpose in buying arsenic?
5   How does she refer to Colonel Sartoris, who is of a higher social class than the rest of the townsfolk and who found a way to remit her taxes without injuring her pride?
6   How does she treat Homer Barron, a handsome man who apparently dresses well when he visits her and rents a top-of-the-line buggy and horses to take her riding on Sunday afternoons?

The role of cultural categories in the town's response to Its African American citizens

Given their concern about it, why do none of the white townsfolk in Jefferson think to ask Tobe about the nature of Emily's relationship with Homer Barron? Why does no one consult Tobe about the reason for Homer's disappearance, about which everyone is so curious? Why does no one ask him about the terrible smell that emanates from the Grierson house shortly after Homer disappears? Apparently, it never occurs to the white folks in Jefferson to consult Tobe about anything because Tobe doesn't exist for them as a human being, only as a Negro servant. That is, he exists for them only in terms of his race and class, only as a cultural category. To see how Tobe and the story's other African American characters are treated as cultural categories by Jefferson's white characters, collect the textual evidence required to respond to the following questions.

1   How is Tobe treated by his employer, Emily Grierson?

   a   Do Emily and Tobe converse together? (Note the narrator's comment about Tobe's voice.)
   b   How does Emily speak to Tobe when she does address him?
   c   Why is it safe to assume that Emily expects Tobe to keep quiet about her murdering Homer, a crime about which Tobe can't help but know?

2 In a town as prone to gossip as Jefferson, why is it that we don't hear a single bit of personal information about Tobe? What does this suggest about the separation of whites and blacks in this town?

3 How does Colonel Sartoris's edict about African American women, to which it seems that no white character objects, reveal that the dominant white culture of Jefferson defines these women, not in terms of their humanity, but in terms of the cultural categories of race, class, and gender?

4 How do Homer's treatment of his African American crew and the narrator's matter-of-fact reference to the black crew members as "niggers" reveal that these black characters are viewed primarily in terms of the cultural categories of race and class, rather than just as human beings?

Focusing your essay

Given the textual data you've already collected, you should be able to write an essay explaining the anticolonialist dimension of "A Rose for Emily." For the Griersons, Homer Barron, and the white townsfolk of Jefferson seem to base their judgments of and behavior toward people on the cultural categories in which society places those people, and the results are disastrous. In fact, it might be reasonable to argue that most of the characters in the story relate to one another not as human beings but as cultural categories. Emily Grierson and Homer Barron are not two people; they're an upper-class southern lady and a lower-class northern laborer. Tobe isn't a human being; he's a Negro servant. The story provides numerous examples like these and illustrates abundantly the negative effects of classifying people in this manner.

Keep in mind that you don't have to limit yourself to the analysis of the story I've offered you. For example, you might expand your essay to argue that the townsfolk's adherence to the cultural categories illustrated in "A Rose for Emily" reveals the ways in which they are colonial subjects. For most of the standards of cultural classification to which they adhere date from the pre-Civil-War south ruled by the wealthy plantation owners, standards by which the townsfolk, themselves, are subalterns in terms of their social class. Whatever your interpretation, be sure you understand the postcolonial concepts you choose to employ, compose a clear statement of your thesis, and support your interpretation with adequate textual evidence.

Appreciating anticolonialist resistance: Interpreting "Don't Explain"

The stories we've analyzed so far in this chapter have all been anticolonialist in their depictions of the harmful effects of some aspect of colonialist ideology. "The Battle Royal" provided us with a rather thorough and chilling view both of the colonialist ideology of America's dominant white culture and of the various ways in which that ideology subjugates subalterns. "Everyday Use" allowed us to focus our attention more specifically on the colonial subject, which is one of the most disturbing creations of colonialist ideology because it traps subalterns into cooperating in the dominant culture's victimization of them. And we saw how "A Rose for Emily" illustrates the ways in which human relations are damaged by the colonialist practice of judging people according to the cultural categories by which the dominant culture defines them. We also found that "The Battle Royal" and "Everyday Use" are anticolonialist in that they depict possibilities for anticolonialist resistance, but that topic is not as prominent in these two literary works as it is in Jewelle Gomez's "Don't Explain" (1987; see Appendix D).

Set in Boston in 1959, "Don't Explain" provides a glimpse into the lives of a small group of working-class African American women who must hide their lesbian orientation for their own protection. In 1959, it was difficult enough for working-class women of color to find adequate employment, housing, and freedom from molestation. Openly acknowledging their lesbianism could easily cost them their jobs, their homes, and their physical safety. It should not be surprising then that Letty, the character through whose eyes we view the events of the story, tries to "shut off" her lesbian sexuality. She is a subaltern in terms of her race, class, and gender. So the last thing she wants is to acquire yet another subaltern category. However, as the story progresses, we see Letty do just that: she realizes that she can no longer deny her sexual orientation, and she finds a group of women whose support offers her the kind of cultural and emotional home she probably thought she would never find.

From a postcolonial perspective, then, "Don't Explain" is a fascinating story because it offers us characters who resist the colonialist ideology to which they are so vulnerable. Letty, Delia, Terry, and Terry's friends could easily have become colonial subjects because they are subaltern in so many ways. Their multiple subaltern status—because it increases the ways in which they are othered by the dominant culture—increases their vulnerability to low self-esteem, which is the key ingredient in creating colonial subjects. Yet these women resist having their consciousness colonized by racism, which tells them they're less intelligent, less reliable, and less attractive than whites; by classism, which tells them they're less hard-working, less ambitious, and less trustworthy than people from higher classes; and by sexism, which tells them they're less rational, less independent, and less capable than men. And at the end of the story, Letty joins the other main characters in resisting the colonization of her consciousness by heterosexism, which tells them they're sick and/or evil.

These characters don't believe they're inferior to others because of their race, class, gender, or sexual orientation, and they don't judge others in terms of those categories. How do they accomplish this rather remarkable feat? They find sources of self-esteem and emotional strength in their African American culture, in the group support of other working-class lesbians of color, and in their ability to survive economically in a world that has placed so many forms of discrimination in their path. To see how "Don't Explain" produces such a thorough illustration of anticolonialist resistance, we'll examine the story's: (1) non-stereotypical, positive characterizations of Letty, Delia, Terry, and Terry's friends; (2) portrayal of the anticolonialist attitudes of these characters; and (3) depiction of the sources of these characters' anticolonialist resistance. Because our postcolonial reading of this story includes the kinds of oppression—and the kinds of resistance to oppression—discussed in our African American, Marxist, feminist, and lesbian interpretations of this story, feel free to consult the readings of "Don't Explain" offered in those chapters to help you understand and gather the textual evidence required for the following postcolonial interpretation of the story.

The story's non-stereotypical characterizations

Because colonialist ideology includes multiple forms of othering, it stereotypes people according to such cultural categories as race, class, gender, and sexual orientation. "Don't Explain" opposes all of these forms of othering by positively portraying characters—Letty, Delia, Terry, and Terry's friends—who do not fit cultural stereotypes. To see how thoroughly the story accomplishes this task, collect the textual evidence requested below.

1   *Antiracist characterizations*—According to racist stereotypes operating in the United States, people of color are less intelligent, less reliable, and less attractive than whites. How does the story combat these stereotypes by showing that Letty, Delia, Terry, and/or Terry's friends are

   a   intelligent (which includes such abilities as learning a job quickly, recognizing and knowing how to deal with a potential danger, and recognizing the needs and feelings of other people),
   b   reliable (which includes, for example, behaving reliably in the performance of one's job, toward one's co-workers, and toward one's friends), and
   c   attractive in a variety of ways that don't conform to the biased standard of "beauty" promoted by the dominant white culture (which includes, for instance, body type, skin color, speaking voice, and clothing style)?

2   *Anticlassist characterizations*—According to classist stereotypes, people from the lower classes are less hard-working, less ambitious, and less trustworthy than people from the higher classes. How does the story combat these stereotypes by showing that Letty, Delia, Terry, and/or Terry's friends are

   a   hard-working (which includes working long hours or late shifts at jobs that are physically or emotionally taxing),
   b   ambitious (which includes doing what it takes to keep one's job, save one's money, and better one's living conditions), and
   c   trustworthy (which includes being allowed to do one's job without the boss's constant supervision and being trusted by co-workers)?

3   *Antisexist characterizations*—According to sexist stereotypes, women are less rational, less independent, and less capable than men. How does the story combat these stereotypes by showing that Letty, Delia, Terry, and/or Terry's friends are:

a   rational (which includes making sound judgments and handling one's emotions appropriately),

b   independent (which includes making one's own living and one's own decisions, even if those decisions don't always conform to the norms of the dominant culture), and

c   capable (which includes doing one's job well and surviving economically even when one is put at a disadvantage by one's subaltern status)?

4   *Antiheterosexist characterizations*—According to heterosexist stereotypes, lesbians are sick and/or evil. As such, they're considered, among other things, sexual predators who care for nothing but the satisfaction of their own desires and for whom other women are sexual objects. How does the story combat these stereotypes by showing that Letty, Delia, Terry, and/or Terry's friends are, rather than sick and/or evil,

a   kind,

b   sensitive to others' feelings, and

c   capable of unselfish acts of friendship toward other women?

The portrayal of anticolonialist attitudes

Given the multiple forms of othering to which the race, class, gender, and sexual orientation of Letty, Delia, Terry, and Terry's friends make them vulnerable, it would not be surprising if they were to try to boost their own self-esteem by seizing any opportunity they could to look down on individuals they could other, individuals who, though subalterns like themselves, have slightly lower status. That is, it would not be surprising if the main characters had become colonial subjects. To see how successfully, these women have, instead, resisted colonialist ideology, collect the following textual evidence.

1   Letty could choose to other the prostitutes that frequent the 411 Lounge, for they are well below her on the ladder of social status. How does Letty feel about the prostitutes?

2   Letty and Delia, who are waitresses, could choose to other Terry and her friends, who clean office buildings and thus hold somewhat less prestigious jobs. How do Letty and Delia feel about Terry and her friends?

3   Delia and Terry, who live in a large apartment in a recently integrated neighborhood, could choose to other those, like Letty, who live in smaller apartments in less prestigious areas of the city. How do Delia and Terry treat Letty?

4   The lighter-skinned African American women who gather in Delia and Terry's apartment could choose to other the darker-skinned women. Do we see any evidence of this attitude anywhere in the story?

5   Because, as the story opens, Letty has renounced her lesbian orientation, she could choose to other Billie Holiday, whom she believes is a lesbian, as well as Delia, Terry, and Terry's friends when she realizes, at the end of the story, that they are lesbians. How does Letty feel about these women?

The sources of anticolonialist resistance

Find as many examples as you can of the sources of anticolonialist resistance demonstrated by Letty, Delia, Terry, and Terry's friends. Include the following sources of cultural belonging, which surely contribute to the self-esteem and emotional strength required to resist colonialist ideology.

1   Find the passages relating to African American culture—for example, African American cuisine, music, and such cultural icons as Billie Holiday—that provide the main characters with a sense of cultural belonging.

2   Describe the instances of interpersonal support, including group support, that the main characters provide for one another.

3   Describe the main characters' ability to survive economically in a world that discriminates against them in so many ways, and explain how you think this accomplishment may contribute to their self-esteem.

Focusing your essay

Using the textual evidence you've gathered, you should be able to write an essay analyzing how "Don't Explain" illustrates the possibilities for anticolonialist resistance even on the part of subalterns who are othered in terms of their race, class, gender, and sexual orientation. Letty, Delia, Terry, and Terry's friends work hard, enjoy one another's company, and are doing well in the world despite the social, economic, and psychological obstacles they face on a daily basis due to the various kinds of discrimination to which they are vulnerable. Although their subaltern status places them under a good deal of psychological pressure to try to boost their self-esteem by othering those below them in social status, they don't do so. Even Billie Holiday, whom we meet through Letty's recollection of the famous singer's visit to the 411 Lounge and who clearly had enormous self-esteem problems, is kind to the employees of the 411 and seems to feel at home in this working-class environment.

As always, you don't have to limit yourself to the analysis of the story I've offered you. For example, you might want to focus your essay only on Letty and do a more thorough analysis of her than you would be inclined to do if you analyzed all of the characters about whom you've collected textual data.

After all, it is through Letty's eyes that we see the events of the story, and she's the character who undergoes a kind of postcolonial transformation. For when she accepts the friendship offered her by the women at Delia and Terry's apartment, she also accepts her lesbian orientation, which, in postcolonial terms, means that she stops othering herself as a lesbian. Or perhaps you'd like to write an essay in which you compare and contrast the kinds of anti-colonialist resistance illustrated in "Don't Explain" and "Everyday Use." What does Mama and Maggie's anticolonialist lifestyle have in common with that of the main characters in "Don't Explain"? How do they differ? How would you compare or contrast the sources of the characters' anticolonialist attitudes in the two stories? Might you compare and contrast the emotional difficulty Letty has with her subaltern status as a lesbian with the emotional difficulty Mama and Maggie have with their subaltern status as women of color? Whatever your interpretation, be sure you understand the postcolonial concepts you choose to employ, compose a clear statement of your thesis, and support your interpretation with adequate textual evidence.

Recognizing the othering of nature: Interpreting "I started Early—Took my Dog"

At first glance, Emily Dickinson's "I started Early—Took my Dog" (c. 1862; see Appendix A) might not seem like a very good candidate for a postcolonial interpretation. The poem doesn't provide enough information for us to know whether or not the female speaker is subaltern in any way other than her gender. And as we saw in Chapters 5 and 8—in which we used, respectively, Marxist and African American concepts to interpret literature—we can't just decide on our own that the relationship between the big frigates and the little mouse, or between the powerful sea and the frightened speaker, symbolizes some theoretical concept, such as the oppression of the lower class by the upper class (a Marxist concept), the racist oppression of black Americans (an African American concept), or the oppression of subalterns by a colonialist culture (a postcolonial concept). For there is nothing in the poem or in any of these theories to justify this kind of symbolic interpretation. A reader could just as easily claim, and with no better justification, that the relationship between the ships and the mouse or between the sea and the speaker symbolizes good versus evil, redemption versus damnation, society versus the nonconformist individual, or any number of other symbolic relationships. Therefore, all of these symbolic readings would rest on the kind of unjustified "symbolic leap" discussed in Chapter 2, "Using concepts from reader-response theory to understand our own literary interpretations."

There is something in Dickinson's poem, however, that might lend itself to a postcolonial interpretation. It's at least worth our giving it some thought and seeing where it takes us. I'm referring to the fact that the speaker others the sea. This might sound odd at first. How can something non-human be othered when othering is the act of treating a *human being* as if he or she were *subhuman*? However, othering isn't a practice limited to human beings. Animals can be othered, as they were in the past when cats were thought to be in the employ of witches, and wolves were thought to be demonically possessed. And nature as a whole can be othered, as it was when the early settlers in New England believed that the wilderness surrounding their towns and villages was Satan's territory, filled with demons and devils and evil spirits of every description. In other words, when we demonize non-human living things—a species of animal, a wilderness area, a type of storm, or nature as a whole—we are, in effect, othering them. We're relating to them as if they were not merely non-human but antihuman. In order to do this, we imagine that these natural elements have the same kind of selfhood or will or consciousness that humans do. That is, we *personify* them: we imagine that they are human-like, capable of human feelings and behavior. And then we imagine that they are consciously and deliberately "against us."

We see this attitude frequently revealed in the language of Western exploration, such as the English and European exploratory voyages to the Americas and the American settlement of the frontier. In both cases, the military language of conquest was used to describe human beings' relationship to nature: the famous explorers "conquered" the "savage" and frightening oceans just as the American pioneers "tamed" and "civilized" the "savage" and frightening frontier. In other words, the othering of nature is part and parcel of colonialist ideology. Think about it. Colonialist ideology others that which is different and, because it is different, frightening. And colonialist ideology others that which it wants to treat unjustly or destroy. Well, just as colonialist cultures have othered native peoples around the globe in order to justify exploiting or destroying them, so colonialist cultures have othered nature in order to justify exploiting or destroying it.

Given that the othering of nature is so built into the Anglo (English)-European colonialist ideology to which America is heir, it shouldn't be too surprising to find examples of the othering of nature in our literary works, even in works by authors who loved nature. Emily Dickinson's numerous nature poems, for example, express her deep appreciation of nature's wonders. Furthermore, she lived in New England at the time when famous writers, such as Ralph Waldo Emerson and Henry David Thoreau, were promoting the view that nature is the key to spiritual knowledge. Dickinson shared this view. In her poem "Some keep the Sabbath going to Church" (c. 1860), for example, the speaker argues that in viewing the beauty available to her in nature, she worships God better than she could do by attending church. So in suggesting that "I started Early—Took my Dog" reflects a colonialist othering of nature, we're assuming that the colonialist ideology expressed in the poem was not embraced by the author. Rather, this interpretation of the poem assumes either that the othering of nature is a part of our Anglo-European colonialist heritage that can influence a writer's literary production without her being aware of it or that the othering of the sea depicted in the poem is a fictional representation that does not reflect the writer's personal feelings about nature. After all, the speaker of a poem is a literary device—as is the narrator of a short story or novel—that may or may not reflect the writer's personal experience or philosophy. In either case, our task here is to find the ways in which the poem's characterization of nature, in the form of the sea, is an example of othering.

In order to understand the poem's othering of nature we'll have to read it literally—take it at face value—as a poem about the speaker's terror of the sea, which she personifies and others as a dangerous, threatening creature. To accomplish this task, we'll analyze the ways in which the poem: (1) others the sea (that is, nature); and (2) positively portrays the products of *human* technology, or that which is *not* nature. The essay this interpretation exercise produces may not be as long as some of the others we've outlined in this chapter, but I believe that the kind of thinking you will do in order to write it will be valuable in helping you understand the variety of insights into literature, history, and human behavior that postcolonial concepts can offer us.

The othering of the sea

Find all the textual evidence you can to show the ways in which the speaker others the sea, which, given how much of the planet it covers and how much animal and plant life it supports, can easily be taken to represent nature as a whole.

1   First, how does the speaker personify the sea? How does she describe it as if it were a human being?
2   How is the personified sea described as dangerous, even life-threatening?
3   How does the presence of mermaids in the poem add to the feeling that the sea is strange, unknown, and unpredictable?
4   How does the disappearance of the dog from the poem (it is mentioned in the opening line only) add to the feeling that the sea is alien and dangerous? (Keep in mind that the dog, as the speaker's companion on her walk, is an image of domesticity, of the world of familiar things, and of protection.)
5   How does the sea's lack of acquaintance with anyone in the town add to the feeling that the sea is alien, an outsider who doesn't belong with human beings?
6   Given the interpretation of the poem being developed in the preceding five questions, how does the "Mighty look" the sea gives the speaker in the final stanza seem like a kind of threat?

The positive portrayal of human technology

Find all the textual evidence you can to show that human technology—"man-made" objects, the products of civilization—is positively portrayed in the poem.

1   How are the frigates in the second stanza positively portrayed? (Note that frigates were capable of crossing oceans; they were advanced examples of the technology of the time.)

   a   How are the frigates trying to help the speaker?
   b   How would a frigate be able to protect her if the speaker boarded one?

2   How is the town in the final stanza positively portrayed?
3   In what ways does a town embody or consist of the products of human technology and thus represent everything that is the opposite of nature?
4   How does the poem indicate that the sea knows it is beaten—this time?
5   Given that human technology is the only protection the speaker has in the poem, how does the insufficiency of the speaker's clothing to protect her (for clothing is, after all, "man-made") increase the frightening, othered quality of the sea analyzed under the previous heading?

Focusing your essay

The textual data you've gathered should allow you to focus your essay on the ways in which "I started Early—Took my Dog" others nature, whether or not it intends to do so, and thus reinforces this aspect of colonialist ideology. Given the poem's frightening depiction of the sea, what we have here is clearly an example of the *demonic other*, which, as we saw in the "Basic concepts" section of this chapter, is considered not just savage but evil. As you may recall, colonialist cultures define themselves as "civilized," while they define the cultures of the peoples they subjugate as "savage," "primitive," or "uncivilized." Similarly, the poem creates an opposition between the "civilized" town, which is positively portrayed, and the "savage" sea, which is negatively depicted.

Remember, as always, that you don't have to limit yourself to the analysis of the poem I've offered. For example, with your instructor's help, you might want to expand your essay to include additional literary examples of the othering of nature. In that case, you might want to consider reading Stephen Crane's "The Open Boat" (1897) or perhaps Jack London's "To Build a Fire" (1908), both of which stories depict attempts to survive the dangers of nature. You might also want to include examples of the othering of nature that occur in real life—for example, the ways in which most people misunderstand the behavior of such animals as wolves, bats, and sharks, believing the horrifying myths about them rather than learning the truth. Or you might want to explain the connection between the othering of nature and the pollution of the earth's air, water, and soil; the destruction of the rain forests and other timberland for commercial profit; or any other ecological threat to the well-being of our planet that interests you. Whatever your interpretation of Dickinson's poem, or of any other literary work you analyze, be sure you understand the postcolonial concepts you choose to employ, compose a clear statement of your thesis, and support your interpretation with adequate textual evidence.

Food for further thought

Thinking it over

If you've worked through all of the interpretation exercises offered in this chapter, you should feel quite familiar with the basic approaches to understanding literature provided by concepts from postcolonial theory. Specifically, we've seen how postcolonial concepts can be used to analyze

1 literary works that are anticolonialist in that they illustrate the harmful effects of colonialist ideology (our example: "The Battle Royal"),
2 literary works that are anticolonialist in that they illustrate the emotional losses suffered by the colonial subject, whose life is one of unhomeliness and mimicry (our example: "Everyday Use"),
3 literary works that are anticolonialist in that they depict the harmful effects of judging individuals according to the cultural categories by which the dominant culture defines people (our example: "A Rose for Emily"),
4 literary works that are anticolonialist in that they positively portray anticolonialist resistance (our example: "Don't Explain"), and
5 literary works that engage, often unwittingly, in the othering of nature that is part of the legacy of colonialist ideology (our example: "I started Early—Took my Dog").

It is interesting to note that the importance of anticolonialist resistance is sometimes a topic even in literary works with a different primary focus. "Don't Explain"—our only literary example in which anticolonialist resistance *is* the primary focus—portrays subaltern characters whose bonds of friendship help them embrace an alternative culture and reject the dominant culture's colonialist othering of subalterns. Yet as we saw earlier, "Everyday Use" also includes an example of anticolonialist resistance: the story illustrates how anticolonialist resistance can take the form of a family heritage that rejects the values of colonialist culture, a family heritage strong enough to give emotional support to those family members whose self-esteem has been damaged by their subaltern status. And even "The Battle Royal," in which the subaltern characters seem to have no power whatsoever, depicts the potential for anticolonialist resistance in subalterns who do not accept the dominant culture's claim to superiority.

Of course, you probably noticed that postcolonial concepts can provide us with literary interpretations that are very similar to, as well as very different from, the literary interpretations provided by concepts from other theories. As we noted in the opening paragraphs of this chapter, postcolonial concepts provide us with ways of combining psychoanalytic, Marxist, feminist, LGBTQ, and African American insights into human experience. We see a good deal of this kind of combination of theoretical insights in our postcolonial reading of "Don't Explain." Because our postcolonial interpretation of this story focuses on the anticolonialist resistance of a group of characters who are subalterns in terms of their race, class, gender, and sexual orientation, our interpretation draws together a good deal of the textual data we gathered in our African American, Marxist, feminist, and lesbian readings of that story.

In addition, a postcolonial reading of a literary work can overlap with a different theoretical interpretation of that work. For example, our African American and postcolonial readings of "Everyday Use" overlap in at least three important ways. Both interpretations discuss at some length the Black Pride Movement that Dee has joined. Both interpretations argue that Dee's participation in the Black Pride Movement is superficial. Finally, both interpretations show the ways in which Mama and Maggie derive a good deal of emotional strength from their family heritage, a heritage that Dee doesn't consider to be of much use. However, these two readings are significantly different, and the difference is one of focus. The African American reading of the story focuses on the harmful effects of internalized racism, which Dee *shares* with Mama and Maggie despite their other differences. In contrast, the postcolonial reading of "Everyday Use" focuses on the ways in which Dee is a colonial subject—both in terms of the dominant white culture she copied in high school and in terms of the Black Pride Movement she follows as an adult—while Mama and Maggie are not.

A striking example of the difference between postcolonial interpretations of literary works and the literary interpretations provided by other theoretical concepts can be seen in the contrast between, on the one hand, our Marxist and African American readings of "I started Early—Took my Dog" and, on the other hand, our postcolonial reading of the poem. As you may recall, we saw how both Marxist and African American concepts are liable to be *misapplied* to Dickinson's poem. In both cases, the large-versus-small or high-versus-low imagery (for example, the images of the tall frigates and the small mouse) tempt us to see the poem as a representation of the upper-class oppression of the lower class or of the racist oppression of African Americans. Yet as we saw in those chapters, there is nothing in the poem itself, or in our Marxist or African American concepts, to justify such a "symbolic leap." In fact, we were unable to find any way to interpret the poem using Marxist or African American concepts. Therefore, we discovered that we should resist the temptation to use concepts from these two theories to analyze this literary work. In contrast, we found that the poem lends itself well to a postcolonial reading as long as we don't make the "symbolic leap" of claiming that the large-versus-small or high-versus-low imagery represents some postcolonial concept, such as the oppression of subalterns by a colonialist culture. Instead, we saw that, by reading the poem literally (at face value), we were able to use postcolonial concepts to show the ways in which "I started Early—Took my Dog" provides us with a vivid example of the othering of nature that is a legacy of Anglo-European colonialist ideology.

As I hope our postcolonial interpretation exercises have illustrated, although the exploitation of colonies by their "mother countries" is largely a thing of the past, colonialist ideology is still alive and well. And this ideology becomes more and more dangerous as our planet "shrinks"—that is, as modern technology shortens the geographical distance between nations and as cultures intermingle or merge through emigration. For colonialist ideology places communication barriers between peoples from different cultures who, more than ever before, need to communicate. In addition, colonialist ideology justifies the oppression of one culture by another, which continues to happen as wealthier, more technologically advanced nations continue to exploit the natural resources and cheap labor of poorer nations. Postcolonial concepts are therefore as important as ever in helping us get a larger, more objective view of world events and learn to appreciate some of the differences between our own culture and the cultures of other countries as well as the cultural differences among people living within our own borders.

Postcolonial theory and cultural criticism

We can also use concepts from postcolonial theory for the purposes of cultural criticism. That is, we can use postcolonial concepts to help us analyze the cultural messages sent, whether deliberately or not, by the everyday productions of the culture in which we live, such as movies, games, television shows, song lyrics, toys and other productions of popular culture discussed in Chapter 1. Indeed, those cultural productions that in some way represent human behavior—that have characters and a plot—can be analyzed using concepts from postcolonial theory just as we use those concepts to analyze literary works. For example, an understanding of colonialist ideology—particularly of the terms *subaltern*, *othering*, and *mimicry*—can offer us insights into the hit film romance *Waiting to Exhale* (directed by Forest Whitaker, 1995), in which we follow the diverse experiences of four thirty-something African American women through a single year of their close friendship.

Of particular interest for postcolonial cultural criticism, I think, are the black characters' multiple positions, or rankings, within the dominant white culture's hierarchy of power. For individuals who are subaltern in two or more areas are especially vulnerable to multiple forms of othering, which is the hallmark of colonialist ideology and oppression. Yes, the film portrays the world of successful middle- and upper-class African American professionals at home, at work, and at play. We don't see, for example, acts of racist or classist oppression in the film. In fact, we don't see many white characters at all: the few there are in the movie have very minor roles. However, viewers know that the members of the upscale African American culture portrayed in the film nevertheless belong to a political minority and must deal with the institutionalized biases of a dominant culture that is still largely racist. And it's often the case that subaltern individuals are liable to other themselves because they've been programmed, despite any successes they may have achieved, to feel inferior. Then, in an effort to identify with the dominant culture, such individuals frequently other anyone who is in any way below them.

A great deal of the positive impact of *Waiting to Exhale* therefore lies in the fact that the movie's four main characters—who are themselves subaltern in terms of race and gender—do not succumb to this destructive pattern of behavior. In fact, their behavior toward themselves and others often serves as an example of anticolonialist resistance. Television producer Savannah Jackson (Whitney Houston), wealthy stay-at-home wife and mother Bernadine Harris (Angela Bassett), beauty-salon owner and single mother Gloria Matthews (Loretta Devine), and insurance underwriter Robin Stokes (Lela Rochon) have different skin colors, facial features, and body types. However, none of the four friends is concerned that her skin is "too dark" or that some feature of her face or body is "too African." They don't relate to one another—nor do they judge the men they date—in terms of physical characteristics related to race. That is, they don't other themselves or anyone else along racial lines.

The four main characters, moreover, do not other those whose subaltern status in terms of class or sexual orientation makes them vulnerable targets. Robin's short-term boyfriend Troy (Mykelti Williamson) is subaltern in terms of class. Gloria's ex-husband David (Giancarlo Esposito) is subaltern in terms of sexual orientation. And we might argue that Joseph (Lamont Johnson), one of the hairdressers Gloria employs, is subaltern in terms of gender as well as sexual orientation. For although he's a man, Joseph's gender behavior is feminine, which means that heterosexist culture ties his gender to his subaltern sexual orientation: in no way is he a "real" man, and this "deficit" makes him an easy target of abuse and discrimination. Even Robin is a vulnerable target, in terms of both her own self-esteem and her friends' view of her, if we contrast her economic status with that of Gloria, Savannah, and Bernadine. For Robin is the only one of the group who lives in a small apartment in a less-than-affluent neighborhood. Gloria owns her own ample home in a quiet middle-class neighborhood; Savannah occupies a modern, upscale home in an upscale location; and Bernadine lives in a mansion complete with extensive grounds and expensive landscaping. Nevertheless, for the four main characters, these differences make no difference.

These women do, however, invest a great deal of themselves in a patriarchal ideology that plays an important role in colonialist ideology: sexism. For all four friends have accepted patriarchy's dictum that a woman who has no man has nothing. Savannah and Robin keep trying to find the "right" man but keep dating the wrong ones. Bernadine, in order to hold a husband who has never reciprocated her willingness to make sacrifices for him, has spent the last eleven years putting John's financial welfare and personal convenience first, against her own best interests and those of her two children. And Gloria, who has raised a fine son, has used the responsibilities and rewards of motherhood to avoid dating altogether. Nevertheless, through the strength of their collective emotional support, each woman is able, over the course of the movie, to grow beyond whatever self-destructive patriarchal fantasy has led her to the romantic dead-end in which she finds herself as the film opens. As the film closes, each is able to place herself, with or without a man by her side, firmly on the path to her own fulfillment.

Finally, in its portrayal of Bernadine's husband John (Michael Beach), *Waiting to Exhale* illustrates the destructive effects of colonialist ideology both on the colonial subject who has internalized it and on his family. Like his enormous, neutral-colored, conservative wardrobe, John doesn't have much originality or personality. His attempts to repress his emotions make him seem, at times, like a robot. Apparently by John's choice, the Harris family live in a mansion-like home in an extremely upscale, predominantly white neighborhood, and in contrast to the homes of Savannah, Gloria, and Robin, the only art displayed is European. In addition, the two Harris children, despite Bernadine's objections, attend an expensive private school at which they are two of the four black students enrolled. So we should not be surprised that the company John has founded is strictly white collar or that John's twelve employees are all affluent-looking and all white. His divorce lawyer, too, is white, male, and upscale. Finally, John has left his wife and children for a pretty, conservative-looking white woman who is one of his corporate employees.

On some level, however, John must believe that he doesn't really belong to the dominant, wealthy white culture to which he aspires. For if he did feel at home in that culture, his practice of mimicry wouldn't have to be so thorough or so vigilant: it wouldn't have to take over every aspect of his life or be, at all times, his emotional focal point. Bernadine doesn't use the words *colonial subject*, but she knows one when she sees one: John tries to get rid of whatever he can that reminds him he is not an upper-crust member of the dominant white culture, and he adopts whatever he can that makes him feel he is.

Waiting to Exhale, then, performs a great deal of anticolonialist cultural work. The film's four main characters don't participate in the othering of individuals based on race, class, or sexual orientation that is still all too common in American society as a whole. In addition, they make great progress, over the course of the film, in rejecting the self-defeating patriarchal ideology that has kept them dissatisfied with their lives despite their legitimate reasons for happiness. By their own antiracist, anticlassist, antihomophobic, and antisexist behavior, Savannah, Bernadine, Gloria, and Robin demonstrate the virtues of these anticolonialist attitudes and show us that life is happier and more harmonious without them. And the characterization of John illustrates the negative effects of colonialist ideology both on the man who internalizes it and on his family.

It is interesting to note, however, that while the main characters do not other those individuals who are culturally different from them, the film itself inadvertently others the poor, it seems to me, in its classist portrayal of Troy. Troy occupies the bottom rung of the economic ladder depicted in the movie, and given that he's the only representative of that class offered in the film, his characterization can easily be taken as representative of his class as a whole. It is significant, therefore, that his characterization is a classist stereotype of the poor man, especially of the poor black man: what little money

Troy has apparently comes from drug dealing; he chronically abuses cocaine and alcohol; he treats Robin like a sex object; he steals money from her, and we can therefore assume that he steals from women whenever he can; he is unrefined in speech, manners, and dress; and as his last scene with Robin implies, he is apparently deficient in personal hygiene.

Does this one exception to its anticolonialist message undercut *Waiting to Exhale*'s constructive cultural work? Yes, I think it does. But while the film's classist portrayal of Troy is disturbing, it's also instructive because it shows us that no cultural production, whatever its positive aims, is likely to be transformative in every way. In many ways, cultural productions are like people. Try as we might to do the right thing, some cultural bias is always liable to sneak in just under our level of awareness. That's one of the reasons why our effort to practice cultural criticism is so important: it helps raise our level of awareness concerning the cultural biases operating both in our society and in ourselves.

★★★

Remember, it's natural to feel a bit uncertain when we encounter a new theory—a new way of looking at ourselves and our world—that may call into question many of the beliefs that have been pressed upon us, and that we've accepted uncritically, for most of our lives. Uncertainty is an unavoidable part of learning and growing. Keep in mind, too, that others may disagree with your opinions. Individuals often disagree in their interpretations of literature, popular culture, or everyday experiences, even when drawing upon the same postcolonial concepts for their analyses. The keys to a good interpretation—besides intellectual curiosity and an open mind—are a clear understanding of the postcolonial concepts you've chosen to use and strong evidence to support your analysis.

Taking the next step

Questions for further practice

1   In Langston Hughes' short story "The Blues I'm Playing" (1934), how might Mrs. Dora Ellsworth be seen as a colonizing force attempting to convince Miss Oceola Jones that the young woman's own cultural heritage is inferior to that of Mrs. Ellsworth? Specifically, what are the many ways in which Mrs. Ellsworth tries to separate Oceola from her cultural roots in the African American community and turn her into an exotic other to be displayed before white "high society"? What are the many ways in which Oceola refuses that colonization and shows that we don't have to reject our own cultural heritage in order to appreciate and participate in others?

2   Leslie Marmon Silko's "Lullaby" (1974), a short story written by and about a Native American woman, illustrates the mistreatment of Native Americans by the descendants of the colonialist invaders who took their

lands. In order to show that this story is anticolonialist, find textual evidence to support the following claims. (a) The story portrays the suffering caused by the exploitation of subalterns (Ayah and Chato) by the dominant culture (the rancher for whom Chato works). (b) The story depicts the erasure of native culture (note the memories Ayah has of the native culture of her childhood) by the dominant culture (the white authorities who take away Danny and Ella). (c) Ayah and Chato are othered by members of the dominant culture and, indeed, by anyone above them in social rank. (d) Ayah, who is positively portrayed, has resisted the pressure to believe herself and her culture inferior to white Americans and white American culture.

3   What can David Sedaris's short story "I Like Guts" (1974) teach us about the postcolonial concept called *othering*? Collect as many examples as you can of the ways in which the story's subalterns—gay young men and people of color—are othered. What does the story suggest are the psychological or social motives of those who practice othering? More subtly, how does the story indicate that sexism, in addition to being a form of othering in itself, is also a factor in the othering of gay men? To accomplish this last task, note the examples of homophobic othering that involve attributing disparaged feminine qualities to gay men.

4   How might we say that the story of Edna Pontellier in Kate Chopin's novel *The Awakening* (1899) is a story of unhomeliness? Does Edna feel she belongs to any of the three cultures she has known in her life: the Presbyterian, Kentucky blue-grass culture of her childhood; the Mississippi plantation culture of her teenage years; or the upper-crust, Catholic Creole culture of New Orleans into which she married? Is there any other culture available to her to which she wants to belong? (If there were, we would surely see her practicing mimicry in order to be accepted by the members of that culture.) Find as many examples as you can of Edna's unhomeliness. Do you think her unhomed condition contributes to her suicide?

5   Use concepts from postcolonial theory to help you interpret some aspect of a movie, television show, song lyric, cartoon, video game, or any other production of popular culture that you find interesting and that seems to lend itself to a postcolonial interpretation. For example, does your chosen cultural production positively portray cultural diversity, which includes diversity created by differences among individuals based on a combination of such cultural factors as gender, social class, race, ethnicity, sexual orientation, religion, and the like? Are subalterns realistically depicted, or are they stereotyped? Does this production represent, in some way, mimicry, othering, or unhomeliness? Based on your observations, what cultural work does your chosen cultural production do relevant to postcolonial theory? Specifically, how does it encourage us to respond to cultural diversity? Be sure to offer evidence from your chosen production to support your ideas.

Suggestions for further reading

Achebe, Chinua. *Hopes and Impediments: Selected Essays*. 1988. New York: Doubleday, 1990. (See, especially, "An Image of Africa: Racism in Conrad's *Heart of Darkness*," 1–20; and "Colonialist Criticism," 68–90.)

Ashcroft, Bill, Gareth Griffiths, and Helen Tiffin, (eds.) *The Post-Colonial Studies Reader*. New York: Routledge, 1995. (See, especially, Charles Larson's "Heroic Ethnocentrism: The Idea of Universality in Literature," 62–65; Edward W. Said's "Orientalism," 87–91; Frantz Fanon's "National Culture," 153–57; Mudrooroo's "White Forms, Aboriginal Content," 228–31; and Philip G. Altbach's "Education and Neocolonialism," 452–56.)

Fanon, Frantz. *Black Skin, White Masks*. 1952. Trans. Charles Lam Markmann. New York: Grove Press, 1967. (See, especially, "The Negro and Language," 17–40; "The Fact of Blackness," 109–40; and "The Negro and Psychopathology," 141–209.)

Kincaid, Jamaica. *A Small Place*. New York: Farrar Strauss Giroux, 1988.

Loomba, Ania. *Colonialism/Postcolonialism*. 2nd ed. New York: Routledge, 2005. (See, especially, "Colonialism and Knowledge," 53–62; "Colonialism and Literature," 62–82; and "Constructing Racial and Cultural Difference," 91–106.)

Tyson, Lois. "Postcolonial Criticism." *Critical Theory Today: A User-Friendly Guide*. 2nd ed. New York: Routledge, 2006. 418–49.

Wisker, Gina. *Key Concepts in Postcolonial Literature*. New York: Palgrave Macmillan, 2007.

Chapter 10

Holding on to what you've learned

If you've read the preceding chapters, you must be wondering, "How can I keep these theories straight in my mind?" So let me help by starting this chapter off with the following bird's-eye view of (1) the eight theories you've encountered in this book, (2) the interpretation exercises provided for each of our five sample literary works, and (3) the range of different perspectives on literary analysis offered by each theory, which our interpretation exercises illustrated. This shorthand overview isn't a substitute for reading the chapters themselves. In fact, one of the best ways to learn to use the theoretical concepts we've employed is to go back and *reread* the chapters that interested you the most (or that confused you the most!). Nevertheless, at this point, a shorthand overview might give you a feeling of clarity that will both reassure you about what you've learned so far and encourage you to learn more.

A shorthand overview of our eight critical theories

One way to keep the critical theories we've studied straight in your mind is to think of each of them as a question about human experience that focuses our attention on a different aspect of our relationship to ourselves and our world. Now, think about that phrase—*our relationship to ourselves and our world*—and you'll see that it includes such elements as our personality traits, our self-image, our relationships with others, our beliefs, our likes and dislikes, our sense of right and wrong, and the like. The only theory we've studied that doesn't address some aspect of our relationship to ourselves and our world is New Criticism, which asks us to put aside such issues in order to focus exclusively and objectively on discovering how the meaning of individual literary texts is communicated by their formal elements, that is, by their language and literary devices. Whether or not such objectivity can be attained is an interesting problem to consider, and the attempt to discover and support your own opinion concerning this problem might result in some useful self-reflection. So each of the following short questions should give you a good deal to think about.

Reader-response theory—How is our relationship to ourselves and our world reflected in our literary interpretations?

New Critical theory—Putting aside our relationship to ourselves and our world, what is the theme—the meaning as a whole—of a given literary text, and how do the text's formal elements support that theme?

Psychoanalytic theory—How is our relationship to ourselves and our world formed by our psychological wounds and our psychological strengths?

Marxist theory—How is our relationship to ourselves and our world formed by the socioeconomic system in which we live?

Feminist theory—How is our relationship to ourselves and our world formed by traditional gender roles?

Lesbian, gay, and queer theories—How is our relationship to ourselves and our world formed by our sexual orientation and by the way in which society defines *sexual orientation*?

African American theory—How is our relationship to ourselves and our world formed by our race and by the attitudes toward race of the society in which we live?

Postcolonial theory—How is our relationship to ourselves and our world formed by the interplay of all the cultural factors—race, class, gender, sexual orientation, religion, ethnicity, and so forth—by which we define ourselves and others?

Let me emphasize that the role played in our lives by such factors as race, traditional gender roles, sexual orientation, and the like depends upon the society in which we live. For example, the role played in our lives by race in a society that believes white people are naturally superior will be different from the role played in our lives by race in a society that believes black people are naturally superior. And the role played in our lives by race in a society that believes no race is naturally superior will be different from both. Similarly, our experience of traditional gender roles will differ depending on the attitude toward these roles encouraged by our ethnic group or our religious faith. Even our experience of our own sexual orientation, socioeconomic class, and psychological wounds will be strongly influenced by our society's ideas about what is good or evil, natural or unnatural, superior or inferior, and normal or abnormal. The more we learn about the critical theories we've used in this book, the more we are able to see—in our own lives as well as in the literary works we read—the intriguing connections between an individual's personal identity and the society in which that individual lives.

A shorthand overview of our literary interpretation exercises

Our goal here is to see the ways in which concepts from different critical theories can sometimes provide very different and sometimes very similar readings of the same literary works. The following shorthand overview simply lists, as briefly as possible, both the focus, or topic, and the *thesis*—the debatable opinion that forms the main point of an argument—of each of the literary interpretation exercises we did in the previous chapters. And as I did in the previous chapters, I address the literary works below in the order in which, for our present purpose, I think they will be most accessible to you. You'll notice that reader-response interpretations aren't included here because the response exercises provided in Chapter 2 are intended to help you analyze your personal responses to literary works, not the literary works themselves. Don't forget that the interpretation exercises summarized in this overview are *sample* interpretations intended to give you practice using a given theory's basic concepts. Many other interpretations are possible using the same theory, and as you may recall, alternative interpretations were offered in the "Focusing your essay" section that closes each of the interpretation exercises provided in the preceding chapters.

"Everyday Use"

Our New Critical interpretation

Our focus—The story's representation of tradition and change.

Our thesis—The story suggests that the adoption of new ideas about cultural heritage should not result in the abandonment of family traditions, for these traditions keep us connected to our family history and contribute to the emotional bond among family members.

Our psychoanalytic interpretation

Our focus—The story's representation of dysfunctional behavior.

Our thesis—Although Mama is a loving parent, she unconsciously projects her own low self-esteem onto Maggie and her own unfulfilled desire for success onto Dee. As a result, Mama holds Maggie back and thus contributes to this daughter's low self-esteem, while Mama pushes Dee away from the nest and thus contributes to this daughter's fear of intimacy and abandonment.

Our Marxist interpretation

Our focus—The story's representation of capitalism.

Our thesis—The story is anticapitalist. It depicts the negative effects of capitalism on all three main characters, and it negatively portrays Dee, who embraces capitalist ideology, while positively portraying Mama and Maggie, who reject capitalist ideology.

Our feminist interpretation

Our focus—The story's representation of patriarchal ideology.

Our thesis—The story has a conflicted attitude toward patriarchal ideology. It is antipatriarchal in its positive portrayal of Mama's violation of traditional gender roles and its sympathetic depiction of Mama and Maggie's victimization by patriarchy. However, the story's negative portrayal of Dee's violation of traditional gender roles supports patriarchal ideology.

Our lesbian interpretation

Our focus—The woman-identified woman beneath the story's heterosexual plot.
Our thesis—By means of a quiet subtext beneath its heterosexual plot, the story suggests that being a woman-identified woman is an emotional orientation that plays an important role in women's lives regardless of their sexual orientation.

Our African American interpretation

Our focus—The story's representation of internalized racism.
Our thesis—The story is antiracist. It illustrates the negative effects of internalized racism on individual self-esteem and family unity even among African Americans who have, in different ways, accomplished a great deal despite the obstacles placed in their paths by a racist world.

Our postcolonial interpretation

Our focus—The story's representation of the colonial subject.
Our thesis—The story is anticolonialist. It depicts the emotional losses suffered by the colonial subject, Dee, who has been unhomed (turned into a cultural outsider) by the dominant culture and, as a result, practices mimicry: she views culture as a lifestyle to be acquired rather than as a way of understanding the world and defining her place within it.

"The Battle Royal"

Our New Critical interpretation

Our focus—The story's representation of alienation.
Our thesis—The story suggests that a sense of belonging can help us in the worst of times, and without it we risk becoming alienated not only from others but from ourselves, as well.

Our psychoanalytic interpretation

Our focus—Using psychoanalytic concepts in service of other theories.

Our thesis—There is no psychological experience represented in the story that can be viewed independently of the characters' socioeconomic class, gender, sexual orientation, race, or cultural identity. If we want to use psychoanalytic concepts to interpret the tale, we'll have to put those concepts in service of another theory. For example, we might analyze the story's depiction of the *psychological* effects on its characters of capitalism, sexism, heterosexism, racism, or colonialist ideology, which would produce, respectively, a Marxist, feminist, gay, African American, or postcolonial interpretation.

Our Marxist interpretation

Our focus—The story's representation of the American Dream.
Our thesis—The story suggests that the American Dream is not only a false ideology—it doesn't keep its promise—but a dangerous ideology. The narrator is so blinded by his belief in the American Dream that he can't see the obvious reality of his own situation.

Our feminist interpretation

Our focus—The story's representation of the objectification of women.
Our thesis—The story is antipatriarchal. Its negative portrayal of the white men's treatment of the exotic dancer rejects the patriarchal belief that it is natural, and therefore acceptable, for men to use women as sex objects and tokens of male power.

Our gay interpretation

Our focus—The story's representation of homophobia.
Our thesis—The story illustrates the ways in which men's homophobia is caused by their insecurity about their own masculinity and, therefore, about their own sexuality.

Our African American interpretation

Our focus—The story's representation of overt forms of institutionalized racism.
Our thesis—The story is antiracist. Is illustrates the evils of institutionalized racism, which, the tale shows, creates an environment of unrestrained power that reduces the white characters to little more than brutes and forces the black characters to scramble for any means of survival—no matter how personally degrading—they can find.

Our postcolonial interpretation

Our focus—The story's representation of colonialist ideology.

Our thesis—The story is anticolonialist. It illustrates the ways in which the relationship between America's dominant culture and its subalterns (those with the least political power) is much like the relationship between a colonialist country and the people it subjugates on foreign shores.

"A Rose for Emily"

Our New Critical interpretation

Our focus—The story's representation of death.
Our thesis—The story suggests that death, as a presence that shadows and depletes the life force, can be stronger than life and is embodied in the desire to live in the past.

Our psychoanalytic interpretation

Our focus—The story's representation of insanity.
Our thesis—Emily's unresolved oedipal attachment to her father, which Mr. Grierson creates by putting his daughter on a pedestal and isolating her from others, is the underlying cause of a fear of abandonment and of intimacy that becomes intense enough to drive Emily insane.

Our Marxist interpretation

Our focus—The story's representation of classism.
Our thesis—The story is anticlassist. It illustrates the evils of classism by showing the negative effects of classist ideology on all of the story's main characters.

Our feminist interpretation

Our focus—The story's representation of patriarchal ideology.
Our thesis—The story is sexist. It endorses the patriarchal ideology it illustrates by portraying Emily more and more negatively as she increasingly violates traditional gender roles and by negatively stereotyping its minor female characters.

Our queer interpretation

Our focus—The story's queer dimension.
Our thesis—The story illustrates the ways in which human sexuality is too complex to be fully understood by the categories *heterosexual* and *homosexual*, the traditional terms by which our sexuality is defined.

Our African American interpretation

Our focus—The function of black characters in a white story.

Our thesis—The story has an antiracist project that doesn't fully succeed. The tale is antiracist in that its minor African American characters are used to remind us of the evils of racism in the time and place in which the story is set. However, these characters function as mere "pointers," not as meaningful characters, and we are thus deprived of any sense of their humanity.

Our postcolonial interpretation

Our focus—The story's representation of cultural categories.

Our thesis—The story is anticolonialist. It illustrates the harmful effects of judging individuals according to the cultural categories by which the dominant culture defines people, categories that depend on such factors as race, class, gender, sexual orientation, ethnicity, and religion.

"Don't Explain"

Our New Critical interpretation

Our focus—The story's representation of nonconformity.

Our thesis—The story suggests that when conformity requires self-negation, then self-acceptance requires nonconformity.

Our psychoanalytic interpretation

Our focus—The story's representation of psychological self-healing.

Our thesis—The story illustrates how emotional identification with another person, even with a relative stranger, can be a source of psychological strength. The story accomplishes this task by showing how Letty is helped psychologically through her emotional identification with Billie Holiday.

Our Marxist interpretation

Our focus—The story's representation of classism.

Our thesis—The story is anticlassist. It encourages readers to reject classism by providing positive portrayals of working-class characters and by illustrating the virtues of an anticlassist attitude.

Our feminist interpretation

Our focus—The story's representation of patriarchal ideology.

Our thesis—The story is antipatriarchal. It encourages readers to resist patriarchal ideology by positively portraying women who do not conform to traditional gender roles and who do not fit the white patriarchal definition of the "true woman."

Our lesbian interpretation

Our focus—The story's representation of lesbian characters.
Our thesis—The story combats negative stereotypes of lesbians through its positive portrayals of lesbian characters.

Our African American interpretation

Our focus—The story's representation of "less visible" forms of institutionalized racism.
Our thesis—The story is antiracist. It subtly illustrates the "less visible" forms of institutionalized racism in American society and positively portrays African American characters who must contend with these racist forces in their daily lives.

Our postcolonial interpretation

Our focus—The story's representation of anticolonialist resistance.
Our thesis—The story is anticolonialist. It illustrates the possibilities for anti-colonialist resistance even on the part of subalterns who are othered in terms of their race, class, gender, and sexual orientation.

"I started Early—Took my Dog"

Our New Critical interpretation

Our focus—The poem's representation of the unknown.
Our thesis—The poem suggests that we fear the unknown largely because we are attracted to it, for our attraction to the unknown makes us feel our vulnerability to it.

Our psychoanalytic interpretation

Our focus—The poem's dream imagery.
Our thesis—Using the psychoanalytic symbolism present in the poem to interpret it as a dream, we can see the speaker's sexual repression. Specifically, she is afraid of her own sexual desire.

Our Marxist interpretation

Our focus—When *not* to use Marxist concepts to interpret a literary work.
Our thesis—The poem does not lend itself well to a Marxist interpretation. If we want to use Marxist concepts to analyze Dickinson's poetry, we will have to choose one of her poems that will work for this purpose.

Our feminist interpretation

Our focus—The poem's representation of the psychological oppression of women.
Our thesis—The poem is antipatriarchal: it illustrates the ways in which patriarchal ideology promotes in women both sexual repression and low self-esteem.

Our lesbian (or gay) interpretation

Our focus—When to draw upon context for a lesbian (or gay) reading.
Our thesis—The poem, on its own, doesn't yield a convincing lesbian interpretation. However, taken in the context of other poetry by Dickinson, the poem helps show that the lesbian dimension of her work as a whole is evident in its rejection of heterosexuality and in its lush, erotic images of female sexuality. Biographical research can also provide a context to support this interpretation.

Our African American interpretation

Our focus—When *not* to use African American concepts to interpret a literary work.
Our thesis—The poem does not lend itself well to an African American interpretation, and there don't seem to be any other poems by Dickinson that we can readily use instead. If we want to use African American concepts to discuss Dickinson's work, we will have to do biographical research in order to speculate as to why there are no direct references to any of the prominent racial issues of her day in Dickinson's poetry, despite her intellectual ties with antiracist thinkers.

Our postcolonial interpretation

Our focus—The poem's representation of nature.
Our thesis—Unlike most of Dickinson's other nature poetry, this poem's depiction of the sea others nature just as colonialist ideology others nature, suggesting that America's Anglo-European colonialist legacy can influence writers without their being aware of it.

A shorthand overview of the range of perspectives offered by each theory

In each of the "Food for further thought" sections found at the end of the preceding chapters, I offered you a list summarizing the different perspectives the theory at hand provided for our interpretation exercises or, in the case of reader-response theory in Chapter 2, for our response exercises. The goal was to give you a sense of the range of interpretation options offered by each theory. I think it might be helpful for you to see all of those lists laid out before you, both as a review of what you've done and to reinforce your awareness of the variety of interpretation possibilities made available by each of our theories.

Reader-response concepts—Reader-response concepts can be used to analyze

1 your personal identification with a literary character,
2 your relationship to a literary character that reminds you of someone important in your life,
3 your relationship to a plot event that reminds you of something important that occurred in your life or in the life of someone close to you,
4 your relationship to a literary setting that reminds you of someplace important in your life.

New Critical concepts—New Critical concepts can be used to analyze

1 literary texts that address the topic of tradition and change (our example: "Everyday Use"),
2 literary texts that address the topic of death (our example: "A Rose for Emily"),
3 literary texts that address the topic of alienation (our example: "The Battle Royal"),
4 literary texts that address the topic of conformity and nonconformity (our example: "Don't Explain"), and
5 literary texts that address the topic of the unknown (our example: "I started Early – Took my Dog").

Psychoanalytic concepts—Psychoanalytic concepts can be used to analyze

1 literary works that illustrate the kind of "everyday" dysfunctional behavior found, to varying degrees, in most families (our example: "Everyday Use"),
2 literary works that illustrate insanity (our example: "A Rose for Emily"),
3 literary works that consist largely of dream imagery (our example: "I started Early—Took my Dog"),
4 literary works that illustrate psychological self-healing (our example: "Don't Explain"), and
5 literary works whose representations of psychological experience should not be analyzed using psychoanalytic theory alone (our example: "The Battle Royal").

Marxist concepts—Marxist concepts can be used to analyze

1 literary works that are anticapitalist in that they illustrate the harmful effects of capitalist ideologies (our example: "Everyday Use"),

2   literary works that are anticapitalist in that they illustrate the harmful effects of one particular capitalist ideology, for example, the American Dream (our example, "The Battle Royal"),

3   literary works that are anticlassist in that they illustrate the harmful effects of classism (our example: "A Rose for Emily"),

4   literary works that are anticlassist in that they provide positive images of working-class people, images that operate against lower-class stereotypes, and/or admirable characters who, themselves, display anticlassist behavior (our example: "Don't Explain"), and

5   literary works whose juxtaposition of large/small or high/low images will tempt us to misinterpret them by imposing a Marxist framework that the literary work does not justify (our example: "I started Early—Took my Dog").

Feminist concepts—Feminist concepts can be used to analyze

1   literary works that are antipatriarchal in that their negative representations of patriarchal ideology encourage us to reject that ideology (our example: "The Battle Royal"),

2   literary works that are antipatriarchal in that their positive representations of characters who violate traditional gender roles encourage us to resist patriarchal ideology (our example: "Don't Explain"),

3   literary works that have a conflicted response to patriarchy in that they both combat and promote patriarchal ideology, for instance, by providing both positive and negative images of characters who violate traditional gender roles (our example: "Everyday Use"),

4   literary works that are patriarchal in that they encourage us to accept patriarchal ideology, for instance, by providing negative images of women who violate traditional gender roles and/or patriarchal stereotypes of women (our example: "A Rose for Emily"), and

5   literary works whose psychoanalytic elements can be used to produce a feminist interpretation by illustrating patriarchy's psychological oppression of women (our example: "I started Early—Took my Dog").

Lesbian, gay, and queer concepts—Lesbian, gay, and queer concepts can be used to analyze

1   literary works that provide positive images of LGBTQ people (our example: "Don't Explain"),

2   literary works that illustrate the operations of homophobia (our example: "The Battle Royal"),

3   literary works with a lesbian, gay, or queer subtext that contributes a subtle but important element to the lives of heterosexual characters (our example: "Everyday Use"),

4 literary works that illustrate the first principle of queer theory: that the opposition of the categories *heterosexual* and *homosexual* is inadequate for understanding the complexities of human sexuality (our example: "A Rose for Emily"), and

5 literary works whose lesbian or gay dimension can be understood best when analyzed in the context of other works by the author and with some support from biographical materials (our example: "I started Early—Took my Dog").

African American Concepts—African American concepts can be used to analyze

1 literary works that are antiracist in that they illustrate the harmful effects of overt operations of institutionalized racism (our example: "The Battle Royal"),

2 literary works that are antiracist in that they provide positive images of African Americans—images that work against racist stereotypes—who deal with "less visible" operations of institutionalized racism (our example: "Don't Explain"),

3 literary works that are antiracist in that they illustrate the harmful effects of internalized racism (our example: "Everyday Use"),

4 literary works by white authors writing about white experience whose portrayals of black characters are antiracist and/or racist in nature (our example: "A Rose for Emily"), and

5 literary works whose juxtaposition of large/small or high/low images will tempt us to misinterpret them by imposing an African American framework that the literary work does not justify (our example: "I started Early—Took my Dog").

Postcolonial concepts—Postcolonial concepts can be used to analyze

1 literary works that are anticolonialist in that they illustrate the harmful effects of colonialist ideology (our example: "The Battle Royal"),

2 literary works that are anticolonialist in that they illustrate the emotional losses suffered by the colonial subject, whose life is one of unhomeliness and mimicry (our example: "Everyday Use"),

3 literary works that are anticolonialist in that they depict the harmful effects of judging individuals according to the cultural categories by which the dominant culture defines people (our example: "A Rose for Emily"),

4 literary works that are anticolonialist in that they positively portray anticolonialist resistance (our example: "Don't Explain"), and

5 literary works that engage in the othering of nature that is part of the legacy of colonialist ideology (our example: "I started Early—Took my Dog").

Remember, this list is intended just to give you an idea of the range of perspectives on literary interpretation provided by each of our theories. The list is by no means complete because the possibilities are limited only by our imagination and by our ability to gather textual evidence to support our interpretations.

Critical theory and cultural criticism revisited

As you may recall from our discussion of critical theory and cultural criticism in Chapter 1, the next step in the study of critical theory actually occurs, for many students, while they're still taking their first step: they begin to notice things in their everyday lives that they probably wouldn't have noticed before. Perhaps this has begun to happen to you, too. For example, you might have begun to notice how people of different races, classes, cultures, and sexual orientations are represented on television shows. Have you observed, for instance, the race, gender, and apparent social class—or, at least, social "style"—of the majority of contestants on various television game shows or reality shows, such as *Let's Make a Deal, Minute to Win It, Deal or No Deal, Jeopardy!* or *Apprentice*? Or have concepts from our critical theories seemed to pop up in the song lyrics you listen to as you drive to school or work? Perhaps you've found yourself having new insights into a movie you had seen in the past, a movie in which there was more to see than you realized at the time.

It makes sense that you *would* see these concepts illustrated rather frequently in your daily life and in a variety of ways. After all, our theoretical concepts weren't invented out of thin air. They are based on observations of human behavior and of the ways in which human behavior has been represented over the centuries in mythology, folklore, and literature. Certainly, the originators of that mythology and folklore and the writers of that literature may not have intended to illustrate the concepts you are now able to see in them. But if the material you're reading, viewing, or hearing represents human experience in some way, then it's a safe bet that it will illustrate such concepts as psychological repression, classism, the American Dream, traditional gender roles, heterosexism, institutionalized racism, unhomeliness, and so forth. That's why, as suggested in Chapter 1, our concepts from critical theory are useful not only for the interpretation of literary works, but also for the purposes of cultural criticism, that is, for the purposes of analyzing popular culture in order to discover the cultural work performed—the cultural messages sent, whether deliberately or not—by movies, television shows, comic strips, song lyrics, advertisements, radio talk-shows, toys, games, cartoons, and, well, just about any cultural production intended for the general public.

Let's consider, for example, the television shows mentioned above. Is there a certain "kind" of contestant associated with each program? For instance, what personal qualities or abilities are required of contestants in order to win? How do contestants dress? How does the show's moderator dress? How do contestants show their enthusiasm for the game and for the prizes offered? What, if anything, do contestants do to "get the audience going"? (Do they address the audience directly? Do they share personal information? If so, what kind?) How do contestants show their happiness upon winning? Do the prizes differ from one show to another depending on the "type" of contestant associated with each show? Taken together, what do these game shows seem to be saying, whether or not they realize it, about the differences among people based on their race, class, gender, or any other cultural category that you can observe? Keeping in mind that contestants' clothing and behavior largely conforms to the clothing and behavior suggested for them by program executives, do any of these shows seem to promote stereotyping in terms of race, class, gender, or any other cultural category? If you attempt to answer these questions, you're engaging in cultural criticism, and you're probably drawing on concepts from African American, Marxist, feminist, psychoanalytic, postcolonial, or gay, lesbian, and queer theories to guide your analysis and to give you the confidence to pursue it. For the study of these theories helps us notice racial, class, gender, and other stereotypes much more readily; helps us analyze how, specifically, those stereotypes are communicated; and helps us perceive the complex ways in which media representations of human beings can sometimes dehumanize those viewed by the camera and desensitize the viewer. In addition, concepts from these same theories can help us understand how a production of popular culture is trying to combat racial, class, gender, or other stereotypes—think, for instance, of the television series *Battlestar Galactica*—for popular-culture productions can also transform the values of the culture that creates them.

Of course, as we've seen in previous chapters, you can also use concepts from a single critical theory to analyze a single cultural production. Let's dip our toes in one last time and do that again here. This time, we'll take a look at a cultural production that's over forty years old. Maybe we will be able to see if the cultural work it performed decades ago is still relevant today. I'm referring to *The Andy Griffith Show*, a television series that originally aired in the United States from 1960 to 1968, the reruns of which remain popular today under the title *Andy of Mayberry*. Drawing on concepts from feminist theory, let's consider the season-seven opening episode, "Opie's Girlfriend" (September 12, 1966), in which Andy Taylor's (Andy Griffith) girlfriend Helen (Aneta Corsaut) has a visit from her young niece.[1]

It seems that Helen's niece Cynthia (Mary Anne Durkin) and Andy's young son Opie (Ronnie Howard) have been spending a good deal of time together, engaging in running and jumping contests and the like. However, when Cynthia intercepts a pass intended for Opie during a touch-football game that includes some of his buddies, Opie dishonestly claims that Cynthia's interception was a foul. He shoves her. She shoves back. The outcome is a black eye for Opie and the end of his short-lived friendship with Cynthia. Upon investigation, Helen learns that her niece has out-performed Opie at every game. The good-natured young girl sees nothing wrong with this state of affairs and doesn't think less of Opie just because he's not a great athlete. But she doesn't understand Opie's negative response to her. Aha! Helen talks with Cynthia—in a scene that plays like the girl's rite of passage into adulthood—and tells her that men have been the breadwinners and the protectors of women for centuries. So it's natural for them to feel the need to be superior to women in acts of physical prowess. Indeed, women need to help men feel that they're superior even when they're not. In short, every woman has a choice to make. She can outplay her man and risk losing him. Or she can deliberately fumble the ball and pretend to need his help. She'll lose the game, but she'll win her man! Needless to say, Cynthia chooses the second option, and the episode closes with everyone in smiles.

Of course, you don't need to study feminist critical theory to understand what this episode is saying about boys and girls. But if you are acquainted with the concepts from feminist theory we studied in Chapter 6, you're probably more likely to ask yourself such questions as those listed below and probably more likely to be able to answer them. As we've seen before, and as I hope this example makes especially clear, you can often generate ideas to help you analyze a cultural production by brainstorming a list of questions about the cultural messages sent by that production and about the culture in which that production emerged. Here's my list.

1   Given the time and place in which the story is set (small-town North Carolina in the early 1960s), does Helen's niece really have much of a choice about whether or not to conform to patriarchal gender roles? That is, are we watching a young girl making a choice, as Helen suggests it is, or are we watching an act of patriarchal programming?

2   Given what we know today, is this kind of deception (on Cynthia's part) and self-deception (on Opie's part) good for either youngster?

3   Isn't Helen's niece getting some unspoken messages here, such as "Boys aren't very bright, and it's okay to manipulate them to get what you want"; "Nothing is as important as having a boyfriend"; and "A female shouldn't have abilities in a field that society considers male-oriented"?

4   Do patriarchal gender roles require that men and women sometimes lie to themselves and to one another?

5   Does the happy ending, including the niece's satisfaction with her "choice," mean that this episode is influencing viewers to agree with Helen, whether it intends to do so or not?

6   Come to think of it, wasn't it unrealistic, in the mid-1960s, to portray an adolescent girl who thinks she can beat a boy at every game and still be liked by him? Had she been living in a cave prior to her visit with Aunt Helen? Doesn't the use of this rather ludicrous plot device mean that the show's producers deliberately wanted to send a patriarchal message to their viewers?

7   What was happening in the United States during the mid-1960s to make the show's producers think that such a message was needed or (the more likely motive) that such a message, even so transparently packaged, would sell?

8   Might not the women's rights movement growing during this period have been a factor in the production of this mini-"morality play" about the importance of patriarchal gender roles for the happiness of both males and females?

9   Do you think the cultural messages sent by this episode would still appeal to some people today? If so, why?

10   Are cultural messages like these still being sent by the television and film industries, though perhaps in a more subtle fashion? Can you give some examples?

The issue here isn't whether or not we believe in traditional gender roles or which roles we accept or reject. Rather, the issue here is our ability to use concepts from our critical theories to think creatively and productively about the cultural messages we receive every day from even what seem to be the least likely sources. The issue here is our power to know when a television show, a toy, a movie, or a popular song is trying to influence our thinking while pretending to merely entertain or inform us. For our thinking is most easily influenced, unfortunately, when we believe we're just being entertained or informed.

Critical theory and an ethics for a diverse world

You may be beginning to notice, by this point, that most of the theoretical approaches to literature you've encountered in this book are trying to help us see something about human relations: the ways in which human relations are influenced by individuals' psychological wounds; by whatever socioeconomic system controls the flow of money and power in a given nation; and by a society's attitudes toward race, class, gender, sexual orientation, and other cultural factors. These critical theories, then, have ethical implications. This simply means that part of their purpose is to help us better understand ourselves, our world, and the variety of people who share this planet. It's not just a matter of being better informed about the issues that affect our world, though increasing our knowledge is certainly a primary goal. Ideally, I think, the theories we've studied help us develop not just our intellect, but our ethical awareness. By trying to show us our world from a variety of vantage points—by helping us experience the world as others experience it—these theories also try to make us more insightful, compassionate human beings whose presence in the world can help make it a better place, in our homes, on our jobs, and in our communities.

Well, once it occurs to us that ethics are involved in learning critical theory, many of us wonder, "If I don't understand or don't like a particular theory, does that mean I will be considered a 'bad person'?" Of course not. It simply means that each theory offers us a number of opportunities to stretch our understanding, to see old ideas in new ways, and, above all, to view our own personal values as "ways of seeing" that can mature and deepen as we mature and deepen over the course of our lives. If you'll pardon the metaphor, you don't have to like all the vegetables on the buffet table to benefit from the variety of choices available. And as you'll see if you continue to study critical theory, there are many more theories you can "sample." Some will appeal to you more than others; some won't appeal to you at all. In studying any theory, you might find that you experience a complete reversal of an opinion you'd previously held, or you might find that the new theory reinforces and helps you define and defend your original opinion. Even if you find that you object to a particular theory, or to some portions of that theory, your objections will be more meaningful and more convincing to others if you understand the theory to which you object.

I'm not suggesting that you should expect some life-changing revelation to occur from studying critical theory, though I have heard students say that critical theory has opened their eyes in some very interesting and important ways. But I do think that the experience will not leave you exactly as it found you. At the very least, you can expect some brain-training, so to speak. If you've read the literary works provided in the appendices of this book and have done your best to follow our interpretation exercises, you have probably experienced some growth in your capacity as a thinker, which you may notice, for example, in an increased awareness of the psychological and social issues addressed in this book as they are represented in the literary works and productions of popular culture you may encounter in the future. Or you may just notice an increased ability to talk about these issues with your friends and family, which is, I think, no small gain.

Indeed, the kinds of ideas critical theory offers us often require that we change our thinking to some extent just in order to be able to fully understand those ideas. I think, in fact, it's safe to say that most education consists not of acquiring information but of changing how we think. How can we grasp new ideas if we don't learn to think in new ways? Does this idea sound a bit frightening? I think it should. Real change, real growth, real education *are* somewhat frightening because we don't always know what we're going to learn, not just about our subject matter but also about ourselves and our world. So let me share with you an old saying that works for me when I get a little nervous about learning something new: "People learn only what they're ready to learn." Maybe, then, the best idea is to trust yourself. You'll be able to learn what you're ready to learn. And if there's one thing I've learned from studying critical theory, it's that we're usually able to learn a great deal more than we first expect.

Note

1 You can view "Opie's Girlfriend" online at http://youtube.com/watch?v=JU9nqOsk0Y.

Appendix A: Poem 520
I started Early—Took my Dog
(c. 1862)

Emily Dickinson (1830–86)

¹ I started Early—Took my Dog—
² And visited the Sea—
³ The Mermaids in the Basement
⁴ Came out to look at me—
⁵ And Frigates—in the Upper Floor
⁶ Extended Hempen Hands—
⁷ Presuming Me to be a Mouse—
⁸ Aground—upon the Sands—
⁹ But no Man moved Me—till the Tide
¹⁰ Went past my simple Shoe—
¹¹ And past my Apron—and my Belt
¹² And past my Bodice—too—
¹³ And made as He would eat me up—
¹⁴ As wholly as a Dew
¹⁵ Upon a Dandelion's Sleeve—
¹⁶ And then—I started—too—
¹⁷ And He—He followed—close behind—
¹⁸ I felt His Silver Heel
¹⁹ Upon My Ankle—Then my Shoes
²⁰ Would overflow with Pearl—
²¹ Until We met the Solid Town—
²² No One He seemed to know—
²³ And bowing—with a Mighty look—
²⁴ At me—The Sea withdrew—

Appendix B: A Rose for Emily
(1931)

William Faulkner (1897–1962)

When Miss Emily Grierson died, our whole town went to her funeral: the men through a sort of respectful affection for a fallen monument, the women mostly out of curiosity to see the inside of her house, which no one save an old man-servant—a combined gardener and cook—had seen in at least ten years.

It was a big, squarish frame house that had once been white, decorated with cupolas and spires and scrolled balconies in the heavily lightsome style of the seventies, set on what had once been our most select street. But garages and cotton gins had encroached and obliterated even the august names of that neighborhood; only Miss Emily's house was left, lifting its stubborn and coquettish decay above the cotton wagons and the gasoline pumps—an eyesore among eyesores. And now Miss Emily had gone to join the representatives of those august names where they lay in the cedarbemused cemetery among the ranked and anonymous graves of Union and Confederate soldiers who fell at the battle of Jefferson.

Alive, Miss Emily had been a tradition, a duty, and a care; a sort of hereditary obligation upon the town, dating from that day in 1894 when Colonel Sartoris, the mayor—he who fathered the edict that no Negro woman should appear on the streets without an apron—remitted her taxes, the dispensation dating from the death of her father on into perpetuity. Not that Miss Emily would have accepted charity. Colonel Sartoris invented an involved tale to the effect that Miss Emily's father had loaned money to the town, which the town, as a matter of business, preferred this way of repaying. Only a man of Colonel Sartoris' generation and thought could have invented it, and only a woman could have believed it.

When the next generation, with its more modern ideas, became mayors and aldermen, this arrangement created some little dissatisfaction. On the first of the year they mailed her a tax notice. February came, and there was no reply. They wrote her a formal letter, asking her to call at the sheriff's office at her convenience. A week later the mayor wrote her himself, offering to call or to send his car for her, and received in reply a note on paper of an archaic shape, in a thin, flowing calligraphy in faded ink, to the effect that she no longer went out at all. The tax notice was also enclosed, without comment.

They called a special meeting of the Board of Aldermen. A deputation waited upon her, knocked at the door through which no visitor had passed since she ceased giving china-painting lessons eight or ten years earlier. They were admitted by the old Negro into a dim hall from which a stairway mounted into still more shadow. It smelled of dust and disuse—a close, dank smell. The Negro led them into the parlor. It was furnished in heavy, leather-covered furniture. When the Negro opened the blinds of one window, they could see that the leather was cracked; and when they sat down, a faint dust rose sluggishly about their thighs, spinning with slow motes in the single sun-ray. On a tarnished gilt easel before the fireplace stood a crayon portrait of Miss Emily's father.

They rose when she entered—a small, fat woman in black, with a thin gold chain descending to her waist and vanishing into her belt, leaning on an ebony cane with a tarnished gold head. Her skeleton was small and spare; perhaps that was why what would have been merely plumpness in another was obesity in her. She looked bloated, like a body long submerged in motionless water, and of that pallid hue. Her eyes, lost in the fatty ridges of her face, looked like two small pieces of coal pressed into a lump of dough as they moved from one face to another while the visitors stated their errand.

She did not ask them to sit. She just stood in the door and listened quietly until the spokesman came to a stumbling halt. Then they could hear the invisible watch ticking at the end of the gold chain.

Her voice was dry and cold. "I have no taxes in Jefferson. Colonel Sartoris explained it to me. Perhaps one of you can gain access to the city records and satisfy yourselves."

"But we have. We are the city authorities, Miss Emily. Didn't you get a notice from the sheriff, signed by him?"

"I received a paper, yes," Miss Emily said. "Perhaps he considers himself the sheriff ... I have no taxes in Jefferson."

"But there is nothing on the books to show that, you see. We must go by the—"

"See Colonel Sartoris. I have no taxes in Jefferson."

"But, Miss Emily—"

"See Colonel Sartoris." (Colonel Sartoris had been dead almost ten years.) "I have no taxes in Jefferson. Tobe!"

The Negro appeared. "Show these gentlemen out."

II

So she vanquished them, horse and foot, just as she had vanquished their fathers thirty years before about the smell. That was two years after her father's death and a short time after her sweetheart—the one we believed would marry her—had deserted her. After her father's death she went out very little; after her sweetheart went away, people hardly saw her at all. A few of the ladies had the temerity to call, but were not received, and the only sign of life about the place was the Negro man—a young man then—going in and out with a market basket.

"Just as if a man—any man—could keep a kitchen properly," the ladies said; so they were not surprised when the smell developed. It was another link between the gross, teeming world and the high and mighty Griersons.

A neighbor, a woman, complained to the mayor, Judge Stevens, eighty years old.

"But what will you have me do about it, madam?" he said.

"Why, send her word to stop it," the woman said. "Isn't there a law?"

"I'm sure that won't be necessary," Judge Stevens said. "It's probably just a snake or a rat that nigger of hers killed in the yard. I'll speak to him about it."

The next day he received two more complaints, one from a man who came in diffident deprecation. "We really must do something about it, Judge. I'd be the last one in the world to bother Miss Emily, but we've got to do something." That night the Board of Aldermen met—three graybeards and one younger man, a member of the rising generation.

"It's simple enough," he said. "Send her word to have her place cleaned up. Give her a certain time to do it in, and if she don't ... "

"Dammit, sir," Judge Stevens said, "will you accuse a lady to her face of smelling bad?"

So the next night, after midnight, four men crossed Miss Emily's lawn and slunk about the house like burglars, sniffing along the base of the brickwork and at the cellar openings while one of them performed a regular sowing motion with his hand out of a sack slung from his shoulder. They broke open the cellar door and sprinkled lime there, and in all the outbuildings. As they recrossed the lawn, a window that had been dark was lighted and Miss Emily sat in it, the light behind her, and her upright torso motionless as that of an idol. They crept quietly across the lawn and into the shadow of the locusts that lined the street. After a week or two the smell went away.

That was when people had begun to feel really sorry for her. People in our town, remembering how old lady Wyatt, her great-aunt, had gone completely crazy at last, believed that the Griersons held themselves a little too high for what they really were. None of the young men were quite good enough for Miss Emily and such. We had long thought of them as a tableau, Miss Emily a slender figure in white in the background, her father a spraddled silhouette in the foreground, his back to her and clutching a horsewhip, the two of them framed by the back-flung front door. So when she got to be thirty and was still single, we were not pleased exactly, but vindicated; even with insanity in the family she wouldn't have turned down all of her chances if they had really materialized.

When her father died, it got about that the house was all that was left to her; and in a way, people were glad. At last they could pity Miss Emily. Being left alone, and a pauper, she had become humanized. Now she too would know the old thrill and the old despair of a penny more or less.

The day after his death all the ladies prepared to call at the house and offer condolence and aid, as is our custom. Miss Emily met them at the door, dressed as usual and with no trace of grief on her face. She told them that her father was not dead. She did that for three days, with the ministers calling on her, and the doctors, trying to persuade her to let them dispose of the body. Just as they were about to resort to law and force, she broke down, and they buried her father quickly.

We did not say she was crazy then. We believed she had to do that. We remembered all the young men her father had driven away, and we knew that with nothing left, she would have to cling to that which had robbed her, as people will.

III

She was sick for a long time. When we saw her again, her hair was cut short, making her look like a girl, with a vague resemblance to those angels in colored church windows—sort of tragic and serene.

The town had just let the contracts for paving the side-walks, and in the summer after her father's death they began the work. The construction company came with niggers and mules and machinery, and a foreman named Homer Barron, a Yankee—a big, dark, ready man, with a big voice and eyes lighter than his face. The little boys would follow in groups to hear him cuss the niggers, and the niggers singing in time to the rise and fall of picks. Pretty soon he knew everybody in town. Whenever you heard a lot of laughing anywhere about the square, Homer Barron would be in the center of the group. Presently we began to see him and Miss Emily on Sunday afternoons driving in the yellow-wheeled buggy and the matched team of bays from the livery stable.

At first we were glad that Miss Emily would have an interest, because the ladies all said, "Of course a Grierson would not think seriously of a North-erner, a day laborer." But there were still others, older people, who said that even grief could not cause a real lady to forget *noblesse oblige*—without calling it *noblesse oblige*. They just said, "Poor Emily. Her kinsfolk should come to her." She had some kin in Alabama; but years ago her father had fallen out with them over the estate of old lady Wyatt, the crazy woman, and there was no communication between the two families. They had not even been represented at the funeral.

And as soon as the old people said, "Poor Emily," the whispering began. "Do you suppose it's really so?" they said to one another. "Of course it is. What else could ... " This behind their hands; rustling of craned silk and satin behind jalousies closed upon the sun of Sunday afternoon as the thin, swift clop-clop-clop of the matched team passed: "Poor Emily."

She carried her head high enough—even when we believed that she was fallen. It was as if she demanded more than ever the recognition of her dignity as the last Grierson; as if it had wanted that touch of earthiness to reaffirm her imperviousness. Like when she bought the rat poison, the arsenic. That was over a year after they had begun to say "Poor Emily," and while the two female cousins were visiting her.

"I want some poison," she said to the druggist. She was over thirty then, still a slight woman, though thinner than usual, with cold, haughty black eyes in a face the flesh of which was strained across the temples and about the eye-sockets as you imagine a lighthouse-keeper's face ought to look. "I want some poison," she said.

"Yes, Miss Emily. What kind? For rats and such? I'd recom—"

"I want the best you have. I don't care what kind."

The druggist named several. "They'll kill anything up to an elephant. But what you want is—"

"Arsenic," Miss Emily said. "Is that a good one?"

"Is ... arsenic? Yes, ma'am. But what you want—"

"I want arsenic."

The druggist looked down at her. She looked back at him, erect, her face like a strained flag. "Why, of course," the druggist said. "If that's what you want. But the law requires you to tell what you are going to use it for."

Miss Emily just stared at him, her head tilted back in order to look him eye for eye, until he looked away and went and got the arsenic and wrapped it up. The Negro delivery boy brought her the package; the druggist didn't come back. When she opened the package at home there was written on the box, under the skull and bones: "For rats."

IV

So the next day we all said, "She will kill herself"; and we said it would be the best thing. When she had first begun to be seen with Homer Barron, we had said, "She will marry him." Then we said, "She will persuade him yet," because Homer himself had remarked—he liked men, and it was known that he drank with the younger men in the Elks' Club—that he was not a marrying man. Later we said, "Poor Emily" behind the jalousies as they passed on Sunday afternoon in the glittering buggy, Miss Emily with her head high and Homer Barron with his hat cocked and a cigar in his teeth, reins and whip in a yellow glove.

Then some of the ladies began to say that it was a disgrace to the town and a bad example to the young people. The men did not want to interfere, but at last the ladies forced the Baptist minister—Miss Emily's people were Episcopal—to call upon her. He would never divulge what happened during that interview, but he refused to go back again. The next Sunday they again drove about the streets, and the following day the minister's wife wrote to Miss Emily's relations in Alabama.

So she had blood-kin under her roof again and we sat back to watch developments. At first nothing happened. Then we were sure that they were to be married. We learned that Miss Emily had been to the jeweler's and ordered a man's toilet set in silver, with the letters H. B. on each piece. Two days later we learned that she had bought a complete outfit of men's clothing, including a nightshirt, and we said, "They are married." We were really glad. We were glad because the two female cousins were even more Grierson than Miss Emily had ever been.

So we were not surprised when Homer Barron—the streets had been finished some time since—was gone. We were a little disappointed that there was not a public blowing-off, but we believed that he had gone on to prepare for Miss Emily's coming, or to give her a chance to get rid of the cousins. (By that time it was a cabal, and we were all Miss Emily's allies to help circumvent the cousins.) Sure enough, after another week they departed. And, as we had expected all along, within three days Homer Barron was back in town. A neighbor saw the Negro man admit him at the kitchen door at dusk one evening.

And that was the last we saw of Homer Barron. And of Miss Emily for some time. The Negro man went in and out with the market basket, but the front door remained closed. Now and then we would see her at a window for a moment, as the men did that night when they sprinkled the lime, but for almost six months she did not appear on the streets. Then we knew that this was to be expected too; as if that quality of her father which had thwarted her woman's life so many times had been too virulent and too furious to die.

When we next saw Miss Emily, she had grown fat and her hair was turning gray. During the next few years it grew grayer and grayer until it attained an even pepper-and-salt iron-gray, when it ceased turning. Up to the day of her death at seventy-four it was still that vigorous iron-gray, like the hair of an active man.

From that time on her front door remained closed, save for a period of six or seven years, when she was about forty, during which she gave lessons in china-painting. She fitted up a studio in one of the downstairs rooms, where the daughters and granddaughters of Colonel Sartoris' contemporaries were sent to her with the same regularity and in the same spirit that they were sent to church on Sundays with a twenty-five-cent piece for the collection plate. Meanwhile her taxes had been remitted.

Then the newer generation became the backbone and the spirit of the town, and the painting pupils grew up and fell away and did not send their children to her with boxes of color and tedious brushes and pictures cut from the ladies' magazines. The front door closed upon the last one and remained closed for good. When the town got free postal delivery, Miss Emily alone refused to let them fasten the metal numbers above her door and attach a mailbox to it. She would not listen to them.

Daily, monthly, yearly we watched the Negro grow grayer and more stooped, going in and out with the market basket. Each December we sent her a tax notice, which would be returned by the post office a week later, unclaimed. Now and then we would see her in one of the downstairs windows—she had evidently shut up the top floor of the house—like the carven torso of an idol in a niche, looking or not looking at us, we could never tell which. Thus she passed from generation to generation—dear, inescapable, impervious, tranquil, and perverse.

And so she died. Fell ill in the house filled with dust and shadows, with only a doddering Negro man to wait on her. We did not even know she was sick; we had long since given up trying to get any information from the Negro. He talked to no one, probably not even to her, for his voice had grown harsh and rusty, as if from disuse.

She died in one of the downstairs rooms, in a heavy walnut bed with a curtain, her gray head propped on a pillow yellow and moldy with age and lack of sunlight.

V

The Negro met the first of the ladies at the front door and let them in, with their hushed, sibilant voices and their quick, curious glances, and then he disappeared. He walked right through the house and out the back and was not seen again.

The two female cousins came at once. They held the funeral on the second day, with the town coming to look at Miss Emily beneath a mass of bought flowers, with the crayon face of her father musing profoundly above the bier and the ladies sibilant and macabre; and the very old men—some in their brushed Confederate uniforms—on the porch and the lawn, talking of Miss Emily as if she had been a contemporary of theirs, believing that they had danced with her and courted her perhaps, confusing time with its mathematical progression, as the old do, to whom all the past is not a diminishing road but, instead, a huge meadow which no winter ever quite touches, divided from them now by the narrow bottle-neck of the most recent decade of years.

Already we knew that there was one room in that region above stairs which no one had seen in forty years, and which would have to be forced. They waited until Miss Emily was decently in the ground before they opened it.

The violence of breaking down the door seemed to fill this room with pervading dust. A thin, acrid pall as of the tomb seemed to lie everywhere upon this room decked and furnished as for a bridal: upon the valance curtains of faded rose color, upon the rose-shaded lights, upon the dressing table, upon the delicate array of crystal and the man's toilet things backed with tarnished silver, silver so tarnished that the monogram was obscured. Among them lay a collar and tie, as if they had just been removed, which, lifted, left upon the surface a pale crescent in the dust. Upon a chair hung the suit, carefully folded; beneath it the two mute shoes and the discarded socks.

The man himself lay in the bed.

For a long while we just stood there, looking down at the profound and fleshless grin. The body had apparently once lain in the attitude of an embrace, but now the long sleep that outlasts love, that conquers even the grimace of love, had cuckolded him. What was left of him, rotted beneath what was left of the nightshirt, had become inextricable from the bed in which he lay; and upon him and upon the pillow beside him lay that even coating of the patient and biding dust.

Then we noticed that in the second pillow was the indentation of a head. One of us lifted something from it, and leaning forward, that faint and invisible dust dry and acrid in the nostrils, we saw a long strand of iron-gray hair.

From *The Collected Stories of William Faulkner*. Reprinted by permission of Random House, Inc., and Curtis Brown, Ltd., London.

Appendix C: The Battle Royal
(1952)

Ralph Ellison (1914–94)

It goes a long way back, some twenty years. All my life I had been looking for something, and everywhere I turned someone tried to tell me what it was. I accepted their answers too, though they were often in contradiction and even self-contradictory. I was naive. I was looking for myself and asking everyone except myself questions which I, and only I, could answer. It took me a long time and much painful boomeranging of my expectations to achieve a realization everyone else appears to have been born with: That I am nobody but myself. But first I had to discover that I am an invisible man!

And yet I am no freak of nature, nor of history. I was in the cards, other things having been equal (or unequal) eighty-five years ago. I am not ashamed of my grandparents for having been slaves. I am only ashamed of myself for having at one time been ashamed. About eighty-five years ago they were told that they were free, united with others of our country in everything pertaining to the common good, and, in everything social, separate like the fingers of the hand. And they believed it. They exulted in it. They stayed in their place, worked hard, and brought up my father to do the same. But my grandfather is the one. He was an odd old guy, my grandfather, and I am told I take after him. It was he who caused the trouble. On his deathbed he called my father to him and said, "Son, after I'm gone I want you to keep up the good fight. I never told you, but our life is a war and I have been a traitor all my born days, a spy in the enemy's country ever since I give up my gun back in the Reconstruction. Live with your head in the lion's mouth. I want you to overcome 'em with yeses, undermine 'em with grins, agree 'em to death and destruction, let 'em swoller you till they vomit or bust wide open." They thought the old man had gone out of his mind. He had been the meekest of men. The younger children were rushed from the room, the shades drawn and the flame of the lamp turned so low that it sputtered on the wick like the old man's breathing. "Learn it to the younguns," he whispered fiercely; then he died.

But my folks were more alarmed over his last words than over his dying. It was as though he had not died at all, his words caused so much anxiety. I was warned emphatically to forget what he had said and, indeed, this is the first time it has been mentioned outside the family circle. It had a tremendous effect upon me, however. I could never be sure of what he meant. Grandfather had been a quiet old man who never made any trouble, yet on his deathbed he had called himself a traitor and a spy, and he had spoken of his meekness as a dangerous activity. It became a constant puzzle which lay unanswered in the back of my mind. And whenever things went well for me I remembered my grandfather and felt guilty and uncomfortable. It was as though I was carrying out his advice in spite of myself. And to make it worse, everyone loved me for it. I was praised by the most lily-white men of the town. I was considered an example of desirable conduct—just as my grandfather had been. And what puzzled me was that the old man had defined it as *treachery*. When I was praised for my conduct I felt a guilt that in some way I was doing something that was really against the wishes of the white folks, that if they had understood they would have desired me to act just the opposite, that I should have been sulky and mean, and that that really would have been what they wanted, even though they were fooled and thought they wanted me to act as I did. It made me afraid that some day they would look upon me as a traitor and I would be lost. Still I was more afraid to act any other way because they didn't like that at all. The old man's words were like a curse. On my graduation day I delivered an oration in which I showed that humility was the secret, indeed, the very essence of progress. (Not that I believed this— how could I, remembering my grandfather?—I only believed that it worked.) It was a great success. Everyone praised me and I was invited to give the speech at a gathering of the town's leading white citizens. It was triumph for our whole community.

It was in the main ballroom of the leading hotel. When I got there I discovered that it was on the occasion of a smoker, and I was told that since I was to be there anyway I might as well take part in the battle royal to be fought by some of my schoolmates as part of the entertainment. The battle royal came first.

All of the town's big shots were there in their tuxedoes, wolfing down the buffet foods, drinking beer and whiskey and smoking black cigars. It was a large room with a high ceiling. Chairs were arranged in neat rows around three sides of a portable boxing ring. The fourth side was clear, revealing a gleaming space of polished floor. I had some misgivings over the battle royal, by the way. Not from a distaste for fighting, but because I didn't care too much for the other fellows who were to take part. They were tough guys who seemed to have no grandfather's curse worrying their minds. No one could mistake their toughness. And besides, I suspected that fighting a battle royal might detract from the dignity of my speech. In those pre-invisible days I visualized myself as a potential Booker T. Washington. But the other fellows didn't care too much for me either, and there were nine of them. I felt superior to them in my way, and I didn't like the manner in which we were all crowded together into the servants' elevator. Nor did they like my being there. In fact, as the warmly lighted floors flashed past the elevator we had words over the fact that I, by taking part in the fight, had knocked one of their friends out of a night's work.

We were led out of the elevator through a rococo hall into an anteroom and told to get into our fighting togs. Each of us was issued a pair of boxing gloves and ushered out into the big mirrored hall, which we entered looking cautiously about us and whispering, lest we might accidentally be heard above the noise of the room. It was foggy with cigar smoke. And already the whiskey was taking effect. I was shocked to see some of the most important men of the town quite tipsy. They were all there—bankers, lawyers, judges, doctors, fire chiefs, teachers, merchants. Even one of the more fashionable pastors. Something we could not see was going on up front. A clarinet was vibrating sensuously and the men were standing up and moving eagerly forward. We were a small tight group, clustered together, our bare uppers touching and shining with anticipatory sweat; while up front the big shots were becoming increasingly excited over something we still could not see. Suddenly I heard the school superintendent, who had told me to come, yell, "Bring up the shines, gentlemen! Bring up the little shines!"

We were rushed up to the front of the ballroom, where it smelled even more strongly of tobacco and whiskey. Then we were pushed into place. I almost wet my pants. A sea of faces, some hostile, some amused, ringed around us, and in the center, facing us, stood a magnificent blonde—stark naked. There was dead silence. I felt a blast of cold air chill me. I tried to back away, but they were behind me and around me. Some of the boys stood with lowered heads, trembling. I felt a wave of irrational guilt and fear. My teeth chattered, my skin turned to goose flesh, my knees knocked. Yet I was strongly attracted and looked in spite of myself. Had the price of looking been blindness, I would have looked. The hair was yellow like that of a circus kewpie doll, the face heavily powdered and rouged, as though to form an abstract mask, the eyes hollow and smeared a cool blue, the color of a baboon's butt. I felt a desire to spit upon her as my eyes brushed slowly over her body. Her breasts were firm and round as the domes of East Indian temples, and I stood so close as to see the fine skin texture and beads of pearly perspiration glistening like dew around the pink and erected buds of her nipples. I wanted at one and the same time to run from the room, to sink through the floor, or go to her and cover her from my eyes and the eyes of the others with my body; to feel the soft thighs, to caress her and destroy her, to love her and murder her, to hide from her, and yet to stroke where below the small American flag tattooed upon her belly her thighs formed a capital V. I had a notion that of all in the room she saw only me with her impersonal eyes.

And then she began to dance, a slow sensuous movement, the smoke of a hundred cigars clinging to her like the thinnest of veils. She seemed like a fair bird-girl girdled in veils calling to me from the angry surface of some gray and threatening sea. I was transported. Then I became aware of the clarinet playing and the big shots yelling at us. Some threatened us if we looked and others if we did not. On my right I saw one boy faint. And now a man grabbed a silver pitcher from a table and stepped close as he dashed ice water upon him and stood him up and forced two of us to support him as his head hung and moans issued from his thick bluish lips. Another boy began to plead to go home. He was the largest of the group, wearing dark red fighting trunks much too small to conceal the erection which projected from him as though in answer to the insinuating low-registered moaning of the clarinet. He tried to hide himself with his boxing gloves.

And all the while the blonde continued dancing, smiling faintly at the big shots who watched her with fascination, and faintly smiling at our fear. I noticed a certain merchant who followed her hungrily, his lips loose and drooling. He was a large man who wore diamond studs in a shirtfront which swelled with the ample paunch underneath, and each time the blonde swayed her undulating hips he ran his hand through the thin hair of his bald head and, with his arms upheld, his posture clumsy like that of an intoxicated panda, wound his belly in a slow and obscene grind. This creature was completely hypnotized. The music had quickened. As the dancer flung herself about with a detached expression on her face, the men began reaching out to touch her. I could see their beefy fingers sink into the soft flesh. Some of the others tried to stop them and she began to move around the floor in graceful circles, as they gave chase, slipping and sliding over the polished floor. It was mad. Chairs went crashing, drinks were spilt, as they ran laughing and howling after her. They caught her just as she reached a door, raised her from the floor, and tossed her as college boys are tossed at a hazing, and above her red, fixed-smiling lips I saw the terror and disgust in her eyes, almost like my own terror and that which I saw in some of the other boys. As I watched, they tossed her twice and her soft breasts seem to flatten against the air and her legs flung wildly as they spun. Some of the more sober ones helped her to escape. And I started off the floor, heading for the anteroom with the rest of the boys.

Some were still crying and in hysteria. But as we tried to leave we were stopped and ordered to get into the ring. There was nothing to do but what we were told. All ten of us climbed under the ropes and allowed ourselves to be blindfolded with broad bands of white cloth. One of the men seemed to feel a bit sympathetic and tried to cheer us up as we stood with our backs against the ropes. Some of us tried to grin. "See that boy over there?" one of the men said. "I want you to run across at the bell and give it to him right in the belly. If you don't get him, I'm going to get you. I don't like his looks." Each of us was told the same. The blindfolds were put on. Yet even then I had been going over my speech. In my mind each word was as bright as flame. I felt the cloth pressed into place, and frowned so that it would be loosened when I relaxed.

But now I felt a sudden fit of blind terror. I was unused to darkness. It was as though I had suddenly found myself in a dark room filled with poisonous cottonmouths. I could hear the bleary voices yelling insistently for the battle royal to begin.

"Get going in there!"

"Let me at that big nigger!"

I strained to pick up the school superintendent's voice, as though to squeeze some security out of that slightly more familiar sound.

"Let me at those black sonsabitches!" someone yelled.

"No, Jackson, no!" another voice yelled. "Here, somebody, help me hold Jack."

"I want to get at that ginger-colored nigger. Tear him limb from limb," the first voice yelled.

I stood against the ropes trembling. For in those days I was what they called ginger-colored, and he sounded as though he might crunch me between his teeth like a crisp ginger cookie.

Quite a struggle was going on. Chairs were being kicked about and I could hear voices grunting as with a terrific effort. I wanted to see, to see more desperately than ever before. But the blindfold was tight as a thick skin-puckering scab and when I raised my gloved hands to push the layers of white aside a voice yelled, "Oh, no you don't, black bastard! Leave that alone!"

"Ring the bell before Jackson kills him a coon!" someone boomed in the sudden silence. And I heard the bell clang and the sound of the feet scuffling forward.

A glove smacked against my head. I pivoted, striking out stiffly as someone went past, and felt the jar ripple along the length of my arm to my shoulder. Then it seemed as though all nine of the boys had turned upon me at once. Blows pounded me from all sides while I struck out as best I could. So many blows landed upon me that I wondered if I were not the only blindfolded fighter in the ring, or if the man called Jackson hadn't succeeded in getting me after all.

Blindfolded, I could no longer control my motions. I had no dignity. I stumbled about like a baby or a drunken man. The smoke had become thicker and with each new blow it seemed to sear and further restrict my lungs. My saliva became like hot bitter glue. A glove connected with my head, filling my mouth with warm blood. It was everywhere. I could not tell if the moisture I felt upon my body was sweat or blood. A blow landed hard against the nape of my neck. I felt myself going over, my head hitting the floor. Streaks of blue light filled the black world behind the blindfold. I lay prone, pretending that I was knocked out, but felt myself seized by hands and yanked to my feet. "Get going, black boy! Mix it up!" My arms were like lead, my head smarting from blows. I managed to feel my way to the ropes and held on, trying to catch my breath. A glove landed in my mid-section and I went over again, feeling as though the smoke had become a knife jabbed into my guts. Pushed this way and that by the legs milling around me, I finally pulled erect and discovered that I could see the black, sweat-washed forms weaving in the smoky-blue atmosphere like drunken dancers weaving to the rapid drum-like thuds of blows.

Everyone fought hysterically. It was complete anarchy. Everybody fought everybody else. No group fought together for long. Two, three, four, fought one, then turned to fight each other, were themselves attacked. Blows landed below the belt and in the kidney, with the gloves open as well as closed, and with my eye partly opened now there was not so much terror. I moved carefully, avoiding blows, although not too many to attract attention, fighting from group to group. The boys groped about like blind, cautious crabs crouching to protect their mid-sections, their heads pulled in short against their shoulders, their arms stretched nervously before them, with their fists testing the smoke-filled air like the knobbed feelers of hypersensitive snails. In one corner I glimpsed a boy violently punching the air and heard him scream in pain as he smashed his hand against a ring post. For a second I saw him bent over holding his hand, then going down as a blow caught his unprotected head. I played one group against the other, slipping in and throwing a punch then stepping out of range while pushing the others into the melee to take the blows blindly aimed at me. The smoke was agonizing and there were no rounds, no bells at three minute intervals to relieve our exhaustion. The room spun around me, a swirl of lights, smoke, sweating bodies surrounded by tense white faces. I bled from both nose and mouth, the blood spattering upon my chest.

The men kept yelling, "Slug him, black boy! Knock his guts out!"

"Uppercut him! Kill him! Kill that big boy!"

Taking a fake fall, I saw a boy going down heavily beside me as though we were felled by a single blow, saw a sneaker-clad foot shoot into his groin as the two who had knocked him down stumbled upon him. I rolled out of range, feeling a twinge of nausea.

The harder we fought the more threatening the men became. And yet, I had begun to worry about my speech again. How would it go? Would they recognize my ability? What would they give me?

I was fighting automatically when suddenly I noticed that one after another of the boys was leaving the ring. I was surprised, filled with panic, as though I had been left alone with an unknown danger. Then I understood. The boys had arranged it among themselves. It was the custom for the two men left in the ring to slug it out for the winner's prize. I discovered this too late. When the bell sounded two men in tuxedoes leaped into the ring and removed the blindfold. I found myself facing Tatlock, the biggest of the gang. I felt sick at my stomach. Hardly had the bell stopped ringing in my ears than it clanged again and I saw him moving swiftly toward me. Thinking of nothing else to do I hit him smash on the nose. He kept coming, bringing the rank sharp violence of stale sweat. His face was a black blank of a face, only his eyes alive—with hate of me and aglow with a feverish terror from what had happened to us all. I became anxious. I wanted to deliver my speech and he came at me as though he meant to beat it out of me. I smashed him again and again, taking his blows as they came. Then on a sudden impulse I struck him lightly and as we clinched, I whispered, "Fake like I knocked you out, you can have the prize."

"I'll break your behind," he whispered hoarsely.

"For *them*?"

"For *me*, sonofabitch!"

They were yelling for us to break it up and Tatlock spun me half around with a blow, and as a joggled camera sweeps in a reeling scene, I saw the howling red faces crouching tense beneath the cloud of blue-gray smoke. For a moment the world wavered, unraveled, flowed, then my head cleared and Tatlock bounced before me. That fluttering shadow before my eyes was his jabbing left hand. Then falling forward, my head against his damp shoulder, I whispered,

"I'll make it five dollars more."

"Go to hell!"

But his muscles relaxed a trifle beneath my pressure and I breathed, "Seven?" "Give it to your ma," he said, ripping me beneath the heart.

And while I still held him I butted him and moved away. I felt myself bombarded with punches. I fought back with hopeless desperation. I wanted to deliver my speech more than anything else in the world, because I felt that only these men could judge truly my ability, and now this stupid clown was ruining my chances. I began fighting carefully now, moving in to punch him and out again with my greater speed. A lucky blow to his chin and I had him going too—until I heard a loud voice yell, "I got my money on the big boy."

Hearing this, I almost dropped my guard. I was confused: Should I try to win against the voice out there? Would not this go against my speech, and was not this a moment for humility, for nonresistance? A blow to my head as I danced about sent my right eye popping like a jack-in-the-box and settled my dilemma. The room went red as I fell. It was a dream fall, my body languid and fastidious as to where to land, until the floor became impatient and smashed up to meet me. A moment later I came to. An hypnotic voice said FIVE emphatically. And I lay there, hazily watching a dark red spot of my own blood shaping itself into a butterfly, glistening and soaking into the soiled gray world of the canvas.

When the voice drawled TEN I was lifted up and dragged to a chair. I sat dazed. My eye pained and swelled with each throb of my pounding heart and I wondered if now I would be allowed to speak. I was wringing wet, my mouth still bleeding. We were grouped along the wall now. The other boys ignored me as they congratulated Tatlock and speculated as to how much they would be paid. One boy whimpered over his smashed hand. Looking up front, I saw attendants in white jackets rolling the portable ring away and placing a small square rug in the vacant space surrounded by chairs. Perhaps, I thought, I will stand on the rug to deliver my speech.

Then the M.C. called to us, "Come on up here boys and get your money."

We ran forward to where the men laughed and talked in their chairs, waiting. Everyone seemed friendly now.

"There it is on the rug," the man said. I saw the rug covered with coins of all dimensions and a few crumpled bills. But what excited me, scattered here and there, were the gold pieces.

"Boys, it's all yours," the man said. "You get all you grab."

"That's right, Sambo," a blond man said, winking at me confidentially. I trembled with excitement, forgetting my pain. I would get the gold and the bills, I thought, I would use both hands. I would throw my body against the boys nearest me to block them from the gold.

"Get down around the rug now," the man commanded, "and don't anyone touch it until I give the signal."

"This ought to be good." I heard.

As told, we got around the square rug on our knees. Slowly the man raised his freckled hand as we followed it upward with our eyes.

I heard, "These niggers look like they're about to pray!"

Then, "Ready," the man said. "Go!"

I lunged for a yellow coin lying on the blue design of the carpet, touching it and sending a surprised shriek to join those rising around me. I tried frantically to remove my hand but could not let go. A hot, violent force tore through my body, shaking me like a wet rat. The rug was electrified. The hair bristled up on my head as I shook myself free. My muscles jumped, my nerves jangled, writhed. But I saw that this was not stopping the other boys. Laughing in fear and embarrassment, some were holding back and scooping up the coins knocked off by the painful contortions of the others. The men roared above us as we struggled.

"Pick it up, goddamnit, pick it up!" someone called like a bass-voiced parrot. "Go on, get it!"

I crawled rapidly around the floor, picking up the coins, trying to avoid the coppers and to get greenbacks and the gold. Ignoring the shock by laughing, as I brushed the coins off quickly, I discovered that I could contain the electricity—a contradiction, but it works. Then the men began to push us onto the rug. Laughing embarrassedly, we struggled out of their hands and kept after the coins. We were all wet and slippery and hard to hold. Suddenly I saw a boy lifted into the air, glistening with sweat like a circus seal, and dropped, his wet back landing flush upon the charged rug, heard him yell and saw him literally dance upon his back, his elbows beating a frenzied tattoo upon the floor, his muscles twitching like the flesh of a horse stung by many flies. When he finally rolled off, his face was gray and no one stopped him when he ran from the floor amid booming laughter.

"Get the money," the M.C. called. "That's good hard American cash!"

And we snatched and grabbed, snatched and grabbed. I was careful not to come too close to the rug now, and when I felt the hot whiskey breath descend upon me like a cloud of foul air I reached out and grabbed the leg of a chair. It was occupied and I held on desperately.

"Leggo, nigger! Leggo!"

The huge face wavered down to mine as he tried to push me free. But my body was slippery and he was too drunk. It was Mr. Colcord, who owned a chain of movie houses and "entertainment palaces." Each time he grabbed me I slipped out of his hands. It became a real struggle. I feared the rug more than I did the drunk, so I held on, surprising myself for a moment by trying to topple *him* upon the rug. It was such an enormous idea that I found myself actually carrying it out. I tried not to be obvious, yet when I grabbed his leg, trying to tumble him out of the chair, he raised up roaring with laughter, and, looking at me with soberness dead in the eye, kicked me viciously in the chest. The chair leg flew out of my hand and I felt myself going and rolled. It was as though I had rolled through a bed of hot coals. It seemed a whole century would pass before I would roll free, a century in which I was seared through the deepest levels of my body to the fearful breath within me and the breath seared and heated to the point of explosion. It'll all be over in a flash, I thought as I rolled clear. It'll all be over in a flash.

But not yet, the men on the other side were waiting, red faces swollen as though from apoplexy as they bent forward in their chairs. Seeing their fingers coming toward me I rolled away as a fumbled football rolls off the receiver's fingertips, back into the coals. That time I luckily sent the rug sliding out of place and heard the coins ringing against the floor and the boys scuffling to pick them up and the M.C. calling, "All right, boys, that's all. Go get dressed and get your money."

I was limp as a dish rag. My back felt as though it had been beaten with wires.

When we had dressed the M.C. came in and gave us each five dollars, except Tatlock, who got ten for being last in the ring. Then he told us to leave. I was not to get a chance to deliver my speech, I thought. I was going out into the dim alley in despair when I was stopped and told to go back. I returned to the ballroom, where the men were pushing back their chairs and gathering in groups to talk.

The M.C. knocked on a table for quiet. "Gentlemen," he said, "we almost forgot an important part of the program. A most serious part, gentlemen. This boy was brought here to deliver a speech which he made at his graduation yesterday."

"Bravo!"

"I'm told that he is the smartest boy we've got out there in Greenwood. I'm told that he knows more big words than a pocket-sized dictionary."

Much applause and laughter.

"So now, gentlemen, I want you to give him your attention:"

There was still laughter as I faced them, my mouth dry, my eye throbbing. I began slowly, but evidently my throat was tense, because they began shouting, "Louder! Louder!"

"We of the younger generation extol the wisdom of the great leader and educator," I shouted, "who first spoke these flaming words of wisdom: 'A ship lost at sea for many days suddenly sighted a friendly vessel. From the mast of the unfortunate vessel was seen a signal: "Water, water, we die of thirst!" The answer from the friendly vessel came back: "Cast down your bucket where you are." The captain of the distressed vessel, at last heeding the injunction, cast down his bucket, and it came up full of fresh sparkling water from the mouth of the Amazon River.' And like him I say, and in his words, 'To those of my race who depend upon bettering their condition in a foreign land, or who underestimate the importance of cultivating friendly relations with the Southern white man, who is his next-door neighbor, I would say: "Cast down your bucket where you are"—cast it down in making friends in every manly way of the people of all races by whom we are surrounded ... '"

I spoke automatically and with such fervor that I did not realize that the men were still talking and laughing until my dry mouth, filling up with blood from the cut, almost strangled me. I coughed, wanting to stop and go to one of the tall brass, sand-filled spittoons to relieve myself, but a few of the men, especially the superintendent, were listening and I was afraid. So I gulped it down, blood, saliva and all, and continued. (What powers of endurance I had during those days! What enthusiasm! What a belief in the rightness of things!) I spoke even louder in spite of the pain. But still they talked and still they laughed, as though deaf with cotton in dirty ears. So I spoke with greater emotional emphasis. I closed my ears and swallowed blood until I was nauseated. The speech seemed a hundred times as long as before, but I could not leave out a single word. All had to be said, each memorized nuance considered, rendered. Nor was that all. Whenever I uttered a word of three or more syllables a group of voices would yell for me to repeat it. I used the phrase "social responsibility," and they yelled:

"What's that word you say, boy?"

"Social responsibility," I said.

"What?"

"Social ... "

"Louder."

" ... responsibility."

"More!"

"Respon—"

"Repeat!"

"—sibility."

The room filled with the uproar of laughter until, no doubt, distracted by having to gulp down my blood, I made a mistake and yelled a phrase I had often seen denounced in newspaper editorials, heard debated in private.

"Social ... "

"What?" they yelled.

" ... equality—"

The laughter hung smokelike in the sudden stillness. I opened my eyes, puzzled. Sounds of displeasure filled the room. The M.C. rushed forward. They shouted hostile phrases at me. But I did not understand.

A small dry mustached man in the front row blared out, "Say that slowly, son!"

"What, sir?"

"What you just said!"

"Social responsibility, sir," I said.

"You weren't being smart, were you, boy?" he said, not unkindly.

"No, sir!"

"You sure that about 'equality' was a mistake?"

"Oh yes, sir," I said. "I was swallowing blood."

"Well, you had better speak more slowly so we can understand. We mean to do right by you, but you've got to know your place at all times. All right, now, go on with your speech."

I was afraid. I wanted to leave but I wanted also to speak and I was afraid they'd snatch me down.

"Thank you, sir," I said, beginning where I had left off, and having them ignore me as before.

Yet when I finished there was a thunderous applause. I was surprised to see the superintendent come forth with a package wrapped in white tissue paper, and, gesturing for quiet, address the men.

"Gentlemen, you see that I did not overpraise the boy. He makes a good speech and some day he'll lead his people in the proper paths. And I don't have to tell you that that is important in these days and times. This is a good, smart boy, and so to encourage him in the right direction, in the name of the Board of Education I wish to present him a prize in the form of this ... "

He paused, removing the tissue paper and revealing a gleaming calfskin brief case.

" ... in the form of this first-class article from Shad Whitmore's shop."

"Boy," he said, addressing me, "take this prize and keep it well. Consider it a badge of office. Prize it. Keep developing as you are and some day it will be filled with important papers that will help shape the destiny of your people."

I was so moved that I could hardly express my thanks. A rope of bloody saliva forming a shape like an undiscovered continent drooled upon the leather and I wiped it quickly away. I felt an importance that I had never dreamed.

"Open it and see what's inside," I was told.

My fingers a-tremble, I complied, smelling the fresh leather and finding an official-looking document inside. It was a scholarship to the state college for Negroes. My eyes filled with tears and I ran awkwardly off the floor.

I was overjoyed; I did not even mind when I discovered that the gold pieces I had scrambled for were brass pocket tokens advertising a certain make of automobile.

When I reached home everyone was excited. Next day the neighbors came to congratulate me. I even felt safe from grandfather, whose deathbed curse usually spoiled my triumphs. I stood beneath his photograph with my brief case in hand and smiled triumphantly into his stolid black peasant's face. It was a face that fascinated me. The eyes seemed to follow everywhere I went.

That night I dreamed I was at a circus with him and that he refused to laugh at the clowns no matter what they did. Then later he told me to open my brief case and read what was inside and I did, finding an official envelope stamped with the state seal; and inside the envelope I found another and another, endlessly, and I thought I would fall of weariness. "Them's years," he said. "Now that one." And I did and in it I found an engraved document containing a short message in letters of gold. "Read it," my grandfather said. "Out loud!"

"To whom It May Concern," I intoned. "Keep This Nigger-Boy Running."

I awoke with the old man's laughter ringing in my ears.

(It was a dream I was to remember and dream again for many years after. But at that time I had no insight into its meaning. First I had to attend college.)

Appendix D: Everyday Use

for your grandmama (1973)

Alice Walker (b. 1944)

I will wait for her in the yard that Maggie and I made so clean and wavy yesterday afternoon. A yard like this is more comfortable than most people know. It is not just a yard. It is like an extended living room. When the hard clay is swept clean as a floor and the fine sand around the edges lined with tiny, irregular grooves, anyone can come and sit and look up into the elm tree and wait for the breezes that never come inside the house.

Maggie will be nervous until after her sister goes: she will stand hopelessly in corners, homely and ashamed of the burn scars down her arms and legs, eying her sister with a mixture of envy and awe. She thinks her sister has held life always in the palm of one hand, that "no" is a word the world never learned to say to her.

You've no doubt seen those TV shows where the child who has "made it" is confronted, as a surprise, by her own mother and father, tottering in weakly from backstage. (A pleasant surprise, of course: What would they do if parent and child came on the show only to curse out and insult each other?) On TV mother and child embrace and smile into each other's faces. Sometimes the mother and father weep, the child wraps them in her arms and leans across the table to tell how she would not have made it without their help. I have seen these programs.

Sometimes I dream a dream in which Dee and I are suddenly brought together on a TV program of this sort. Out of a dark and soft-seated limousine I am ushered into a bright room filled with many people. There I meet a smiling, gray, sporty man like Johnny Carson who shakes my hand and tells me what a fine girl I have. Then we are on the stage and Dee is embracing me with tears in her eyes. She pins on my dress a large orchid, even though she has told me once that she thinks orchids are tacky flowers.

In real life I am a large, big-boned woman with rough, man-working hands. In the winter I wear flannel nightgowns to bed and overalls during the day. I can kill and clean a hog as mercilessly as a man. My fat keeps me hot in zero weather. I can work outside all day, breaking ice to get water for washing; I can eat pork liver cooked over the open fire minutes after it comes steaming from the hog. One winter I knocked a bull calf straight in the brain between the eyes with a sledge hammer and had the meat hung up to chill before nightfall. But of course all this does not show on television. I am the way my daughter would want me to be: a hundred pounds lighter, my skin like an uncooked barley pancake. My hair glistens in the hot bright lights. Johnny Carson has much to do to keep up with my quick and witty tongue.

But that is a mistake. I know even before I wake up. Who ever knew a Johnson with a quick tongue? Who can even imagine me looking a strange white man in the eye? It seems to me I have talked to them always with one foot raised in flight, with my head turned in whichever way is farthest from them. Dee, though. She would always look anyone in the eye. Hesitation was no part of her nature.

"How do I look, Mama?" Maggie says, showing just enough of her thin body enveloped in pink skirt and red blouse for me to know she's there, almost hidden by the door.

"Come out into the yard," I say.

Have you ever seen a lame animal, perhaps a dog run over by some careless person rich enough to own a car, sidle up to someone who is ignorant enough to be kind to him? That is the way my Maggie walks. She has been like this, chin on chest, eyes on ground, feet in shuffle, ever since the fire that burned the other house to the ground.

Dee is lighter than Maggie, with nicer hair and a fuller figure. She's a woman now, though sometimes I forget. How long ago was it that the other house burned? Ten, twelve years? Sometimes I can still hear the flames and feel Maggie's arms sticking to me, her hair smoking and her dress falling off her in little black papery flakes. Her eyes seemed stretched open, blazed open by the flames reflected in them. And Dee. I see her standing off under the sweet gum tree she used to dig gum out of; a look of concentration on her face as she watched the last dingy gray board of the house fall in toward the red-hot brick chimney. Why don't you do a dance around the ashes? I'd wanted to ask her. She had hated the house that much.

I used to think she hated Maggie, too. But that was before we raised the money, the church and me, to send her to Augusta to school. She used to read to us without pity; forcing words, lies, other folks' habits, whole lives upon us two, sitting trapped and ignorant underneath her voice. She washed us in a river of make-believe, burned us with a lot of knowledge we didn't necessarily need to know. Pressed us to her with the serious way she read, to shove us away at just the moment, like dimwits, we seemed about to understand.

Dee wanted nice things. A yellow organdy dress to wear to her graduation from high school; black pumps to match a green suit she'd made from an old suit somebody gave me. She was determined to stare down any disaster in her efforts. Her eyelids would not flicker for minutes at a time. Often I fought off the temptation to shake her. At sixteen she had a style of her own: and knew what style was.

I never had an education myself. After second grade the school was closed down. Don't ask my why: in 1927 colored asked fewer questions than they do now. Sometimes Maggie reads to me. She stumbles along goodnaturedly but can't see well. She knows she is not bright. Like good looks and money, quickness passed her by. She will marry John Thomas (who has mossy teeth in an earnest face) and then I'll be free to sit here and I guess just sing church songs to myself. Although I never was a good singer. Never could carry a tune. I was always better at a man's job. I used to love to milk till I was hoofed in the side in '49. Cows are soothing and slow and don't bother you, unless you try to milk them the wrong way.

I have deliberately turned my back on the house. It is three rooms, just like the one that burned, except the roof is tin; they don't make shingle roofs any more. There are no real windows, just some holes cut in the sides, like the portholes in a ship, but not round and not square, with rawhide holding the shutters up on the outside. This house is in a pasture, too, like the other one. No doubt when Dee sees it she will want to tear it down. She wrote me once that no matter where we "choose" to live, she will manage to come see us. But she will never bring her friends. Maggie and I thought about this and Maggie asked me, "Mama, when did Dee ever *have* any friends?"

She had a few. Furtive boys in pink shirts hanging about on washday after school. Nervous girls who never laughed. Impressed with her they worshiped the well-turned phrase, the cute shape, the scalding humor that erupted like bubbles in lye. She read to them.

When she was courting Jimmy T she didn't have much time to pay to us, but turned all her faultfinding power on him. He *flew* to marry a cheap city girl from a family of ignorant flashy people. She hardly had time to recompose herself.

When she comes I will meet—but there they are!

Maggie attempts to make a dash for the house, in her shuffling way, but I stay her with my hand. "Come back here," I say. And she stops and tries to dig a well in the sand with her toe.

It is hard to see them clearly through the strong sun. But even the first glimpse of leg out of the car tells me it is Dee. Her feet were always neat-looking, as if God himself had shaped them with a certain style. From the other side of the car comes a short, stocky man. Hair is all over his head a foot long and hanging from his chin like a kinky mule tail. I hear Maggie suck in her breath. "Uhnnnh," is what it sounds like. Like when you see the wriggling end of a snake just in front of your foot on the road. "Uhnnnh."

Dee next. A dress down to the ground, in this hot weather. A dress so loud it hurts my eyes. There are yellows and oranges enough to throw back the light of the sun. I feel my whole face warming from the heat waves it throws out. Earrings gold, too, and hanging down to her shoulders. Bracelets dangling and making noises when she moves her arm up to shake the folds of the dress out of her armpits. The dress is loose and flows, and as she walks closer, I like it. I hear Maggie go "Uhnnnh" again. It is her sister's hair. It stands straight up like the wool on a sheep. It is black as night and around the edges are two long pigtails that rope about like small lizards disappearing behind her ears.

"Wa-su-zo-Tean-o!" she says, coming on in that gliding way the dress makes her move. The short stocky fellow with the hair to his navel is all grinning and he follows up with "Asalamalakim, my mother and sister!" He moves to hug Maggie but she falls back, right up against the back of my chair. I feel her trembling there and when I look up I see the perspiration falling off her chin.

"Don't get up," says Dee. Since I am stout it takes something of a push. You can see me trying to move a second or two before I make it. She turns, showing white heels through her sandals, and goes back to the car. Out she peeks next with a Polaroid. She stoops down quickly and lines up picture after picture of me sitting there in front of the house with Maggie cowering behind me. She never takes a shot without making sure the house is included. When a cow comes nibbling around the edge of the yard she snaps it and me and Maggie *and* the house. Then she puts the Polaroid in the back seat of the car, and comes up and kisses me on the forehead.

Meanwhile Asalamalakim is going through the motions with Maggie's hand. Maggie's hand is as limp as a fish, and probably as cold, despite the sweat, and she keeps trying to pull it back. It looks like Asalamalakim wants to shake hands but wants to do it fancy. Or maybe he don't know how people shake hands. Anyhow, he soon gives up on Maggie.

"Well," I say. "Dee."

"No, Mama," she says. "Not 'Dee,' Wangero Leewanika Kemanjo!"

"What happened to 'Dee'?" I wanted to know.

"She's dead," Wangero said. "I couldn't bear it any longer, being named after the people who oppress me."

"You know as well as me you was named after your aunt Dicie," I said. Dicie is my sister. She named Dee. We called her "Big Dee" after Dee was born.

"But who was *she* named after?" asked Wangero.

"I guess after Grandma Dee," I said.

"And who was she named after?" asked Wangero.

"Her mother," I said, and saw Wangero was getting tired. "That's about as far back as I can trace it," I said. Though, in fact, I probably could have carried it back beyond the Civil War through the branches.

"Well," said Asalamalakim, "there you are."

"Uhnnnh," I heard Maggie say.

"There I was not," I said, "before 'Dicie' cropped up in our family, so why should I try to trace it that far back?"

He just stood there grinning, looking down on me like somebody inspecting a Model A car. Every once in a while he and Wangero sent eye signals over my head.

"How do you pronounce this name?" I asked.

"You don't have to call me by it if you don't want to," said Wangero.

"Why shouldn't I?" I asked. "If that's what you want us to call you, we'll call you."

"I know it might sound awkward at first," said Wangero.

"I'll get used to it," I said. "Ream it out again."

Well, soon we got the name out of the way. Asalamalakim had a name twice as long and three times as hard. After I tripped over it two or three times he told me to just call him Hakim-a-barber. I wanted to ask him was he a barber, but I didn't really think he was, so I didn't ask.

"You must belong to those beef-cattle peoples down the road," I said. They said "Asalamalakim" when they met you, too, but they didn't shake hands. Always too busy: feeding the cattle, fixing the fences, putting up salt lick shelters, throwing down hay. When the white folks poisoned some of the herd the men stayed up all night with rifles in their hands. I walked a mile and a half just to see the sight.

Hakim-a-barber said, "I accept some of their doctrines, but farming and raising cattle is not my style." (They didn't tell me, and I didn't ask, whether Wangero (Dee) had really done and married him.)

We sat down to eat and right away he said he didn't eat collards and pork was unclean. Wangero, though, went on through the chitlins and corn bread, the greens and everything else. She talked a blue streak over the sweet pota- toes. Everything delighted her. Even the fact that we still used the benches her daddy made for the table when we couldn't afford to buy chairs.

"Oh, Mama!" she cried. Then turned to Hakim-a-barber. "I never knew how lovely these benches are. You can feel the rump prints," she said, run- ning her hands underneath her and along the bench. Then she gave a sigh and her hand closed over Grandma Dee's butter dish. "That's it!" she said. "I knew there was something I wanted to ask you if I could have." She jumped up from the table and went over in the corner where the churn stood, the milk in it clabber by now. She looked at the churn and looked at it.

"This churn top is what I need," she said. "Didn't Uncle Buddy whittle it out of a tree you all used to have?"

"Yes," I said.

"Uh huh," she said happily. "And I want the dasher, too."

"Uncle Buddy whittle that, too?" asked the barber.

Dee (Wangero) looked up at me.

"Aunt Dee's first husband whittled the dash," said Maggie so low you almost couldn't hear her. "His name was Henry, but they called him Stash."

"Maggie's brain is like an elephant's," Wangero said, laughing. "I can use the churn top as a centerpiece for the alcove table," she said, sliding a plate over the churn, "and I'll think of something artistic to do with the dasher." When she finished wrapping the dasher the handle stuck out. I took it for a moment in my hands. You didn't even have to look close to see where hands pushing the dasher up and down to make butter had left a kind of sink in the wood. In fact, there were a lot of small sinks; you could see where thumbs and fingers had sunk into the wood. It was beautiful light yellow wood, from a tree that grew in the yard where Big Dee and Stash had lived.

After dinner Dee (Wangero) went to the trunk at the foot of my bed and started rifling through it. Maggie hung back in the kitchen over the dishpan. Out came Wangero with two quilts. They had been pieced by Grandma Dee and then Big Dee and me had hung them on the quilt frames on the front porch and quilted them. One was in the Lone Star pattern. The other was Walk Around the Mountain. In both of them were scraps of dresses Grandma Dee had worn fifty and more years ago. Bits and pieces of Grandpa Jarrell's Paisley shirts. And one teeny faded blue piece, about the size of a penny matchbox, that was from Great Grandpa Ezra's uniform that he wore in the Civil War.

"Mama," Wangero said sweet as a bird. "Can I have these old quilts?"

I heard something fall in the kitchen, and a minute later the kitchen door slammed.

"Why don't you take one or two of the others?" I asked. "These old things was just done by me and Big Dee from some tops your grandma pieced before she died."

"No," said Wangero. "I don't want those. They are stitched around the borders by machine."

"That'll make them last better," I said.

"That's not the point," said Wangero. "These are all pieces of dresses Grandma used to wear. She did all this stitching by hand. Imagine!" She held the quilts securely in her arms, stroking them.

"Some of the pieces, like those lavender ones, come from old clothes her mother handed down to her," I said, moving up to touch the quilts. Dee (Wangero) moved back just enough so that I couldn't reach the quilts. They already belonged to her.

"Imagine!" she breathed again, clutching them closely to her bosom.

"The truth is," I said, "I promised to give them quilts to Maggie, for when she marries John Thomas."

She gasped like a bee had stung her.

"Maggie can't appreciate these quilts!" she said. "She'd probably be backward enough to put them to everyday use."

"I reckon she would," I said. "God knows I been saving 'em for long enough with nobody using 'em. I hope she will!" I didn't want to bring up how I had offered Dee (Wangero) a quilt when she went away to college. Then she had told me they were old-fashioned, out of style.

"But they're *priceless*!" she was saying now, furiously; for she has a temper. "Maggie would put them on the bed and in five years they'd be in rags. Less than that!"

"She can always make some more," I said. "Maggie knows how to quilt."

Dee (Wangero) looked at me with hatred. "You just will not understand. The point is these quilts, *these* quilts!"

"Well," I said, stumped. "What would *you* do with them?"

"Hang them," she said. As if that was the only thing you *could* do with quilts.

Maggie by now was standing in the door. I could almost hear the sound her feet made as they scraped over each other.

"She can have them, Mama," she said, like somebody used to never winning anything, or having anything reserved for her. "I can 'member Grandma Dee without the quilts."

I looked at her hard. She had filled her bottom lip with checkerberry snuff and it gave her face a kind of dopey, hangdog look. It was Grandma Dee and Big Dee who taught her how to quilt herself. She stood there with her scarred hands hidden in the folds of her skirt. She looked at her sister with something like fear but she wasn't mad at her. This was Maggie's portion. This was the way she knew God to work.

When I looked at her like that something hit me in the top of my head and ran down to the soles of my feet. Just like when I'm in church and the spirit of God touches me and I get happy and shout. I did something I never had done before: hugged Maggie to me, then dragged her on into the room, snatched the quilts out of Miss Wangero's hands and dumped them into Maggie's lap. Maggie just sat there on my bed with her mouth open. "Take one or two of the others," I said to Dee.

But she turned without a word and went out to Hakim-a-barber.

"You just don't understand," she said, as Maggie and I came out to the car.

"What don't I understand?" I wanted to know.

"Your heritage," she said. And then she turned to Maggie, kissed her, and said, "You ought to try to make something of yourself, too, Maggie. It's really a new day for us. But from the way you and Mama still live you'd never know it."

She put on some sunglasses that hid everything above the tip of her nose and her chin.

Maggie smiled; maybe at the sunglasses. But a real smile, not scared. After we watched the car dust settle I asked Maggie to bring me a dip of snuff. And then the two of us sat there just enjoying, until it was time to go in the house and go to bed.

Appendix E: Don't Explain
(1987)

Jewelle Gomez (b. 1948)

Boston 1959

Letty deposited the hot platters on the table effortlessly. She slid one deep-fried chicken, a club steak with boiled potatoes, and a fried porgy plate down her arm as if removing beaded bracelets. Each one landed with a solid clink on the shiny Formica in its appropriate place. The last barely settled before Letty turned back to the kitchen to get Savannah and Skip their lemonade and extra biscuits. Then to put her feet up. Out of the corner of her eye she saw Tip come in the lounge. His huge shoulders, draped in sharkskin, narrowly cleared the doorframe.

Damn! He's early tonight! she thought, but kept going. Tip was known for his extravagance; that's how he'd gotten his nickname. He always sat at Letty's station because they were both from Virginia, although neither had been back in years.

Letty had come up to Boston in 1946 and been waiting tables in the 411 Lounge since '52. She liked the casual community formed around it. The pimps were not big thinkers but good for a laugh; the musicians who played the small clubs around Boston often ate at the 411, providing some glamour and now and then a jam session. The "business" girls were usually generous and always willing to embroider a wild story. After Letty's mother died there'd been no family to go back to down in Burkeville.

Letty took her newspaper from the locker behind the kitchen and filled a tall glass with the tart grape juice punch for which the cook, Henrietta, was famous.

"I'm going on break, Henrietta. Delia's takin' my station."

She sat in the back booth nearest the kitchen, beside the large blackboard which displayed the menu. When Delia came out of the bathroom, Letty hissed to get her attention. The reddish-brown of Delia's face was shiny with a country freshness that always made Letty feel a little shy.

"What's up, Miss Letty?" Her voice was soft and saucy. "Take my tables for twenty minutes. Tip just came in."

The girl's already bright smile widened as she started to thank Letty.

"Go 'head, go 'head. He don't like to wait. You can thank me if he don't run you back and forth fifty times."

Delia hurried away as Letty sank into the coolness of the over-stuffed booth and removed her shoes. After a few sips of her punch she rested her head on the back of the seat with her eyes closed. The sounds around her were as familiar as her own breathing: squeaking Red Cross shoes as Delia and Vinnie passed, the click of high heels around the bar, the clatter of dishes in the kitchen, and ice cascading into glasses. The din of conversation rose, leveled, and rose again over the jukebox. Letty had not played her record in days, but the words spun around in her head as if they were on a turntable:

Right or wrong don't matter
When you're with me sweet
Hush now, don't explain
You're my joy and pain.

Letty sipped her cool drink; sweat ran down her spine, soaking into the nylon uniform. July weather promised to give no breaks, and fans were working overtime like everybody else.

She saw Delia cross to Tip's table again. In spite of the dyed red hair, no matter how you looked at her, Delia was still a country girl.

Long, self-conscious, shy—she was bold only because she didn't know any better. She'd moved up from Anniston with her cousin a year before and landed the job at the 411 immediately. She was full of fun, but that didn't get in the way of her working hard. Sometimes she and Letty shared a cab going uptown after work, when Delia's cousin didn't pick them up in her green Pontiac.

Letty caught Tip eyeing Delia as she strode on tight-muscled legs back to the kitchen. That lounge lizard! Letty thought to herself. Letty had trained Delia how to balance plates, how to make tips, and how to keep the customer's hands on the table. She was certain Delia would have no problem putting Tip in his place. In the year she'd been working at the 411, Delia hadn't gone out with any of the bar flies, though plenty had asked. Letty figured that Delia and her cousin must run with a different crowd. They talked to each other sporadically in the kitchen or during their break, but Letty never felt that wire across her chest like Delia was going to ask her something she couldn't answer.

She closed her eyes again for the few remaining minutes. The song was back in her head, and Letty had to squeeze her lips together to keep from humming aloud. She pushed her thoughts onto something else. But when she did she always stumbled upon Maxine. Letty opened her eyes. When she'd quit working at Salmagundi's and come to the 411 she'd promised herself never to think about any woman like that again. She didn't know why missing Billie so much brought it all back to her.

She heard the bartender, Duke, shout a greeting from behind the bar to the owner as he walked in. Aristotle's glance skimmed his dimly lit domain before he made his way to his stool, the only one at the bar with a back. That was Letty's signal. No matter that it was her break: she knew white people didn't like to see their employees sitting down, especially with their shoes off. By the time he was settled near the door, Letty was up, her glass in hand, and on her way through the kitchen's noisy swinging door.

"You finished your break already?" Delia asked.

"Ari just come in."

"Uh oh, let me git this steak out there. Boy, he sure is nosy!"

"Who, Tip?"

"Yeah. He ask me where I live, who I live with, where I come from, like he supposed to know me!"

"Well, just don't take nothing he say to heart and you'll be fine. And don't take no rides from him!"

"Yeah. He asked if he could take me home after I get off. I told him me and you had something to do." Letty was silent as she sliced the fresh bread and stacked it on plates for the next orders.

"My cousin's coming by, so it ain't a lie, really. She can ride us."

"Yeah," Letty said as Delia giggled and turned away with her platter. Vinnie burst through the door like she always did, breathless and bossy. "Ari up there, girl! You better get back on station."

Letty drained her glass with deliberation, wiped her hands on her thickly starched white apron, and walked casually past Vinnie as if she'd never spoken. She heard Henrietta's soft chuckle float behind her. She went over to Tip, who was digging into the steak like his life depended on devouring it before the plate got dirty.

"Everything all right tonight?" Letty asked, her ample brown body towering over the table.

"Yeah, baby, it's all right. You ain't working this side no more?"

"I was on break. My feet can't wait for your stomach, you know."

Tip laughed. "*Break*. What you need a break for, big and healthy as you is!"

"We all get old, Tip. But the feet get old first, let me tell you that!"

"Not in my business, baby. Why you don't come on and work for me and you ain't got to worry 'bout your feet."

Letty sucked her teeth loudly, the exaggeration a part of the game they'd played over the years. "Man, I'm too old for that mess!"

"You ain't too old for me."

"Ain't nobody too old for *you*. Or too young, neither, looks like."

"Where you and that gal goin' tonight?"

"To a funeral," Letty responded dryly.

"Aw, woman, get on away from my food!" The gold cap on his front tooth gleamed from behind his greasy lips when he laughed. Letty was pleased. Besides giving away money, Tip liked to hurt people. It was better when he laughed.

The kitchen closed at 11:00. Delia and Letty slipped off their uniforms in the tiny bathroom and were on their way out the door by 11:15. Delia looked even younger in her knife-pleated skirt and white cotton blouse. Letty felt old in her slacks and long-sleeved shirt as she stood on Columbus Avenue in front of the neon 411 sign. The movement of car headlights played across her face, which was set in exhaustion. The dark green car pulled up and they got in quietly, both anticipating Sunday, the last night of their work week.

Delia's cousin was a stocky woman who looked about thirty-five, Letty's age. She never spoke much. Not that she wasn't friendly. She always greeted Letty with a smile and laughed at Delia's stories about the customers. Just close to the chest like me, that's all, Letty often thought. As they pulled up to the corner of Cunard Street, Letty opened the rear door. Delia turned to her and said, "I'm sorry you don't play your record on break no more, Miss Letty. I know you don't want to, but I'm sorry just the same."

Delia's cousin looked back at them with a puzzled expression but said nothing. Letty said goodnight, shut the car door, and turned to climb the short flight of stairs to her apartment. Cunard Street was quiet outside her window, and for once the guy upstairs wasn't blasting his record player. After her bath, Letty lay awake and restless in her bed. The electric fan was pointed at the ceiling, bouncing warm air over her, rustling her sheer nightgown.

Inevitably the strains of Billie Holiday's songs brushed against her, much like the breeze that moved around her. She felt silly when she thought about it, but the melody gripped her like a solid presence. It was more than the music. Billie was her hero. Letty saw Billie as big, like herself, with big hungers and a hard secret she couldn't tell anyone. Two weeks before, when Letty had heard that Lady was dead, sorrow had enveloped her. A door had closed that she could not consciously identify to herself or to anyone. It embarrassed her to think about. Like it did when she remembered how she'd felt about Maxine.

Letty had met Billie soon after she started working at the 411 when the singer had stopped in the club with several musicians on their way back from the Jazz Festival. There the audience, curious to see what a real, live junkie looked like, had sat back waiting for Billie to fall on her face. Instead she'd killed them dead with her liquid voice and rough urgency. Still, in the bar, the young, thin horn player had continued to reassure her: "Billie, you were the show, the whole show!"

Soon the cloud of insecurity receded from her face and it lit up with a center-stage smile. Once convinced, Billie became the show again, loud and commanding. She demanded her food be served up front, at the bar, and sent Henrietta, who insisted on waiting on her personally, back to the kitchen fifteen times. Billie laughed at jokes that Letty could barely hear as she bustled back and forth between the abandoned kitchen and her own tables. The sound of that laugh from the bar penetrated her bones. She'd watched and listened, certain she saw something no one else did. Vulnerability was held at bay, and behind that, a hunger even bigger than the one for food or heroin. Letty found reasons to walk up to the front—to use the telephone, to order a drink she paid for and left in the kitchen—just to catch the scent of her, the scent of sweat and silk emanating from her.

"Hey, baby," Billie said when Letty reached past her to pick up her drink from Duke.

"Henny sure can cook, can't she," Letty responded, hoping to see into Billie's eyes.

"Cook? She in these pots, sister!" the horn player shouted from down the bar, sitting behind his own heaping plateful of food.

Billie laughed, holding a big white napkin in front of her mouth, her eyes watering. Letty enjoyed the sound even though she still sensed something deeper, unreachable.

When Billie finished eating and gathered her entourage to get back on the road, she left a tip, not just for Henrietta but for each of the waitresses and the bartender. Generous just like the "business" girls, Letty was happy to note. She still had the two one-dollar bills in an envelope at the back of her lingerie drawer.

After that, Letty felt even closer to Billie. She played one of the few Lady Day records on the jukebox every night during her break. Everyone at the 411 had learned not to bother her when her song came on. Letty realized, as she lay waiting for sleep, that she'd always felt if she had been able to say or do something that night to make friends with Billie, it might all have been different. The faces of Billie, her former lover Maxine, and Delia blended in her mind in half-sleep. Letty slid her hand along the soft nylon of her gown to rest it between her full thighs. She pressed firmly, as if holding desire inside herself. Letty could have loved her enough to make it better.

Sunday nights at the 411 were generally quiet. Even the pimps and prostitutes used it as a day of rest. Letty came in early to have a drink at the bar and talk with Duke before going to the back to change into her uniform. She saw Delia through the window as the younger woman stepped out of the green Pontiac, looking as if she'd just come from Concord Baptist Church. "Satin Doll" played on the jukebox, wrapping the bar in mellow nostalgia for the Sunday dinners they'd serve.

Aristotle let Henrietta close the kitchen early on Sunday, and Letty looked forward to getting done by 9:30 or 10:00 and maybe enjoying some of the evening. When her break time came, she started for the jukebox automatically. She hadn't played anything by Billie in two weeks. Now, looking down at the inviting glare, she knew she still couldn't do it. She punched the buttons that would bring up Jackie Wilson's "Lonely Teardrops" and went to the back booth.

She'd almost dropped off to sleep when she heard Delia whisper her name. Letty opened her eyes and looked up into the girl's smiling face. Her head was haloed in tight, shiny curls.

"Miss Letty, won't you come home with me tonight?"

"What?"

"I'm sorry to bother you, but your break time almost up. I wanted to ask if you'd come over to the house tonight ... after work. My cousin'll bring you back home after."

Letty didn't speak. Her puzzled look prompted Delia to start again.

"Sometime on Sunday my cousin's friends from work come over to play cards, listen to music, you know. Nothin' special, just some of the girls from the office building down on Winter Street where she work, cleaning. She, I mean we, thought you might want to come over tonight. Have a drink, play some cards—"

"I don't play cards much."

"Well, not everybody play cards … just talk … sitting around talking. My cousin said you might like to for a change."

Letty wasn't sure she liked the last part—*for a change*—as if they had to entertain an old aunt.

"I really want you to come, Letty. They always her friends, but none of them is my own friends. They all right, I don't mean nothin' against them, but it would be fun to have my own personal friend there, you know?"

Delia was a good girl. Perfect words to describe her, Letty thought, smiling. "Sure, honey. I'd just as soon spend my time with you as lose my money with some fools."

By ten o'clock the kitchen was clean. Once they'd changed out of their uniforms and were out on the street Delia apologized that they had to take a cab uptown. She explained that her cousin and her friends didn't work on Sunday so they were already at home. Letty almost declined, tempted to go home. But she didn't. She stepped into the street and waved down a Red and White cab with brisk, urban efficiency. All the way uptown Delia explained that the evening wasn't a big deal and cautioned Letty not to expect much. "Just a few friends, hanging around, drinking and talking." She was jumpy, and Letty tried to put her at ease. She had not expected her visit would make Delia so anxious.

The apartment was located halfway up Blue Hill Avenue in an area where a few blacks had recently been permitted to rent. They entered a long, carpeted hallway and heard the sounds of laughter and music ringing from the rooms at the far end.

Inside, with the door closed, Delia shed her nervousness. This was clearly her home turf, and Letty couldn't believe she ever really needed an ally to back her up. Delia stepped out of her shoes at the door and walked to the back with her same long-legged gait. They passed a closed door, which Letty assumed to be one of the bedrooms, then came to a kitchen ablaze with light. Food and bottles were strewn across the blue-flecked table top. A counter opened from the kitchen into the dining room, which was the center of activity. Around a large mahogany table sat five women in smoke-filled concentration, playing poker.

Delia's cousin looked up from her cards with the same slight smile she displayed when she picked them up at work. Here it seemed welcoming, not guarded as it did in those brief moments in her car. She wore brown slacks and a matching sweater. The pink, starched points of her shirt collar peeked out at the neck.

Delia crossed to her and kissed her cheek lightly. Letty looked around the table to see if she recognized anyone. The women all seemed familiar in the way that city neighbors can, but Letty was sure she hadn't met any of them before. Delia introduced them, and each acknowledged Letty without diverting her attention from her cards: Karen, a short, round woman with West Indian bangles almost up to her elbow; Betty, who stared intently at her cards through thick eyeglasses encased in blue cat's-eye frames; Irene, a big, dark woman with long black hair and a gold tooth in front. Beside her sat Myrtle, who was wearing army fatigues and a gold Masonic ring on her pinkie finger. She said hello in the softest voice Letty had ever heard. Hovering over her was Clara, a large redbone woman whose hair was bound tightly in a bun at the nape of her neck. She spoke with a delectable Southern accent that drawled her "How're you doin'" into a full paragraph draped around an inquisitive smile.

Letty felt Delia tense again. Then she pulled Letty by the arm toward the French doors behind the players. There was a small den with a desk, some books, and a television set. Through the second set of glass doors was a living room. At the record player was an extremely tall, brown-skinned woman. She bent over the wooden cabinet searching for the next selection, oblivious to the rest of the gathering. Two women sat on the divan in deep conversation punctuated with constrained laughter.

"Maryalice, Sheila, Dolores … this is Letty. She work with me at the 411."

They looked up at her quickly, smiled, then went back to their preoccupations. Two of them resumed their whispered conversation; the other returned to the record collection. Delia directed Letty back toward the foyer and the kitchen.

"Come on, let me get you a drink. You know, I don't even know what you drink!"

"Delia?" Her cousin's voice reached them over the counter, just as they stepped into the kitchen. "Bring a couple of beers back when you come, okay?"

"Sure, babe." Delia went to the refrigerator and pulled out two bottles. "Let me just take these in. I'll be right back."

"Go 'head, I can take care of myself in this department, girl." Letty surveyed the array of bottles on the table. Delia went to the dining room and Letty mixed a Scotch and soda. She poured slowly as the reality settled on her. These women were friends, perhaps lovers, like she and Maxine had been. The name she'd heard for women like these burst inside her head: *bulldagger.* Letty flinched, angry she had let it in, angry that it frightened her. "Ptuh!" She blew through her teeth as if spitting the word back at the air.

She did know these women, Letty thought, as she stood at the counter looking out at the poker game. They were oblivious to her, except for Terry. Letty finally remembered that that was Delia's cousin's name.

As Letty took her first sip, Terry called over to her, "We gonna be finished with this hand in a minute, Letty, then we can talk." This time her face was filled by a large grin.

"Take your time," Letty said. She went out through the foyer door and around to the living room. She walked slowly on the carpet and adjusted her eyes to the light, which was a bit softer. The tall woman, Maryalice, had just put a record on the turntable and sat down on a love seat across from the other two women. Letty stood in the doorway a moment before the tune began:

Hush now, don't explain
Just say you'll return
I'm glad you're back
Don't explain …

Letty was stunned. She realized the song sounded different among these women: Billie sang just to them. Letty watched Maryalice sitting with her long legs stretched out tensely in front of her. She was wrapped in her own thoughts, her eyes closed. She appeared curiously disconnected after what had clearly been a long search for this record. Letty watched her face as she swallowed several times. Then Letty sat beside her. They listened to the music while the other two women spoke in low voices.

Maryalice didn't move when the song was over.

"I met her once," Letty said.

"I beg your pardon?"

"Kinda met her. At the 411 Lounge where me and Delia work."

"Naw!" Maryalice said as she sat up.

"She was just coming back from a gig."

"Honestly?" Maryalice's voice caught with excitement.

"She just had dinner—smothered chicken, potato salad, green beans, side of stewed tomatoes, and an extra side of cornbread."

"Big eater."

"Child, everybody is when Henrietta's cooking. Billie was … ," Letty searched for the words, "she was sort of stubborn."

Maryalice laughed. "You know, that's kinda how I pictured her."

"I figure she had to be stubborn to keep going," Letty said. "And not stingy, either!"

"Yeah," Maryalice said, enjoying the confirmation of her image of Billie.

Letty rose from the sofa and went to the record player. Delia stood tentatively watching from the doorway of the living room. Letty picked up the arm of the phonograph and replaced it at the beginning of the record. Letty noticed the drops of moisture on Maryalice's lashes, but she relaxed as Letty settled onto the seat beside her. They listened to Billie together, for the first time.

Appendix F
Additional literary works for further practice

If you wish to improve your ability to interpret literature using concepts from the critical theories we've studied, I think you will find that the following literary works lend themselves readily to the critical theories under whose headings they appear. Where possible, I've listed literary works under more than one theoretical heading so that you can continue to see the ways in which the concepts you use to interpret a literary work tend to change what you're likely to notice in that work. While I personally like all of the works listed below, and I hope you do too, I chose them for you because of their readability and their accessibility to theoretical interpretations.

Please note, however, one exception. The selections listed under "Reader-response theory" were chosen because, in my own experience and in that of many of my colleagues, these works tend to elicit a relatively strong personal response from most readers as well as a variety of responses from different readers.

Of course, these titles are offered only as a sample of what's to come if you continue to read literature. I sincerely hope you will consider my suggestions as a starting point for your own independent adventures in the surprising, intriguing, comforting, and often astonishing world of literary exploration.

Reader-response theory

Short stories

"The Girls in Their Summer Dresses" (Irwin Shaw, 1939)
"I Stand Here Ironing" (Tillie Olsen, 1953)
"Johnnieruth" (Becky Birtha, 1987)
"The Secret Sharer" (Joseph Conrad, 1910)
"Son in the Afternoon" (John A. Williams, 1962)
"The Storm" (Kate Chopin, 1898)
"When I Was Thirteen" (Denton Welch, 1948)
"The Yellow Wallpaper" (Charlotte Perkins Gilman, 1892)

Poems

"After great pain, a formal feeling comes—" #341 (Emily Dickinson, c. 1862)
"The Little Black Boy" (William Blake, 1789)
"Missing Lips" (Phebe Hanson, 1974)
"My Papa's Waltz" (Theodore Roethke, 1948)

Plays

Death of a Salesman (Arthur Miller, 1949)
The Piano Lesson (August Wilson, 1990)

Novels

The Awakening (Kate Chopin, 1899)
The Bluest Eye (Toni Morrison, 1970)

New Critical theory

Short stories

"The Chrysanthemums" (John Steinbeck, 1937)
"Girls in Their Summer Dresses, The" (Irwin Shaw, 1939)
"A Pair of Tickets" (Amy Tan, 1989)
"The Storm" (Kate Chopin, 1898)
"When I Was Thirteen" (Denton Welch, 1948)
"The Yellow Wallpaper" (Charlotte Perkins Gilman, 1892)

Poems

"After great pain, a formal feeling comes—" #341 (Emily Dickinson, c. 1862)
"Birches" (Robert Frost, 1916)
"Missing Lips" (Phebe Hanson, 1974)
"Pocahontas to Her English Husband John Rolfe" (Paula Gunn Allen, 1988)
"Suicide Note" (Janice Mirikitani, 1987)
"Tour 5" (Robert Hayden, 1966)

Plays

The Piano Lesson (August Wilson, 1990)
Trifles (Susan Glaspell, 1916)

Novels

Heart of Darkness (Joseph Conrad, 1902)
Sula (Toni Morrison, 1970)

Psychoanalytic theory

Short stories

"The Birthmark" (Nathaniel Hawthorne, 1843)
"The Chaser" (John Collier, 1951)
"The Girls in Their Summer Dresses" (Irwin Shaw, 1939)
"I Stand Here Ironing" (Tillie Olsen, 1953)
"The Secret Sharer" (Joseph Conrad, 1910)
"Son in the Afternoon" (John A. Williams, 1962)
"The Yellow Wallpaper" (Charlotte Perkins Gilman, 1892)

Poems

"Birches" (Robert Frost, 1916)
"Missing Lips" (Phebe Hanson, 1974)
"My Papa's Waltz" (Theodore Roethke, 1948)
"Prowling the Ridge" (Judith Minty, 1981)

Plays

A Doll's House (Henrik Ibsen, 1879)
The Piano Lesson (August Wilson, 1990)

Novels

As I Lay Dying (William Faulkner, 1930)
Frankenstein (Mary Shelley, 1801)
Heart of Darkness (Joseph Conrad, 1902)

Marxist theory

Short stories

"The Chaser" (John Collier, 1951)
"The Circuit" (Francisco Jiménez, 1973)
"I Stand Here Ironing" (Tillie Olsen, 1953)
"The Lesson" (Toni Cade Bambara, 1972)
"On the Road" (Langston Hughes, 1952)
"Son in the Afternoon" (John A. Williams, 1962)
"The Stolen Party" (Liliana Heker, 1982)

Poems

"Missing Lips" (Phebe Hanson, 1974)
"The Secretary Chant" (Marge Piercy, 1973)

"What Soft – Cherubic Creatures" #401 (Emily Dickinson, c. 1862)
"What Work Is" (Philip Levine, 1991)

Plays

A Doll's House (Henrik Ibsen, 1879)
The Piano Lesson (August Wilson, 1990)

Novels

Frankenstein (Mary Shelley, 1801)
The Grapes of Wrath (John Steinbeck, 1939)
Heart of Darkness (Joseph Conrad, 1902)

Feminist theory

Short stories

"The Birthmark" (Nathaniel Hawthorne, 1843)
"The Chaser" (John Collier, 1951)
"The Chrysanthemums" (John Steinbeck, 1937)
"Girl" (Jamaica Kincaid, 1983)
"The Girls in Their Summer Dresses" (Irwin Shaw, 1939)
"The Yellow Wallpaper" (Charlotte Perkins Gilman, 1892)

Poems

"Daystar" (Rita Dove, 1986)
"Missing Lips" (Phebe Hanson, 1974)
"Prowling the Ridge" (Judith Minty, 1981)
"Suicide Note" (Janice Mirikitani, 1987)

Plays

A Doll's House (Henrik Ibsen, 1879)
Trifles (Susan Glaspell, 1916)

Novels

The Autobiography of My Mother (Jamaica Kincaid, 1996)
Frankenstein (Mary Shelley, 1801)
Sula (Toni Morrison, 1973)

Autobiography

I Know Why the Caged Bird Sings (Maya Angelou, 1969)

Lesbian, gay, and queer theories

Short stories

"A Birthday Remembered" (Ann Allen Shockley, 1980)
"Johnnieruth" (Becky Birtha, 1987)
"The Outing" (James Baldwin, 1951)
"The Secret Sharer" (Joseph Conrad, 1910)
"When I Was Thirteen" (Denton Welch, 1948)

Poems

"Café: 3 A.M." (Langston Hughes, 1951)
"Christopher St. Liberation Day, June 28, 1970" (Fran Winant, 1971)
"How to Watch Your Brother Die" (Michael Lassell, 1990)
"I Think the New Teacher's a Queer" (Perry Brass, 1986)
"When I Heard at the Close of Day" (Walt Whitman, 1860)

Plays

The Normal Heart (Larry Kramer, 1985)
Springtime (Maria Irene Fornes, 1989)

Novels

A Boy's Own Story (Edmund White, 1982)
Equal Affections (David Leavitt, 1989)
Oranges Are Not the Only Fruit (Jeanette Winterson, 1985)
Sula (Toni Morrison, 1973)

African American theory

Short stories

"Blood-Burning Moon" (Jean Toomer, 1923)
"Everything That Rises Must Converge" (Flannery O'Connor, 1965)
"The Lesson" (Toni Cade Bambara, 1972)
"On the Road" (Langston Hughes, 1952)
"Son in the Afternoon" (John A. Williams, 1962)

Poems

"Harlem" (Langston Hughes, 1951)
"I, Too" (Langston Hughes, 1932)
"nikki-rosa" (Nikki Giovanni, 1968)
"Song of the Law Abiding Citizen" (June Jordan, 1985)
"Tour 5" (Robert Hayden, 1966)

Plays

A Raisin in the Sun (Lorraine Hansberry, 1959)
Fences (August Wilson, 1985)

Novels

Black Boy (Richard Wright, 1945)
The Bluest Eye (Toni Morrison, 1970)
Sula (Toni Morrison, 1973)

Autobiography

I Know Why the Caged Bird Sings (Maya Angelou, 1969)

Postcolonial theory

Short stories

"The Circuit" (Francisco Jiménez, 1973)
"The Man to Send Rain Clouds" (Leslie Marmon Silko, 1969)
"Marriage Is a Private Affair" (Chinua Achebe, 1972)
"A Pair of Tickets" (Amy Tan, 1989)
"Son in the Afternoon" (John A. Williams, 1962)
"The Stolen Party" (Liliana Heker, 1982)

Poems

"The Little Black Boy" (William Blake, 1789)
"Lost Sister" (Cathy Song, 1983)
"Pocahontas to her English Husband, John Rolfe" (Paula Gunn Allen, 1988)
"Powwow 79, Durango" (Paula Gunn Allen, 1982)

Plays

"Master Harold" ... and the Boys (Athol Fugard, 1982)

Novels

The Autobiography of My Mother (Jamaica Kincaid, 1996)
Frankenstein (Mary Shelley, 1801)
The Grapes of Wrath (John Steinbeck, 1939)
Heart of Darkness (Joseph Conrad, 1902)
Things Fall Apart (Chinua Achebe, 1958)

Index

affective fallacy 39
African American culture 209–10; and "Everyday Use" 222–23; and history 206–7, 210; and
literary tradition, 210; and *Waiting to Exhale* 240
African American Vernacular English (AAVE) 210; and "The Blues I'm Playing" 242
ambiguity 42; and "Everyday Use" 117–18; and "I started Early—Took my Dog" 73, 74
American Dream 110–11, 115; and "The Battle Royal" 104, 119–23, 289; and "Everyday Use" 117–18; and *Pretty Woman* 135–36
The Andy Griffith Show: and feminist cultural criticism 298–300
anticolonialist resistance 250–51; and "The Battle Royal" 255–57, 277; and "Don't Explain" 268–73, 277; and "Everyday Use" 263, 277; and *Waiting to Exhale* 280
antiSemitism 249
Asian Americans 8, 108–9, 202–3, 209, 246, 248
authorial intention 11, 38, 39
avoidance 84; and "Everyday Use" 88; and reader-response theory 26; and "A Rose for Emily" 93–94
The Awakening: and African American theory 243; and feminist theory 169; and lesbian theory 203; and Marxist theory 137; and New Critical theory 79; and postcolonial theory 283; and psychoanalytic theory 108
"The Battle Royal" 288–90, 311–22; and African American theory 213–17; and feminist theory 44–47; and gay theory

182–85, 194; and Marxist theory 119–24; and New Critical theory 57–63. 75; and postcolonial theory 251–57, 277; and psychoanalytic theory 103–4, 105; and reader-response theory 28

Beauvoir, Simone de 143
Bennett, Paula 196–97
biological essentialism 174
Black Pride Movement 222, 261–62; and "Everyday Use" 29–30, 50, 117, 151–52, 222–23, 225, 226-7, 258–59, 261–63, 278
Black Vernacular English (BVE) *see* African American Vernacular English (AAVE)
"The Blues I'm Playing": and African American theory 242; and feminist theory 169; and Marxist theory 137; and New Critical theory 78; and postcolonial theory 283; and psychoanalytic theory 108
"Breaking Tradition": and psychoanalytic theory 108

capitalism 113–16; and *Death of a Salesman* 137; and "Everyday Use" 116–20; and "I started Early—Took my Dog" 131
cardboard characters *see* one-dimensional characters
character analysis 29–30
"A Chinese Banquet" 205n5; and lesbian theory 202
Chopin, Kate *see The Awakening*
classism 112–13; and "The Battle Royal" 124; and "Don't Explain" 129–31; and *Frankenstein* 133–34; and "I started Early—Took my Dog" 131–32; and *Pretty Woman* 135; and "A Rose for Emily"124–29, 134;